IMPERFECT KNOWLEDGE ECONOMICS

IMPERFECT KNOWLEDGE ECONOMICS

EXCHANGE RATES AND RISK

ROMAN FRYDMAN
MICHAEL D. GOLDBERG

FOREWORD BY EDMUND S. PHELPS

Princeton University Press

PRINCETON AND OXFORD

Requests for permission to reproduce material from this work should be sent to Permissions, Princeton University Press

Published by Princeton University Press, 41 William Street, Princeton, New Jersey 08540

In the United Kingdom: Princeton University Press, 3 Market Place, Woodstock, Oxfordshire OX20 1SY

ISBN-13: 978-0-691-12160-4
ISBN-10: 0-691-12160-5

Library of Congress Control Number: 2007927611

British Library Cataloging-in-Publication Data is available

This book was composed in ITC New Baskerville and Eurostile using ZzTEX by Princeton Editorial Associates, Inc., Scottsdale, Arizona

Printed on acid-free paper. ∞

www.press.princeton.edu

Printed in the United States of America

10 9 8 7 6 5 4 3 2 1

To Halina, Julia, and Marcella
R.F.

To my parents
M.G.

Our capacity to predict will be confined to . . . general characteristics of the events to be expected and not include the capacity
for predicting particular individual events. . . . [However,] I am
anxious to repeat, we will still achieve predictions which can be
falsified and which therefore are of empirical significance. . . .
Yet the danger of which I want to warn is precisely the belief that in
order to be accepted as scientific it is necessary to achieve more.
This way lies charlatanism and more. I confess that I prefer true
but imperfect knowledge . . . to a pretence of exact knowledge
that is likely to be false.

FRIEDRICH A. HAYEK,
"The Pretence of Knowledge," Nobel Lecture

Contents

Foreword

Edmund S. Phelps

Much has been written by historians and sociologists as well as business commentators about the modern economy—the kind that supplanted the traditional economy in several nations in the nineteenth century and many more in the latter half of the twentieth century. The pre-capitalist system dominated by the self-employed and the self-financed gave way to finance capitalism. To call this a "great transformation" was no overstatement.

A traditional economy is one of routine. In the usual illustrative example, rural folk periodically exchange their produce for the goods of the town. The sole disturbances are not of their doing and are beyond their control—rainfall, temperature, and other exogenous shocks. This was the economy modeled in the neoclassical theory of economic equilibrium from Ricardo and Böhm-Bawerk to Walras and Samuelson. It is also the economy described in the subsequent stochastic models of "rational expectations equilibrium" in the face of shocks that were pioneered by Arrow, Samuelson, Muth, and Lucas.

The modern economy is marked by the feasibility of endogenous change. Modernization opens the door for individuals to engage in novel activity—most importantly, the financing, developing, and marketing of new products and methods. Furthermore, such innovations, when successful in the marketplace, have unforeseen effects on production possibilities, prices, the differentiation of goods, and the specialization of work.

The author is McVickar Professor of Political Economy at Columbia University; director of the Center on Capitalism and Society, Earth Institute, at Columbia University; and the winner of the 2006 Nobel Prize in Economics.

For decades, economics students have quietly asked themselves whether the equilibrium theory of the classroom is adequate for modeling the modern economy. It is one thing to know the prices at hand, another to know all prices far and wide and over the whole future and for every state of the world that shocks might land the economy in. Equilibrium theory implicitly takes the mechanisms that constitute the economy to be completely known: participants have a full understanding of how this organism works, so everyone knows the probability distribution of outcomes to expect in this or that state. This in turn implies that everyone knows this understanding to be common knowledge, so there is no diversity of views that would have to be guessed at in estimating what others intend to do.

History records a small band of economists who have called attention to points of dissonance between the modern economy and equilibrium theory, including the theory of rational expectations equilibrium, in which expectations (and thus prices) are taken to be appropriate for equilibrium in each possible current state.[1] In fact the growing perception, starting from the turn of the century, that the new modern economies were generally out of equilibrium, sometimes frighteningly so, is one of the hallmarks of twentieth-century thought.

The great interwar theorist at Chicago, Frank Knight, pondering the arrival of capitalism, took the unprecedented position in his 1921 classic *Risk, Uncertainty and Profit* that virtually all business decisions other than the routine ones are to an appreciable extent a step into the unknown. The possible outcomes might have probabilities but those probabilities were unknown, or "unmeasurable"—the radical sort of uncertainty now called "Knightian uncertainty." Viewing from London and Cambridge a similarly modern economy, John Maynard Keynes proposed in his 1921 *Treatise on Probability* a rewrite of probability theory that would take account of radical uncertainty. His 1936 *General Theory* was an attempt to overthrow equilibrium theory. In subsequent years, economists from Vienna to Copenhagen critiqued "perfect foresight" and its generalization, now known as rational expectations equilibrium.[2] In the glorious 1960s several American economists broke from equilibrium theory.[3]

---

1. I discuss some of the implications of this anti-equilibrium view for economic activity and inflation-unemployment tradeoffs in the context of my early expectations-driven macroeconomic models in my Nobel Prize lecture (Phelps, 2007).

2. I am thinking of the game theorists Morgenstern (1949) and Zeuthen (1955).

3. Ambiguity and vagueness were introduced by Ellsberg (1961) and Fellner (1961), personal knowledge by Polanyi (1958). Several applied papers followed in this spirit. For example, in a macroeconomic context, Friedman (1961, p. 449) pointed out that long and variable lags in the effects of monetary policy imply that forecasting the consequences of monetary action is "not an easy requirement in the present state of our knowledge." Phelps (1968a) argued that a (expectational) disequilibrium may be created by an undiagnosed structural shift.

Trained professionals in that decade had a sense of what this anti-equilibrium literature was getting at. We thought that, empirically, equilibrium theory would not work well. For one thing, the economies (at least the world economy) we lived in had become too rich for equilibrium theory to fit at all well: forming correct expectations about a sole experiment, such as a lower price or a new variation on a product, is one thing, but forming expectations when most or all firms are simultaneously experimenting is qualitatively different. For another thing, these economies were not really fluctuating around the stationary state or steady-growth path of neoclassical theory; they were constantly evolving in their structure and were changing too fast for economic relationships (between prices and quantities, for example) to have the durability that would be necessary for formation of accurate expectations about present and future data.[4]

Yet, a few years later, the community of macroeconomists, far from distancing themselves farther and farther from equilibrium theory, proceeded almost unanimously to embrace the rational expectations models of business activity introduced in the early 1970s. Keynes and the Cantabridgians were out. Hayek and the Austrians were out. So was Spiethoff and his German school.

This marvelous book by Frydman and Goldberg documents in its first two chapters invaluable insights of the "early modern" theory of capitalism that were lost when the profession endorsed rational expectations equilibrium. And it exposes to the light the arguments offered by the advocates of the premise of rational expectations. There can't be many readers who won't be fascinated by this story. In letting the two sides speak in their own carefully chosen words the authors allow the expressed points of disagreement to come into sharp focus.

These chapters, however, soon probe to a deeper level. It isn't just that the postulate of rational expectations is unrealistic in the same way that the postulate of rational choice is conceded to be unrealistic. We agree to work with rational choice in spite of its limitations, so why not rational expectations too? The primary issue is not an empirical one. Even if no firms at the current time were actually venturing a new price list, conceiving a new way to cut costs, devising new financial vehicles, contemplating a new product, and so forth, there would still be a problem: rational expectations equilibrium theory as an element of our models of the modern sort of economies contradicts the very essence of an economy in which economic actors are free to exercise their "creativity" by venturing to do something innovative.

---

4. The former argument is the theme of Frydman (1982). The latter argument is the theme of a recent paper of mine (Phelps, 2006a).

The authors argue that if we aspire to build models that apply to modern economies—economies whose central functioning is the manufacture of change through their innovative activity and their adoption and mastery of the innovations made available—it is contradictory to adopt the rational expectations postulate that whatever change takes place in the future is already knowable and known in the present: that the economic change to be experienced is in a sense predetermined. Yet contemporary model builders embracing rational expectations have been undeterred or unaware of the contradiction: they either specify that there is no change in the world (the world they would describe with their models) or that whatever process of change is going on in the world can be incorporated in their models in a fully predetermined way.

This criticism is not a narrow point that would be straightforward to remedy. The authors are not referring to the fact that the archetypal models of an economy enjoying rational expectations equilibrium have built into them an invariant trend-growth path to which the economy is constantly returning (as described by some transition dynamics). It is obvious that such a trend path is predetermined; the possibilities and probabilities are "prespecified" (in the authors' preferred term). The authors' argument is broader than that. If a rational expectations model supposed instead that the future was governed by a probabilistic linear birth process, so the model has no trend path to which the economy is tethered, there is still a fundamental predeterminacy: the possible states at a given future date are all known already and there is at present a calculable probability, conditional on the present state, of each such future state's occurrence. In this model too, then, there is implicitly no possibility for the actors in the economy to create something unforeseeable, surprising, genuinely innovative. Thus, there is a methodological choice: to model on the premise of fully prespecified future possibilities, which rational expectations requires, or to model an economy capable of endogenous change, which the modern economy is.

A recent case in point is the state-of-the-art model of the real business cycle type, where recognition is given to the accepted idea that opportunities are rosier at some times than others—the notion of "regimes" in which there are outsize rates of return in prospect for investment.[5] At first blush this construct appears to capture an economy undergoing the occasional boom and the occasional slump at unpredictable times and having a future that feels not fully predetermined—and all this without sacrificing the precision of rational expectations equilibrium. The truth is, however, that this is

5. See Beaudry and Portier (2004).

a highly mechanical apparatus implying a finite number of states at any future date and imputing to each a calculable probability conditional on the economy's present state.

An older case of equilibrium theory in macroeconomics is Joseph Schumpeter's great 1911 work *Theory of Economic Development*. He saw the need to go beyond the Spiethoff-Cassel model, in which no entrepreneur appears and none is needed, only the occasional discovery of an exogenous scientist or explorer. Forced to choose whether to remain with the equilibrium perspective of his idol Walras or instead to regard entrepreneurs as creators in their own—figures creating the future—Schumpeter clung to the equilibrium perspective. The Schumpeterian entrepreneurs were merely the vessels the economy needs to carry out the commercial innovations made possible by the technology. The stock of undeveloped innovations were all "in the air," each waiting for one of Schumpeter's "entrepreneurs" to find it convenient to take on its financing, developing, and marketing. The rate of return of every project was known, at any rate to the experienced banker. The Schumpeterian model makes determinate (at least probabilistically) the rate of innovative activity and the time path of productivity—as if the creativity is all science and no commerce.

In contrast, to elaborate on earlier remarks, Keynes saw the rate of return as quite unknown and the demand for investment funds as driven by entrepreneurs' "animal spirits." Hayek saw that every participant has little or no knowledge of how the economy works as a whole, contrary to rational expectations; that a participant is apt to have only some highly specialized knowledge about his or her industry, which is itself apt to be quite specialized; that in some cases it is so deep as to be "private knowledge"; and that such knowledge may permit a creative person to conceive some new business strategy or new business product that is *not* in the air, *not* already known by all. In the struggle between these two worldviews, Keynes and Hayek were right but did not carry the day.[6]

As the rational expectations view has come under increasing suspicion, parts of the profession have jumped to the conclusion that the problem is "sticky" prices or some sort of rote behavior or "irrational exuberance" in asset prices or all of these. What Keynes and Hayek in the 1930s and Phelps in the 1960s understood is that there may be a problem with expectational equilibrium and it need not be sticky prices or irrationality but mainly the

---

6. I would add that in relatively recent work (Phelps, 1994) I simply treat every shock as de novo, so the state it brings was fully unanticipated. Obviously this treatment is at odds with rational expectations. However, I regard the implications of that model to fit more closely with the behavior of national economies than do the models that invoke a stochastic stationary state with no room for parametric shifts.

ever-imperfect knowledge of the structure of the economy and the attempt of purposeful market participants and policy makers to cope with it.[7]

If rational expectations equilibrium and its doppelganger predeterminacy must be regarded as inapplicable to the modern economy, the profession needs to embark on its own voyage of discovery. The present book is devoted to setting out a fresh approach, one that is neither rational-expectationist nor behavioralist.

The authors of this book show that if we want to do coherent macroeconomic theorizing about a modern economy we are going to have to allow in our models for non-routine decision making and unforeseeable changes in the social context within which individuals make decisions. How do we build such a *theory* for modern economies?

The authors devote most of the book to developing such a theory, which they dub "imperfect knowledge economics." This economics builds in mathematical microfoundations of aggregate outcomes and yet it allows for non-routine ways in which market participants might alter the way they deploy resources. The remarkable feature of these imperfect knowledge models is that, while they do not assume away non-routine activities, they nevertheless generate implications that allow an economist to compare empirically the performance of alternative explanations of outcomes.

How is this done? The key point is that imperfect knowledge economics focuses on *change* and looks for *qualitative* regularities, not quantitative ones. The authors' models impose qualitative restrictions on the way forecasting strategies are revised. While placing enough structure on an economist's model, these restrictions are general enough to be compatible with a myriad of ways in which market participants might revise their views of the future. Moreover, these restrictions recognize that *sharp* forecasts of what an individual will do are beyond the reach of any economic analysis of *modern* economies.

This approach resolves Knight's and Keynes's problem of how to reconcile the use of probability theory in modeling decisions under uncertainty. As Knight and Keynes recognized, neither the actors nor the economist-modeler knows the probability distribution of outcomes. The key innovation of the authors is to model the change across time in these distributions and in a purely qualitative way (the authors refer to these as "partially predetermining restrictions") rather than to model the probability distribution at each point in time.

---

7. Leijonhufvud (1968) also attributes this view to Keynes, and he identifies himself with that view. I should add that, although I participated in the New Keynesian venture in the 1970s to rewrite Keynesian economy on the basis of rational expectations coupled with non-synchronous wage/price setting, my heart was always with the model in which wages and prices were continually being revised.

The three-decade-long debate between the neoclassical and "Keynesian" schools over whether prices are sticky or flexible appears to be a mere distraction. In the context of the foreign exchange market, the authors show that, with incomplete knowledge, long swings in real exchange rates do not depend on whether prices are sticky or flexible. Rather, they arise from the imperfection of knowledge concerning the structure of the economy and market participants' attempts to cope with it. Moreover, in contrast to recently fashionable behavioral models, the authors' explanation of swings does not abandon the long tradition in economics that individuals behave in largely rational, or reasonable, ways.

Remarkably, once the authors allow for imperfect knowledge on how fundamentals influence the exchange rate, long swings can arise even if all market participants' diverse forecasting strategies depend solely on the macroeconomic fundamentals. It would not be surprising, therefore, if it is later found that a similar mechanism generates swings in overall business activity. (This possibility suggests that if modified by the authors' imperfect knowledge framework, my models of "structural slumps" would generate not a monotone shift from the initial steady state to the new one but rather a cyclical transition.)

In the conventional conception, as I pointed out above, market outcomes are mere vibration around a steady state path. Swings are viewed as anomalous and puzzling. Once imperfect knowledge is placed at the center of the analysis, swings arise as part of the discovery process of how prices are related to macroeconomic fundamentals.

The authors' imperfect knowledge economics sees the modern economy as possessing bounded instability around historical benchmark values, which themselves may be evolving over time. The importance of historical benchmarks in characterizing individual behavior and aggregate outcomes was emphasized by almost all important early modern economists: Wicksell, Keynes, and Tobin, who built on this in his work on "behavior toward risk." (I imagine this view will be found to link well to my own work on movements of the medium-term natural unemployment rate.)

Another hallmark of the imperfect knowledge view is its qualification of fixed policy rules. The necessary point is that the optimum rule is not the same from one structure of the economy to another. As with the rest of macroeconomics, the issues have to be rethought in a way that makes the ever-imperfect knowledge of market participants and policymakers an integral part of the analysis.

I had the great good fortune in the 1960s to initiate the profession's work on plausible microfoundations for macroeconomic modeling, taking into account the knowledge and the information that the micro-actors could reasonably be supposed to have—a revolutionary movement, it seems. Unfortunately, the rational expectations models, appearing in the 1970s, sidestepped the problem of expectations formation under uncertainty by blithely supposing that the model's actors (tellingly dubbed "agents") knew the "correct" model and the correct model was the analyst's model—whatever that model might be that day. The stampede toward "rational expectations"—widely thought to be a "revolution," though it was only a generalization of the neoclassical idea of equilibrium—derailed the expectations-driven model building that had just left the station. In the end, this way of modeling has not illuminated how the world economy works. Happily for me and, I believe, for the profession of economics, this deeply original and important book gives signs of bringing us back on track—on a road toward an economics possessing a genuine microfoundation and at the same time a capacity to illuminate some of the many aspects of the modern economy that the rational expectations approach cannot by its nature explain.

Acknowledgments

We have benefited tremendously from illuminating discussions on modern macroeconomics, stretching over decades, with Edmund Phelps, and we are grateful for his support of this project from the outset. George Soros's insights into the role of imperfect knowledge in the workings of financial markets and historical change have likewise stimulated and sustained the development of our ideas over the years. Stephan Schulmeister's work on modeling asset markets has given impetus to our search for an approach that accords imperfect knowledge the central role in economic analysis. Pentti Kouri has unstintingly encouraged us in our attempt to develop such an alternative and has contributed penetrating ideas and reactions at every step along the way. We are grateful to Katarina Juselius for taking an early interest in Imperfect Knowledge Economics, and for her continuing efforts to examine econometrically the implications of imperfect knowledge for the empirical record in macroeconomics.

Thought-provoking discussions with many other colleagues and friends have led us to countless revisions of our ideas and arguments. An early version of our analysis of the epistemological flaws of the rational expectations approach, which we build on and substantially extend in the introductory chapters of this book, was presented at the Conference on Rational Expectations at New York University in 1981. The supportive reactions from Frank Hahn, Peter Howitt, Alan Kirman, Axel Leijonhufvud, and Fritz Machlup, as well as sharp criticism from Robert Lucas and Tom Sargent, led us to rethink and elaborate our arguments. Visits to Stanford University during the 1980s and 1990s led to several provocative discussions with Kenneth Arrow and Milton Friedman. Their trenchant comments and suggestions helped shape the development of our thinking. Over the years, we were also fortunate to have received important comments on—and reactions to—our evolving arguments from Alan Blinder, Jorge Braga de Macedo, Rudiger Dornbusch, Bruce Elmslie, Jean-Paul Fitoussi, Lejb Fogelman, Halina Frydman, Jan Gross, David Hendry, Soren Johansen, Niels Thygesen, James Tobin, James Wible, and Charles Wilson.

We are indebted to Olga Amsterdamska, Rebecca Berlow, Irena Grosfeld, Helena Hessel, Melvyn Krauss, Joel Owen, Andrzej Rapaczynski, Richard Robb, Robert Shiller, Klaudiusz Weiss, and Michael Woodford for taking the time to read parts of an early version of the manuscript. Their queries and astute suggestions have led to refinements and revisions of some of our key arguments. We also thank Jess Benhabib, Steven Brams, Daniel Cohen, Helmut Frisch, Giancarlo Gandolfo, Irena Grudzinska-Gross, Stephen Holmes, Damien King, Kenneth Monahan, Gene Moore, Kenneth Murphy, Luigi Spaventa, and Susan Weiler for their encouragement and helpful comments on earlier drafts.

We are grateful to Peter Dougherty of Princeton University Press for taking on this project, for his unfailing support at every stage, and for many important suggestions. We are deeply indebted to Marcella Frydman and Jonathan Stein for their extraordinary editorial efforts, which have greatly improved the book's style, presentation, and readability. Jan W. Zakrzewski generously allowed us to use an image of one of his paintings for the cover. We much appreciate the time he devoted to the initial design. We were extremely fortunate to have Maria Lindenfeldar develop the final design for the cover, which comes as close as seems possible to conveying the main ideas of this book in abstract art. Cyd Westmoreland provided expert copyediting, and Ellen Foos and Peter Strupp were instrumental in accomplishing the rare feat of making the book's production a painless process.

We are pleased to acknowledge support at various stages of this project from the Alfred P. Sloan Foundation, the C. V. Starr Center for Applied Economics at New York University, Ewing Marion Kauffman Foundation, the Ford Foundation, the Hoover Institution at Stanford University, the Institute for Advanced Studies in Vienna, the Institute of Economics at the University of Copenhagen, the Nathan Cummings Foundation, and the Reginald F. Atkins Chair at the University of New Hampshire.

Finally, we thank Halina, Sybille, Ben, Julia, and Marcella for their infinite patience with our sacrifice of time and attention that was rightfully theirs.

Abbreviations

ADL	autoregressive distributive lag
AMEX	American Express Banking Corporation
ARCH	autoregressive conditional heteroskedastic
BF	Bilson and Fama (regression)
BP	British pound
CCA	cumulative current account
CPI	consumer price index
CRRA	constant relative risk aversion (utility function)
DCS	direction of change statistic
DF	Dornbusch and Frankel sticky-price (model)
DM	German mark
ESTAR	exponential smooth transition autoregressive model
FIML	full information maximum likelihood
FB	Frenkel and Bilson flexible-price (model)
GP	gap plus (model)
HM	Hooper and Morton sticky-price hybrid model
IFP	international financial position
IKE	Imperfect Knowledge Economics
JY	Japanese yen
LCP	local-currency pricing
MMSI	Money Market Services International
NOEM	New Open Economy Macroeconomics
OLG	overlapping generations
PCP	producer-currency pricing
PPP	purchasing power parity
QR	Quandt ratio
RAUIP	risk-adjusted uncovered interest parity
REH	Rational Expectations Hypothesis
RMSE	root mean square error
TCEH	Theories Consistent Expectations Hypothesis
UAUIP	uncertainty-adjusted uncovered interest parity
UIP	uncovered interest parity

PART I

From Early Modern Economics
to Imperfect Knowledge Economics

1 Recognizing the Limits of Economists' Knowledge

> I prefer to use the term "theory" in a very narrow sense, to refer to an explicit dynamic system, something that can be put on a computer and *run*. This is what I mean by the "mechanics" of economic development—the construction of a mechanical, artificial world, populated by the interacting robots that economics typically studies.
>
> ROBERT E. LUCAS, JR.,
> *Lectures on Economic Growth*, p. 21

> Policymakers often have to act, or choose not to act, even though we may not fully understand the full range of possible outcomes, let alone each possible outcome's likelihood. As a result, . . . policymakers have needed to reach to broader, though less mathematically precise, hypotheses about how the world works.
>
> ALAN GREENSPAN,
> "Risk and Uncertainty in Monetary Policy,"
> *American Economic Review*, p. 38

1.1. The Overreach of Contemporary Economics

On the occasion of his 1974 Nobel lecture, Friedrich Hayek appealed to fellow economists to resist the "pretence of exact knowledge" in economic analysis. Drawing on his prescient analysis of the inevitable failure of central planning, Hayek warned against the lure of predetermination: no economist's model would ever render *fully* intelligible the causes of market outcomes or the consequences of government policies. Decades later, experience as a Federal Reserve chief led Alan Greenspan to concur with Hayek. He told the economists assembled at a 2004 meeting of the American Economic Association that central banking requires creativity. Central bankers, just as all individuals, act in a world of imperfect knowledge; hence, they can comprehend neither "the full range of possible [market] outcomes" nor their likelihoods.

In contrast to these skeptical views, contemporary economists have been much less circumspect about the ability of economic analysis to uncover the causal mechanism that underpins market outcomes. In fact, over the past three decades, economists have come to believe that, to be worthy of scientific status, economic models should generate "sharp" predictions that account for the full range of possible market outcomes and their like-lihoods.[1] To construct such models, which we refer to as *fully predetermined,* contemporary economists must fully prespecify how market participants alter their decisions and how resulting aggregate outcomes unfold over time. By design, contemporary models rule out the importance of individual creativity in coping with inherently imperfect knowledge and unforeseen changes in the social context.

In modeling individual decision making and market outcomes, economists make use of a variety of assumptions and insights. The vast majority appeal to a set of a priori assumptions that putatively characterize how "rational" individuals make decisions. In contrast to these *conventional economists,* the increasingly influential *behavioral economists* appeal to empirical observations of how individuals "actually" behave. However different the conventional and behavioral approaches may appear, they share one key feature: both instruct economists to search for fully predetermined models of the causal mechanism that underpins change. Because of this common feature, we regard the conventional and behavioral approaches as branches of the *contemporary approach.*

Economists fully predetermine their models by first representing individual decision making in terms of causal variables, although they sometimes leave the particular set of causal variables unspecified. They also usually specify a set of qualitative conditions that restrict how the causal variables enter their representations of individual behavior at an arbitrary "initial" point in time.[2] While their representations at the initial point in time are qualitative, the insistence on sharp predictions of change leads economists to impose restrictions that relate exactly the properties of their representation at all points in time, past and future, to the properties of the representation at the initial point in time.

Contemporary models usually involve random error terms, the properties of which are also fully prespecified. These standard probabilistic representations imply a highly restricted view of uncertainty as mere random deviations from a fully predetermined model of behavior. Though they may appear to be different from their deterministic counterparts, contemporary probabilistic models represent market participants as "robots" who revise their behavior according to rules that are prespecified by an economist.

The insistence on models that fully prespecify change has led many economists to an extreme position concerning how policymaking should be

---

1. See chapters 3 and 4 for a formal discussion of the concept of sharp predictions in contemporary economics. For an early comprehensive treatment, see Sargent (1987).

2. For example, it is common for economists to assume that an individual's utility depends positively on her consumption of goods or that her forecast of a future market price depends positively on the current value of this price.

conducted. Academic economists have argued that discretion on the part of policymakers is likely to result in "inferior" (according to a given "social welfare" criterion) macroeconomic performance. The belief in the scientific status of such conclusions has been so strong that leading economists have advocated far-reaching institutional changes to eliminate all discretion on the part of policymakers.[3] In a seminal paper, for example, Finn Kydland and Edward Prescott advocate

> institutional arrangements which make it difficult and time-consuming to change the policy rules in all but emergency situations. One possible institutional arrangement is for Congress to legislate monetary and fiscal policy rules and these rules to become effective only after a 2-year delay. This would make discretionary policy all but impossible. (Kydland and Prescott, 1977, p. 487)

The trouble with such proposals is that, in reducing policymakers to passive executors of rules based on a fully predetermined economic model, they ignore the multifarious ways in which economies change over time. As Governor Mervyn King of the Bank of England once put it, "Our understanding of the economy is incomplete and constantly evolving, sometimes in small steps, sometimes in big leaps." Because neither economists nor policymakers can adequately prespecify all possible outcomes and their likelihoods, Governor King continued,

> Any monetary policy rule that is judged to be optimal today is likely to be superseded by a new and improved version tomorrow. . . . So learning about changes in the structure of the economy lies at the heart of the daily work of central banks. To describe monetary policy in terms of a constant rule derived from a known model of the economy is to ignore this process of learning. (King, 2005, pp. 8–10)

Although central bankers are always on guard for "changes in the structure of the economy," contemporary models presume that such changes are

---

3. To avoid misunderstanding, we should stress that what we question here is the scientific status of proposals for rules based on fully predetermined models. Nevertheless, some "rules" or guidelines, such as inflation or exchange rate targets, intended to anchor the decisions of market participants, may play a useful role in policymaking. For example, see Atkins (2006) for a report on how the Norwegian Central Bank uses guidelines and announces long-term forecasts in an attempt to influence market participants' decisions. However, as we discuss in section 1.7, to shed light on the consequences of such policy tools for individual decision making and aggregate outcomes, they would have to be analyzed in models that are not fully predetermined.

unimportant for understanding market outcomes and the consequences of government policies.

1.2. The Aim of This Book

This book arose from our conviction that the contemporary approach to economic analysis of market outcomes is fundamentally flawed. The practice of fully prespecifying the causal mechanism that underpins change leads to insuperable epistemological problems in modeling aggregate outcomes and lies at the root of contemporary models' failure to explain these outcomes in many markets. Our critique rests on the premise that the causal mechanism that underpins the way market participants alter their decisions is not fully intelligible to anyone, including economists or market participants themselves. We hope to persuade our colleagues that the exclusive pursuit of models that "can be put on the computer and *run*" has been misguided; the view that only such models are "scientific" has impeded economic research.

Our goal is to contribute to the development of a more insightful approach to modeling market outcomes and the consequences of government policies. As the first step toward such an approach, we place imperfect knowledge on the part of market participants and economists at the center of our analysis. Our proposed approach, which we call *Imperfect Knowledge Economics* (IKE), does not seek to explain exactly how market outcomes unfold over time. That is, we eschew the contemporary practice that relates change in outcomes precisely to a set of causal factors that has, in turn, been prespecified by an economist.

Following the tradition of early modern economics,[4] IKE constructs its models of aggregate outcomes by relating them to individual behavior. Like the contemporary approach, it represents this behavior mathematically. But IKE attempts to come to terms with early modern economists' justified modesty about how complete their representations of individual behavior could be. As in any scientific theory, IKE must presume that purposeful behavior exhibits regularities, even if these regularities are context-dependent.

---

4. For lack of a better term, we refer to Friedrich Hayek, John Maynard Keynes, and Frank Knight as *early modern* economists. These economists and some of their contemporaries were early modern in that they attempted to explain aggregate outcomes in reference to individual behavior. But their analyses were far more flexible than contemporary economists' because they understood that the causal factors underpinning individual behavior are often not fully intelligible to individuals themselves, let alone to outsiders such as economists. For further elaboration of this point, see the remainder of this chapter as well as the succeeding chapter.

However, IKE explores the possibility that these regularities, the ways in which market participants make and alter their decisions, may be formalized with *qualitative* conditions. In contrast to both conventional and behavioral models, these conditions only *partially* predetermine economists' representations of change.

IKE solves an intractable epistemological problem that is inherent to fully predetermined, microfounded models of market outcomes. These models, which aim to explain market outcomes on the basis of explicit representations of individual behavior, have become hallmarks of contemporary economics. Yet these models, in both their conventional and behavioral forms, are internally inconsistent in a world of imperfect knowledge: the aggregate outcomes that they predict deviate systematically from their representations of market participants' forecasts of those outcomes. Recognizing the imperfection of knowledge—the fact that no one, including economists, can fully prespecify change—is the key to solving the inconsistency problem that has plagued fully predetermined models. IKE begins with this premise.

In contemporary models, change in the composition of the set of causal variables and in their influences on outcomes is fully prespecified. By contrast, partially predetermined models do not fully specify which causal variables may become relevant in the future or how these variables may enter an economist's representation.[5] By design, IKE models do not imply sharp predictions of change, but they do generate qualitative implications. Moreover, we do not abandon the key aim of all scientific endeavor: IKE restricts its models sufficiently to enable an economist to distinguish empirically among alternative explanations of economic phenomena. At the same time, opening economics to models that generate *only* qualitative predictions is important to understanding salient features of the empirical record that extant approaches have found anomalous.

We use the foreign exchange market as a testing ground for the development of our alternative approach. We find that IKE sheds new light on features of the empirical record that have long resisted adequate explanations by fully predetermined models. We construct IKE models that deliver new, empirically relevant explanations of exchange rate dynamics, particularly their persistent and often large misalignments, as well as movements in the market premium (that is, excess return) on holding a speculative asset, such as foreign exchange.[6] Once we understand market outcomes with IKE

---

5. In our IKE model of exchange rate swings in chapter 14, we do not need to specify, even in a qualitative way, how a set of causal variables influences individual decision making at any point in time.

6. We develop IKE models of the market premium and long swings in the exchange rate in chapters 12 and 14, respectively.

models, some of the important "findings" that have been reported in the literature are rendered artifacts of a world viewed through the prism of fully predetermined models.

1.3. Contemporary Models in a World of Imperfect Knowledge

Our critique of the contemporary approach rests on the crucial premise that market participants and economists have only imperfect knowledge of the causal mechanism that underpins market outcomes. We recognize that, despite considerable effort by philosophers, the meaning of the term *knowledge,* let alone *imperfect knowledge,* cannot be encapsulated easily. In this book, we make use of a relatively narrow definition of imperfect knowledge that is closely tied to the idea of a fully predetermined model in contemporary economics. We refer to knowledge as *imperfect* if no one has access to a fully predetermined model that adequately represents, as judged by whatever criteria one chooses, the causal mechanism that underpins outcomes in all time periods, past and future. Because knowledge is imperfect, individuals are not constrained to view the world through the prism of a common model. Consequently, one of the main premises of our approach is that market participants, who act on the basis of different preferences, constraints, and causal factors, will likewise adopt different strategies in forecasting the future as well as the consequences of their decisions.

According to Hayek (1945), such a division of knowledge among market participants is the key feature that distinguishes the "rational economic order" from an "optimal" allocation of resources by a single individual:

> The economic problem of society is . . . not merely a problem of how to allocate "given" resources—if "given" is taken to mean given to a single mind which deliberately solves the [resource-allocation] problem. . . . It is rather a problem of how to secure the best use of resources known to any of the members of society, for ends whose relative importance only these individuals know. Or, to put it briefly, *it is a problem of the utilization of knowledge which is not given to anyone in its totality.* (Hayek, 1945, pp. 519–20, emphasis added)

An individual's forecasts of future market outcomes underpin her purposeful choices among alternative uses of her resources.[7] But, as Hayek indi-

---

7. The distinction between an economist and an individual whose behavior an economist is trying to explain plays a key role in our analysis. Thus, to facilitate our presentation, we have chosen

cated, market participants' choices and, hence, market outcomes, arise out of a division of knowledge whose totality remains opaque to any one individual.[8] As economic knowledge is diffuse and evolves in ways that cannot be fully foreseen, economists' fully predetermined models cannot adequately represent the causal mechanism that underpins purposeful actions, regardless of whether these actions are motivated by self-interest or other objectives.

Nevertheless, we suspect that some of our colleagues may find our critique of the contemporary approach uncompelling. They might argue that economics, like every other field of human inquiry, must abstract from many features of the real world, and that its fully predetermined models are simply particularly bold abstractions. In response to the claim that the assumptions of their models are unrealistic, economists often invoke Milton Friedman's argument:

> The relevant question to ask about the "assumptions" of a theory is not whether they are descriptively "realistic," for they never are, but whether they are sufficiently good approximations for the purpose in hand. And this question can be answered only by seeing whether the theory works[,] which means whether it yields sufficiently accurate predictions. (Friedman, 1953, p. 15)

Useful assumptions in science are therefore those that abstract from features of reality considered irrelevant for the problems under study. The hope is that the omitted considerations are relatively unimportant for one's understanding of a problem.

In general, the assumptions underlying the model of a phenomenon reflect a combination of extant knowledge, convention among scientists, and, at least in part, an investigator's luck and intuition as to what will "work" empirically. Thus, no one can prove on purely logical grounds that the contemporary approach will never succeed in explaining market outcomes. We can, however, appeal to the many epistemological and empirical failures of the contemporary approach and show how these failures stem precisely from contemporary economists' insistence that their models should fully prespecify change. Fully predetermined models are flawed not because they are abstract, but because they disregard a *key* feature that drives outcomes

---

to refer to an economist (or any other outsider) by different gender than that of an individual (a market participant). Of course, the specific choice of whom we refer to as "he" or "she" is without any significance.

8. Building on Hayek, Frydman (1982) formally shows that, in a world of imperfect knowledge, self-interest would lead to a division of knowledge. See chapter 2 for an extensive discussion and further references.

in real world markets: market participants must cope with imperfect knowledge in making decisions that underpin those outcomes.[9]

1.3.1. The Flawed Microfoundations of Fully Predetermined Models

The recognition of ever-imperfect knowledge requires a substantial revision of the contemporary approach to modeling aggregate outcomes on the basis of individual foundations:[10] fully predetermined models lack plausible microfoundations.

Just as any science, economics seeks to uncover and explain empirical regularities. This uncontroversial observation has an important implication for modern economic theory. On the one hand, models of aggregate outcomes are based on mathematical representations of individual behavior; on the other hand, individual behavior depends on forecasts of aggregate outcomes. This inherent two-way interdependence opens up the possibility of the inconsistency that we noted earlier: the forecasts of aggregate outcomes that an economist attributes to individuals may differ systematically from the predictions of an economist's aggregate model.

Lucas argued that models embodying such an inconsistency are "the wrong theory." For example, suppose an economist attributes to firms in each period the forecast that a given market price will remain constant at its current level, while the resulting aggregate model predicts that this price will rise period after period. "In such a model, you could *see* profit opportunities that firms were passing up. Why couldn't they see these opportunities too? But if they did, the model couldn't be right. If your theory reveals profit opportunities, you have the wrong theory" (Lucas, 2001, p. 13).

To rid economic models of this modeling inconsistency, Lucas (1972) and others embraced the Rational Expectations Hypothesis (REH). REH instructs an economist to choose only that representation of individual forecasting behavior that coincides exactly with the causal mechanism implied by the aggregate model that he himself constructs. As Lucas later put it, "John Muth's [REH] focused on this inconsistency . . . and showed how it can be removed" (Lucas, 1995, p. 255). In his Nobel lecture, Lucas recounted this revolutionary moment in the development of the contemporary approach to modeling aggregate outcomes:

> The prevailing strategy for macroeconomic modeling in the early 1960s held that the individual or sectoral models arising out of this

---

9. For an early critique of conventional models along similar lines, see Frydman (1982, 1983), Frydman and Phelps (1983), and Phelps (1983). Independently, Soros (1987), drawing on the concept of an open society (Popper, 1946), argued that the imperfection of knowledge on the part of market participants is the key to understanding financial markets.

10. See chapter 3 for a formal argument.

intertemporal theorizing could then simply be combined in a single model. But models of individual decisions over time necessarily involve expected future prices. . . . However, . . . [aggregate] models assembled from such individual components implied behavior of actual prices . . . that bore no relation to, and were in general *grossly inconsistent* with, the price expectations that the theory imputed to individual agents. (Lucas, 1995, pp. 254–55, emphasis added)

In the wake of such statements, achieving consistency between representations on the individual and aggregate levels is widely perceived as the solution to the problem of modeling rational forecasting behavior. Moreover, because economists believe that REH delivers such consistency, it has become the key building block of most economic models of aggregate outcomes.

1.3.1.1. REH Models

Lucas's insight concerning the key theoretical importance of avoiding internal inconsistency in models of aggregate outcomes that are based on representations of individual behavior is compelling. But what he and other followers of REH seem to have overlooked is that the outcomes that their models try to explain stem from decisions by individuals who must all cope with ever-imperfect knowledge. Although Lucas formulated his argument against fully predetermined non-REH models, it also applies to REH models.

Building on Frydman (1982), we argue that, *in a world of imperfect knowledge*, REH models presume that individual market participants endlessly disregard systematic information in their forecast errors. REH supposes that an economist's fully predetermined model of aggregate outcomes adequately represents, at least in the aggregate, market participants' forecasting strategies. Recalling Lucas, if an REH model were to capture adequately empirical regularities in aggregate outcomes, and some individuals did not use this model to forecast, it would mean there were profit opportunities that individual market participants were seeing and endlessly passing up. In a world of imperfect knowledge, market participants make use of diverse forecasting strategies; to account for this diversity, therefore, an REH model has to presume gross irrationality. If Lucas's alarm at the prospect of inconsistent models was appropriate, as we think it was, we must conclude that REH models, too, are the "wrong theory" for modeling aggregate outcomes on the basis of individual foundations.[11]

11. For a more complete discussion of this issue, see chapter 3.

1.3.1.2. Behavioral Models

Behavioral economists, for their part, have uncovered many inconsistencies between the way market participants "actually" behave and conventional representations of rational behavior. They have not, however, interpreted their findings as evidence that the main problem with conventional representations is that they do not adequately represent rational behavior. Instead, they have concluded that market participants are irrational.

Behavioral economists justify this striking conclusion by arguing that market participants are, after all, human beings with inadequate foresight, unpredictable emotions, and limited computational abilities. But, despite their putative embrace of "psychological realism," behavioral economists emulate their conventional colleagues by disregarding the importance of individual creativity, which is arguably one of the defining features of human behavior. They do so by prespecifying "[h]ow *exactly* people deviate from the [conventional representation of rationality]" (Barberis and Thaler, 2003, p. 1056, emphasis added).

By design, a non-REH behavioral model embodies an inconsistency between its representations on the individual and aggregate levels: it represents an individual's forecasting strategy as one whose predictions are systematically inconsistent with the predictions of the aggregate model.[12] Lucas has argued forcefully that models, such as non-REH behavioral ones, in which market participants endlessly disregard systematic information in their forecast errors, posit the "wrong theory."

This reasoning leads us to conclude that there is an inherent conflict between the objective of searching for models of aggregate outcomes based on explicit microfoundations and the insistence of both conventional and behavioral approaches that these models be fully predetermined. The methodology raises an intractable epistemological problem: in real world markets, the "microfoundations" of fully predetermined models prove specious.

1.3.2. Structural Instability of Contemporary Models

Although fully predetermined representations of individual behavior cannot serve as the microfoundations of any theory of aggregate outcomes, this conclusion does not rule out the possibility that fully predetermined models of aggregate outcomes, even if they are based on explicit microfoundations, might be useful. With insightful selection of the causal variables and a bit of luck, fully predetermined models may capture adequately, according to

---

12. Puzzlingly, although Lucas argued that this inconsistency provided the main motivation for the REH revolution, behavioral economists, who developed their approach after REH, have disregarded Lucas's arguments.

statistical or other, less stringent criteria, the past relationship between the causal variables and the aggregate outcomes in a selected historical period.

But as time passes, market participants eventually alter the way that they make decisions and the social context changes in ways that cannot be fully foreseen by anyone. Disregarding these key determinants of change restricts the usefulness of such models for illuminating the historical record to limited periods of time. The well-known debacle of the hedge fund Long Term Capital Management suggests how fully predetermined models eventually become inadequate. After all, trading in financial markets cannot be reduced to mere financial engineering, even if it is based on the most recent advances in contemporary finance theory.

We are thus led to one of the key empirical implications of imperfect knowledge: even if a fully predetermined model's structure adequately represents outcomes in terms of a set of causal variables during a particular period of time, it will be inadequate during other periods. When such models are used to analyze time-series data—or as aids for policymakers, bankers, traders, and others—they should always be tested for possible structural changes. These test procedures should not require an economist to fully prespecify when structural change might occur or which causal variables might enter the structure of the postchange representation. In chapters 12 and 15, we develop such an approach in the context of modeling the premium on foreign exchange and the exchange rate, respectively.

1.4. The Non-Fully Intelligible Individual

The observation that extant models lack plausible microfoundations leads us to a re-examination of how individual decision making ought to be represented. Conventional economists often use the same fully predetermined representation to explain individual self-interested behavior and aggregate outcomes over many decades or in different economies or markets. They impute such generality to their "theory" because they believe that self-interest is a universal human trait and that they have found a way to represent it with fully predetermined rules. Behavioral economists share this view of rationality. This understanding leads them to diagnose the inconsistency between the actual behavior of market participants and conventional representations of "rational" behavior as a symptom of market participants' "irrationality."

IKE is compatible with—but does not necessarily require—the presumption that market participants in capitalist economies are motivated by purely self-interested concerns. The focus on self-interest in economic analysis has elided a central issue: even if self-interestedness were universal, such a presumption would not enable an outsider to fully prespecify his representations of self-interested behavior or their implications both for aggregate outcomes and for the consequences of economic policies. The reasons for this assertion are already implicit in our foregoing discussion. Individual decisions depend on forecasts of future market outcomes. These outcomes are not only a result of the actions of many individuals, but they also depend on future economic policies, political developments, and institutional changes. Thus, even if individuals are presumed to be purely self-interested, the way that they deploy resources depends as much on the social context as it does on their personal motivations.[13]

An individual herself, let alone an outsider, cannot fully prespecify how she will form and revise her forecasts. Even if an economist were able to attribute clear objectives to a market participant, he would still be unable to assess the participant's rationality.[14] IKE supposes, therefore, that an economist cannot ascertain completely whether an individual behaves rationally or irrationally; that is, he cannot completely evaluate whether she pursues her objectives reasonably or unreasonably.

1.5. IKE Models

How can economic analysis recognize the centrality of imperfect knowledge while continuing to represent individual and aggregate behavior in mathematical terms? How can it acknowledge the importance of individual creativity and the inevitability of unpredictable changes in social contexts while still generating "predictions which . . . are of empirical significance"? The future relevance of economics to understanding real world markets and policy analysis lies in its ability to articulate answers to these questions; the IKE framework offers one response.

Like contemporary models, IKE models consist of representations of an individual's preferences, constraints, and forecasts of future outcomes that are relevant to her well-being. IKE also imposes qualitative conditions on its representations at an initial arbitrary point in time. But, in sharp contrast to the contemporary approach, IKE does not fully prespecify how its representations of preferences and forecasting behavior change between an initial point and all other points in time.

IKE recognizes that without some regularity in economic life, no economic theory that aimed for generality would be possible. IKE considers two types of regularities on the individual level. First, *an individual's preferences or forecasting strategy at different points in time may share certain qualitative features.*

---

13. Foley (2003) has advanced a related criticism of the notion of rationality invoked in economic analysis.

14. Kay (2004, p. 16) has called this fundamental difficulty "obliquity." As he quipped, "no one will ever be buried with the epitaph 'He maximized shareholder value,' . . . because even with hindsight there is no way of recognising whether the objective has been achieved."

For example, at each point in time, her utility may depend positively on changes in her wealth or her forecast of a future market price may depend on a changing subset of causal variables that is contained in an unchanging larger set.

Second, although the way that any of the causal variables affect an individual's preferences or forecasting behavior may change with time, these changes may share certain qualitative features. For example, although an individual might substantially revise her preferences or forecasting strategy, the effect of such revisions may be "conservative," that is, her pre- and postchange preferences or forecasts may not be "too" different.

IKE instructs an economist to search for regularities in individual behavior but presumes that they can at best be formalized with qualitative restrictions on its representations. Because IKE's restrictions only partially prespecify change in a model, we refer to them as *partially predetermining*. Just as in extant models, IKE represents future outcomes as uncertain. However, instead of the standard (fully predetermined) conditional probability distributions implied by a contemporary model, an IKE model relates the distribution of the outcome variables at a future time to its distribution at an initial time in only a qualitative way. Thus, IKE's partially predetermined probabilistic representations of change are compatible with Knight (1921) and Keynes's (1921, 1936) insight that economists cannot fully prespecify the consequences of individual decisions or future market outcomes and their chances of occurrence.[15]

In contrast to the fully predetermining restrictions of a contemporary model, the restrictions of an IKE model do not force an economist to take a position on how a set of causal variables or their influences on individual decision making may change between any two points in time. Because IKE only partially prespecifies its representations, a change in a causal variable back to its initial value does not lead an IKE model to devolve to its initial structure. Thus, historical change plays an essential role in an IKE model: as time passes, partially predetermined representations make allowance for the possibility that market participants' knowledge and their decisions concerning the use of resources will evolve in ways that cannot be fully foreseen.[16]

---

15. See chapter 4 for a formal treatment.

16. This point has an important implication for supply and demand analysis, which is basic to economics. Under IKE, the unique equilibrium implied by the usual fully predetermined supply and demand curves is replaced by a myriad of equilibria implied by partially predetermined *supply and demand paths*. Although these paths are not unique, they share common features: all demand paths are downward sloping and all supply paths are upward sloping. It is these common features that enable supply and demand analysis of aggregate outcomes under IKE to replace the usual analysis implied by fully predetermined models. See chapter 5.

1.5.1. Individual Preferences

Many studies have found that conventional representations of preferences, which usually involve expected utility theory and the assumption of risk aversion, are grossly inconsistent with the way individuals actually behave. Much of the evidence on how individuals make choices is based on laboratory experiments in which the structure of payoffs from various gambles is predetermined by the experimenter. This common experimental design allows the investigator to examine the nature of an individual's preferences without the confounding problem of having to represent her forecasts of the potential payoffs from gambling. The findings concerning the importance of loss aversion and the seminal formulation of prospect theory by Kahneman and Tversky (1979) and Tversky and Kahneman (1992) made use of such a setup.

Building on prospect theory, we develop an alternative representation of preferences for modeling decision making that is consistent with the experimental evidence. This representation, which we call *endogenous prospect theory*, supposes that an individual's preferences share certain qualitative features at every point in time. This utility ranking depends on her forecast of the outcomes of her decisions regarding the allocation of her resources, in particular, on her forecast of future returns and on her forecast of the size of the potential loss that she might incur. The representation also presumes that an individual's degree of loss aversion increases as her forecast of the size of the potential loss increases.[17] Because we represent this forecast with partially predetermining restrictions, the way in which an individual's degree of loss aversion changes between any two points in time is also partially predetermined in our models.

Although laboratory experiments have been the key to uncovering new ways to model preferences, their typical design effectively limits the economist's view of an individual's decision making; the economist is only able to observe the subject's responses to an experimenter's stimuli. This basic framework, which is used extensively in psychological research, sidesteps a key problem: participants in real world markets forecast payoffs, the experimenter's "stimuli," on the basis of imperfect knowledge. Moreover, these forecasts depend not only on the subject's creativity, her analytical abilities, and other personal characteristics, but also on the unfolding social context.[18] As a result, the basic type of model used in these psychological ex-

---

17. In chapter 9, we show that this assumption, which we call *endogenous loss aversion*, is needed to model an individual's decision about how much capital to gamble at any point in time solely on the basis of prospect theory.

18. Kahneman and Tversky (1979) recognized that, while laboratory experiments are useful in uncovering the properties of the utility function over single outcomes, they may be much less informative about an individual's choices over gambles with two or more uncertain outcomes in real world markets.

periments is grossly insufficient as a foundation for representing economic behavior.

1.5.2. Individual Forecasting Behavior

The premise that self-interested or, more broadly, purposeful behavior is to an important degree context dependent does not dispute the usefulness of insights from psychology in modeling individual behavior. Indeed, we make use of some of these insights in representing how an individual revises her forecasting strategy. For example, researchers have uncovered much evidence that individuals are conservative in how they revise their beliefs in the face of new evidence.[19] In our model of exchange rate swings, we formulate this finding in terms of partially predetermining restrictions that limit the change in a market participant's forecast that arises from the change in her forecasting strategy.

However, the importance of the social context in an individual's decision making implies that, in searching for empirical regularities that might be useful in modeling an individual's decisions, economists will need to look beyond laboratory experiments and insights from psychology. To represent individual behavior, an economist must search for—and attempt to formalize—the findings of other social sciences. Other social scientists have knowledge and intuitions concerning the social context within which individuals make decisions that may complement economists' work in modeling individual forecasting behavior.[20]

We make use of the insight that conventions among market participants play an important role in individual decision making.[21] We also draw on our understanding of the qualitative regularities that have characterized aggregate outcomes; we suppose that market participants must also be aware of these regularities when they are forming their forecasts. For example, the tendency of exchange rates to undergo long swings that revolve around historical benchmark levels plays a key role in our model of the premium on foreign exchange. Our representations of individual behavior, on the basis of which we construct our model for the market premium, involve specifications for bulls' and bears' forecasts of the potential loss from holding

---

19. See Edwards (1968) and Shleifer (2000).

20. The use of insights concerning the social context in modeling individual behavior has a venerable tradition in sociology. Perhaps best known is Weber's argument that Protestantism—an important aspect of the social context within which individuals made decisions—is key to understanding "rational" behavior at the time of the emergence of capitalism. See chapter 2 for a discussion and references.

21. For early insights on the role of social conventions in individual decision making and its implications for market outcomes, see Keynes (1936).

speculative positions.[22] These representations constrain, in a qualitative way, the revisions of market participants' forecasts of the potential loss to depend on the gap between the exchange rate and their assessments of its historical benchmark.[23]

The gap and conservative restrictions, because they only partially pre-specify change in our models, are consistent with myriad possible ways that an individual's forecasting strategy may develop over time. Nevertheless, the possible ways that this strategy could unfold in a model share certain qual-itative features. It is this partially predetermined aspect of IKE models that enables them to deliver testable implications.

The distinguishing feature of our IKE models of exchange rate swings and the market premium is that they do not require an economist to pre-specify either the potential set of causal variables that underpin change in outcomes or the influences of these variables in his representation. This feature is important, as the presumption that an economist can prespec-ify, even partially, the set of causal variables and their influences is very bold.

Nevertheless, in addressing some problems, we acknowledge that an economist is required to represent these aspects of the causal mechanism. For example, to examine whether macroeconomic fundamentals matter for exchange rate movements, an economist must prespecify, at least partially, a representation of the causal mechanism that involves the set of potential fun-damentals (potential causal factors) and how they influence the exchange rate. To this end, we consider the idea that the stock of extant economic models summarizes economists' insights concerning the causal factors that underpin market outcomes. Presumably, these insights are shared by market participants. This idea underlies the *Theories Consistent Expectations Hypoth-esis* (TCEH) proposed by Frydman and Phelps (1990). TCEH recognizes that a set of extant economic models at best indicates to a market par-ticipant, or to an economist attempting to represent her behavior, which causal variables may be important for forecasting market outcomes; it also suggests, in a qualitative way, how these variables may influence those out-comes.

In chapter 15, we propose a simple procedure that enables an econo-mist to decipher qualitative features of the reduced forms of a set of models under imperfect knowledge. TCEH provides a way to take into account the qualitative features of more than one model in constructing its representa-

---

22. A bull (a bear) is a market participant who speculates on the belief that the asset price will rise (fall).

23. This idea, that the convention concerning the historical benchmark level plays an important role in understanding individual forecasting behavior in an asset market, was put forth by Keynes (1936). It was formalized by Tobin (1958) as a key component of his model of the speculative demand for money.

tions of market participants' forecasting strategies.[24] Although TCEH may seem to be a qualitative analog of REH, there are two fundamental differences. To account for the social context within which market participants act, TCEH recognizes that an economist cannot ignore the pluralism of models. And, furthermore, TCEH only partially prespecifies change.

1.5.3. How IKE Avoids Modeling Inconsistency

Lucas (2001) has argued that fully predetermined models that embody an inconsistency between their representations on the individual and aggregate levels do not constitute a theory of persistent regularities. Lucas's argument makes the general claim that, if a model predicts an unchanging feature of the causal mechanism underpinning aggregate outcomes regardless of whether the feature is qualitative or quantitative, then an economist's representation of individual behavior should not be inconsistent with this regularity.

Our argument that REH does not solve the inconsistency problem in a world of imperfect knowledge begs the question of how IKE avoids it. IKE does so by recognizing the limits of economists' knowledge, that is, by instructing economists only to partially prespecify their representations of change. IKE avoids the inconsistency in different ways, depending on whether an economist represents the same or distinct aspects of the causal mechanism on the individual and aggregate levels. If he represents the same features on the individual and aggregate levels, he must choose a representation of individual forecasting behavior that leads to the same qualitative predictions concerning the causal mechanism as that implied by his aggregate model.

In chapter 15, for example, we construct a model that generates qualitative predictions about the relationship between the exchange rate and macroeconomic fundamentals. We illustrate TCEH by using the qualitative features of three extant monetary models to represent an individual's forecasting strategy. If the models all agree on how a particular causal variable influences the future exchange rate, then our TCEH representation constrains the sign of the weight that is attached to this variable to be consistent with these models. Otherwise, TCEH leaves this sign unconstrained. Thus, although TCEH uses a variety of models to represent forecasting behavior, it avoids, by construction, the inconsistency between an economist's representations on the individual and aggregate levels.

Although TCEH offers a way to avoid an inconsistency in models that involve representations of the same aspect of the causal mechanism, some

---

24. For an early implementation of TCEH in modeling exchange rates, see Goldberg and Frydman (1996a).

features of the empirical record may only require that an economist represent different aspects of the causal mechanism in modeling individual and aggregate behavior. If an economist were to set out to construct a fully predetermined model of such phenomena, he could not avoid an internal inconsistency under imperfect knowledge. However, because IKE constrains its representations only partially, it enables an economist to model distinct aspects of the causal mechanism on the individual and aggregate levels, while avoiding the inconsistency problem.

For example, our IKE model of the premium implies that the excess return on foreign exchange depends positively on the gap between the exchange rate and market participants' assessments of its historical benchmark. Our representations on the individual level, however, involve predictions concerning a different aspect of the causal mechanism, namely, the potential loss from holding a speculative position. Moreover, because our model is partially predetermined, the qualitative prediction on the aggregate level places no constraints on how the gap should influence an individual's forecast of her potential loss. In this way, our IKE model of the premium avoids an internal inconsistency and, in contrast to fully predetermined models of the premium, it does not presume that market participants are grossly irrational.

1.6. IKE of Exchange Rates and Risk

In parts II and III of this book, we focus on many of the aspects of behavior in currency markets that are particularly difficult to reconcile with the conventional approach to exchange rate dynamics. The exchange rate modelers of the 1960s and 1970s believed that currency movements depended largely on macroeconomic fundamentals and that market participants acted in "rational" ways.[25] But the empirical failures of conventional exchange rate models have led economists to abandon these tenets; many now believe that macroeconomic fundamentals do not play an important role in currency movements and that market participants forgo obvious profit opportunities in making their speculative decisions.

1.6.1. Exchange Rate Swings and Macroeconomic Fundamentals

It is clear from the past three decades of floating currencies that exchange rates have a tendency to undergo large and persistent swings away from historical benchmark levels, such as those based on purchasing power parity

---

25. The seminal open-economy model is from Mundell (1963) and Fleming (1962). Other early milestone studies include Dornbusch (1976), Frenkel (1976), and Kouri (1976).

(PPP). Economists have found this kind of behavior difficult to explain with models that use REH, such as those based on Dornbusch (1976).[26] It is striking that, by 1983, Rudiger Dornbusch himself had reached the conclusion that his own overshooting theory could not explain the long-swings behavior of exchange rates. He asserted, "A theory is needed that will explain why the dollar—real or nominal—is both high and stuck [away from parity]" (Dornbusch, 1983, p. 83). The failure to explain swings, to which Dornbusch alluded, led to the view that exchange rate fluctuations are driven by "irrational noise" traders who do not rely on macroeconomic fundamentals. This view was further reinforced by economists' unsuccessful search for a fully predetermined, mostly invariant, relationship between the exchange rate and macroeconomic fundamentals during the current period of floating rates.

However, there is much evidence in the literature that movements in macroeconomic fundamentals *do* influence exchange rates, but in different ways during different time periods. To account for this temporal instability, we replace REH with an IKE representation of forecasting behavior in the context of the Dornbusch model. Remarkably, swings can occur in our model even if all market participants form their forecasts solely on the basis of macroeconomic fundamentals. Indeed, it is the influence of persistent trends in such fundamentals on market participants' forecasts that cause them to bid the exchange rate away from PPP. Because we recognize that market participants must cope with imperfect knowledge, our model does not rely on the presumption that they are irrational.[27]

1.6.2. Returns on Foreign Exchange

Relying on invariant empirical relationships, many researchers report that future returns in currency markets co-vary negatively with the current value of the forward premium.[28] To explain this behavior, conventional economists have constructed exchange rate models in which risk-averse individuals require a positive return, a premium, to hold risky positions in currency markets. It is widely recognized, however, that this research effort has been unsuccessful.[29]

---

26. Conventional economists have recently generalized the sticky-price model of Dornbusch (1976) to include complete intertemporal microfoundations. We discuss this literature of "new open economy macroeconomics" in chapter 7.

27. For early analyses that also make use of qualitative assumptions about individual forecasting in explaining long swings in the exchange rate, see Schulmeister (1983, 1987) and Soros (1987). Soros (1998, 2006) uses a similar framework to analyze historical change more generally.

28. The forward premium depends on the difference between the forward and spot exchange rates.

29. See chapter 8 for a discussion of this literature.

The failure of REH risk-premium models has led many economists to the view that market participants forgo obvious profit opportunities. IKE does not rely on the presumption of irrationality. We thus explain returns as the compensation for the risk of capital loss from holding speculative positions in foreign exchange. To this end, we develop an IKE model of returns on foreign exchange that is based on endogenous prospect theory.[30]

Our alternative representation of preferences implies that all market participants require a minimum premium before they commit any capital to speculating in the foreign exchange market. This result, in turn, leads to a new equilibrium condition in the foreign exchange market, which we refer to as *uncertainty-adjusted uncovered interest parity*.

But experimental evidence on individuals' preferences is not enough to model their decisions about how much capital to hold in foreign exchange. We also need to represent individuals' forecasting behavior. We do so by replacing REH with partially predetermined IKE representations of forecasting strategies and their revisions.

Our IKE model of the premium is able to capture the fact that market participants differ in their forecasting strategies: bulls gamble on appreciation, while bears bet on depreciation. This difference between bulls and bears proves crucial to explaining the behavior of foreign exchange returns.

1.6.3. Is the Market Really Grossly Inefficient?

Unable to explain the negative co-variation between the return on foreign exchange and the forward premium that their studies report, economists have reached the startling conclusion that "one can make predictable profits by betting against the forward rate" (Obstfeld and Rogoff, 1996, p. 589). The apparent anomaly that these profits remain unexploited has become one of the major "puzzles" in the international finance literature.

There are several well-known studies in the literature that indicate that the relationship between the return on foreign exchange and the forward premium is temporally unstable. In part III, we add to this evidence and show that the correlation between the return on foreign exchange and the forward premium is sometimes negative, sometimes positive, and sometimes insignificantly different from zero.

---

30. Some economists have begun to recognize that the failure of conventional models to explain returns in asset markets stems from ignoring ever-imperfect knowledge on how the structure of the economy unfolds over time. In a recent study along these lines, Weitzman (2006) introduces "perennial" uncertainty concerning the variance of the future growth of consumption into a standard consumption-based asset-pricing model.

Acknowledging the importance of temporal instability goes a long way toward resolving the forward-rate "puzzle." A returns process that gives rise to both negative and positive correlations with the forward premium implies that betting against the forward rate will be profitable during some time periods but not in others. We show that a trading rule based on betting against the forward rate does not deliver significant profits over the modern period of floating in the major currency markets.

Because the contemporary approach has led economists to construct fully predetermined, mostly invariant models of foreign exchange returns that ignore temporal instability, the "finding" of a negative correlation between returns and the forward premium has led them to conclude that there is easy money to be made in the foreign exchange market. But, because the correlation is not always negative, fully predetermined trading rules based on the forward rate do not deliver profits. As in the case of the disjunction between the exchange rate and macroeconomic fundamentals, the forward-rate "puzzle" is another artifact of the epistemological flaws inherent in the contemporary approach. The existence of literally hundreds of studies attempting to explain this "puzzle" provides an example par excellence of how contemporary economics' insistence on sharp predictions has misdirected research and impeded its progress.

1.7. Imperfect Knowledge and Policy Analysis

As in the case of modeling aggregate outcomes, the validity of policy prescriptions based on fully predetermined models should be reexamined under imperfect knowledge. Although this task is outside the scope of this book, our analysis of exchange rate swings provides a strong indication that fully predetermined models are unsuitable for policy analysis in a world of imperfect knowledge.

The vast majority of contemporary economists presume that, once the policy environment is fixed, invariant models adequately represent market participants' behavior. However, we find that, if invariant representations were to represent individual behavior in a traditional monetary model under conditions of imperfect knowledge, then a policy rule that set money supply to grow at a fixed rate would imply an unbounded swing in the exchange rate away from PPP.[31] Stated succinctly, a fixed money-growth rule exacerbates, rather than limits, the magnitude of the exchange rate swing.

---

31. See chapter 14.

Our conclusion that fully predetermined models provide inadequate bases for policy prescriptions still leaves open the possibility that guidelines intended to anchor the forecasts of market participants, such as exchange rate or inflation targets or central bank forecasts, may play a useful role in a world of imperfect knowledge.[32] But this possibility will need to be analyzed in models that do not presume that economists can fully prespecify change.[33]

1.8. From Contemporary Economics to Imperfect Knowledge Economics

The research program of contemporary economics is predicated on the belief that it is possible to prespecify economic change over stretches of time as long as decades. The premise that seems, at least implicitly, to motivate this mechanistic way of modeling market outcomes is that there exists a fully predetermined causal mechanism that underpins actual behavior on the individual and aggregate levels.

But aggregate outcomes and individual forecasting behavior are not governed by an overarching causal mechanism in many, if not all, markets in capitalist economies. Creative forecasting behavior on the part of purposeful individuals alters the causal mechanism that underpins market outcomes in ways—and at points in time—that cannot be fully prespecified. Moreover, changes in the social context, including the evolution of institutions, values, and norms, are all important in engendering temporal instability in causal relationships in real world markets.

If change in capitalist economies is not governed by a fully predetermined causal mechanism, then attempting to explain individual behavior and aggregate outcomes on the basis of representations that presume the existence of such a mechanism is clearly misguided. It is not surprising, then, that the contemporary approach has had great difficulties in discovering the "mechanics of economic development" in many markets where

32. Indeed, a number of central banks have been using such tools in their policymaking. See footnote 3.

33. We have begun such a line of research in Frydman and Goldberg (2004) and Frydman, Goldberg, and Cavusoglu (2007), where we show that our IKE model of the premium leads to a new view of how policy officials can limit the magnitude of long swings in floating-rate regimes. In a manuscript under preparation (Frydman and Goldberg, 2008), we also examine other policy issues, such as inflation targeting, in the context of an IKE model.

profit-seeking inherently involves individual creativity in coping with ever-imperfect knowledge.

Economics calls for a new approach that represents individual behavior and aggregate outcomes mathematically, and that, at the same time, refrains from fully prespecifying economic change. Taking up this task, the following pages propose IKE as the beginnings of such a new approach.

2   A Tradition Interrupted

> The peculiar character of the problem of a rational economic order is determined precisely by the fact that the knowledge of the circumstances of which we must make use never exists in concentrated or integrated form but solely as the dispersed bits of incomplete and frequently contradictory knowledge which all the separate individuals possess.
>
> FRIEDRICH A. HAYEK,
> "The Use of Knowledge in Society,"
> *American Economic Review*, p. 519

> **Evans and Honkapohja**: Do you think differences among people's models are important aspects of macroeconomic policy debates?
>
> **Sargent**: The fact is that you simply cannot talk about those differences within the typical rational expectations model. There is a communism of models. All agents inside the model, the econometrician, and God share the same model. The powerful and useful empirical implications of rational expectations . . . derive from that communism of models.
>
> GEORGE EVANS AND SEPPO HONKAPOHJA,
> "An Interview with Thomas J. Sargent,"
> *Macroeconomic Dynamics*, pp. 566–67

Relating aggregate outcomes to individual decision making has been a hallmark of modern economics. The largely narrative mode of analysis used by Friedrich Hayek, Frank Knight, John Maynard Keynes, and their contemporaries enabled these giants of early modern economics to examine the importance of individual creativity, the division of knowledge and its unfolding over time, and the roles of social norms and institutions for understanding how individual behavior and aggregate outcomes develop. Indeed, their great insight was to place at the center of economic analysis the inextricable connection between imperfect knowledge, non-routine behavior, and the pursuit of profits in capitalist economies. Although the early modern economists recognized the importance of explaining aggregate outcomes on the basis of individual behavior, they also pointed to a fundamental difficulty inherent in any attempt to do so: purposeful behavior, whether motivated by pure self-interest or other objectives, is not completely intelligible to outsiders, whether they are economists, policy officials, or social planners. Consequently, market outcomes that result from the decisions of many individuals are not completely intelligible either.

Post-1945 models of aggregate outcomes recognized the inherent tension between the early modern insights and the attempt to relate aggregate outcomes precisely to individual behavior.[1] "For this and other reasons, [these] macro-economic models . . . were only loosely linked to optimizing behavior of individual agents" (Tobin, 1981, p. 14).

Phelps (1968a) and Phelps et al. (1970) are generally credited with pioneering the modeling of aggregate outcomes on the basis of explicit mathematical representations of individual behavior. These studies acknowledged the importance of the key early modern insight that the way an individual forecasts the future consequences of her decisions cannot be completely understood by an economist. However, it was not apparent how to incorporate this insight into mathematical representations of individual behavior and its implications for aggregate outcomes.[2] Evidently, the hope was that future research would continue to search for ways to resolve the fundamental tension between the non-fully intelligible individual and attempts to represent her behavior mathematically. In the event, subsequent researchers disregarded this vision and have undertaken an intensive effort to construct the "mechanics" of economic development.

2.1. The Stranglehold of the Contemporary Approach

Hayek's (1978) dismissal in his Nobel lecture of the search for "exact knowledge" carried a corollary warning against the common "belief that in order to be accepted as scientific it is necessary to achieve more" than qualitative predictions. Ignoring Hayek's warning, contemporary economists have embraced that belief and have undertaken an intensive empirical effort to uncover "exact knowledge" of aggregate relationships based on fully predetermined representations of individual behavior.

2.1.1. REH

Initially, the contemporary approach to economic analysis of aggregate outcomes was based on representations of "rational" behavior, with its models of an individual's forecasting strategy and its revisions over time employing REH. Such representations presume that an economist can capture adequately what Hayek (1945) referred to as "the use of knowledge in society" with his own fully predetermined model of aggregate outcomes. "In rational

---

1. For a discussion of this issue, see Tobin (1981) and Hahn and Solow (1995).

2. In the absence of a better alternative, these early "microfounded" models represented individual forecasting behavior with a fixed error-correcting rule, called "adaptive expectations." See chapter 3.

expectations models, people's beliefs are among the outcomes of our theorizing. They are not inputs."[3]

Frydman (1982) argued that there is an inherent conflict between REH's presumption that people's beliefs can be adequately represented as one of the outcomes of an economist's theorizing and the premise that market participants are motivated by self-interest: purposeful individuals would not, in general, adhere to a single forecasting strategy.[4] In contrast, REH presupposes an agreement among market participants to rely on one common forecasting strategy. Phelps sharply criticized this "communism of models":

> In the theory of macroeconomic disturbances . . . to which the rational expectations hypothesis has frequently been applied, it is difficult to justify the premise that each agent presumes his expectations to be universal—as if some Jungian collective unconscious existed to bring expectations into an understood agreement. There is no nationwide expectation of Reagan's economic policy *the existence of which is public knowledge*. (Phelps, 1983, p. 32, emphasis in original)

REH is often believed to represent the way rational individuals use information to formulate and revise their forecasting strategies. As Sargent put it:

> The idea of rational expectations is sometimes explained informally by saying that it reflects a process in which individuals are inspecting and altering their forecasting records in ways to eliminate systematic forecast errors. . . . It is also sometimes said that [REH embodies] the idea that economists and the agents they are modeling should be placed on equal footing: the agents in the model should be able to forecast and profit-maximize and utility-maximize as well as . . . the econometrician who constructed the model. (Sargent, 1993, p. 21)

---

3. Thomas J. Sargent, in an interview with Evans and Honkapohja (2005, p. 566). All further quotes that appear in this section without explicit citation are taken from that interview. From the quotes in this section, it may appear that Thomas Sargent, one of the pioneers of the REH approach, has lately become one of its critics. We should acknowledge, however, that in personal communication with Frydman, Sargent emphasized that he does not regard himself as participating in any critique of REH.

4. Frydman showed that popular "learning" models that are often used to justify REH representations of forecasting behavior presume that market participants somehow agree to use the same fully predetermined learning rule. The subsequent literature has disregarded this difficulty and continued to prespecify common learning mechanisms to justify REH models. For a survey of the numerous studies that have attempted to do so, see Evans and Honkapohja (2001) and references therein.

Like Frydman (1980, 1983), and Frydman and Phelps (1983), however, he then pointed out that "these ways of explaining things are suggestive, but misleading, because they make [REH] sound less restrictive and more behavioral than it really is" (Sargent, 1993, p. 21).

Despite the fundamental flaws of REH as a representation of how rational individuals do or should behave, its proponents have been extraordinarily successful in persuading their colleagues to join the REH revolution. But, just as the number of economists embracing this approach and working out its implications has increased, so has empirical evidence of its predictive failures accumulated.

The failure of REH models is particularly apparent in financial markets. After reviewing many empirical studies, Maurice Obstfeld and Kenneth Rogoff concluded in their magisterial book on the REH approach to international economics that "the undeniable difficulties that international economists encounter in empirically explaining nominal exchange rate movements are an embarrassment, but one shared with virtually any other field that attempts to explain asset price data" (Obstfeld and Rogoff, 1996, p. 625).

The dismal performance of REH models in markets in which forecast revisions drive movements in prices and returns stands in sharp contrast to the widespread belief that these models have provided *the* solution to the problem of adequately representing the forecasting behavior of rational individuals. But, as Lucas (2003a,b) recently acknowledged, the problems with the conventional approach are not confined to financial markets. For example, he pointed out that little progress has been made in the three decades since Phelps et al. (1970) examined the persistent effects of changes in monetary policy on a nation's real output:

> New frameworks—contracts, monopolistic competition—are introduced, motivated by the inability of earlier theory to resolve [the] difficulty [of explaining persistent real responses to monetary shocks], but the problem of persistence has proved to be persistent itself. . . . Ever since the January, 1969, conference that Ned Phelps invited us to, the 14 authors of the Phelps volume have been apologetic about the fact that we couldn't resolve these issues. (Lucas, 2003b, p. 140)

Lucas is acknowledging that the conventional approach could not remedy its failures by modifying ancillary assumptions, such as the nature of contracts, market structure, and other institutional arrangements.

Behavioral economists, for their part, have focused on the lack of "psychological realism" of conventional models. However, instead of questioning whether conventional models adequately capture rational behavior, behavioral economists concluded from the empirical failure of these models that individuals are irrational. Indeed, they proceeded to prespecify fully "irrational" behavior. This intellectual development illustrates par excellence the stranglehold the contemporary approach has maintained on the direction and methods of economic research.

2.1.2. The Retreat from Statistical Inference

Conventional economists have responded to the empirical failures of REH models in an even more startling way than their behavioral colleagues. They disregard the significance of the disappointing findings and continue to build their models on the basis of REH, while refining the microfoundations of their models.

In recent years, for example, international macroeconomists have been engaged in an intensive effort to salvage the older overshooting models of the exchange rate originated by Dornbusch (1976) by basing these models on representations of "intertemporally optimizing agents." This effort has required economists to prespecify fully the forecasting behavior of market participants over the indefinite future. As we discuss in chapter 7, this research effort, now called the *New Open Economy Macroeconomics* (NOEM), has been launched despite Dornbusch and Frankel's assessment that "the chief problem with the overshooting theory, indeed, with the more general rational expectations approach, is that it does not explain well the shorter-term [long-swings] dynamics in exchange rates" (Dornbusch and Frankel, 1995, p. 16).

To help rationalize this steadfast adherence to REH modeling in the face of its empirical failures, conventional economists have redefined the notion of empirical failure. Prior to the ascendancy of the conventional approach, economists, like *all* scientists, relied primarily on standard methods of statistical inference to confront their models with empirical data. By contrast, REH theorists have decided that these methods were too stringent for judging the adequacy of their models, so they have sought to develop an alternative methodology.

The structure of economic models embodies economists' hypotheses concerning individual behavior and its implications for aggregate outcomes. Assuming that an economist's model is an adequate representation of the causal mechanism underlying an economic outcome, such as the market price, the methods of statistical inference enable him to ascertain the likelihood that his model's restrictions are consistent with the observed data on the outcome and causal variables. The so-called likelihood ratio tests of restrictions that such hypotheses imply for the structure of economic models enable economists to distinguish between alternative explanations of economic phenomena.

As Sargent recounts, early REH theorists also relied on standard statistical methods to assess the adequacy of their fully predetermined models:

My recollection is that Bob Lucas and Ed Prescott were initially very enthusiastic about rational expectations econometrics, [which relied on standard statistical methods to test its models.] After all, it simply involved imposing on ourselves the same high standards we had criticized the Keynesians for failing to live up to.

But,

after about five years of doing likelihood ratio tests on rational expectations models I recall Bob Lucas and Ed Prescott both telling me that those tests were rejecting *too many good models.* (p. 568, emphasis added)

Instead of concluding that REH might not be as useful as originally believed, REH theorists responded to these failures "by lowering [their] standards relative to maximum likelihood," and began to rely on computer simulations—so-called "calibration"—to "match" the selected aspects of their models to the data.[5] According to Sargent, the decision to ignore the often gross inconsistency of the REH models with the data was "a sensible opinion that the time had come to . . . first devote resources to learning how to create a range of *compelling* [REH] equilibrium models to incorporate *interesting mechanisms. We will be careful about estimation in later years* when we have mastered modeling technology" (p. 569, emphasis added).

As intended, lowering the standards of what constitutes an adequate model has obscured many of the inconsistencies of REH models with the data, inevitably increasing the number of REH models that are not rejected. However, this does not necessarily mean that the nonrejected models capture "interesting mechanisms" underpinning real world outcomes. The calibration methodology may suggest to an economist that he has found an explanation of an economic phenomenon. Even so, however persuasive such an explanation may be to his colleagues, according to standard statistical criteria, it may nonetheless be grossly inconsistent with empirical evidence. For example, although NOEM models appear reasonable when viewed through the prism of calibration exercises, they are unable to explain even the most basic features of floating exchange rates, such as their tendency to undergo large and protracted swings away from historical benchmark levels.[6]

---

5. See Kydland and Prescott (1996) and references therein for an exposition and numerous examples of the calibration methodology.

6. See chapter 7 and references therein. See also chapter 12, where we show that the recent REH model of Barberis, Huang, and Santos (2001), which appears to provide an adequate characterization of equity returns when based on the calibration methodology, is strongly rejected by standard statistical tests when applied to the foreign exchange market.

Sims, who pioneered the search for empirical regularities in macroeconomic data using statistical methods, has commented on the use of the calibration methodology in testing economic models:

> Economics is not physics. Science in general does not consist of formulating theories, testing them against data and accepting or rejecting them. But we can recognize these points without losing sight of the qualitative difference between modern science and classical or medieval natural philosophy: . . . in scientific discourse certain types of apparently persuasive arguments are not legitimate.

Defending "the language of statistical inference" in order "to communicate about the central questions of the discipline," he then argues:

> The fact that economics is not physics does not mean that we should not aim for the same *fundamental* standards for what constitutes legitimate argument; we can insist that the ultimate criterion for judging economic ideas is the degree to which they help us order and summarize the data, that is, it is not legitimate to try to protect attractive theories from the data. (Sims, 1996, pp. 111–12, emphasis added)

Sims's call against protecting "attractive theories from the data" is important for the advancement of economic science. Yet, as Sargent reveals in his interview, the retreat from standard statistical methods was at least in part motivated by nonscientific considerations: the leaders of the REH revolution believed that these methods were rejecting "too many good [fully predetermined] models."

2.1.3. *Lost Fundamentals and the Escape from Reality*

The field of financial economics provides a particularly clear example of the detrimental effect of the belief that only models that generate sharp predictions are worthy of scientific status. Consider, for example, how the contemporary approach has impeded economists' thinking about the often wide price fluctuations in financial markets, such as those in the foreign exchange market. A key question for exchange rate modelers and policymakers is whether the long swings in exchange rates are linked to movements in fundamental macroeconomic variables, such as interest rates and current account balances.

There is much anecdotal evidence in the popular media, backed up by survey research, that participants in the foreign exchange market pay close attention to fundamental variables in forming their forecasts of future exchange rates. It is obvious, for example, that market participants hang on every word that central bank officials utter, listening for hints of a change in monetary policy. Similarly, in the year or so preceding the writing of this book, market participants clearly responded to announcements of large and growing U.S. current account deficits by selling the dollar. Because individuals' forecasts drive their behavior in financial markets, we would expect fundamental variables to have considerable influence on exchange rate fluctuations.

But to build models on the foundation of individual rational behavior while remaining faithful to the contemporary approach, conventional exchange rate theorists modeled behavior, on the individual and aggregate levels, with fully predetermined representations.[7] These conventional models were thought to offer *the* way to understand how macroeconomic fundamentals and rational behavior affect the exchange rate.

When the search failed to find an overarching relationship between the exchange rate and macroeconomic fundamentals, conventional economists concluded that swings in exchange rates away from benchmark levels were unconnected to changes in these fundamentals. Obstfeld and Rogoff (2000) have referred to this "anomalous" finding as the "exchange rate disconnect puzzle." Yet this "anomaly" disregards empirical evidence, much of it reported by conventional economists themselves, that, while macroeconomic fundamentals matter for exchange rate movements, the causal mechanism that underpins these movements is temporally unstable: not only do the coefficients of empirical models change from one sub-period of floating to another, but the sets of fundamentals that seem to matter for exchange rates also change.[8] Fully predetermined models cannot account for such structural change: the nature and timing of structural change depend on how market participants revise their forecasting strategies and on unforeseeable changes in the social context.[9]

As we noted in chapter 1, the constraint that economists should consider only explanations that are based on fully predetermined representations

---

7. Although the contemporary exchange rate models of the 1970s rely on REH, these models do not derive other individual decision variables, such as money demand and consumption, on the basis of an explicit mathematical model of individual choice. Instead, they use ad hoc functions to represent aggregate outcomes whose connection to individual choice is only implicit. Subsequent research added complete representations of individual behavior based on intertemporal optimizing decisions (for example, see Lucas, 1982; Obstfeld and Rogoff, 1996).

8. See chapters 7 and 15.

9. When and how market participants revise their forecasting strategies depend, in part, on historical events, such as the appointment of a new Federal Reserve chairman or the economic policies pursued by elected officials. Recent popular attempts to prespecify fully the nonlinearity between the exchange rate and macroeconomic fundamentals, therefore, are tantamount to a presumption that economists can prespecify fully the timing and consequences of such historical events.

has led many to presume not only that macroeconomic fundamentals are irrelevant to individual forecasting behavior—and thus, to long swings in the exchange rate—but that some or all market participants behave irrationally.

2.1.4. *Misinterpreting the Failure of Conventional Theory*

There is a breathtaking irony in the unfailing belief that contemporary economics' mechanistic approach is the only way to model change in individual decision making—whether rational or irrational—and aggregate outcomes, as well as to analyze the consequences of government policies. During the three decades in which economists increasingly embraced the contemporary approach, an experiment in economic planning that hoped to replace markets with mechanical instructions based on fully prespecified economic models was heading inexorably to its demise. As Hayek and Knight clearly understood, the dynamism of capitalist economies could not be captured adequately with fully predetermined models that "can be put on a computer and *run*."

Odd but true, the demise of central planning failed to diminish contemporary economists' reliance on fully predetermined representations of economic outcomes. Perhaps this failure is because many of our colleagues find Hayek's argument that central planning is impossible *in principle* to be too far removed from the practice of contemporary analysis of capitalist economies. Like central planners in socialist times, the failure to appreciate Hayek's argument has given rise to a belief among contemporary economists that their approach can be reformed.

Hence the split in contemporary economics between the conventional and behavioral approaches. Behavioral economists—the "reformers"— "built on the premise that mainstream economic *methods* are great, [and] so too are mainstream economic *assumptions*" (Rabin, 2002, p. 658, emphasis in original). We disagree with that premise. The conventional approach cannot be rescued by introducing more "psychological realism" into its models. Representing psychological insights with fully predetermined behavioral models merely replaces one mechanistic representation of individual behavior with another. Moreover, as early modern economists compellingly argued, understanding the social context within which an individual makes decisions is at least as important in modeling her behavior as insights from psychology.

2.2. The Non-Fully Intelligible Individual in Early Modern Economics

Economists have long understood that the way individuals decide on the allocation of resources available to them cannot be fully prespecified. In their analyses of individual behavior and its implications for market outcomes, Adam Smith, Frank Knight, Friedrich Hayek, and John Maynard Keynes actually went so far as to argue that the economic importance of many decisions made by purposeful individuals stems from the fact that they are not fully intelligible to an outsider.[10]

2.2.1. *Individual Preferences, Knowledge, and the Social Context*

Prior to extolling the virtues of self-interest in *The Wealth of Nations,* Smith (1759) emphasized in *The Theory of Moral Sentiments* that even a purely selfish individual ranks the consequences of the alternative ways to deploy her resources differently in different social settings. For Smith, the social context, particularly the strength of common norms, was important to understanding the reasons underlying the choices of a self-interested individual regarding how to deploy her resources.[11]

Weber (1897) pursued a similar line of analysis. He devoted considerable attention to the question of whether and, if so, how an outsider could make sense of an individual's behavior, pointing out a number of difficulties in ascertaining whether an individual acts rationally in the sense of pursuing intelligible objectives. He argued, however, that an outsider might be able to gain some understanding of an individual's behavior if institutions, such as bureaucracies and organized religions, shape the values that an individual attaches to her actions.

In his analysis of the emergence of capitalist economic arrangements, Weber (1930) did precisely that, appealing to the social context to explain individual preferences. In his view, the post-Reformation emergence of Protestantism was associated with largely unanticipated and drastic changes in individuals' values and preferences. Protestantism, Weber argued, led individuals to eschew consumption, particularly of luxuries, and to attach great value to work and the accumulation of capital. According to Weber, once one understands Protestant ethics, an outsider can begin to make sense of the objectives and preferences that underpin individual behavior. He went so far as to argue that Protestantism had such a strong influence on values that it dominated all other factors shaping individual preferences: "In this case we are dealing with the connection of the spirit of

---

10. Frydman and Rapaczynski (1993, 1994) relate Knight's argument that an outsider cannot adequately imitate the creative aspects of self-interested behavior to the central importance of private ownership for economic performance. For econometric evidence on this point in the context of post-communist transition economies, see Frydman et al. (1999).

11. For many reasons why Smith's work on moral philosophy continues to be important for understanding contemporary capitalist arrangements see Dougherty (2002).

modern economic life [including individual preferences and values] with the *rational* ethics of ascetic Protestantism" (Weber, 1958, p. 27, emphasis added).

Weber's view that an outsider might be able to make sense of an individual's behavior by examining the social context has important implications for economic analysis of individual behavior. In the language of contemporary economics, institutions and other social factors help shape both an individual's assessment of the future consequences of her actions (her forecasts), as well as the ranking she attaches to these consequences (her preferences).

Smith and Weber did not attempt to pin down the precise strength of the effect of the social context or altruistic concerns on an individual's ranking of the consequences of alternative decisions for her well-being. They also did not attempt to pin down how the influence of social factors might change over time. The early modern thinkers nonetheless implicitly assumed that such influences arise through a complex process in which the interdependence of individual preferences and the social context unfold over time.

This view suggests that strongly shared values or dominant institutions are not enough for the social context to serve as a prism through which an outsider could make sense of an individual's behavior. For this to be the case, the social context would have to remain relatively stable. After all, Weber would certainly agree that if Protestantism were to diminish in importance, the analysis of Protestant attitudes—for example, attitudes toward saving and investment—would also become less informative for understanding individual behavior. Moreover, what actually matters are not changes in the environment per se, but rather an individual's perception of such changes and her forecasts of their future effects. Thus, an individual's preferences might be intimately linked to her knowledge of the social context within which she acts and her forecasts of its future changes.

Contemporary economists typically do not explicitly incorporate social factors in their representations of individual preferences.[12] This practice may be reasonable in some contexts: for some decision problems, the influence of social factors may not vary across individuals or may remain relatively stable over time. But such considerations as the state of knowledge, its division among individuals, and its unfolding over time cannot be ignored in constructing representations of individual forecasting behavior. Individual forecasts are ipso facto based on an individual's knowledge of the social setting and on how aggregate outcomes unfold over time.

---

12. For examples of ways in which behavioral economists have fully prespecified the effects of the social context, such as concern for the well-being of others or social norms, on individual preferences, see Charness and Rabin (2002) and references therein.

2.2.2. *Individual Forecasting, Knowledge, and the Social Context*

The giants of early modern economics cogently argued that no group of individuals, including economists or market participants, could represent fully and adequately the division of knowledge and its evolution in society. They would have been quite surprised, therefore, by the contemporary practice of fully prespecifying an individual's forecasting strategy and its revisions.

Knight (1921, pp. 231–32) argued that forecasts of returns from innovative entrepreneurial activities "deal with situations which are far *too unique* . . . for any sort of statistical tabulations to have any value for guidance." Knight's position points to a fundamental flaw in the contemporary attempt to fully prespecify change: only if creative behavior cannot be fully prespecified can individual creativity be truly indispensable.[13]

Like Knight, Keynes (1921, p. 34) also questioned the efficacy of fully prespecifying an individual's decision making. He noted that one of the main reasons why "[not] all probabilities are measurable" is that it is impossible to prespecify fully all the potential consequences of many economic and social decisions. Consequently, Keynes emphasized that many important individual decisions in market and broader societal settings necessarily involve forecasting strategies that mix rules and models based on probabilistic and statistical calculations with more informal procedures:

> We are merely reminding ourselves that human decisions affecting the future, whether personal or political or economic, *cannot* depend on strict mathematical expectation, since the basis for making such calculations does not exist; and . . . that our *rational selves* [are] choosing between alternatives as best as we are able, calculating where we can, but often falling back for our motive on whim or sentiment or chance. (Keynes, 1936, p. 162, emphasis added)

What is truly insightful about this description of individual decision making is that Keynes explicitly claims that rational individuals would adopt forecasting strategies that, in general, include factors, formal or informal, that cannot be adequately represented by standard probability theory.[14]

---

13. This interpretation of Knight draws on the analysis of the role of creative activities and private ownership in the postcommunist transition in Grosfeld and Roland (1997) and Frydman et al. (2006b).

14. For an early discussion of the fundamental difficulties in using probability theory to understand economic outcomes in a world of imperfect knowledge, see Peirce (1878). For a modern treatment of Peirce's ideas, see Wible (2007).

2.3. Jettisoning Insights from Early Modern Analysis

The foregoing discussion highlights two fundamental difficulties that severely limit the empirical relevance of contemporary models. The first stems from the uncontroversial observation that creative activities do not completely follow pre-existing rules and procedures. The second difficulty arises from ignoring the dependence of purposeful individual decisions on the relevant social context.

2.3.1. Ruling Out Autonomy in Forecasting Behavior

While, by design, both conventional and behavioral representations disregard the importance of individual creativity, contemporary models that use REH go even further: they rule out an autonomous role for market participants' forecasts in driving market outcomes. REH representations of an individual's forecasting strategy are derivative of an economist's specifications of preferences and constraints. Thus the causal variables that enter such a representation are limited to those that the economist uses in representing the other components of his model. Moreover, the parameters of his representation are restricted to be particular functions of the parameters of his specifications of preferences and constraints and the way that the policy and other causal variables unfold through time.

By design, REH precludes the introduction of so-called "free parameters"—those arising from the autonomous role of market participants' forecasting strategies and their revisions—in explaining outcomes. Proponents of the conventional approach proclaim this tightness as the greatest virtue of REH-based models. All graduate students of economics— and, increasingly, undergraduates, too—are taught that to capture rational, self-interested behavior in a scientific way, they must use REH.

By ruling out any autonomy for forecasting behavior, REH severely impedes economists' ability to develop empirically relevant explanations of market outcomes. For example, in attempting to explain the equity premium—the excess return of stocks over bonds—REH has led economists to an intensive search for alternative specifications of preferences.[15]

---

15. Mehra and Prescott (1985) and many others have found that the historical average return on stocks over risk-free bonds is too high to be consistent with conventional asset market models. As we discuss in chapter 8, these models are also unable to explain excess returns in the foreign exchange market. Much work has been invested in searching for an alternative specification of preferences that would improve the ability of conventional models to explain the data. For example, see Epstein and Zin (1989, 1991), Constantinides (1990), Campbell and Cochrane (1999), and Barberis et al. (2001).

2.3.2. Reintroducing Autonomous Representations of Individual Behavior

Despite its behavioral implausibility and empirical failures, some behavioral economists continue to rely on REH to represent individual forecasting. By retaining REH, however, they have ruled out any autonomous role for forecasting behavior in driving asset prices.[16]

In contrast to the conventional approach, however, the behavioral approach does not oblige an economist to use REH. This freedom enables a behavioral economist to specify his representation of forecasting behavior as an autonomous component of his model alongside, but not derivative of, his representation of preferences and constraints. Yet their "reformist" objective—"behavioral economics is not meant to be a separate approach [of contemporary economics] in the long run" (Camerer and Loewenstein, 2004, p. 42)—has led behavioral economists to fully prespecify forecasting behavior and thereby contradict one of their core beliefs: economic models require "greater psychological realism."[17]

2.3.3. Individual Behavior and the Social Context

The opportunities, incentives, and institutional arrangements that propel individuals to engage in creative activities vary, often substantially, among different capitalist economies, and even among different markets within the same economy. Capitalist economies are particularly effective in tying an individual's creativity in coping with inherently imperfect knowledge of the unfolding social context to her self-interest. The intrinsic links between creativity, the social context, individual incentives, and the resulting aggregate outcomes are, of course, not unique to capitalist economies. A revealing and relatively transparent historical example of these links comes from the former centrally planned socialist economies. As is well known, these economies repudiated private ownership of productive assets and other institutional arrangements that motivate the economic activities of self-interested individuals in capitalist economies. The results are equally

---

16. For a widely cited model that mixes preferences motivated by behavioral and conventional considerations with REH, see Barberis et al. (2001). As we discuss in chapter 9, because it disregards some of the key experimental findings of Kahneman and Tversky (1979) and others, even the specification of preferences used in this model suffers from shortcomings on purely behavioral grounds.

17. Some economists, most notably Phelps (2006b), have emphasized that the motivation for being creative stems not only from the profit motive, but from a basic human desire to make a unique personal contribution to the world. For earlier arguments on the importance of creativity for understanding the implications of population growth, see Phelps (1968b).

well known: individuals allocated as little effort as possible to creative activities aimed at producing goods and services in the official, state sector, which resulted in chronic shortages, narrow assortments, and execrable quality. Nevertheless, although individuals in these economies pursued mostly routine activities intended to signal compliance with state directives, there was abundant evidence of individual creativity and entrepreneurship. For example, faced with the lack and poor assortment of goods and services provided by the state sector, individuals innovated by diverting resources from state-controlled firms to private use. In turn, this allocation of individual creative effort away from the state-controlled sector compounded shortages and poor assortments, providing further stimulus to creative activities in the unofficial economy. Despite central planners' efforts, prespecified instructions for individual behavior and aggregate outcomes, such as output targets and quotas in the Soviet Union, could never capture the existing links among individual creativity, social context, individual behavior, and aggregate outcomes. This failure may explain why reading contemporary economics often reminds one of nothing so much as a model of some fictitious planned economy.

3   Flawed Foundations

The Gross Irrationality of "Rational Expectations"
and Behavioral Models

[M]any . . . values toward which experience shows that human action may
be oriented . . . often cannot be understood completely.

MAX WEBER,
Economy and Society, p. 5

Beware of theorists bearing free parameters.
ATTRIBUTED TO ROBERT E. LUCAS, JR., BY THOMAS J. SARGENT,
in *The Conquest of American Inflation*, p. 73

Modern economics constructs models of market outcomes on the basis of
representations of individual decision making. This *methodological individ-
ualism* is inherently in conflict with the contemporary economists' insistence that their models should imply sharp predictions. In this chapter,
we illustrate this conflict in the context of a simple algebraic model of a
market outcome—the equilibrium price that equates the supply and demand for a single good. In specifying the microfoundations of this model,
we sketch how conventional and behavioral economists construct their fully
predetermined representations of "rational" and "irrational" behavior. This
example enables us to show how fully predetermined models presume that
participants in real world markets endlessly disregard obvious systematic information in their forecast errors. This presumption of gross irrationality
holds true regardless of whether contemporary models are based on REH
or behavioral representations of forecasting behavior.

All graduate students of economics—and, increasingly, undergraduates, too—are taught that to capture rational, self-interested behavior in a
scientific way, they must use REH. In an attempt to shed light on how economists came to espouse such extreme views, we use our algebraic example
to highlight the milestones in the development of contemporary macroeconomics over the past four decades. In doing so, we illustrate Lucas's
argument that fully predetermined models, such as non-REH behavioral
models, suffer from glaring internal inconsistencies. Our algebraic example also reveals a simple, but important, point: in real world markets, where
knowledge about the future course of market outcomes is imperfect, REH,

too, implies that individual market participants ignore obvious systematic information in their forecast errors and thus, to paraphrase Lucas's own argument, REH models are also the "wrong theory."

We also illustrate another fundamental difficulty with using REH to construct the microfoundations of aggregate models. REH instructs an economist to determine his individual and aggregate representations jointly. While an REH theorist would specify individual preferences and constraints autonomously from his aggregate model, his representation of an individual's forecasting behavior is derivative of these other components. Thus, explanations of aggregate outcomes that rely on REH are not based on bona fide microfoundations.

By contrast, a behavioral economist who does not rely on REH specifies his representation of forecasting strategies and their revisions autonomously. This autonomy allows him to complete his specification of individual behavior without having to construct his aggregate model. However, because these models are fully predetermined, they entail, by design, an inconsistency between their representations on the individual and aggregate levels. As Lucas compellingly argued, such models presume gross irrationality on the part of market participants and thus cannot serve as plausible microfoundations of models of aggregate outcomes.

3.1. Conventional and Behavioral Representations of Preferences with Uncertain Outcomes

Economists represent an individual's decision as a choice among alternative ways to deploy her resources. This opportunity set includes options that an economist may be able to infer from his understanding of the social setting (institutional constraints, legislation, and the like). In general, however, some of the options that an individual contemplates are creative, and these are not, ipso facto, completely intelligible to an economist. Nevertheless, the contemporary approach leads an economist to disregard the importance of such alternatives. To represent the opportunity set, an economist specifies a set of outcome variables that represent the consequences of each of these alternatives. For example, the variable that contemporary finance models typically use to represent the consequences of an individual's decisions is the level of her wealth or consumption. In contrast, as we discuss below and in chapter 9, behavioral finance models sometimes use the change in an individual's wealth or consumption relative to a reference level to represent individual behavior.

**Table 3.1   Representation of Uncertainty
Faced by an Individual**

	Option 1		Option 2	
Value	y_{t+1}^{11}	y_{t+1}^{12}	y_{t+1}^{21}	y_{t+1}^{22}
Probability	p_{t+1}^{11}	p_{t+1}^{12}	p_{t+1}^{21}	p_{t+1}^{22}

3.1.1. Fully Predetermined Probabilistic Representations of Uncertain Outcomes

The key feature of the contemporary approach is that, to represent uncertainty concerning the future consequences of an individual's decisions, it uses conditional probability distributions whose change over time is fully prespecified. In keeping with the simplicity of our presentation, we suppose that, at some time t, an individual contemplates only two alternative deployments of her resources. We refer to these alternative deployments as "option 1" and "option 2." We also suppose that an economist represents the uncertainty of the future consequences of each of these options by the probability distribution of the future, time $t + 1$, values of some outcome variable, y_{t+1} shown in table 3.1.

In the table, y_{t+1}^{ij} ($i = 1, 2$ and $j = 1, 2$) is the jth outcome implied by the ith option to deploy resources and p_{t+1}^{ij} is the probability associated with that outcome, so that $p_{t+1}^{11} + p_{t+1}^{12} = 1$ and $p_{t+1}^{21} + p_{t+1}^{22} = 1$.

3.1.2. Preferences of a "Rational" Individual: The Expected Utility Hypothesis

To determine whether his representation implies that an individual would choose option 1 or 2, an economist must specify a preference ranking for options whose outcomes are uncertain. To this end, economists specify a parametric utility function $u(\cdot)$, which converts the values of an outcome variable into utilities. For example, if y_{t+1} is the level of consumption at $t + 1$, $u(y_{t+1})$ associates each potential level of consumption with a utility number; a higher utility number implies a higher level of well-being.

To select and justify the particular parametric functions that they use to represent rational preferences, economists appeal to a set of a priori assumptions that are supposed to characterize how a rational individual chooses among the consequences of her decisions. These assumptions postulate that an individual's choices among the available options follow a consistent pattern. For example, one of these conditions is that preferences are transitive: if an individual prefers outcome A to outcome B and outcome B to outcome C, then she is assumed to always prefer A to C. Such consistency is thought to capture the way rational individuals choose among the alternatives available to them. The a priori assumptions concerning individual preferences that are adopted by the contemporary approach are thus often thought of as axioms of rational choice.

To represent the choice of a particular option, an economist typically picks the option that yields the greatest utility. However, an economist's representation of the ranking of the outcomes in terms of his parametric utility function is insufficient to determine which option yields the highest utility. Although the utility numbers generated by $u(\cdot)$ imply a ranking of the outcomes if they were certain to occur, the consequences of each of the options are uncertain. Option 1, for example, can result in one of the two outcomes, y_{t+1}^{11} or y_{t+1}^{12}.

Thus, an economist must construct a specification of preferences that ranks options whose outcomes are uncertain. To this end, conventional economists have relied on the expected utility hypothesis (von Neumann and Morgenstern, 1944): the utility of option $i = 1, 2$, which we denote by U^i, is equal to the expected value of the utilities of the outcomes that are associated with the option:

$$U_{t+1}^1 = p_{t+1}^{11} u(y_{t+1}^{11}) + p_{t+1}^{12} u(y_{t+1}^{12}) \tag{3.1}$$

$$U_{t+1}^2 = p_{t+1}^{21} u(y_{t+1}^{21}) + p_{t+1}^{22} u(y_{t+1}^{22}). \tag{3.2}$$

In addition to the axioms of rational choice, conventional representations of preferences are often based on the assumption of risk aversion: an individual is risk averse if replacing an uncertain final wealth by its expected value makes her better off.[1] In the appendix to chapter 6, we make use of a typical functional form for $u(\cdot)$ to represent the well-being of risk-averse rational individuals. That function relates an individual's utility to the level of her consumption.

3.1.3. Behavioral Representations of Preferences: Prospect Theory

Kahneman and Tversky and many others have used experiments to examine the adequacy of the axioms of rational choice and the assumption of risk aversion. They present numerous findings that the a priori assumptions

---

1. For a recent exposition of the expected utility hypothesis and risk aversion, see Gollier (2001).

underpinning conventional representations of preferences are grossly inconsistent with observed behavior.

The empirical failure of the axioms of rational choice led Kahneman and Tversky (1979) and Tversky and Kahneman (1992) to develop a seminal alternative to modeling individual preferences, dubbed "prospect theory." Prospect theory represents well-being in terms of *changes* in the relevant outcome variables, called losses and gains, relative to a reference value, rather than their postchoice *levels*. Moreover, a utility function based on prospect theory has a different functional form than its conventional risk-averse counterparts.[2]

As with the expected utility hypothesis, prospect theory represents preferences over gambles with weighted sums of utilities of the single outcomes that are implied by an option. Kahneman and Tversky (1979) present experimental evidence that these weights, which they call "decision-weights," are nonlinear functions of probabilities. Prospect theory, therefore, leads to the following counterparts to the expected utilities in equations (3.1) and (3.2), which are called "prospective utilities":

$$V_{t+1}^1 = \pi(p_{t+1}^{11})v(y_{t+1}^{11}) + \pi(p_{t+1}^{12})v(y_{t+1}^{12}) \tag{3.3}$$

$$V_{t+1}^2 = \pi(p_{t+1}^{21})v(y_{t+1}^{21}) + \pi(p_{t+1}^{22})v(y_{t+1}^{22}), \tag{3.4}$$

where $\pi(\cdot)$ denotes decision weight, $v(\cdot)$ is the prospect–theory based counterpart of $u(\cdot)$ in equations (3.1) and (3.2), and y is the change in the level of wealth or consumption relative to some reference value.

3.2. Self-Interest, Social Context, and Individual Decisions

Equations (3.1)–(3.4) make clear that specifying the utilities of the outcomes, $u(\cdot)$ or $v(\cdot)$, is insufficient to model individual decisions in real world markets. The use of the expected utility hypothesis or prospect theory also requires that an economist represent the way individuals form forecasts of future outcomes and their associated probabilities.

To fix ideas, we consider a typical conventional problem and suppose that the outcome variable y is the quantity of a composite good that an individual consumes.[3] We assume that the decision problem facing an individual is to choose in the current period how much of her current and future real

---

2. Behavioral economists have developed other alternatives to risk-averse preferences. For example, see Epstein and Zin (1990) and Gul (1991).

3. We focus here on conventional preferences because their use is simpler to present.

income, x_t and X_{t+1}, she would like to spend on the consumption good in the current and future periods. She has the option of saving some of her current income to consume more in the future and less in the present, or she can borrow from her future income to consume more in the present and less in the future. In so doing, she locks in a nominal rate of interest in the current period. Her real rate of interest, then, and thus her future real income, depends on the future price level P_{t+1}. Consequently, in making her decision about y_t and y_{t+1}, the individual must forecast her future real income and the future price level, which are uncertain in the current period t.[4]

This typical setup illustrates the key point emphasized by early modern economists: the assumption of self-interested behavior—that an individual acts to maximize her well-being—is far from sufficient to represent her decision concerning how much of her income she should spend on consumption today. How an individual chooses to deploy her resources and forecast payoffs from those choices depends at least as much on the social context within which she forms forecasts of the future consequences of her decisions as it does on her personal motivations. In our example, the social context is represented by X_{t+1}, P_{t+1} and the aggregate forecast of the future market price. The future real income is sometimes related to the way monetary authorities set money supply. The future equilibrium price depends on decisions of all market participants, which, in turn, stem from their forecasting strategies.

The utility maximization problem in our example gives rise to a representation for quantity demanded by a self-interested individual in the current period t, which we denote by Q_t^D. It depends on the price and real income in the current period, p_t and x_t, respectively, as well as on an individual's point forecasts of the price and real income in the future period, $\widehat{P}_{t|t+1}$ and $\widehat{X}_{t|t+1}$, respectively.[5] For simplicity, we use the following linear form to represent quantity demanded at time t:

$$Q_t^D \left(p_t, \widehat{P}_{t|t+1}, x_t, \widehat{X}_{t|t+1}\right) = \alpha_{0_t} + \beta_t \left[\widehat{P}_{t|t+1} - p_t\right] + \gamma_{1_t} x_t + \gamma_{2_t} \widehat{X}_{t|t+1}, \quad (3.5)$$

where $\beta_t > 0$. The variables $\widehat{P}_{t|t+1}$ and p_t enter with coefficients that are opposite in sign, because a rise in the current (future) market price, ceteris paribus, raises (lowers) the return from saving current income. Moreover, because both current and future consumption raise utility, higher current

---

4. This decision problem of how best to allocate current and future income over an individual's lifetime is common in contemporary macroeconomics. See, for example, Blanchard and Fischer (1989) and Obstfeld and Rogoff (1996). See also chapter 6.

5. The subscript $t|t+1$ indicates that a forecast of the future period's price or income is formed on the basis of the current period's information and the forecasting strategy that an individual uses in that period.

or future income, ceteris paribus, is associated with an increase in current consumption, that is, $\gamma_1 > 0$, and $\gamma_2 > 0$. We note that, in conventional applications, the parameters α_{0_t}, β_t, γ_{1_t}, and γ_{2_t} are functions of the parameters of the utility function $u(\cdot)$ and of the parameters of the processes driving the causal variables (X in the present case) that are used to represent the causal factors.[6]

Contemporary models typically assume that the structure of the utility function is unchanging over time.[7] Moreover, most economists not only fully prespecify change in the process underpinning the causal variables that represent the social context, but they also do not allow for any change in institutions, government policies, the state of knowledge, and other determinants of change in modern societies.

In this chapter, we adopt a particularly simple invariant representation for real income:

$$X_{t+1} = \rho x_t + \mu + \epsilon_{t+1}, \tag{3.6}$$

where ρ and μ are constant parameters, ϵ_{t+1} is an error term whose distribution is unchanging over time, and $E(\epsilon_{t+1}|X_t) = 0$, $E(\epsilon_{t+1}\epsilon_\tau) = 0$ for all t and τ.

We also follow the usual practice and constrain the structure of the utility function to be invariant over time, which results in the following representation for the quantity demanded on the individual level:

$$Q_t^{\mathrm{D}}(p_t, \widehat{P}_{t|t+1}, x_t) = \alpha + \beta \left[\widehat{P}_{t|t+1} - p_t \right] + \gamma x_t, \tag{3.7}$$

where $\alpha = \alpha_0 + \gamma_2\mu$, and $\gamma = \gamma_1 + \gamma_2\rho$.

To represent an individual's forecast of the future market price $\widehat{P}_{t|t+1}$, a contemporary economist either invokes REH, which attributes to individuals the conditional probability distribution of the aggregate outcome implied by his own model, or he makes use of a specification that is motivated by empirical observations on how individuals forecast. Before we consider the implications of both approaches, we need to sketch how an economist would construct his representation of an aggregate outcome—the price that would equate the aggregates of individual demand and supply—on the basis of his representation of individual behavior.

---

6. See the appendix to chapter 6 for an example of how the parameters in equation (3.5) are related to the parameters of the utility function and the representations of the causal variables.

7. In general, an individual's future preferences differ from her current preferences, as she experiences different levels of outcome variables and as her social context changes. But even if the contemporary representations allow for such change, they fully prespecify it. A widely used representation that fully prespecifies change is the so-called "habit formation" model of preferences. See Constantinides (1990).

3.3. Individual Behavior and Aggregate Outcomes

In real world markets, there is a diversity of preferences, forecasting strategies, and decision rules among participants. In moving from the individual to the aggregate level, such diversity might be important for explaining aggregate outcomes. But even if a contemporary economist allows for diversity among the ways market participants make decisions, he fully prespecifies how this diversity unfolds over time.

Contemporary economists often disregard the importance of heterogeneity: they attempt to capture an aggregate (some weighted sum) of market participants' decisions with a representation of the decisions of an average, so-called "representative," individual. With this assumption, we interpret the specification of an individual's demand in equation (3.7) and her forecast of the next period's price as also representing aggregate (market) demand and the average of the forecasts across market participants.

As with an individuals' demand decision, economists sometimes represent an individual's supply decision to depend on her forecast of the future price.[8] But to simplify our presentation, we assume that the supply decision Q_t^s depends only on the current market price. Moreover, we adopt the following (invariant) linear specification:

$$Q_t^s(p_t) = \delta + \lambda p_t, \tag{3.8}$$

where $\delta \leq 0$ and $\lambda > 0$ are constant parameters. We invoke the representative agent assumption and interpret the specification in equation (3.8) as representing the total supply in the market.

Equating aggregate demand in equation (3.7) with aggregate supply in equation (3.8) yields the following representation for the equilibrium price:

$$p_t = a + b\widehat{P}_{t|t+1} + cx_t, \tag{3.9}$$

where

$$a = \frac{\alpha - \delta}{\lambda + \beta}, \; b = \frac{\beta}{\lambda + \beta} > 0, \text{ and } c = \frac{\gamma}{\lambda + \beta} > 0. \tag{3.10}$$

The positive signs of b and c are implied from the considerations highlighted above that set $\beta > 0$, $\gamma > 0$, and $\lambda > 0$.

---

8. For example, in the seminal paper that introduced rational expectations into economic analysis, Muth (1961) relates supply for period t to the forecast of P_t formed by suppliers at time $t - 1$.

3.4. From Early Modern to Phelps's Microfoundations

To express his model of the market price in equation (3.9) solely in terms of a set of causal variables, an economist must show how a representative agent forms and revises her forecasts. In a series of papers, Phelps (1968a) and Phelps et al. (1970) pioneered an approach to modeling aggregate outcomes on the basis of explicit mathematical microfoundations. Phelps accorded "a crucial [autonomous] role" to individuals' expectations in his explanation of aggregate outcomes (Phelps et al., 1970, p. 5). To capture the idea that individuals do not form the same expectation, he formulated his well-known island model involving informationally isolated labor markets. As he put it, individuals on each island "have to cope ignorant of the future and even much of the present. Isolated and apprehensive, these Pinteresque figures construct expectations of the state of the economy . . . and maximize relative to that *imagined* world" (Phelps, 1970, p. 22, emphasis added).

Because the island model specified that a market participant maximizes utility relative to the world she "imagines," it was not apparent how to represent an individual's forecasting behavior. In the absence of a better alternative, the early "microfounded" models represented individual forecasting behavior with the following fixed error-correcting rule, called "adaptive expectations":[9]

$$\widehat{P}_{t|t+1} - \widehat{P}_{t-1|t} = \lambda \left[\widehat{P}_{t-1|t} - p_t \right]. \qquad (3.11)$$

The early proponents of the explicit microfoundations approach used their models to examine particular historical episodes, such as the looming inflation at the end of the 1960s. They did not claim their fixed representations of individual behavior and aggregate outcomes, including the adaptive expectations rule, were general enough to apply to other historical episodes.[10]

3.5. "Rational Expectations": Abandoning the Modern Research Program

Lucas set out to construct a theory of aggregate outcomes that would apply across social settings and for long stretches of time. His early work followed Phelps closely in the use of the island model involving individuals acting in the context of informationally isolated markets. But, in a momentous break,

---

9. Modeling expectations with an error-correcting mechanism, such as in equation (3.11), was originally proposed by Cagan (1956) and Friedman (1956).

10. See Phelps (1972).

Lucas replaced Phelps's metaphor of "Pinteresque figures" on each island with a mechanistic image of "rational" robots. Lucas's research program instructed economists to search for the "'mechanics' of economic development" (Lucas, 2002, p. 21) based on fully predetermined representations of rational behavior.

3.5.1. Imposing Consistency in Fully Predetermined Models

Lucas argued that economic theory that is based on rational individual behavior should not involve an inconsistency between its representations on the individual and aggregate levels. But, beyond ruling out inconsistency, Lucas and others also believed that economic theory should imply sharp predictions. Aiming to develop economic theory that would meet both of these objectives, Lucas and others embraced REH introduced by Muth (1961). REH imposes complete consistency within a fully predetermined model: it instructs an economist to choose only that representation of individual behavior whose probabilistic predictions coincide exactly with the probabilistic predictions implied by the aggregate model that he himself constructs. REH became the main building block of contemporary models based on putatively rational behavior.

To illustrate how REH removes the inconsistency within a fully predetermined model, we write the REH representation of an individual's forecasting strategy as a linear function in x_t:

$$\widehat{P}_{t|t+1} = \hat{a} + \hat{c}x_t. \tag{3.12}$$

To solve for the REH representation, we determine the coefficients $\hat{a}$ and $\hat{c}$ to be specific functions of the parameters a, b, and c in equation (3.9) so as to ensure the required consistency between the individual and aggregate representations:

$$\widehat{P}_{t|t+1}^{\text{RE}} = E[P_{t+1}^{\text{EM}}|x_t] \text{ for all } x_t, \tag{3.13}$$

where the superscripts RE and EM denote REH representation and the economist's model, respectively.

It readily follows that the solutions for $\hat{a}$ and $\hat{c}$ that imply that equation (3.13) holds for any x_t are:

$$\hat{c} = \frac{c\rho}{1 - b\rho}, \text{ and } \hat{a} = \frac{a(1 - b\rho) + c\mu_0}{(1 - b)(1 - b\rho)}. \tag{3.14}$$

Substituting equations (3.12) and (3.14) into equation (3.9) implies the following REH representation for the aggregate outcome:

$$P_t^{\text{RE}} = a + \frac{ba(1 - b\rho) + bc\mu_0}{(1 - b)(1 - b\rho)} + \frac{c(1 - b\rho) + bc\rho}{(1 - b)(1 - b\rho)}x_t. \tag{3.15}$$

In contrast to fully predetermined non-REH representations (see below), the forecast error implied by the REH representation in equation (3.15), $fe^{RE}_{t|t+1}$ is, by construction, not systematically correlated with the causal variable x that represents market participants' information:

$$fe^{RE}_{t|t+1} = P^{RE}_{t+1} - \widehat{P}^{RE}_{t|t+1} = \frac{c}{1 - b\rho}\epsilon_{t+1}. \tag{3.16}$$

3.5.2. Lack of Autonomous Microfoundations in REH Models

The foregoing example illustrates how the imposition of REH implies that the structure of an economist's representation of an individual's forecasting behavior—her knowledge—is completely derivative of the other components of his model. The causal variable that appears in the model, x_t, enters from the representation of an individual's preferences and the constraint that links consumption at t to current and future income. The parameters $\hat{a}$ and $\hat{c}$ are particular functions of the parameters a, b, c, μ_0, and ρ, which arise from preferences, constraints, and social context. Thus, REH models are not based on autonomous microfoundations in that they rule out an autonomous role for expectations.

As on the individual level, REH representations of aggregate outcomes, such as in equation (3.15), include the causal variable and parameters that enter through preferences and constraints. Remarkably, this lack of an autonomous role for expectations in REH models has been viewed as their principal virtue: it rules out "free parameters" and, thereby, disciplines economic analysis in a way that was absent in previous models of aggregate outcomes. But precisely the opposite premise—that empirical relevance requires that economic models allow for an autonomous role for individual forecasting behavior—is shared by the early modern giants and the founders of the modern microfounded approach to modeling aggregate outcomes (Phelps et al., 1970). In this sense, the REH approach represents a significant departure from the program of modern economic research, which attempts to explain market outcomes on the basis of autonomous representations of individual behavior.

3.6. Diversity of Forecasting Strategies: The Gross Irrationality of "Rational Expectations"

There is an even more fundamental way in which the REH approach departs from the modern attempt to explain aggregate outcomes on the basis of individual foundations. Under imperfect knowledge, REH models not only lack autonomous microfoundations, but they are best interpreted as representations of aggregate outcomes with *no* basis in reasonable individual behavior. Indeed, under the interpretation that REH models are based on individual foundations, they necessarily presume gross irrationality on the part of market participants in real world markets.

3.6.1. REH in a World of Imperfect Knowledge

Muth understood that, although REH removes the knowledge inconsistency from an economist's model, it should not be viewed as a normative hypothesis about how rational individuals should forecast the future: "At the risk of confusing this *purely descriptive* hypothesis with a pronouncement as to what firms ought to do, we call such expectations 'rational'" (Muth, 1961, p. 316, emphasis added). Muth was well aware of the danger that the term *rational expectations* might suggest some notion of individual rationality. But, despite his warning, REH is commonly interpreted as a pronouncement as to what firms (or other market participants) ought to do. However, self-interested, rational individuals would collectively adhere to one forecasting strategy in perpetuity only if "all agents have solved their 'scientific problems'" (Sargent, 1993, p. 23). In such an imaginary world, REH would indeed be a plausible hypothesis. All market participants would have discovered an overarching causal mechanism that characterizes aggregate outcomes, as well as how the causal factors unfold over time, and thus, individual creativity would cease to be economically important. Economic decisions would become purely routine and passive, and thus capable of being captured with fully predetermined representations. In this fanciful world, contemporary representations would adequately explain individual behavior and would be completely consistent with the model of aggregate outcomes. Moreover, in such an *REH world*, the heterogeneity of forecasts among market participants would stem solely from differences in information.

Of course, in the real world, where the scientific problem has not been solved, there is a division of knowledge among market participants, who forecast not only on the basis of different factors (their information sets), but also on the basis of different strategies (their knowledge) that map these factors into forecasts. No one knows precisely how knowledge differs among individuals.

To clarify how, in a world of imperfect knowledge, fully predetermined REH representations of individual behavior imply that individual market participants endlessly disregard systematic information in their forecast errors, we assume that there are two types of market participants who use two different forecasting strategies. We denote fully predetermined representations of these strategies by $\widehat{P}_{t|t+1}^{(1)}$ and $\widehat{P}_{t|t+1}^{(2)}$.

Suppose that the model of aggregate outcomes in equation (3.9) were to represent adequately the causal mechanism that underpins the behavior of the equilibrium price. Also suppose that this model results from the aggregation of representations of individual behavior. Thus, the forecast appearing in that model is an average of market participants' forecasts. Without loss of generality, we suppose that this average forecast is given by:

$$\widehat{P}_{t|t+1} = \omega_1 \widehat{P}^{(1)}_{t|t+1} + \omega_2 \widehat{P}^{(2)}_{t|t+1}, \tag{3.17}$$

where the weights ω_1 and ω_2, which sum to unity, represent the importance of each type of individual in influencing the behavior of the equilibrium price. If the REH representation in equation (3.15) actually does represent the causal mechanism that underpins the behavior of the equilibrium price, then the representation in equation (3.12), along with equation (3.14), would adequately represent the average of forecasts across market participants. This conclusion immediately implies that for equations (3.17) and (3.12) to hold for every value of x_t, the fully predetermined representations of the forecasting strategies that underpin the average forecast take the form:

$$\widehat{P}^1_{t|t+1} = \hat{a}^1 + \hat{c}^1 x_t \tag{3.18}$$

$$\widehat{P}^2_{t|t+1} = \hat{a}^2 + \hat{c}^2 x_t, \tag{3.19}$$

where heterogeneity implies that $\hat{a}^1 \neq \hat{a}^2$ and $\hat{c}^1 \neq \hat{c}^2$. Moreover, the parameters of these functions must satisfy the following restriction:

$$\hat{a} = \omega_1 \hat{a}^1 + \omega_2 \hat{a}^2 \text{ and } \hat{c} = \omega_1 \hat{c}^1 + \omega_2 \hat{c}^2. \tag{3.20}$$

Although, by design, the forecast errors implied by the average forecast are uncorrelated with x_t, this is not the case with the representations attributed to type 1 and 2 individuals. For example, for type 1:

$$fe^{1,\text{RE}}_{t|t+1} = P^{\text{RE}}_{t+1} - \widehat{P}^{1,\text{RE}}_{t|t+1}$$

$$= (1 - \omega_1)[(\hat{a}^2 - \hat{a}^1) + (\hat{c}^2 - \hat{c}^1)x_t] + \frac{c\rho}{1 - b\rho}\epsilon_{t+1}. \tag{3.21}$$

Thus, in a world in which individuals have not solved their scientific problems, but where an REH model nonetheless adequately represents the behavior of market outcomes, fully predetermined representations of forecasting strategies imply that individuals disregard endlessly the obvious systematic information contained in their forecast errors. To paraphrase Lucas

(2001), in such a world, REH implies that there would be profit opportunities that market participants could see. If they *did* see these opportunities, they would revise their forecasting strategies. Not doing so—ever—would be grossly irrational.

3.6.2. Abandoning Individual Foundations

Some economists might argue that REH forecasting rules are intended to capture adequately only the aggregate average forecast that underpins aggregate outcomes. This view presumably underlies the common claim that "the market" behaves as if its forecasting behavior were consistent with an REH model. But even if we suppose that an REH model adequately represents aggregate outcomes, the foregoing argument shows that, under imperfect knowledge, REH-based models of those outcomes are not based on plausible individual foundations.

3.7. Inconsistency in Behavioral Models

3.7.1. Autonomous but Fully Predetermined Microfoundations

REH models have also turned out to be grossly inconsistent with actual behavior in real world markets, particularly in financial markets, leading economists to search for alternative, behaviorally based representations. A behavioral economist who does not rely on REH specifies his representation of an individual's forecasting strategy and its revisions autonomously. This autonomy allows him to complete his specification of individual behavior without having to construct his aggregate model. Embracing the conventional belief that economic models should generate sharp predictions, however, behavioral economists have relied on fully predetermined representations of forecasting behavior.

3.7.2. Gross Irrationality of Non-REH Fully Predetermined Models

Representing market participants as "robots" acting according to rules that are fully prespecified by an economist is odd for an approach that focusses on "psychological realism."[11] But what makes the behavioral approach's reliance on fully predetermined models particularly puzzling is that this approach was developed after the REH revolution. Lucas's argument that gave

---

11. Camerer and Loewenstein (2004) argue that greater "psychological realism" is the main advantage of behavioral models relative to their conventional counterparts.

rise to the REH revolution applies to non-REH behavioral representations: they involve an inherent inconsistency between their probabilistic implications at the individual and aggregate levels. As such, these models presume not just irrationality, but gross irrationality.

This point is easily illustrated with the model in equation (3.9). To this end, suppose that, as in Lucas's (2001) example, an economist sets the representative individual's point forecast of the next period's price equal to its realization in the current period:

$$\widehat{P}_{t|t+1} = p_t. \tag{3.22}$$

Substituting equation (3.22) into equation (3.9) and solving for the equilibrium price at time t yields:

$$p_t = \frac{a}{1-b} + \frac{c}{1-b}x_t. \tag{3.23}$$

We now presume—as indeed Lucas does—that equation (3.22) and equation (3.23) adequately represent forecasting behavior and the aggregate outcome (the market price) at time $t+1$. We also suppose that the causal variable, which here represents government policy or other aspects of the social context, is adequately prespecified at $t+1$ by the representation in equation (3.6). These assumptions result in the following fully predetermined representation for P_{t+1}:

$$P_{t+1} = \frac{a+c\mu}{1-b} + \frac{c\rho}{1-b}x_t + \frac{c}{1-b}\epsilon_{t+1}, \tag{3.24}$$

where we recall that ρ and μ are constant parameters and ϵ_{t+1} is an error term that is uncorrelated with X_t. Using equation (3.23) in equation (3.22) leads to the following representation for the forecast error implied by the fully predetermined model in equation (3.24):

$$fe^{\text{EM}}_{t|t+1} = P_{t+1} - \widehat{P}_{t|t+1} = \frac{c\mu}{1-b} + \frac{c(1-\rho)}{1-b}x_t + \frac{c}{1-b}\epsilon_{t+1}, \tag{3.25}$$

where the superscript EM denotes that the forecast error has been computed under the null hypothesis that an economist's model adequately represents the market price.

Equation (3.25) shows that if the model in equation (3.24) were to represent adequately the future course of the market price, and the representation in equation (3.22) were to represent adequately an individual's forecasting strategy, the economist's model would entail what Lucas (1995, p. 255) called a "glaring" inconsistency. It would presume that an individual ignores *endlessly* a systematic component in her forecast errors: $\frac{c\mu}{1-b} + \frac{c(1-\rho)}{1-b}x_t$. This observation led Lucas to conclude that such models presume gross irrationality on the part of market participants, and are thus the "the wrong theory."

3.7.3. Behavioral Representations of Diversity

In contrast to conventional economists, behavioral economists sometimes attempt to capture the fact that individuals in real world markets use more than one forecasting model. One of the earliest examples that anticipated the behavioral approach is the seminal exchange rate model of Frankel and Froot (1986). This model was developed in response to the empirical failure of conventional exchange rate models, which we discuss at length in chapters 7 and 8. This behavioral alternative and its extensions have by now become a popular way to explain persistent swings in the exchange rate away from fundamental values such as those based on PPP.

The Frankel and Froot model makes use of two forecasting rules to represent individual behavior. One of these rules is based on a particular macroeconomic model that relates the exchange rate to a specific set of macroeconomic fundamentals, while the other is based on a specific technical (chartist) trading model that relates future changes in the exchange rate to its past changes. To represent an individual's forecast at a point in time, Frankel and Froot use a weighted average of the predictions implied by their fundamental and chartist rules. They also specify a fixed quantitative updating rule that determines precisely how the weights attached to their two forecasting rules should be revised over time. We show in chapter 6 that, by fully predetermining the rule governing the revision of forecasting strategies, Frankel and Froot, in effect, presume that individuals adhere endlessly to one fully predetermined overarching forecasting strategy. Such non-REH representations imply that individuals ignore systematic information in their forecast errors in perpetuity.

Whereas the conventional approach uses REH—and thus presumes that diversity among individual forecasting strategies is unimportant for explaining market outcomes—the behavioral approach sometimes attempts to represent heterogeneity of forecasting strategies across individuals. For example, an important class of models in the behavioral finance literature, originated by DeLong et al. (1990a,b), contrasts the behavior of "fully rational" (often called "smart") investors with those who are "less-than-fully rational."

Of course, to construct models that involve these two types of market participants, an economist must define the notion of full rationality, and here behavioral economists have relied on the same a priori assumptions, including REH, as the conventional approach. Models based on representations of fully rational and less than fully rational investors play a key role in the behavioral finance literature. However, the DeLong et al. model, as well as that of Frankel and Froot, entail an inconsistency between probabilistic implications on the individual and aggregate levels, and thus lack plausible microfoundations.

4   Reconsidering Modern Economics

> We cannot predict, by rational and scientific methods, the future growth
> of our scientific knowledge.
>
> KARL POPPER,
The Poverty of Historicism, p. xii

An economist formalizes his assumptions on how an individual alters the
way she makes decisions and how aggregate outcomes unfold over time
with restrictions that constrain change in the structure of his model. Alternative sets of restrictions permit economists to formalize alternative explanations of outcomes on the individual and aggregate levels. That much
is common to all modern approaches to economic analysis. IKE, however,
does not construct models that fully prespecify change. In this chapter,
we make use of a simple algebraic example to contrast IKE with extant
approaches. This example highlights how IKE partially predetermines its
models.

We begin by focusing on the inherent connection between the insistence that economic models should generate sharp predictions and the
contemporary practice of fully prespecifying change. We highlight this connection for both deterministic and probabilistic models. The latter are usually constructed by adding stochastic error terms to representations of the
outcome variables on the individual and aggregate levels. Economists commonly believe that such error terms adequately represent uncertainty concerning individual decisions and how aggregate outcomes unfold over time.
Contemporary representations fully prespecify how the probability distributions of the error terms might change over time, past or future, conditional
on the probability distributions of these errors at some initial time. These
probabilistic models are therefore as restrictive as their stochastic counterparts: both ignore the importance of individual creativity and unforeseen
changes in the social context.

The probabilistic representations of contemporary economics embody
an odd conception of economists' knowledge. By adding a stochastic component to his representation, an economist recognizes that his knowledge
concerning the causal mechanism that drives individual behavior and market outcomes is imperfect. But by fully predetermining how the probability

distributions of the stochastic terms in his model evolve over time, contemporary economists, in effect, fully prespecify how their own imperfection of knowledge unfolds between the initial time and *all* other times, past and future.

Some economists may think that our characterization of contemporary models is misleading. They may argue that, although their models generate sharp predictions, it is the qualitative predictions that constitute the real content of their models. We show, however, that what contemporary economists refer to as "qualitative predictions" are in fact particular sharp predictions that result from imposing *additional* qualitative restrictions in an already fully predetermined model of change. In contrast to extant approaches, IKE imposes qualitative restrictions on its representations *instead of,* rather than in addition to a fully predetermining restrictions. Consequently, its models generate only qualitative predictions about the causal mechanism driving outcomes.

The qualitative restrictions of an IKE model presume that there is some regularity in economic life. IKE considers two types of regularities on the individual level. First, although the way that any of the causal variables affect an individual's preferences or forecasting behavior may change from one point in time to another, these changes may share certain qualitative features. The IKE restrictions that formalize such regularities prespecify neither the potential set of causal variables that underpin change in outcomes nor the influences of these variables in its representations. To address some problems, however, an economist may have to look for some regularities in representing these aspects of the causal mechanism. In such cases, IKE prespecifies only partially the causal variables that might enter its representations at every point in time and how they may influence outcomes. We sketch examples of how IKE attempts to capture both types of regularities.

Regardless of which type of regularity an economist may formalize with qualitative restrictions, his IKE model only partially relates the probability distribution of the outcome variables at any point in time to the distribution of those variables at some initial time. At each point in time, the qualitative restrictions of an IKE model allow for myriad possible changes in the probability distribution characterizing outcomes. Nevertheless, because these restrictions, which we refer to as *partially predetermining,* constrain change to share common features, they allow an economist to distinguish empirically between alternative explanations of outcomes. Such specifications of uncertainty, which we refer to as "partially predetermined probabilistic representations of change," replace standard conditional probability distributions as the basic tool of analysis.

Contemporary economists often construct models in which change is represented as either a movement along an invariant equilibrium price function or as fully predetermined (unique) transitions across such functions. By contrast, equilibrium price outcomes in an IKE model are represented as any sequence of transitions across probabilistic representations of the causal mechanism, from among many, that satisfy its partially predetermining restrictions. In so doing, IKE replaces the equilibrium price functions of contemporary economics with what we call "IKE causal-transition paths."

4.1. Sharp Predictions and Fully Predetermined Representations

In this section, we set up a particularly simple example of the causal mechanism that underpins some generic economic outcome. We formulate both a deterministic and probabilistic version of the example and show how the insistence on sharp predictions leads economists to fully prespecify change.

Consider the following deterministic representation of a causal mechanism at some arbitrary initial point in time, which we denote by $t = 0$:

$$y_0 = a_0 + b_0 x_0, \qquad (4.1)$$

where y and x are the outcome and causal variables, respectively.

The outcome variable could represent an aspect of behavior on the individual level, such as an individual's forecast of a future market price or her quantity demanded. It could also stand for an aggregate outcome, such as the market price or market demand. The causal variable, x, represents causal factors that underpin behavior. We refer to the pair of parameters (a_0, b_0) and the composition of the set of causal variables (which in this case consists of only one variable, x) as the structure of an economist's representation of the causal mechanism that underpins y at $t = 0$.[1]

In general, as time passes, individuals alter the way they make decisions, which influences the way aggregate outcomes move over time. Thus, a representation with different structures may be needed to model adequately the causal mechanism that underpins individual behavior or market outcomes in different time periods.

To model change in a particularly simple way, we suppose that an economist presets change to occur at $t = 1$. Beyond the timing of change, an

---

1. Typically, the structure of an economist's representation also includes the properties of the joint probability distribution of the causal variables and error terms. For a formal definition of the structure of a model, see chapter 6.

economist must specify the postchange representation, which we suppose takes the same form as the prechange one:

$$y_t = a_1 + b_1 x_t \quad \text{for } t \geq 1. \tag{4.2}$$

In the context of this example, change in the causal mechanism is represented by A_{10} and B_{10}:[2]

$$A_{10} = a_1 - a_0 \text{ and } B_{10} = b_1 - b_0, \tag{4.3}$$

which relate the postchange structure of an economist's representation, (a_1, b_1), to its prechange structure, (a_0, b_0).

4.1.1. Fully Predetermining Restrictions

Conventional and behavioral representations invoke different assumptions to specify the structures of their representations and how they change over time. All models constructed according to the contemporary approach, however, share one fundamental feature: they generate sharp predictions of outcomes on the individual and aggregate levels. To construct such models, an economist fully predetermines all changes in the structure of his model; that is, he relates the structure in any time period, past or future, exactly to the structure he uses in the initial period.

The vast majority of contemporary models set $A_{10} = 0$ and $B_{10} = 0$. Such restrictions do not allow for any change in the way individuals make decisions or in how aggregate outcomes unfold over time.

Sometimes, however, contemporary economists allow for change in their models. The simplest way to do so in a fully predetermined way is to set A_{10} and B_{10} equal to particular values $\overline{A}_{10}$ and $\overline{B}_{10}$, respectively:

$$A_{10} = a_1 - a_0 = \overline{A}_{10}, \text{ and } B_{10} = b_1 - b_0 = \overline{B}_{10}. \tag{4.4}$$

We refer to such restrictions, which relate a model's pre- and postchange structures, as *fully predetermining*. Sometimes fully predetermining restrictions are probabilistic. For example, an influential class of contemporary models prespecifies A_{10} and B_{10} as functions of the change in the values of the causal variable as well as the initial structure.[3] Because change in the

---

2. Except for purely formal complications, our critique of the contemporary approach also applies to nonlinear representations. For example, suppose that the representation of the causal mechanism when $t \geq 1$ is a nonlinear function of the causal variable. In such a case, A_{10} and B_{10} would be nonlinear functions of the causal variable.

3. See Hamilton (1989, 1994).

causal variable is typically represented with a probability distribution, these representations imply that A_{10} and B_{10} are characterized by a probability distribution, conditional on the initial structure, (a_0, b_0), as well as the change in the causal variable. We present examples of such models below and in appendix 4.B.

4.1.2. Sharp Probabilistic Predictions of Change

The concept of sharp prediction in contemporary analysis usually involves probabilistic, rather than point, predictions of outcomes. In the present example, imposing equation (4.4) on change in equation (4.2) implies the following fully predetermined representation of the causal mechanism that underpins y at $t \geq 1$:

$$y_t = (a_0 + \overline{A}_{10}) + (b_0 + \overline{B}_{10})x_t \quad \text{for } t \geq 1. \tag{4.5}$$

Regardless of whether $\overline{A}_{10}$ and $\overline{B}_{10}$ are constants or random variables, as long as the representation of the causal variable x is probabilistic, equation (4.5) implies that the outcome is represented as a random variable. The probability distribution for y_1 is related exactly to the initial probability distribution and is referred to as a *sharp* prediction of y.

Sometimes economists allow for more than one way in which an individual may alter her decision making strategy, without prespecifying fully the timing of such change. As in other contemporary models, however, such multiple equilibrium models fully prespecify the set of decision making strategies to which an individual may switch from an initial strategy. Thus, although the implications of these models are not unique, they are nonetheless sharp: a decision making strategy to which a market participant may switch is prespecified to come from a set of fully predetermined representations.[4]

The vast majority of economists construct models that generate not just sharp, but also unique, predictions. In the remainder of this chapter, we focus on such models because their exposition is simpler, and yet they highlight the key differences between extant and IKE approaches to economic analysis.

We begin with the basic case in which $\overline{A}_{10}$ and $\overline{B}_{10}$ are particular constants, rather than random variables. To illustrate how the fully predetermin-

---

4. Such models include the so-called "multiple equilibrium" models that make use of REH to predetermine fully each of the forecasting strategies that an individual may switch to. For a formal demonstration of how such models disregard individual creativity and unforeseen changes in the social context, see chapter 6.

Table 4.1   Probability Distribution for ϵ_1

Value	Probability
$\epsilon_{1,1}$	p
$\epsilon_{1,2}$	$1-p$

Table 4.2   Fully Predetermined Probabilistic Representation of Change

Value	Probability
$\bar{y}_1 + \epsilon_{1,1}(b_0 + \overline{B}_{10})$	p
$\bar{y}_1 + \epsilon_{1,2}(b_0 + \overline{B}_{10})$	$1-p$

ing restrictions in equation (4.4) imply a unique probability distribution of outcomes, given some initial probability distribution, we suppose that the causal variable can be represented by a particularly simple mechanism:

$$x_1 = x_0 + \mu_0 + \epsilon_1 = \overline{x}_1 + \epsilon_1, \tag{4.6}$$

where ϵ_1 represents influences on the change in the causal variable that are not adequately captured by the deterministic trend μ_0.[5] We refer to $\overline{x}_1 = x_0 + \mu_0$ as a deterministic prediction of x_1, conditional on x_0 and μ_0. For simplicity, we suppose that the probability distribution for ϵ_1 is given in table 4.1. The error term is assumed not to matter on average, that is, $\epsilon_{1,1}p + \epsilon_{1,2}(1-p) = 0$.

The distribution for ϵ_1 in table 4.1, together with equations (4.5) and (4.6), imply the conditional probability distribution for the outcome variable at $t=1$ shown in table 4.2,[6] where $\overline{y}_1 = (a_0 + \overline{A}_{10}) + (b_0 + \overline{B}_{10})(x_0 + \mu_0)$ is the deterministic prediction of y_1. The sharp prediction in table 4.2 is conditional on:

5. We are assuming that the distribution for ϵ_1 is the same as the one for ϵ at $t=0$. If we were to allow for change in this distribution, then to generate a sharp prediction, the model would have to fully prespecify this change. For an influential class of models that does so, see Engle (1982, 2003).

6. The arguments in this section also apply to models that include error terms in components other than those representing the causal factors.

1. The representation's structure of the causal mechanism in the initial period, a_0 and b_0, and how this structure changes over time, $\overline{A}_{10}$ and $\overline{B}_{10}$; and

2. The value of the causal variable in the initial period, x_0, the parameter μ_0, and the distribution of the error, ϵ_1.

Since the expected value of ϵ_1 is equal to zero, the expected value of y_1 is equal to its deterministic prediction $\overline{y}_1$. Table 4.2 also makes clear that a sharp probabilistic prediction of change involves simply random deviations from a deterministic prediction. We conclude that, as different as they may appear, contemporary probabilistic representations are as restrictive as their deterministic counterparts, linear or nonlinear: they presume that, conditional on his representation in the initial period, an economist can fully prespecify how an individual's decision making and aggregate outcomes change over time.

4.1.3. Prespecifying Change in the Social Context

Economists sometimes recognize that the social context, particularly policy rules, might change over time and attempt to capture this change with a probabilistic rule that governs how one or more of the causal variables change over time.[7] In appendix 4.A, we illustrate how such models fully prespecify change in the social context and show that they are as restrictive as those that do not allow for any change in the way the social context unfolds over time.

4.1.4. Modeling Change in Outcomes with Fully Prespecified Probabilistic Rules

In our simple example, the timing of change is preset to occur at $t = 1$. As with change in the social context, contemporary economists sometimes represent with probabilistic rules uncertainty about when change in the causal mechanism might take place.[8] In appendix 4.B, we show that such an extension does not alter the validity of our conclusion that contemporary probabilistic representations are as restrictive as their deterministic counterparts.

---

7. For example, see Hamilton (1989) and chapter 6.

8. See chapter 6 for a discussion of such models constructed according to both the conventional and behavioral approaches.

4.2.   Qualitative Predictions of Change in Fully Predetermined Models

The vast majority of contemporary economists do not allow for any changes in their representations of the way y unfolds over time; that is, they set $a_1 = a_0$ and $b_1 = b_0$. This fully predetermining invariance restriction is not sufficient, however, to generate a qualitative prediction about how the outcome variable would change as the value of the causal variable changes between any two points in time. To generate such a prediction, an economist would also have to restrict the slope of his representation in the initial period to be either positive or negative. Once the invariance restriction is imposed, constraining the sign of b_0 to be, say, positive, ensures that the representation generates a qualitative prediction in all periods, past and future: as the value of the causal variable increases (decreases) the outcome variable also increases (decreases).

   To generate qualitative predictions in a fully predetermined model that allows for change, further qualitative restrictions beyond the one on the sign of b_0 are needed. To illustrate this point, suppose that an economist sets out to fully prespecify change. To do so, he would relate the structure of his postchange representation in equation (4.2)—the parameters a_1 and b_1—exactly to his prechange representation—the parameters a_0 and b_0. If, in addition, he wants to ensure a qualitative prediction, say, that y always changes in the same direction as x, he would have to pick both $\overline{A}_{10}$ and $\overline{B}_{10}$ in equation (4.4) to satisfy the following relationship for *each* realization of x_1:[9]

$$\overline{A}_{10} + \overline{B}_{10} x_1 = 0 \text{ and } \overline{B}_{10} > -b_0. \tag{4.7}$$

   To see that equation (4.7) must hold for the representation in equation (4.1) and equation (4.5) to imply both sharp and qualitative predictions, suppose that, for a realization of x_1, which we denote by $x_1^{(j)}$, equation (4.7) does not hold. Suppose, for example, that, given $x_1^{(j)}$, the parameters $\overline{A}_{10}^{(j)}$ and $\overline{B}_{10}^{(j)}$ are chosen so that:

$$\overline{A}_{10}^{(j)} + \overline{B}_{10}^{(j)} x_1^{(j)} > 0 \text{ and } \overline{B}_{10}^{(j)} > -b_0, \tag{4.8}$$

which, in turn, implies that:

$$y_1^{(j)} - y_0 = \overline{A}_{10}^{(j)} + \overline{B}_{10}^{(j)} x_1^{(j)} + b_0 \left(x_1^{(j)} - x_0 \right) \quad \text{and} \quad \overline{B}_{10}^{(j)} > -b_0.$$

---

9. The first constraint joins the two linear segments of the representation at x_1 when graphed in x-y space. The second preserves a positve slope beyond x_1.

**Table 4.3   Fully Predetermined Probabilistic
Representation of Change with
a Qualitative Prediction**

Value	Probability
$a_0 + b_0(x_0 + \mu_0 + \epsilon_{1,1})$	p
$a_0 + b_0(x_0 + \mu_0 + \epsilon_{1,2})$	$1 - p$

It is clear that, if the realization $x_1^{(j)}$ implies a fall in the causal variable between $t = 0$ and 1, but the magnitude of this fall is not greater than $\left(\overline{A}_{10}^{(j)} + \overline{B}_{10}^{(j)} x_1^{(j)}\right)/b_0$, then y would move in the opposite direction. Consequently, for this $x_1^{(j)} - x_0$, the assumption that both the fully predetermining and qualitative conditions are satisfied would be violated.

Imposing fully predetermining restrictions on equations (4.1) and (4.5) that lead to both sharp and qualitative predictions implies the probabilistic representation of change for y_1 given in table 4.3. This distribution, unlike that in table 4.2, is based on choosing $\overline{A}_{10}^{(j)}$ and $\overline{B}_{10}^{(j)}$ so that the model delivers the desired qualitative prediction for each realization of x; that is, so that equation (4.7) is satisfied.

Thus, although contemporary economists often focus on the qualitative predictions of their models, such predictions are derived in models that are fully predetermined in the first place. These "qualitative predictions," therefore, rest on the same presumption as their invariant counterparts: individual creativity and unforeseen changes in the way the social context unfolds over time are unimportant in driving individual behavior and market outcomes.

4.3. IKE Models of Change

In constructing IKE models, the economist only partially prespecifies change. IKE requires an economist to search for regularities in individual behavior, but presumes that such regularities can at best be formalized with qualitative, partially predetermining, restrictions on its representations. IKE models of aggregate outcomes imply only qualitative predictions concerning those outcomes.

4.3.1. *Partially Predetermining Restrictions*

The IKE models that we construct in later chapters attempt to account for different types of regularities on the individual level. One regularity that plays an important role in some of our models is a phenomenon observed by psychologists: individuals are conservative in how they revise their beliefs in the face of new evidence. What constitutes conservative behavior depends on the context being modeled. Our formulation implies that an individual is conservative when a revision of her forecasting strategy, ceteris paribus, leads to a new forecast that is not too different from the forecast that she would have formed had she left her forecasting strategy unchanged.

As we show in chapter 10, our conservative restrictions do not constrain the change in an individual's forecast to be small. This change may also stem from changes in the causal variables, which if large, could lead to a large change in the forecast. Moreover, these restrictions require an economist to presume very little about the causal mechanism that underpins an outcome, such as an individual's forecast. This property is important, as the presumption that an economist can prespecify, even partially, the set of causal variables and their influences is very bold.

Nevertheless, based on theoretical or empirical considerations, an economist may feel reasonably confident that his representation of an individual's behavior should include particular variables. For example, in most applications to asset markets of demand and supply analysis, including those in this book, it is usual to represent an individual's forecast of the future price to depend positively on the current price at every point in time.

The model of the preceding section illustrates how a contemporary economist would represent the connection between an individual's forecast and the market price. He would usually assume that this forecast depends positively on the current price at every point in time and fully prespecify when and how this influence changed between the initial point and all other points. By contrast, although some of our IKE models of currency markets presume that an individual's exchange rate forecast depends positively on the current exchange rate at every point in time, they only partially prespecify change in their representations of individual behavior over time.

To illustrate this difference and to sketch how we formulate partially predetermined conservative restrictions, we construct an IKE analog of the example in the preceding section. To this end, we preset the change in the causal mechanism to occur at $t = 1$.[10] This specification leads to the following pre- and postchange representations:

$$y_t = a_0 + b_0 x_t \quad \text{when } t < 1 \tag{4.9}$$

$$y_t = a_1 + b_1 x_t = (a_0 + A_{10}) + (b_0 + B_{10}) x_t \quad \text{when } t \geq 1, \tag{4.10}$$

10. In general, IKE does not require an economist to preselect when change occurs in his models.

where we impose, as before, the qualitative restrictions that b_0 and b_1 are both positive.

Now suppose that, as before, an economist wants his representation to generate the qualitative prediction that the outcome variable always moves in the same direction as the causal variable. In the fully predetermined model, this constraint required that the economist impose qualitative restrictions in addition to fully predetermining ones that uniquely predetermine $\overline{A}_{10}$ and $\overline{B}_{10}$ in terms of the initial structure and the value of the causal variable at $t = 1$. IKE, however, eschews fully predetermining restrictions and recognizes that to generate qualitative predictions from its models, an economist need only make use of partially predetermining restrictions.

To guarantee that y moves in the same direction as x for t between 0 and 1, all that is needed are the following partially predetermining restrictions on change:

$$\frac{\left(A_{10} + B_{10}x_1^{(j)}\right)}{b_0} < -\left(x_1^{(j)} - x_0\right) \quad \text{for every } j \text{ such that } \left(x_1^{(j)} - x_0\right) < 0$$

$$(4.11)$$

$$\frac{\left(A_{10} + B_{10}x_1^{(j)}\right)}{b_0} > -\left(x_1^{(j)} - x_0\right) \quad \text{for every } j \text{ such that } \left(x_1^{(j)} - x_0\right) > 0.$$

$$(4.12)$$

Unlike the fully predetermining restrictions discussed earlier, these qualitative constraints imply a range of functions that relate A_{10} and B_{10} to $x_1^{(j)}$ for each realization of the causal variable.

To see how these restrictions ensure the desired qualitative prediction, consider a realization of the causal variable at $t = 1$, so that x increases $(x_1^{(j)} - x_0 > 0)$. The change in the outcome variable is given by:

$$y_1^{(j)} - y_0 = \left(A_{10}^{(j)} + B_{10}^{(j)}x_1^{(j)}\right) + b_0\left(x_1^{(j)} - x_0\right). \quad (4.13)$$

If there is no change in the representation at $t = 1$, so that the first term in equation (4.13) is zero, then, with $b_0 > 0$, y will necessarily also move up relative to its initial value. In the model, however, the rise in x in general will be associated with a change in its structure. This change can either reinforce or impede the change in the outcome variable that occurs solely because of the increase in x. A reinforcing change would imply that, when evaluated at $x_1^{(j)}$, y is higher, that is, $A_{10}^{(j)} + B_{10}^{(j)} x_1^{(j)} > 0$. In this case, y necessarily rises relative to its initial value.

However, the change in structure at $t = 1$ may be nonreinforcing; that is, $A_{10}^{(j)} + B_{10}^{(j)} x_1^{(j)} < 0$, so that when evaluated at $x_1^{(j)}$, y is lower. In this case, the degree to which change is nonreinforcing must be limited to ensure that the outcome variable nevertheless rises for t between 0 and 1. The necessary conservative condition is given in equation (4.12).

Thus, to ensure the qualitative prediction that the value of the outcome variable always rises with the causal variable, we need to constrain change in the model to be either reinforcing and/or conservative. Because such constraints on change are qualitative, they are consistent with myriad postchange representations for each realization of x_1. Each one of these representations implies a probability distribution for y. Consequently, the model does not relate the postchange distribution for the outcome variable uniquely to its prechange distribution. It thus implies a qualitative prediction without also implying a sharp prediction.

4.3.2. *Partially Predetermined Probabilistic Representations*

As seen in table 4.3, fully predetermined probabilistic representations of change imply standard probabilistic predictions, which relate each possible realization of the causal variables to a unique value for the outcome variable. By contrast, an IKE model implies what we refer to as a *partially predetermined probabilistic representation of change,* which implies many possible values for y for each realization of x.

To illustrate the meaning of this concept, we continue to represent the process behind the causal variable as $x_1 = x_0 + \mu_0 + \epsilon_1$ and use the distribution for ϵ_1 given in table 4.1. The partially predetermining restrictions in equations (4.11) and (4.12) generate the qualitative prediction concerning the outcome variable, conditional on x_0 and the structure of the initial representation (a_0, b_0) that is displayed in table 4.4. In this table, we suppose

Table 4.4   Partially Predetermined Probabilistic Representation of Change

Value	Probability
$y_1 < a_0 + b_0 x_0$	p
$y_1 > a_0 + b_0 x_0$	$1 - p$

that $\mu_0 + \epsilon_{1,1} < 0$ and $\mu_0 + \epsilon_{1,2} > 0$. The simple IKE model in our example predicts that for t between 0 and 1, the outcome variable will rise with probability p and fall with probability $1 - p$.[11] However, the magnitude of the change in y for each realization of x is left unconstrained.

4.4. IKE Causal-Transition Paths

In a more general IKE model, change can occur beyond $t = 1$. To generate testable implications, IKE presumes that change at different points in time share certain qualitative features. For example, if we make use of the partially predetermining restrictions in equations (4.11) and (4.12) at every point in time, then change in the model between all adjacent points in time will be either reinforcing and/or conservative. By imposing only qualitative conditions on change at every point in time, these restrictions are compatible with innumerable possible changes in the model at a point in time for each realization of the causal variable. They are consistent, therefore, with countless transition paths that characterize how the causal mechanism for y may develop over time. Each of these causal-transition paths is based on a sequence of transitions between conditional probability distributions for y that are consistent with the qualitative prediction in table 4.4.

However, because all of these causal-transition paths are consistent with the restrictions in equation (4.11) and (4.12), they all share a common feature: the outcome variable changes in the same direction as the causal variable between any two adjacent points in time. Consequently, to represent how the causal mechanism unfolds over an extended period, IKE would use any one of these causal-transition paths.

The basic tool of contemporary analysis is the so-called "equilibrium price function," which economists use to represent the movement of a market price over time. An IKE model can also represent movements of a market price as a sequence of equilibrium outcomes. However, in contrast to extant approaches, such a sequence is modeled as partially predetermined transitions across probabilistic representations of the causal mechanism. Any one of the causal-transition paths that is consistent with the partially predetermining restrictions of the model can be used to represent behavior.

---

11. In general, IKE models could imply qualitative predictions concerning both the potential values and their probabilities, which would be the case, for example, if the causal variables were assumed to change in a partially predetermined way.

Table 4.5 Probability Distribution of ϵ_0

Value	Probability
0.5	0.6
−0.75	0.4

Appendix 4.A:
Fully Prespecifying Change in the Social Context

To illustrate the issues involved in modeling changes in the social context, we suppose that the probability distribution of the error term is given in table 4.5.

For simplicity, we also suppose that as time passes between $t = 0$ and $t = 1$, the causal variable increases continuously at a constant rate. This rate at $t = 0$ is μ_0, but the value of this parameter could change between $t = 0$ and $t = 1$ to μ_1. Thus, we specify the deterministic component of the representation of change in the causal factors μ_{10}:

$$\mu_{10} = t_{sw}\mu_0 + \left(1 - t_{sw}\right)\mu_1 = \mu_0 + \left(1 - t_{sw}\right)\triangle\mu, \qquad (4.14)$$

where t_{sw}, which lies between 0 and 1, denotes the time at which the deterministic component might switch from μ_0 to μ_1, and $\triangle\mu = \mu_1 - \mu_0$.

In this setup, as time passes, the initial specification of the causal variable in equation (4.14) with $\mu_{10} = \mu_0$ may cease to be an adequate representation of the causal factors. To allow for this possibility, we set $x_0 = 2$ and $\mu_0 = 1$, and suppose that a switch between the initial and new representation occurs at the time that x reaches its conditional mean of $\bar{x}_1 = 3$:[12]

$$x_1 = x_0 + \mu_0 + \epsilon_1 \quad \text{if } x \leq 3 \qquad (4.15)$$

$$x_1 = x_0 + \mu_0 + \left(1 - t_{sw}\right)\triangle\mu + \epsilon_1 \quad \text{if } x > 3. \qquad (4.16)$$

This simple probabilistic rule implies that if the realization of ϵ_1 is equal to 0.5, which is prespecified to occur with probability of 0.6, then the representation of the causal factors is prespecified to remain unchanged and is given by equation (4.15). Otherwise, the structure of this representation is prespecified to switch at $t_{sw} = 0.5$ and is given by equation (4.16). We also

---

12. We note that this setup also illustrates more complex representations of changes in the social context, for example, those specified with a Markov process. See chapter 6.

Table 4.6   Conditional Probability Distribution of x_1

Value	Probability
$3.5 + \left(1 - t_{sw}\right) \Delta \mu$	0.6
2.25	0.4

note that because x is assumed to change at the constant rate $\mu_0 = 1$, the switching time is given by:

$$t_{sw} = \frac{x_{sw} - (\mu_0 + \epsilon_1)}{\mu_0} = 0.5, \tag{4.17}$$

where we assume that the value of ϵ_1 is realized at $t = 0$.[13] Then the conditional probability distribution of x_1 is given in table 4.6. It immediately follows that unless $\Delta \mu$ is constrained to take on a particular value, equations (4.15) and (4.16) have no implications for the value of $3.5 + \left(1 - t_{sw}\right) \Delta \mu$, and thus, do not generate a conditional distribution for x_1.

Thus, to ensure that his representation implies a unique conditional prediction of y_1, an economist must also prespecify fully any change in the way the social context unfolds over time. In our example he must prespecify the parameter $\Delta \mu$.

Appendix 4.B:

Modeling Change in Outcomes with Fully Predetermined Probabilistic Rules

To illustrate how contemporary models fully prespecify the timing of change with probabilistic rules, we use the fully prespecified error process in table 4.5 and again assume that the value of ϵ_1 is realized at time $t = 0$. We also continue to suppose that as time passes between the initial point, $t = 0$, and the future, $t = 1$, the causal variable increases continuously at a constant rate.

To focus on the change in the way outcomes, rather than causal factors, unfold over time, we suppose that the deterministic component of the

---

13. A straightforward interpretation of equations (4.15) and (4.16) in a macroeconomic context is that x stands for the log of the money supply. Under this interpretation, a switch means that if the rate of monetary growth exceeds 3 percent, the authorities are expected to change the average rate of growth of money from μ_0 to μ_1.

Table 4.7 **Fully Predetermined Conditional
Probability Distribution of y_1**

Value	Probability
$(a_0 + \overline{A}_{10}) + (b_0 + \overline{B}_{10})(x_0 + \mu_0) + 0.5b_0$	0.6
$a_0 + b_0(x_0 + \mu_0) - 0.75b_0$	0.4

representation of x in equation (4.15) is constrained to be unchanging be-
tween $t = 0$ and $t = 1$; that is, we set $\triangle\mu = 0$, so that $\mu_{10} = \mu_0$. Instead, we
allow for the possibility that as time passes, the initial specification of the
causal mechanism in equation (4.1) may cease to be an adequate representation of market outcomes.[14] To do so, we suppose that a switch between the
initial and new representations occurs at the same time as x reaches some
value x_{sw}:

$$y = a_0 + b_0x \quad \text{if } x \leq x_{sw} \tag{4.18}$$

$$y = a_1 + b_1x \quad \text{if } x > x_{sw}. \tag{4.19}$$

To see how this simple probabilistic rule works, we set $x_0 = 2$, $\mu_0 = 1$,
and $x_{sw} = 3$. These values imply that if the realization of x_1 is the lower value
(table 4.5), which is prespecified to occur with probability of 0.4, the representation for y_1 is prespecified to remain unchanged in equation (4.18).
Otherwise, the structure of this representation is prespecified to change at
$t_{sw} = 0.5$ (see equation (4.19)).

Moreover, the contemporary approach also fully prespecifies the structure of the representation for y if the switch were to occur:

$$y = (a_0 + \overline{A}_{10}) + (b_0 + \overline{B}_{10})x \quad \text{if } x \geq 3. \tag{4.20}$$

The distribution of ϵ_1 implies that the fully predetermined prediction for y_1
is given in table 4.7.

Thus, even if a contemporary economist allows for a probabilistic timing
of change, his model still implies sharp predictions. Moreover, because an
economist fully prespecifies a probabilistic rule that governs change, his
probabilistic representation of the timing of change is as restrictive as the
deterministic rule that presets the exact time at which change occurs.

---

14. A change in the structures of the x and y processes could be represented together without
altering any of our conclusions.

5 Imperfect Knowledge Economics of Supply and Demand

> Indeed, the chief point was already seen by those remarkable anticipators of modern economics, the Spanish schoolmen of the sixteenth century, who emphasized that what they called *pretium matematicum,* the mathematical price, depended on so many particular circumstances that it could never be known to man but was known only to God.
>
> FRIEDRICH A. HAYEK,
> "The Pretence of Knowledge,"
> Nobel Lecture, p. 28

Capitalist economies rely on the movement of market prices to coordinate the decisions of its many actors. Supply and demand analysis, which most economists use to explain such movements, is thus basic to economics. In the simplest microeconomic problems, an individual is represented as choosing between alternatives on the basis of current market prices and a set of causal factors. For example, in modeling an individual's demand for some good, an economist assumes that she allocates her income to the good and to other alternative uses in a way that maximizes her utility for each set of current market prices. This simple model specifies the quantity demanded with a one-to-one mapping—a demand function, which predicts that a given change in market prices, income, or other causal variables results in a unique revision of the quantity demanded. Moreover, an economist usually imposes additional qualitative constraints on his representation of preferences that leads him to model an individual's demand for a good by a downward-sloping function: ceteris paribus, a fall (increase) in its price leads to an increase (fall) in the quantity demanded. This simple setup has only limited relevance as a representation of change in capitalist economies, where individual decisions in many markets inherently involve not just current prices but also forecasts of future prices. Thus, to represent supply and demand on the individual and aggregate levels in terms of market prices and some set of causal factors, an economist must represent market participants' forecasting strategies and their revisions.

In chapter 4, we used a simple algebraic example to compare how extant and IKE approaches represent the causal mechanism that underpins an outcome variable in terms of a set of factors. In this chapter, we use the same algebraic example to examine the implications of extant and IKE approaches to supply and demand analysis.

We show that representations of supply and demand continue to imply one-to-one mappings of market prices and other causal variables as long as the economist fully prespecifies when and how market participants revise their forecasting strategies, as well as how the social context within which they make decisions unfolds over time. But such fully predetermined models, regardless of whether they are constructed by following the conventional or the behavioral approach, disregard the importance of individual creativity and unforeseen changes in the social context for the movement of aggregate outcomes. Thus, the familiar representations of supply and demand as functions of market prices and other causal variables ignore key factors underpinning the movements of supply, demand, and prices in many real world markets.

To highlight the key differences between extant and IKE approaches to supply and demand, and yet keep the analysis simple, we use a typical upward-sloping supply function to represent the supply side of a market but rely on IKE to represent its demand side. The usual demand and supply analysis examines how quantity demanded changes as the market price adjusts to its equilibrium level while holding the values of the causal variables unchanged. In general, however, a change in the market price may cause market participants to revise their forecasting strategies. To account for such revisions, IKE imposes only partially predetermining restrictions on its representations of forecasting behavior.

By design, there is nothing in an IKE model that prespecifies the exact path that an individual's forecast will follow as the market price adjusts to a disequilibrium situation. Consequently, IKE does not fully prespecify how an individual may modify her demand as price changes. Instead, the partially predetermining restrictions imposed on forecasting behavior imply myriad possible partially predetermined *demand paths,* each one characterizing how quantity demanded may change as the market price changes. Partially predetermined demand paths differ from the causal-transition paths that we discussed in the preceding chapter. The former characterize how quantity demanded changes at a point in time given a change in the market price, while the latter represent how the causal mechanism evolves over time.[1]

In sharp contrast to the usual fully predetermined representation of demand, an IKE model does not represent demand as a one-to-one mapping— a function—of the market price. However, the partially predetermining

---

1. See chapter 11 for an example of equilibrium transition paths in the context of modeling behavior in the foreign exchange market.

restrictions that we impose in the model constrain all of its demand paths to slope downward. Consequently, all of these paths imply that, given excess supply or demand, the market price will adjust to some equilibrium level. Although there is nothing in the model that prespecifies at which price this equilibration process will end, we show that our IKE model generates a testable qualitative prediction: a rise (fall) in income (its causal variable) leads to a rise (fall) in the equilibrium price.

The vast majority of contemporary models represent change as if it were fully reversible: a sequence of two changes in some causal variable that are equal in magnitude but opposite in sign is presumed to have no effect on the way market participants make decisions or how aggregate outcomes unfold over time. By contrast, history in an IKE model is not presumed to be reversible: progress in capitalist economies frequently has irreversible effects on how individuals think about the future, how they make decisions, and how the social context evolves.

5.1. Fully Predetermined Representations of Supply and Demand

Economic decisions in many markets inherently involve not just current prices, but also forecasts of future prices. In chapter 3, we considered an individual's decision concerning how much of her current and future real income she would like to spend on the consumption good in the current and future periods. In making this decision, an individual has to forecast the future price and future real income. By fully prespecifying future real income in terms of current income we were able to represent an individual's demand as follows:

$$Q_t^{\mathrm{D}}(p_t, \widehat{P}_{t|t+1}, x_t) = \alpha + \beta \left[\widehat{P}_{t|t+1} - p_t \right] + \gamma x_t, \tag{5.1}$$

where as in chapter 3 (equation 3.7), Q_t^{D} denotes quantity demanded, p_t is the market price at t, $\widehat{P}_{t|t+1}$ is an economist's representation of an individual's forecast of the market price at $t + 1$, and x_t is an individual's real income at t. The parameters γ and β are positive and depend on the parameters of the utility function and the representation of the way real income unfolds over time. As in chapter 3, we assume here that the specification of the utility function and the representation for x_t are time invariant, which implies that γ and β are constrained to be constants; that is, they vary neither over time nor with the value of x_t.

5.1.1. Forecast Revisions and Price

In general, a representation of an individual's forecasting strategy concerning the price at $t+1$ involves the market price and other causal variables, such as consumers' income, at time t and earlier. In this chapter, however, we contrast extant and IKE representations of the relationship between demand on the individual or aggregate level and the market price while holding the values of the causal variables constant. To focus on this relationship, we suppose that the representation of forecasting behavior that underpins the quantity demanded by an individual depends only on the market price. Extant and IKE approaches to demand and supply analysis differ in terms of how they represent change. To keep our fully predetermined example simple, however, we allow for the possibility that as the price changes and crosses a threshold value, which we denote by p_{sw}, an individual might switch from one forecasting strategy to another:

$$\widehat{P}^0_{t|t+1} = \hat{a}^0 + \hat{b}^0 p_t \quad \text{if } p_t < p_{sw} \tag{5.2}$$

$$\widehat{P}^1_{t|t+1} = \hat{a}^1 + \hat{b}^1 p_t \quad \text{if } p_t > p_{sw}, \tag{5.3}$$

where we use the superscripts 0 and 1 to signify the representations associated with a market price below and above its threshold, respectively. Because the change in structure stems solely from a change in the price across the threshold, we suppress the time subscripts on the parameters $\hat{a}$ and $\hat{b}$.[2]

To fully predetermine the representation of forecasting behavior in equations (5.2) and (5.3), an economist presets the value of the threshold, p_{sw}, at which an individual is presumed to switch from one forecasting strategy to another.[3] He also relates the structure of his postchange representation—$(\hat{a}^1, \hat{b}^1)$—exactly to the structure of his prechange representation—$(\hat{a}^0, \hat{b}^0)$.[4] That is, he sets $\hat{a}^1 = \hat{a}^0 + \overline{A}_{10}$ and $\hat{b}^1 = \hat{b}^0 + \overline{B}_{10}$, where $\overline{A}_{10}$ and $\overline{B}_{10}$ are equal to particular values. These fully predetermining restrictions allow him to relate uniquely his representations of an individual's forecasting strategy when the market price is above and below p_{sw}:

$$\widehat{P}^1_{t|t+1} = \hat{a}^1 + \hat{b}^1 p_t = (\hat{a}^0 + \overline{A}_{10}) + (\hat{b}^0 + \overline{B}_{10})p_t \quad \text{if } p_t > p_{sw}. \tag{5.4}$$

---

2. A more general fully predetermined model could allow for a change in an individual's forecast to arise not only from changes in the market price but also from movements in other factors.

3. In general, the threshold could be a function of the initial structure of the model or the history of prices.

4. For convenience, we refer to equations (5.2) and (5.3) as the pre- and postchange representations, respectively. Of course, if the market price were intially above the threshold, then a fall in its value below p_{sw} would cause a change in the representation from equation (5.3) to equation (5.2).

5.1.2. Standard Demand Function

Substituting equations (5.2) and (5.4) into (5.1) implies the following fully predetermined representation for an individual's demand:

$$Q_t^{D1} = (\alpha + \beta \hat{a}^0) + \beta(\hat{b}^0 - 1)p_t + \gamma x_t \quad \text{if } p_t < p_{sw} \qquad (5.5)$$

$$Q_t^{D2} = \left[\alpha + \beta(\hat{a}^0 + \overline{A}_{10})\right] + \beta \left[(\hat{b}^0 + \overline{B}_{10}) - 1\right] p_t + \gamma x_t \text{ if } p_t > p_{sw}. \quad (5.6)$$

The fully predetermining restrictions do indeed imply the usual representation of demand as a function relating quantity demanded to price. But such restrictions presume that an economist can adequately represent revisions of forecasting strategies as a one-to-one mapping of the change in the market price. As a result, the standard supply and demand curves, regardless of whether they are constructed by following the conventional or the behavioral approach, disregard individual creativity and unforeseen changes in the social context that underpin demand and supply in many markets in capitalist economies.

5.1.3. The Downward-Sloping Demand Curve

The fully predetermined model in equations (5.5) and (5.6) implies that a change in the market price, while holding the causal variables unchanged, results in a unique change in quantity demanded. It does not, however, imply that an individual's demand curve at any point in time is necessarily downward sloping. For the model to imply this familiar relationship, an economist must impose additional qualitative restrictions on his representation of forecasting behavior in equations (5.2) and (5.3). The specification in equation (5.1) reveals what is required: the demand curve at any point in time will be downward-sloping as long as an individual's forecast moves in the same direction as the market price but is less than one for one:

$$0 < \Delta\widehat{P}(p_a, p_b) < \Delta p \quad \text{for any } p_a \text{ and } p_b, \qquad (5.7)$$

where $\Delta\widehat{P}(p_a, p_b)$ denotes a change in $\widehat{P}$ that arises because of a change in the market price from p_a to p_b.

The qualitative constraint in equation (5.7) is similar to the one that we imposed on the model in section 4.2. It is clear from the analysis there that imposing the following qualitative restrictions on equations (5.2) and (5.3) would ensure the desired qualitative prediction for any change in the market price:

$$0 < \hat{b}^0 < 1, -\hat{b}^0 < \overline{B}_{10} < 1 - \hat{b}^0, \text{ and } \overline{A}_{10} + \overline{B}_{10}p_{sw} = 0. \qquad (5.8)$$

With these additional restrictions, the representation of an individual's demand implies not only unique predictions concerning the magnitude of the change in demand following a change in the price: it also implies that as the market price increases (falls), quantity demanded falls (increases).

5.2. Supply and Demand Analysis in Contemporary Models

To construct a model of aggregate outcomes, we follow the usual practice and invoke the representative-individual assumption. Consequently, we interpret the specifications of an individual's forecast and quantity demanded as also representing the forecast and demand in the aggregate (market).

To complete the model, we adopt the simple fully predetermined representation of market supply that we used in chapter 3, equation (3.8):

$$Q_t^s(p_t) = \delta + \lambda p_t, \tag{5.9}$$

where $\delta \leq 0$ and $\lambda > 0$ are constant parameters.

Equating quantity demanded with quantity supplied yields the specification for the equilibrium price:

$$p_t = a^0 + c^0 x_t \quad \text{if } p_t < p_{sw} \tag{5.10}$$

$$p_t = a^1 + c^1 x_t \quad \text{if } p_t > p_{sw}, \tag{5.11}$$

where a^0, a^1, c^0, and c^1 are functions of the parameters in equations (5.5), (5.6), and (5.9).

To illustrate the usual supply and demand analysis, we suppose that the market is initially ($t = 1$) in equilibrium at point fp_1, with an equilibrium price of 1.5. Suppose that as time t passes from 1 to 2, the value of income increases. Because income does not enter into the representation of forecasting behavior, its increase leaves an individual's forecast unchanged. Furthermore, because γ is prespecified to remain fixed over time, the representation of demand in equations (5.5) and (5.6) implies that the rise in x leads to parallel upward shifts in both parts of the demand curve.[5] Figure 5.1 shows that at the initial price of 1.5, Q^D shifts up to point a in the diagram. At this price, the market is characterized by a situation in which quantity demanded exceeds quantity supplied.

---

5. With a more general specification, the increase in x would influence quantity demanded indirectly through its effect on the representation of forecasting behavior. In this case, the shift in the demand curve may not be parallel, but none of our conclusions would be altered. Furthermore, allowing for γ to change in a fully prespecified way would also not affect any of our conclusions.

Figure 5.1   Contemporary Approach to Supply and Demand Analysis

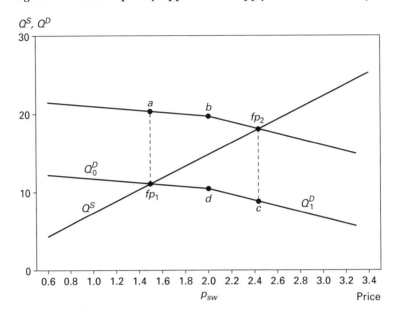

With supply and demand analysis, economists usually assume that a mechanism exists by which the market price rises whenever demand exceeds supply and falls whenever supply exceeds demand.[6] During this price adjustment process, the values of all causal variables are assumed to be constant. Under this assumption, the excess demand associated with $p = 1.5$ causes the market price to rise. Initially, as p rises, the representation in equations (5.5) and (5.6) implies that the quantity demanded falls from point a in figure 5.1 with a prespecified elasticity of $-\beta(\hat{b}^0 - 1)/Q_t^D$.

In real world markets, participants revise the way they form forecasts. The representation in equations (5.2) and (5.4) models such behavior with a fully prespecified change in the relationship between the forecast and price. Once the market price reaches its threshold value, which we set equal to 2, market participants are presumed to revise their forecasting strategies. The representation accounts for such behavior by prespecifying exactly how the new forecasting strategy is related to the initial strategy.

---

6. Economists often portray this price mechanism with the aid of what is called a "Walrasian auctioneer": no trades take place out of equilibrium and the market price increases when excess demand prevails in the market and falls when there is excess supply.

Thus, once the value of p rises above 2, the quantity demanded implied by equation (5.6) continues to fall, but with a prespecified elasticity of $-\beta\left[(\hat{b}^0 + \overline{B}_{10}) - 1\right]/Q_t^D$. This behavior is shown in figure 5.1 by a new piece of the demand curve starting at point b.

As is clear from figure 5.1, the representations of supply and demand in our example imply that the excess demand initially created by the rise in income declines as the market price rises. Because these changes are fully predetermined, there is a unique p at which $Q_{t+1}^D = Q_{t+1}^S$. With the higher value of x, this equilibrium is depicted at point fp_2 in the figure, which corresponds to an equilibrium $p = 2.5$. This equilibrium price is uniquely determined in terms of: (1) the parameters of the initial forecasting strategy; (2) the fully predetermining restrictions, which uniquely relate the initial and revised forecasting strategies; (3) the unchanging parameters of the representations for quantity supplied and quantity demanded; and (4) the values of x_1 and x_2. It follows that, with the equilibrium values of the market price uniquely determined at $t = 1$ and $t = 2$, the fully predetermined model of supply and demand in our example implies a unique change in the equilibrium price for a given change in income.

5.3. History as the Future and Vice Versa

An important implication of most contemporary models, such as the one illustrated above, is that they represent change as if it were fully reversible. This implication is easily seen in our example by considering a fall in x back to its initial value as time t progresses from 2 to 3. It is immediately clear that quantity demanded shifts down to point c on the initial demand curve, and that the sequence of equal but opposite changes in the causal variable has absolutely no effect on how market participants make decisions or on the way aggregate outcomes unfold.

To see how striking this implication of the contemporary approach is, consider the representation of forecasting in our example. As the causal variable increases with the passage of time t from 1 to 2, an individual is supposed to revise her strategy at the time and in a way that is fully prespecified by an economist. Then, as x subsequently declines for t between 2 and 3 and reaches its threshold, market participants are presumed to revert to using the same forecasting strategy as the one they started with. This representation of change is tantamount to presupposing that they have not come up with any genuinely new ways of thinking about the future. In this sense, the contemporary approach presumes, puzzlingly, that history does not play an essential role in altering either individual behavior or the social context within which individuals make decisions.[7]

5.4. Supply and Demand Analysis in IKE Models

The partially predetermining restrictions of an IKE model allow for change in the way individuals forecast the future at every point in time. Such revisions could arise either from movements in the causal variables and market price or merely from the passage of time. However, the key elements of supply and demand analysis in IKE models can be illustrated with an example that, as in the previous section, assumes that an individual's forecasting strategy does not depend on x and that there is only one value of p at which a switch in the structure of the representation occurs. Our example also makes use of linear structures to represent an individual's forecasting strategy for values of the market price below and above the threshold:

$$\widehat{P}^0_{t|t+1} = \hat{a}^0_t + \hat{b}^0_t p_t \quad \text{if } p_t < p_{sw} \tag{5.12}$$

$$\widehat{P}^1_{t|t+1} = \hat{a}^1_t + \hat{b}^1_t p_t \quad \text{if } p_t > p_{sw}, \tag{5.13}$$

where the superscripts 0 and 1 are again used to denote the forecasting strategies associated with a p below and above p_{sw}, respectively. As will become clear shortly, change in an IKE model is not reversible. Thus, unlike in the fully predetermined case, the forecasting strategies that are associated with $p < p_{sw}$ and $p > p_{sw}$ will, in general, be distinct at each point in time. The subscript t on the parameters in equations (5.12) and (5.13) reflects this possibility. Finally, we continue to represent demand and supply with the specifications in equations (5.1) and (5.9).

We begin our illustration by assuming that the market at time $t = 1$ is initially in equilibrium at a price that is lower than the threshold. Then the individual's forecasting strategy at this equilibrium point is given by equation (5.12). We also suppose that as time t passes from 1 to 2, the value of income increases. The representation of demand in equation (5.1) implies that the rise in x leads to an increase in the quantity demanded, which in

---

7. We note that change in a multiple-equilibrium model is not, in general, reversible: a return of a causal variable to its initial value could be associated with a move to an equilibrium other than the initial one. Economists sometimes construct so-called "hysteresis models" in which the movement of an outcome variable is path dependent. For example, see Krugman (1987b). Nevertheless, both types of models fully prespecify the equilibria to which the system does move. Consequently, they both presume that individuals have not invented any genuinely new ways of thinking about the future as history unfolds.

turn produces an excess demand in the market at the old price. As with the fully predetermined model, we assume that this excess demand causes the market price to rise.[8]

5.4.1. IKE Forecast-Revision Paths

Prior to any rise in the market price at $t = 2$, the individual's forecasting strategy is given by equation (5.12). If we were to assume that $\hat{b}_t^0 > 0$, then as p begins to rise, so would $\widehat{P}_{t|t+1}$. But as the market price rises, the individual may revise her forecasting strategy. Our simple example represents such behavior by allowing for a switch in structure as p crosses the threshold value. In general, this switch may involve a rise or fall in an individual's forecast at p_{sw}. Moreover the change in structure could imply a $\hat{b}_t^1 < 0$, in which case a further rise in p would lead to a fall in $\widehat{P}_{t|t+1}$.

We will refer to the relationship that characterizes how an individual's forecast develops as the market price changes, while holding the causal variables unchanged, as a *forecast-revision path*. To generate qualitative predictions from our model, we need to constrain the forecast-revision paths that it generates. To this end, we constrain change in the model so that an individual's forecast moves in the same direction as the market price but is less than one for one, for any change in p; that is, we impose the qualitative constraint in equation (5.7). In our simple example, this constraint implies the following qualitative restrictions on the relationship between the representations associated with a p below and above p_{sw}, respectively:

$$0 < \hat{b}_t^0 < 1, \quad -\hat{b}_t^0 < B_{10} < 1 - \hat{b}_t^0, \text{ and } A_{10} + B_{10}p_{sw} = 0. \quad (5.14)$$

The key difference with the fully predetermined model is that with IKE, these restrictions are imposed instead of, rather than in addition to, the fully predetermining restrictions that require an economist to choose unique values for A_{10} and B_{10}.[9] Because our IKE model of demand and supply does not exactly determine A_{10} and B_{10}, it is consistent with myriad possible forecast-revision paths. However, all of these paths are consistent with the partially predetermining restrictions in equation (5.14). Consequently, they

---

8. If we had assumed that an individual's forecast depended on income as well as the market price, the shift in excess demand that results from an increase in x would also stem from a change in the structure of the representation. None of the conclusions of our analysis would be affected by such a complication. If, for example, we assumed that this change was either conservative or reinforcing (see chapter 4), quantity demanded would still shift up, although there would be nothing in the model that would determine the magnitude of this shift. Nevertheless, the model would continue to predict a rise in quantity demanded and a rise in the market price.

9. See chapter 4.

Figure 5.2   Partially Predetermined Forecast-Revision Paths

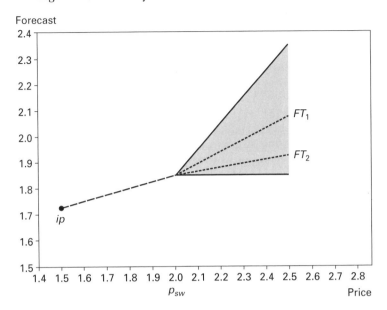

all share a common feature: their slopes are everywhere positive and less than 1. It is this feature that ensures that excess demand necessarily falls in the model as the market price rises. We provide just two examples of the forecast-revision paths that are generated by the model at $t = 2$ in figure 5.2, which we denote by FT_1 and FT_2. The shaded region in the figure depicts all possible forecast revision paths that are consistent with the partially predetermining restrictions in equation (5.14) and *ip* denotes the initial point.

5.4.2. IKE Demand Paths

The IKE representation of forecasting behavior constructed in the preceding section does not presume that an economist can fully prespecify how an individual would revise her forecast as the market price changes. Consequently, it does not fully prespecify how an individual alters the way she make decisions, which in our example concerns how she modifies her demand as price changes during the equilibration process. IKE only constrains the change between representations of demand to be consistent with the partially predetermining restrictions of the model.

The qualitative restrictions in equation (5.14) constrain the model's forecast-revision paths to imply that as the market price rises, an individual's

Figure 5.3   Supply and Demand Analysis in an IKE Model

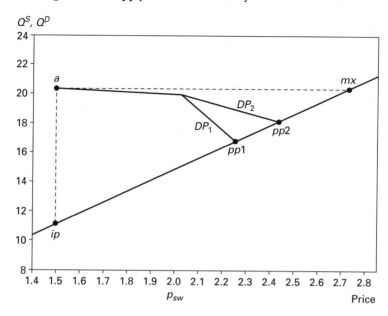

forecast rises, but by less than one for one. This shared feature immediately ensures that each one of these paths is associated with a corresponding partially predetermined demand path that is downward sloping: as the market price rises at a point in time, quantity demanded falls. Figure 5.3 displays the two demand paths that are implied by the forecast-revision paths in figure 5.2, which we denote by DP_1 and DP_2.[10] We emphasize that these examples are purely illustrative: any other set of partially predetermined demand paths consistent with equation (5.14) could be used to illustrate how our IKE model represents the change in demand during the equilibration process.

5.4.3. Partially Predetermined Equilibria

We consider now the implications of our IKE model of demand and supply for the market price given the one-time increase in income between $t = 1$ and $t = 2$. As in figure 5.2, the increase in x causes quantity demanded to rise to point a in figure 5.3, creating excess demand in the model at the initial price of 1.5. Consequently, the market price rises from this value. However, unlike before, there are myriad demand paths that could describe how

---

10. In this figure, *ip* is the initial point and *mx* is the maximum equilibrium point consistent with the partially predetermining restrictions in equation (5.14).

quantity demanded will change as the price rises. Moreover, by design, there is nothing in the model that determines which of these paths quantity demanded might follow. In this sense, IKE does not represent the relationship between quantity demanded and price with a one-to-one mapping (that is, a demand function). Nevertheless, because all demand paths slope downward, they imply that the initial excess demand in the model will decline and eventually reach 0 as the market price rises from 1.5. In general, then, an IKE model of supply and demand implies myriad possible equilibrium points. For example, path DP_1 in figure 5.3 implies that the equilibration process would push the market price to the equilibrium at point $pp1$, whereas path DP_2 would imply an equilibrium price at point $pp2$.

The fully predetermined model considered in the previous section implies that the equilibrium price associated with x_2 can be expressed uniquely in terms of the model's initial structure and x_0. It thus implies a unique positive change in price given $\triangle x$. By contrast, our IKE model implies only that the market will reach some equilibrium at which the higher x will be associated with a higher p.[11] But because IKE imposes partially predetermining restrictions instead of, rather than in addition to, fully predetermining restrictions, the model depicted in figure 5.3 generates no prediction concerning the magnitude of the rise in p following the rise in x.

5.5. Irreversibility of History in IKE Models

In contrast to its predetermined counterpart, history in an IKE model is not presumed to be reversible: a change in x between $t = 2$ and $t = 3$ back to its initial value at $t = 1$ does not lead to a mere unwinding in the model to its initial structure. Rather, such a decline in x from any one of the partially predetermined equilibrium points in figure 5.3 would lead to excess supply and an equilibration process that would, in general, result in an equilibrium other than at point ip.

Consider, for example, the fall from $pp1$, which we depict in figure 5.4 as a decline in Q^D to point c. As the market price falls because of the excess supply, market participants may revise their forecasting strategies. As before, our IKE model, with its partially predetermining restriction in equation (5.7), represents this behavior with myriad partially predetermined upward-sloping forecast-revision paths. Each of these paths presumes that

---

11. In general, an IKE model would also allow the causal variables to enter its representation of forecasting behavior. In this case, the model would need additional partially predetermining restrictions on revisions of forecasting strategies to generate qualitative predictions concerning the impact of a change in one of the causal variables on the market price.

Figure 5.4   Irreversibility of History in an IKE Model

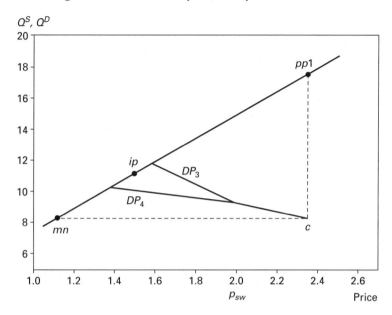

individuals will revise their forecasting strategies in ways and at times that differ from how they acted in the past.

Consequently, the corresponding partially predetermined demand paths imply that individuals will revise their demand decisions differently than when x initially increased to x_2. In general, then, the myriad partially predetermined demand paths implied by the model intersect the supply curve at an equilibrium other than at initial point ip. Figure 5.4 depicts two such demand paths, which we denote by DP_3 and DP_4.[12]

There is nothing in the model that determines the precise path that forecast revisions will take. Consequently, the model makes no prediction concerning the precise path for quantity demanded. But because all of its demand paths are consistent with the partially predetermining restrictions in equation (5.14), they all slope downward. Thus, the model predicts that the fall in x back to its initial value will result in an equilibrium price that is lower than at $pp1$, but that, in general, differs from its initial value of 1.5. This irreversibility follows directly from IKE's reliance on restrictions that only partially prespecify change.

---

12. In the figure, *mn* is the minimum equilibrium point that is consistent with the partially predetermining restrictions in equation (5.14).

PART II

"Anomalies" in Contemporary Models of Currency Markets

6 The Overreach of Contemporary Models of Asset Markets

It is better to be roughly right than precisely wrong.
ATTRIBUTED TO JOHN MAYNARD KEYNES BY ALAN GREENSPAN,
Federal Reserve Bulletin, May 1997

In part I, we argued that the contemporary approach is flawed because it fully prespecifies change. In this part, we show that these arguments help us to understand the widespread failures of contemporary models in explaining outcomes in financial markets. These markets are, in most respects, prototypes of the markets for which much of contemporary economic analysis was designed. They are characterized by a large number of buyers and sellers, few if any barriers to entry and exit, no impediments to the adjustment of prices, and a plethora of available information that is quickly disseminated around the world. We thus would expect that financial markets would offer the best opportunity for contemporary economic models to provide reasonable explanations of market outcomes. But it is precisely in these markets that the contemporary approach has encountered many of its most glaring empirical difficulties.

Outcomes in financial markets are primarily driven by market participants' forecasts. In coping with ever-imperfect knowledge, individuals do not merely follow pre-existing rules and procedures: they search for new ways to forecast future market outcomes. Yet contemporary models represent this forecasting process as a routine activity that can be fully prespecified by an economist. Seen in this light, the empirical difficulties that the conventional models have had in explaining outcomes are hardly surprising.

We have used a simple algebraic example to exposit the meaning of the terms *the structure of* and *fully predetermined* representations of change. In this chapter, we develop a more complete definition of these terms. Although our definitions apply to any component of a contemporary model, we focus on fully predetermined representations of market participants' forecasting strategies.

We illustrate, in the context of a model of the foreign exchange market, how conventional and behavioral economists fully prespecify revisions of market participants' forecasting strategies and the resulting movements in the exchange rate. We demonstrate formally that contemporary representations that fully prespecify when and how change occurs are analogous to those that ignore change altogether: both represent economic behavior with a single, overarching rule. Such models fully prespecify change up to random error terms, the probability distributions of which are also restricted to evolve in a fully predetermined way.

Sometimes economists construct models (primarily based on REH) that, under certain parameter values, imply more than one fully predetermined equilibrium function for an asset price and, therefore, more than one representation of an individual's forecasting strategy at each point in time. In these multiple-equilibrium models, extrinsic factors can cause market participants to switch at a point in time from one forecasting strategy to another. This switch, in turn, causes the equilibrium price function implied by the model to jump from one fully predetermined equilibrium relationship to another.[1] In multiple-equilibrium models neither the timing of jumps nor the particular forecasting strategy that market participants switch to is determined. However, these models fully prespecify the set of equilibrium price functions to which the system could jump. And, because these price functions are themselves fully predetermined, each one implies sharp predictions concerning the movements of the market price. Thus, as with other contemporary models, multiple-equilibrium models disregard the importance of non-routine changes in the way individuals make decisions.

6.1. Describing Forecasting Behavior

To describe an individual's forecasting behavior in formal, succinct language, we distinguish between her information set, her forecasting strategy, and her forecasting process.

6.1.1. *Information Set*

A market participant bases her forecasts on the information she considers relevant. In general, an individual's information set, which we denote by h_t^i, includes current and past realizations on fundamental variables (for example, money supply or income) as well as on nonfundamental factors, such as those based on technical trading or market sentiment.

---

1. For excellent treatments of multiple-equilibrium models, see Blanchard and Fischer (1989) and Farmer (1999).

6.1.2. Forecasting Strategy

To fix ideas, we let z_{t+1} denote the future value of some variable that an individual considers relevant for her well-being, such as the market price in our example in chapter 3. At each point in time, individual i chooses a forecasting strategy to transform her information set h_t^i into a forecast of z_{t+1}. We denote an individual's forecasting strategy by $\mathcal{F}_t^i$ and her forecast of z_{t+1} by $z_{t|t+1}^i$, and write this transformation as:

$$\mathcal{F}_t^i : h_t^i \to z_{t|t+1}^i. \tag{6.1}$$

The forecasting strategies used by market participants are not limited to a set of formal rules: in general, the transformation $\mathcal{F}_t^i$ may consist of a mix of procedures based on formal (perhaps econometric) models and informal intuitive guesses concerning the potential future values of z_{t+1}. For example, an individual may form her forecast by combining the predictions generated by some macroeconomic model with her own guesses of market sentiment.

6.1.3. Forecasting Process

Over time, an individual revises her forecasts as she observes new values of the variables in her information set. Forecast revisions are not limited to mechanistic updates based on an unchanging strategy: in a world of imperfect knowledge, a profit-seeking individual alters, at least intermittently, the mix and/or types of strategies that she uses to form her forecasts. We summarize this creative forecasting process by the set of forecasting strategies an individual uses during some analytically relevant time interval (t_1, t_2):

$$\mathcal{FP}^i = (\mathcal{F}_{t_1}^i, \mathcal{F}_{t_1+1}^i, \ldots, \mathcal{F}_{t_2}^i). \tag{6.2}$$

The meaning of an "analytically relevant time interval" depends on the particular modeling context. In this book, we focus on modeling the behavior in the foreign exchange market over the recent era of floating exchange rates. Thus, (t_1, t_2) spans any subperiod between 1973 and the present.

6.2. Fully Predetermined Representations of Forecasting Strategies and Their Revisions

Market participants' forecasts underpin aggregate outcomes in financial and many other markets. To construct a model of these outcomes on the

basis of individual behavior, an economist must represent the forecasting
process $\mathcal{FP}^i$. To this end, he would construct a representation of $\mathcal{F}_t^i$ at each
point time, which we denote by R_t^i:

$$R_t^i : \mathcal{F}_t^i \to Z_{t|t+1}^{i,\mathrm{RP}}. \tag{6.3}$$

$Z_{t|t+1}^{i,\mathrm{RP}}$ is a function that relates an economist's representation of an individual's forecast of Z_{t+1} to a set of causal variables X_t^i and an error term
$\epsilon_t^{i}.$[2]

$$Z_{t|t+1}^{i,\mathrm{RP}} = F_t^i(X_t^i) + \epsilon_t^i, \tag{6.4}$$

where both X_t^i and ϵ_t^i are assumed to be random variables, and the error
term represents all factors influencing an individual's forecast that are not
captured by X_t^i; that is, $E[\epsilon_{t+\tau}^i | X_t^i] = 0$ for all t and τ.

The set of causal variables X_t^i is assumed by an economist to capture
adequately the factors, both formal and informal (in h_t^i), that underpin an
individual's forecasting strategy $\mathcal{F}_t^i$ in equation (6.1). The composition of
this set depends on the economic problem under study. For example, in the
analysis of macroeconomic problems, the causal variables typically include
policy variables, such as the money supply or tax rates. Such exogenous
variables are determined outside the economist's model. The set X_t^i may
also include current and lagged values of endogenous variables, such as the
current and past values of market prices.

Economists formalize their assumptions concerning individual behavior and aggregate outcomes with a list of properties that characterizes their
representations at a particular point in time and a set of restrictions that
characterize how these representations change over time. The list of properties S_t^i includes:

1. The composition of the set of causal variables X_t^i.

2. The properties of the joint probability distribution of X_t^i and ϵ_t^i.

3. A functional form for $F_t^i(\cdot)$, typically including the signs of its derivatives.
    In cases in which $F_t^i(\cdot)$ is an explicit parametric function, S_t^i may include
    the signs of its parameters.

We refer to S_t^i as the *structure of an economist's representation* at time t.
We note that, to represent the forecasting process $\mathcal{FP}^i$ in equation (6.2),

---

2. More generally, the error term could enter nonlinearly in equation (6.4). The use of an
additive specification, however, is customary and simplifies our presentation without altering any of
the arguments in this chapter.

which, in general, involves forecasting strategies at many points in time, an economist must define a sequence of structures S^i:

$$S^i = (S^i_{t_1}, S^i_{t_{1+1}}, \ldots, S^i_{t_2}). \tag{6.5}$$

The structure S^i_t defines a set of functions that characterize an economist's representation at time t. This structure at time t has no implications concerning which among the many possible sequences of structures in equation (6.5) an economist should choose to represent the forecasting process.

In general, a representation with different structures may be needed to characterize adequately the forecasting strategies used in two different time periods. We denote this structural change by ${}_tSC^i_{t+\tau}$ and write this transformation as:

$$ {}_tSC^i_{t+\tau} : S^i_t \rightarrow S^i_{t+\tau}. \tag{6.6}$$

Because market participants do not merely follow pre-existing rules and procedures and the social context may change in unforeseen ways, the transformation ${}_tSC_{t+\tau}$ is, in general, not one-to-one: for a given structure at time t, there are myriad possible structures that may have to be used at $t + \tau$ to represent adequately economic change between t and $t + \tau$.

Thus, to construct a model of the movement of market outcomes that can be tested against time-series data, an economist must invoke additional assumptions concerning how individuals alter the way they make decisions and how aggregate outcomes unfold over time. He formalizes these assumptions about economic change with restrictions on the transformation ${}_tSC^i_{t+\tau}$.

As we discussed in chapter 3, conventional and behavioral representations invoke different assumptions to specify the structure of their representations and its changes over time. All extant models constructed according to the contemporary approach, however, share one fundamental feature: they fully prespecify change in the structure of their representations between t and any other point in time $t + \tau$. We define such fully predetermined representations as follows:

Definition 1 *An economist's representation is said to be* fully predetermined *if, conditional on S^i_t, restrictions imposed on* change *in his representation select* only *one* structure, $S^i_{t+\tau}$, *at any other point in time, $t + \tau$, past and future. Formally, fully predetermined representations reduce ${}_tSC^i_{t+\tau}$ in equation (6.6) to a one-to-one transformation, which we denote by FP_τ:*

$$FP^i_\tau : S^i_t \rightarrow S^i_{t+\tau}. \tag{6.7}$$

FP$_\tau$ is indexed by τ. However, this transformation is time invariant in that it fully prespecifies a representation of change between any two points in time separated by τ. In general, FP$_\tau$ specifies deterministic or stochastic rules that govern the timing of structural changes, as well as the specifications of alternative structures from which FP$_\tau$ selects one structure at $t + \tau$. We refer to FP$_\tau$ as an invariant or overarching transformation and write $S_{t+\tau}$ as:

$$S^i_{t+\tau} = \mathrm{FP}^i \left(S^i_t, \tau \right). \tag{6.8}$$

*We also refer to the set of restrictions that ensure that the forecasting process $\mathcal{FP}^i$ is represented with an overarching one-to-one transformation, FP$^i_\tau$, as fully pre-*determining.

Note that the properties of the error term in an economist's representation in equation (6.4) are part of the structure. Thus, our definition of fully predetermined representations also applies to the way the probability distribution of the error term changes over time. Typically, error terms are characterized with time-invariant probability distributions, but sometimes economists allow these distributions to change in a fully predetermined way. A class of such models that has been particularly important in modeling financial markets prespecifies the variance of the error term to follow the so-called "ARCH [autoregressive conditional heteroskedastic] process" or its extensions.[3] We refer to the properties of the distributions of the error terms that are included in fully predetermined representations as also being fully predetermined.

The overarching function in equation (6.8) implies a probability distribution of the forecast that an economist attributes to an individual at time $t + \tau$ conditional on the structure of his representation at t. Thus, contemporary representations of forecasting strategies and their revisions ignore Popper's (1957, p. xii) fundamental insight that "we cannot predict . . . the future growth of our . . . knowledge": they fully prespecify the way market participants' knowledge concerning the causal mechanism evolves over time.

6.3. Modeling Economic Change with a Time-Invariant Structure

In this section, we use a simple exchange rate model, whose structure is constrained to be unchanging over time, to illustrate how contemporary models

---

3. See Engle (1982) and Bollerslev et al. (1992).

represent change as a random deviation from a fully predetermined structure. This analysis sets the stage for an examination in the next section of conventional and behavioral models that allow for change in how individuals make decisions or in how the social context unfolds over time. Though our conclusions would remain valid were we to use models with nonlinear structures, we follow the usual practice and rely on linear models to simplify the presentation.

6.3.1. REH Models

In the appendix, we sketch a typical model of the exchange rate based on individual foundations. As is common for contemporary models in finance and macroeconomics, the representative individual is assumed to derive utility from holding consumption and money balances in every period. Her problem is to choose, simultaneously at time t, a level of consumption and money balances in the current time period and all future time periods so as to maximize her lifetime utility. In setting up this intertemporal optimization problem, we make use of a standard utility function that is consistent with the axioms of rational choice and that assumes that individuals are risk averse.

The semi-reduced form of our exchange rate model is given by equation (6.36) in the appendix, which we write as:

$$S_t^{RP} = \frac{\lambda}{1+\lambda}\widehat{S}_{t|t+1} + \frac{1}{1+\lambda}(M_t - \phi Y_t), \tag{6.9}$$

where S_t^{RP}, M_t, and Y_t denote log levels of an economist's representation of the spot exchange rate, domestic money supply, and the real value of world output, respectively, at time t.[4] M_t and Y_t are typically treated as causal variables. $\widehat{S}_{t|t+1}$ is the representation of the point forecast of the next period's exchange rate that an economist attributes to the representative (average) individual. The coefficients λ and ϕ are restricted to be particular functions of the parameters used in specifying individual preferences and the processes governing the causal variables. Moreover, M_t and Y_t enter the model through the specification of the utility function and budget constraint.

REH instructs an economist to set the structure of his representation on the individual level, $\widehat{S}_{t|t+1}$, to be identical to the conditional expectation implied by the aggregate model in equation (6.9), which we denote by

---

4. We use the superscript RP to distinguish between an economist's representation of an aggregate outcome, such as S_t, and the actual distribution of the exchange rate at time t.

$E[S_{t+1}^{\mathrm{RE}}|X_t]$. Imposing REH in equation (6.9) yields:

$$S_t^{\mathrm{RE}} = \frac{\lambda}{1+\lambda} E[S_{t+1}^{\mathrm{RE}}|X_t]] + \frac{1}{1+\lambda}(M_t - \phi Y_t). \qquad (6.10)$$

Assuming that the structure of the utility function is unchanging over time, we can shift equation (6.9) forward repeatedly and express $E[S_{t+1}^{\mathrm{RE}}|X_t]$ as:[5]

$$E[S_{t+1}^{\mathrm{RE}}|X_t] = \frac{1}{1+\lambda} \sum_{s=t+1}^{\infty} \left(\frac{\lambda}{1+\lambda}\right)^{s-t} E[(M_s - \phi Y_s)|X_t]. \qquad (6.11)$$

Equation (6.11) reveals that to construct his REH representation of exchange rate forecasts in terms of the realizations at time t of the causal variables M_t and Y_t, an economist must prespecify fully the social context, which is represented by these variables, between t and all future time periods.[6]

REH theorists typically constrain their representation of the social context to remain fixed. In this section, we follow this practice and assume, for simplicity, that M_t and Y_t are random walks with drift:

$$M_t = \mu + M_{t-1} + \eta_t \text{ and } Y_t = g + Y_{t-1} + v_t. \qquad (6.12)$$

where μ and g are drift terms and η_t and v_t are white noise errors. Using equation (6.12) in equation (6.11) yields the following REH representation of a representative individual's forecasting strategy at time t:

$$\hat{S}_{t|t+1}^{\mathrm{RE}} = E[S_{t+1}^{\mathrm{RE}}|(M_t, Y_t)] = M_t - \phi Y_t + (\lambda + 1)(\mu - \phi g). \qquad (6.13)$$

Substituting equation (6.13) into equation (6.9) results in the following REH representation of the exchange rate at time t:[7]

$$S_t^{\mathrm{RE}} = M_t - \phi Y_t + \lambda(\mu - \phi g). \qquad (6.14)$$

The representation S_t^{RE} illustrates how REH constrains economists to adhere strictly to Lucas's dictum: "beware of [theories] bearing free parameters" (Sargent, 2001, p. 73). This representation does not include any causal

---

5. If a contemporary economist were to allow preferences to change over time, he would fully predetermine such change. Allowing for such fully predetermined change would not affect any of the conclusions presented in this chapter.

6. Such a representation of the social context is also needed to derive the semi-reduced equation in equation (6.9). See the appendix to this chapter.

7. More generally, the REH solution to the dynamic equation (6.9) does not rule out the possibility a "bubble" term. See below.

variables or parameters that do not enter through representations of preferences, constraints, and policy and other exogenous factors. Moreover, the coefficients λ and ϕ are restricted to be particular functions of the parameters used in specifying individual preferences and the social context. By design, REH presumes that the forecasting behavior of market participants plays no autonomous role in driving market outcomes.

The model of this section represents change as a random deviation from an unchanging structure. The representation in equation (6.13) implies the following representation of the REH-based forecast revision between t and any other time period $t + \tau$, past or future:

$$\hat{S}^{RE}_{t+\tau|t+\tau+1} - \hat{S}^{RE}_{t|t+1} = E[S^{RE}_{t+\tau+1}|M_{t+\tau}, Y_{t+\tau}] - E[S^{RE}_{t+1}|M_t, Y_t]. \quad (6.15)$$

$$= (M_{t+\tau} - M_t) - \phi(Y_{t+\tau} - Y_t).$$

Using the representations for M_t and Y_t in equation (6.12), the expression in equation (6.15) implies:

$$\hat{S}^{RE}_{t|t+\tau+1} - \hat{S}^{RE}_{t|t+1} = \tau(\mu - \phi g) + \sum_{j=1}^{\tau} \left(\eta_{t+j} - \phi v_{t+j} \right)$$

$$= E[(\hat{S}^{RE}_{t+\tau+1} - \hat{S}^{RE}_{t+1})|(M_t, Y_t)] + \sum_{j=1}^{\tau} \left(\eta_{t+j} - \phi v_{t+j} \right). \quad (6.16)$$

This REH representation of how an individual revises her forecast is identical to the REH representation of the τ-period change in the market price of foreign exchange:

$$S^{RE}_{t+\tau} - S^{RE}_t = E[(S^{RE}_{t+\tau} - S^{RE}_t)|(M_t, Y_t)] + \sum_{j=1}^{\tau} \left(\eta_{t+j} - \phi v_{t+j} \right). \quad (6.17)$$

Expressions (6.16) and (6.17) illustrate that, by design, the only difference between an economist's prediction of the forecast revision or the change in the exchange rate between any two points in time, and what the model supposes actually happens on the individual and aggregate levels, is equal to the summation of random error terms, whose probability distributions are restricted to evolve in a fully predetermined way.

6.3.2. *Behavioral Models*

In contrast to REH models, behavioral models are based on autonomous representations of individual behavior. However, the conclusions of the preceding section hold true for these behavioral models as well. In this section, we illustrate this point in the context of our simple model.

For simplicity, suppose that empirical research leads an economist to attribute to the representative individual a forecasting rule that depends only on M_t:

$$\hat{S}^{\mathrm{BE}}_{t|t+1} = \beta M_t, \tag{6.18}$$

where β is restricted to be constant and the superscript BE denotes a behavioral representation.

Substituting equation (6.18) into equation (6.9) yields the following example of a behavioral representation for the exchange rate:

$$S^{\mathrm{BE}}_t = \frac{1}{1+\lambda}[(\lambda\beta + 1)M_t - \phi Y_t]. \tag{6.19}$$

The behavioral representations in equations (6.18) and (6.19) imply the following expressions for the revision of an individual's forecasting strategy and the change in the exchange rate:

$$\hat{S}^{\mathrm{BE}}_{t+\tau|t+\tau+1} - \hat{S}^{\mathrm{BE}}_{t|t+1} = \beta(M_{t+\tau} - M_t) = \tau\beta\mu + \sum_{j=1}^{\tau}\eta_{t+j}$$

$$= E[(\hat{S}^{\mathrm{BE}}_{t+\tau+1} - \hat{S}^{\mathrm{BE}}_{t+1})|(M_t, Y_t)] + \sum_{j=1}^{\tau}\eta_{t+j} \tag{6.20}$$

and

$$S^{\mathrm{BE}}_{t+\tau} - S^{\mathrm{BE}}_t = E[(S^{\mathrm{BE}}_{t+\tau} - S^{\mathrm{BE}}_t)|(M_t, Y_t)] + \frac{\lambda\beta + 1}{1+\lambda}\sum_{j=1}^{\tau}\eta_{\tau+j} - \frac{\phi}{1+\lambda}\sum_{j=1}^{\tau}v_{\tau+j}.$$

$$\tag{6.21}$$

Comparing equations (6.16) and (6.17) with equations (6.20) and (6.21) makes clear that, although behavioral and conventional economists rely on different assumptions to represent forecasting behavior and aggregate outcomes, their models share one key feature: they represent change as a random deviation from a fully predetermined structure. This way of representing individual decisions and aggregate outcomes makes no allowance whatsoever for the possibility that economic change may occur either because (1) individuals decide at some point in time to think about the future differently from how they thought about it in the past and thereby alter the way they make decisions or (2) policymakers decide to change the way they conduct policy.

6.4. Models with Fully Predetermined Changes in Structure

Contemporary economists sometimes recognize the importance of building into their models the fact that participants in real world markets do not adhere endlessly to one forecasting strategy, or, more broadly, to one decision rule. They also sometimes take into account the fact that the social context, particularly economic policy, changes over time, at least intermittently. However, both behavioral and conventional economists fully predetermine their representations of the ways in which individual decisions and the social context may unfold over time.

To represent such change, economists have used piecewise linear models in which the separate linear pieces and points of structural change are fully prespecified; each linear piece represents a different way in which individuals and policy officials make decisions. Alternatively, fully predetermined piecewise linear models can be viewed as nonlinear models with time-invariant structures.

6.4.1. REH Models: Prespecifying the Course of Macroeconomic Policy

Although both conventional and non-REH behavioral models fully predetermine their representations, REH models are substantially more restrictive. They represent all revisions of forecasting strategies as derivative of the changes in the other components of an economist's model. With utility functions usually assumed to be unchanging over time, REH requires an economist to represent changes in an individual's forecasting strategy in lockstep with changes in the variables and parameters that represent policy and other aspects of the social context.

An influential way to represent change in the policy environment in REH models was proposed by Hamilton (1988, 1990). To illustrate this approach in the context of our foreign exchange example, suppose that there are two possible monetary policy regimes that are fully prespecified, as in equation (6.12). At each point in time, μ can take on one of two values, μ_1 and μ_2, where $\mu_1 > \mu_2$. Hamilton's proposal for fully predetermining changes in the policy regime is to represent these changes with a Markov chain that is independent of current and past values of the causal variables.[8]

---

8. Hamilton's Markov switching model can be generalized so that the switching probabilities depend on X_t^i. See, for example, Kaminsky (1993). Our arguments concerning the original Hamilton model also apply to this more general version.

We denote the transition matrix for this chain by

$$
\begin{pmatrix} p_{11} & (1 - p_{11}) \\ (1 - p_{22}) & p_{22} \end{pmatrix}, \tag{6.22}
$$

where p_{ik} ($i = 1, 2$ and $k = 1, 2$) denotes transition probabilities between μ_1 and μ_2.

This representation of change in the social context is breathtakingly facile. It presumes that monetary policy can be adequately represented by fixed rules. But even if monetary policy could be represented by such rules over some limited period of time in the past, there is no fixed set of rules that can adequately represent all monetary policy regimes in all future periods.[9] Moreover, REH representations of an individual's forecasting behavior are derivative of precisely such a narrow and mechanistic view of how monetary policy is conducted.

Substituting equation (6.11) into equation (6.9) and using the Markov switching representation of monetary policy results in the following REH representation for the exchange rate:

$$
S_t^{RE} = \frac{1}{1 + \lambda} \sum_{j=0}^{\infty} \left(\frac{\lambda}{1 + \lambda} \right)^j E[(M_{t+j} - \phi Y_{t+j}) | X_t]
$$

$$
= \Pi(X_t; \theta) - \phi(Y_t + \lambda g), \tag{6.23}
$$

where $\theta = (\lambda, \mu_1, \mu_2, p_{11}, p_{22}, \sigma_\eta^2)$ and σ_η^2 denotes the variance of η_t in equation (6.12).

We note that the values of the parameter vector θ are presumed by an economist to be unchanging over time.[10] We also note that $E[M_{t+j}|X_t] < M_t + j\mu_1$, which in turn implies that $\Pi(X_t; \theta)$ in equation (6.23) is bounded for each realization of X_t:

$$
\Pi(x_t; \theta) \leq \frac{m_t}{1 + \lambda} \sum_{j=0}^{\infty} \left(\frac{\lambda}{1 + \lambda} \right)^j + \frac{\mu_1}{1 + \lambda} \sum_{j=1}^{\infty} \left(\frac{\lambda}{1 + \lambda} \right)^j j = m_t + \lambda \mu_1. \tag{6.24}
$$

The representation in equation (6.23) shows that even if REH models allow for change in the process governing macroeconomic policy, they characterize behavior on the individual and aggregate levels with a single, overarching

9. For empirical evidence on this point, see Frydman and Rappoport (1987).

10. See Hamilton (1994, chapter 22) for a thorough analysis of the inference problem involved in computing $E(M_{t+j}|M_t, M_{t-1}, \ldots)$ for models involving Markov switching between "hidden" policy regimes, which are unknown to market participants.

function. This is because they fully prespecify when and how such change occurs.

Thus, as with REH models that restrict their structures to be unchanging over time, REH representations that fully predetermine structural change presume that the *only* difference between an economist's predictions and what the model supposes actually happens on the individual and aggregate levels is equal to a random forecast error, which we denote by $fe_{t+\tau}^{RE}$. In the context of our REH exchange rate model, this error is given by:

$$fe_{t+\tau}^{RE} = S_{t+\tau}^{RE} - E[S_{t+\tau}^{RE}|X_t]$$

$$= \{\Pi(X_{t+\tau};\theta) - E[\Pi(X_{t+\tau};\theta)|X_t]\} - \phi\{Y_{t+\tau} - E[Y_{t+\tau}|X_t]\}, \quad (6.25)$$

where $X_t = (M_t, M_{t-1,...})$, and by construction $E[fe_{t+\tau}^{RE}|X_t] = 0$.

Because the REH representation for the exchange rate in equation (6.25) is fully predetermined, all other moments of the distribution of $fe_{t+\tau}^{RE}$ conditional on X_t are functions of θ. Moreover, although the process driving the policy variable is allowed to change over time, the conditional distribution of the forecast errors implied by the REH representation is time invariant, for the evolution of the policy variable is fully prespecified in equations (6.12) and (6.22). Thus, REH models that incorporate structural change represent change in the same way as do REH models that restrict their structures to be unchanging over time: both presume that an economist can prespecify change up to a random deviation, which is itself restricted to evolve in a fully predetermined way.

6.4.2. Behavioral Models

REH represents the forecasting process as a passive, routine activity that is derivative of the other components of the model. In contrast, the *bona fide* microfoundations of non-REH behavioral models' allow an economist to model revisions of forecasting strategies that are independent of changes in policy. However, because these models also fully predetermine their representations, they, too, represent the forecasting process as a passive, purely mechanistic activity.

To illustrate this point in the context of modeling the foreign exchange market, consider the seminal exchange rate model of Frankel and Froot (1986). They prespecify the set of forecasting strategies attributed to individuals to consist of two fully predetermined rules: a chartist rule that sets the forecast of next-period exchange rate equal to the current period's rate, and a so-called "fundamental rule," which they assume is given by an REH representation—equation (6.14) in our example—and which ignores the possibility that individuals might use the chartist rule. They also prespecify a meta-rule, which selects the set of weights ω_t and $(1 - \omega_t)$, both less than 1, that represents the way an individual combines her two forecasting strategies. This setup represents an individual's point forecast of the exchange rate as:

$$\hat{S}^{BE}_{t|t+1} = \omega_t \left[M_t - \phi Y_t + (\lambda + 1) \left(\mu - \phi g \right) \right] + (1 - \omega_t) S_t. \qquad (6.26)$$

Frankel and Froot prespecify the evolution of the weight ω_t in two ways, one deterministic and the other probabilistic.[11] These specifications of ω_t fully predetermine the way that the structure of the representation in equation (6.26) evolves over time. Consequently, although the Frankel and Froot model recognizes that individuals in currency markets do revise their forecasting strategies, they represent this forecasting process with a single, overarching function. This representation, together with the semi-reduced form in equation (6.9), results in the following fully predetermined behavioral representation for the exchange rate:

$$S^{BE}_t = (1 + \lambda) \left(M_t - \phi Y_t \right) + \frac{(1 + \lambda) \lambda \omega_t}{1 + \lambda \omega_t} \left(\mu - \phi g \right). \qquad (6.27)$$

As with all other fully predetermined models, regardless of whether they allow for structural change, behavioral models presume that an economist can prespecify how individuals revise the way they think about the future up to a random deviation, the probability distribution of which is also constrained to remain unchanging or to evolve in a fully predetermined way. In this sense, behavioral representations are a rather odd way to represent how individuals actually behave in real world markets.

6.5. Prespecifying Collective Beliefs in Currency Markets: Bubble Models

Sometimes economists construct models that, for certain parameter values, imply more than one fully predetermined equilibrium price function. In these multiple-equilibrium models, extrinsic factors can cause market participants to switch at a point in time from one forecasting strategy to another. The probabilistic representation of each of these strategies corresponds to one of the equilibrium price functions implied by an REH model.

---

11. In the deterministic case, ω_t is set equal to the weight that would have predicted the exchange rate correctly. In the probabilistic case, ω_t is updated according to Bayes' or some other probabilistic rule.

Multiple-equilibrium models have been used in many contexts, for example, to model slowly adjusting goods prices and the role of money.[12] In international macroeconomics, they have been used to model swings in exchange rates and currency crises.[13] Unlike the Hamilton model discussed in the preceding section, neither the timing of jumps nor the particular REH forecasting strategy to which market participants switch is determined in these models.

In this section, we sketch an REH bubble model to show that multiple-equilibrium models generate predictions that, although not unique, are sharp. We argue that these models, as with those that generate unique predictions, disregard completely the importance of individual creativity and unforeseen changes in the social context.

6.5.1. *A Bubble Model of Exchange Rate Swings*

The REH representation in equation (6.14) is often referred to as the "fundamental solution" for the exchange rate. In general, the imposition of REH does not yield a unique representation of individual and aggregate behavior. In the present monetary model, for example, consistency is also compatible with an infinite number of equilibrium price functions:

$$E\left[S_{t+1}^{RE}|I_t\right] = E\left[S_{t+1}^{RE_f}|I_t\right] + E\left[B_{t+1}|I_t\right], \tag{6.28}$$

where $S_{t+1}^{RE_f}$ denotes the fundamental solution in equation (6.14) shifted forward one period, I_t is an information set that includes X_t, and the bubble term B_{t+1} must satisfy:

$$E\left[B_{t+1}|I_t\right] = \frac{1+\lambda}{\lambda}B_t. \tag{6.29}$$

A common practice in the literature is to follow Blanchard and Watson (1982) and assume that B_t is governed by the following stochastic process:

$$B_{t+1} = \begin{cases} aB_t + \epsilon_{t+1} & \text{with probability } \rho \\ \epsilon_{t+1} & \text{with probability } 1-\rho, \end{cases} \tag{6.30}$$

---

12. For these and other applications, see Farmer (1999) and references therein.

13. For REH models of swings, see Evans (1986) and Meese (1986), and for REH models of currency crises, see Obstfeld (1994, 1996). Non-REH models with multiple equilibria have been used to model what has been called the "exchange-rate-regime puzzle": the finding that exchange rate volatility is much higher during floating-rate than fixed-rate regimes despite the similarity in the volatility of macroeconomic fundamentals across those regimes. See Flood and Rose (1999) and Jeanne and Rose (2002).

where $a = \frac{1+\lambda}{\lambda\rho} > 1$ and $E\left[\epsilon_{t+\tau}|B_t\right] = 0$ for all $\tau > 0$.[14] We note that because $a\rho > 0$, any bubble that does not burst explodes in expected value:[15]

$$\text{Lim}_{j\to\infty}E\left[B_{t+j}\,\Big|\,I_j\right] = \text{Lim}_{j\to\infty}\,(a\rho)^j\,B_t = \begin{cases} +\infty & \text{if } B_t > 0 \\ -\infty & \text{if } B_t < 0. \end{cases}$$

The exchange rate modelers of the 1970s believed that exchange rates were driven largely by macroeconomic fundamentals. This belief led REH theorists to ignore the bubble trajectories in their models and presume that individuals consider only macroeconomic fundamentals in forming their forecasts. They therefore set $B_t = 0$ at every point in time and represented individuals' forecasting strategies with the fundamental solutions of their REH models. But, as we discuss in chapter 7, the fundamental solutions of REH models are difficult to reconcile with the observed tendency of floating exchange rates to move persistently away from historical benchmark values, such as those based on PPP. This inability to explain swings in currency and other asset markets led economists to consider the bubble trajectories of REH models.

The representation in equations (6.28) and (6.30) presumes that when forming their forecasts at time t, individuals may somehow come to believe that a bubble has begun and collectively set B_t to some nonzero value.[16] The origin of this uniform belief and the particular value of B_t agreed on by individuals are not specified in the model. But each bubble trajectory (there is one for each nonzero value of B_t) is fully predetermined in the model. Once a bubble has formed, it is prespecified to grow in expected value at a constant rate: $\frac{E[B_{t+1}|I_t]}{B_t} = a\rho$. Moreover, every bubble is prespecified to continue with probability ρ or collapse with probability $1 - \rho$. Consequently, this multiple-equilibrium model fully prespecifies the forecasting strategies to which market participants can switch and assumes that each one is invariant.

---

14. Blanchard and Watson (1982) point out that the bubble process in equation (6.30) can be generalized to allow ρ to be a random variable and to depend on other factors.

15. Some REH models generate an infinite number of convergent time paths. See Azariadis and Guesnerie (1986) and Woodford (1984, 1990). See also Blanchard and Fischer (1989) and Farmer (1999).

16. Tirole (1982) shows that, if the information set I_t is assumed to differ among market participants, then the model attributes to them a different intial value for B_t. But consistency between the model's representations of individual behavior and aggregate outcomes requires a unique set of individual bubble terms for each value of the asset price at time t. Thus, the bubble model with heterogeneous information presumes collective agreement on the set of individual beliefs about the bubble term.

In addition to specifications of preferences, constraints, and the processes driving the causal variables, the REH representation of forecasting behavior along any bubble trajectory also depends on the unspecified factor B_t. This bubble term is usually interpreted as "market sentiment" and is supposed to capture the *collective* "belief" of market participants who forecast "what average opinion expects average opinion to be" (Keynes, 1936, p. 156). However, such an interpretation of the bubble term is not plausible, because the bubble solution presumes that an economist can fully prespecify how market sentiment evolves over time. This implausibility can also be seen from the following implications of equation (6.30):

$$\hat{S}^{i,\,\mathrm{RE}_b}_{t+\tau|t+\tau+1} - \hat{S}^{i,\,\mathrm{RE}_b}_{t|t+1} = E[B_{t+\tau+1}|B_{t+\tau}] - E[B_{t+1}|B_t]$$

$$= \rho a[B_{t+\tau} - B_t]$$

$$\hat{S}^{i,\,\mathrm{RE}_b}_{t|t+\tau+1} - \hat{S}^{i,\,\mathrm{RE}_b}_{t|t+1} =$$

$$\begin{cases} \rho a \left\{ E[B_{t+\tau}|B_t] - B_t \right\} + \rho a \sum_{j=1}^{\tau} a^{\tau-j}\epsilon_{t+j} & \text{with probability } \rho^\tau \\ \epsilon_{t+\tau} & \text{with probability } (1 - \rho^\tau). \end{cases}$$

Thus, by design, the only difference between an economist's prediction of the market sentiment and what the model supposes market sentiment will actually be is equal to the summation of random error terms, the probability distributions of which are restricted to evolve in a fully predetermined way.

Appendix 6.A:
A Conventional Macroeconomic Model

We now sketch a conventional model of individual and aggregate outcomes. This model allows us to illustrate more explicitly than in chapter 3 some of the steps and typical assumptions macroeconomists employ in constructing their models. Because we develop IKE in the context of the foreign exchange market, we illustrate the contemporary approach with a simple model of the exchange rate.

To model the exchange rate, economists often assume that the exchange rate adjusts, at each point in time, to ensure PPP, a condition implying that the purchasing power of a nation's currency is the same regardless of the country in which it is used to purchase goods.[17] To simplify matters, we assume that the foreign price level at every time t is exogenous and equal to 1. According to PPP, then, we have:

$$S_t = P_t \text{ for all } t, \tag{6.31}$$

where P_t denotes the domestic price level and S_t denotes the spot exchange rate.

To model the exchange rate in this setup, we need to model the domestic price level. But, unlike our example in chapter 3, we follow a common practice in macroeconomics by assuming that the price level is determined by the equality of the demand for and supply of money in the economy.[18] On the supply side, we assume for simplicity that monetary authorities set the money supply and its growth rate exogenously.[19]

To model an individual's demand for money, economists typically make use of a utility function that embodies the a priori assumptions of "rational" decision making discussed in chapter 3. They also usually specify a utility function that is consistent with risk-averse behavior: the idea that individuals strictly prefer a sure sum of money to a risky gamble whose expected payoff is the same. Economists also assume that a lone perishable consumption good and real money balances adequately represent the outcome variables on which a consumer's well-being depends in a monetary economy.

The following utility function, which embodies the foregoing preference assumptions, is standard in the literature:

$$U_t^i = \frac{C_t^{i^{1-\rho^i}}}{1 - \rho^i} + \log\left(\frac{M_t^i}{P_t}\right), \tag{6.32}$$

where C_t^i and M_t^i denote the quantity of the consumption good consumed and the nominal value of money balances held by domestic consumer i in period t, respectively. The utility function in equation (6.32), which is additive in consumption and real balances, is a constant relative risk-aversion

17. The assumption of PPP is common despite its obvious empirical difficulties. See the next chapter for a discussion. See Obstfeld and Rogoff (1996) for contemporary models that do not assume PPP.

18. An alternative assumption that is used in contemporary macroeconomics is to suppose that monopolistic firms set goods prices. See Obstfeld and Rogoff (1996), Betts and Devereux (2000), and Mark (2001).

19. It is also common to assume that monetary authorities set nominal interest rates according to some quantitative rule based on deviations in the inflation rate and income levels from their targets. In such a setup, money supply becomes endogenous. See Woodford (2003).

(CRRA) utility function, with a coefficient of relative risk aversion of ρ^i.[20] A higher ρ^i implies a greater degree of risk aversion.

In our example, domestic consumers are assumed to earn a known disposable real income in the current period t, which we denote by Y_t^i, and an uncertain income in all future periods. Income is paid in units of the perishable consumption good. The problem that individual consumers are assumed to face is to choose simultaneously, at time t, a level of consumption and money balances in the current and all future time periods.

To choose a level of consumption that differs from the income level in any period t, a consumer must buy or sell nominal and/or real assets. In addition to money balances, it is typical to assume the existence of domestic and foreign nominal bonds, as well as equity shares in a domestic and foreign mutual fund. The net value of domestic- (foreign-) currency bonds held by a consumer in period $t - 1$ and carried over into period t, which we denote by B_t^i $(B_t^{*^i})$, pays a certain $(1 + i_{t-1})\, B_t^i$ in domestic money $\left(\left(1 + i_{t-1}^*\right) B_t^{*^i}\right.$ in foreign money) in period t, where i_{t-1} (i_{t-1}^*) denotes the nominal interest rate on domestic (foreign) money.[21] Each equity share of the domestic (foreign) mutual fund carried into period t is assumed to pay a dividend, denominated in the perishable domestic (foreign) consumption good that is equal to the domestic (foreign) country's national income divided by the total number of domestic (foreign) shares outstanding.

The foregoing individual decision problem involves choice under uncertainty. From the perspective of an individual consumer, uncertainty arises because both her income and the price level in all future time periods are unknown at time t. To represent an individual's decision rule in our example, a contemporary economist would assume that an individual chooses, at time t, the levels of C_t^i and M_t^i in all time periods that maximize her expected lifetime utility, subject to her budget constraint. An individual's expected lifetime utility, evaluated at time t, which we denote by $\bar{U}_t^i$, can be represented as:

$$\bar{U}_t^i = E_t^i \sum_{\tau=t}^{T^i} \beta^{i^{\tau-t}} \left[\frac{C_\tau^{i^{1-\rho^i}}}{1 - \rho^i} + \log\left(\frac{M_\tau^i}{P_\tau}\right) \right], \tag{6.33}$$

20. The additive nature of the utility function in equation (6.32) is popular in the literature because it helps to ensure that changes in the money supply have no effect on the consumption decision.

21. We use a lower case i to denote either a realization of the nominal interest rate or a random variable.

where T^i denotes the end of an individual's life; β^i is a constant subjective discount factor, which is normally assumed to be less than one; and E_t^i is an operator denoting the expectation conditional on the information that the economist attributes to an individual at time t, X_t^i.

The representation of expected lifetime utility in equation (6.33) assumes that an individual's well-being can be represented adequately by the same utility function in each time period. In the real world, individuals have finite lives that differ in duration. But the economy can be thought of as having no end, as one generation replaces another. One could imagine that the mix of preferences of one generation of individuals would differ from that of another as the social context changes over time.

Economists usually abstract from such intergenerational complexities and assume that the aggregate of all individual decisions is tantamount to the decision of a representative individual whose life never ends. In this infinite-horizon, representative "agent" setup, all individual and aggregate variables are assumed to be one and the same; for example, $\bar{U}_t^i = \bar{U}_t$ for all t.[22] Thus, to model individual and aggregate outcomes, a contemporary economist sets $T = \infty$ and chooses C_t and M_t to maximize equation (6.33), subject to a budget constraint. By design, this setup fully predetermines the mix of preferences and forecasting strategies not only among individuals at a given point in time, but among generations over time. It does so by assuming away the importance of all heterogeneity among individuals and of changes in the mix of preferences and forecasting strategies among generations yet to be born.

The foregoing representation of individual behavior and aggregate outcomes enables an economist to generate sharp predictions not only about consumption, money demand, price level, and the exchange rate, but also about the overall well-being of a society in every time period. These sharp predictions about a society's well-being are then used to analyze the welfare implications of various economic policies, such as the choice of the exchange rate regime. This "apparatus for the formal analysis of macroeconomic policies" is viewed as one of the "big payoff[s] from . . . an intertemporal framework" (Obstfeld and Rogoff, 1996, p. xxi).

The particular utility function in equation (6.33) implies a simple solution for the optimal consumption level in each time period under the usual assumptions that the domestic and foreign representative consumers have identical utility functions and identical forecasting strategies in all time periods. Under these assumptions, no domestic or foreign bonds are held. The

---

22. The other workhorse of modern macroeconomics is the overlapping-generations (OLG) setup. In the OLG setup, individuals are usually assumed to live two time periods. See Blanchard and Fischer (1989) for a discussion of the infinite-horizon and OLG setups in modern macroeconomics.

representative domestic consumer sells claims to a part of her (national) income (in the form of equity shares) to the representative foreign consumer, who, in turn, sells claims to part of her foreign income. This risk sharing between domestic and foreign consumers enables the representative domestic consumer to consume a constant fraction φ of world income, $Y_t = Y_t + Y_t^*$, in every time period. We follow standard practice and invoke this solution for individual and aggregate consumption.

We note that, with fully predetermined preferences and forecasting behavior, the representative consumer never revisits her decision rule to consume a fixed proportion φ of world income. There is thus little difference between the intertemporal decision problem considered in this chapter and the one-period decision problem discussed in chapter 2: in both setups, all key decisions are made in period t. Once preferences and forecasting behavior in all periods have been fully prespecified, economic change in the model occurs only because of new realizations of the driving variables. A new realization of Y_t, together with the same decision rule, leads mechanically to a new level of consumption: $C_t = \varphi Y_t$.

The utility function in equation (6.33) also implies the following invariant rule for the representative consumer's demand for money in any period t:

$$M_t = \frac{P_t \left(\varphi Y_t\right)^\rho}{1 - \beta E_t \left[\frac{P_t Y_t^\rho}{P_{t+1} Y_{t+1}^\rho}|X_t\right]}, \tag{6.34}$$

where we substituted in the solution $C_t = \varphi Y_t$. In general, this difference equation does not have a closed-form solution. Obstfeld and Rogoff (1996) show, however, that for the special case where the log of the money supply and world income are represented to follow stationary stochastic processes with independent, normally distributed, homoskedastic innovations and deterministic trends, $\log(1 + \mu)$ and $\log(1 + \gamma)$, respectively, a log approximation to equation (6.34) around the nonstochastic steady state equilibrium can be derived:

$$M_t = P_t + \rho Y_t - \frac{1}{i} E_t \left[(P_{t+1} - P_t)|X_t\right] - \frac{\rho}{i} E_t \left[(Y_{t+1} - Y_t)|X_t\right], \tag{6.35}$$

where $\bar{i} = [(1 + \mu)/\beta] - 1$ is the nominal interest rate in the nonstochastic steady state, and all other variables represent log deviations from this steady state.[23]

---

23. We have omitted a constant term that stems from the variance of the price and income processes.

We use equation (6.35), which, except for the last term involving income growth, is similar to the money demand equation used in many of the older monetary models, to motivate the following semi-reduced form:

$$S_t = \frac{\lambda}{1+\lambda} E^i \left[(S_{t+1}) | X_t^i \right] | + \frac{1}{1+\lambda} (M_t - \phi Y_t), \qquad (6.36)$$

where $\lambda = 1/\bar{i}$ and we omit, for convenience, the income growth term.

7 The "Puzzling" Behavior of Exchange Rates

Lost Fundamentals and Long Swings

> The chief problem with the overshooting theory, and indeed with the more general rational expectations approach, is that it does not explain well the shorter-term [long-swings] dynamics. . . . Exchange rates are moved largely by factors other than the obvious, observable, macroeconomic fundamentals. Econometrically, most of the "action" is in the error term.
>
> RUDIGER DORNBUSCH AND JEFFREY A. FRANKEL,
> "The Flexible Exchange Rate System: Experience and Alternatives,"
> *International Finance and Trade,* p. 16

In chapter 6, we showed that, even if a contemporary economist allows for revisions of forecasting strategies, he represents market participants' forecasting strategies with the same overarching function at every point in time. In this and the next chapters, we argue that the practice of fully prespecifying change lies at the root of the failure of contemporary models to provide plausible explanations of outcomes in markets for foreign exchange. Moreover, we argue that the reliance on fully predetermined, mostly invariant models has misdirected research aimed at understanding the movements in exchange rates and the market premium. Our aim is not to provide an exhaustive review of the empirical record on contemporary exchange rate models, but to examine their main failures and discuss how these failures result from the underlying methodology.

The conventional exchange rate models of the 1970s were based on two insights: market participants are rational and exchange rate movements depend largely on macroeconomic fundamentals. The failure of these and subsequent REH models to explain monthly or quarterly exchange rate movements can be interpreted in three ways. First, economists have not yet found the right conventional macroeconomic model. Second, macroeconomic fundamentals and/or rationality are unimportant for exchange rate movements. Or, third, fully predetermined representations provide an inadequate basis to capture the importance of macroeconomic fundamentals and rational behavior.

The contemporary approach's imperative that models should generate sharp predictions has led economists to consider only the first two interpretations. NOEM represents an intensive effort at developing increasingly sophisticated REH models. As we discussed in chapter 2, these models were developed at roughly the same time that both conventional and behavioral economists adopted less stringent tests of their models' adequacy, so that they would not "reject too many good models." Consequently, to test their theories, many NOEM researchers have attempted to match the first and second moments of simulated and actual data, instead of confronting the predictions of their models directly with time-series data.[1] As we argue in this chapter, although NOEM models have had some success in matching moments, their ability to explain key features of the contemporary era of floating rates is as limited as the original overshooting model.

When attempting to model directly the causal mechanism that underpins monthly or quarterly exchange rate movements, most international economists have concluded that they are largely unrelated to macroeconomic fundamentals. We argue that this conclusion is an artifact of the contemporary approach: as reported by conventional economists themselves, fundamentals do matter for exchange rate movements, but they do so in a way that is unstable over time. The insistence on fully predetermined models, however, led to the view that exchange rates are driven by decisions of "irrational" individuals, who do not pay attention to macroeconomic fundamentals. We argue that a more plausible interpretation of the empirical evidence is that market participants do pay attention to macroeconomic fundamentals, but in coping with inherently imperfect knowledge, they intermittently revise their views as to which fundamentals are important and how they influence the exchange rate.

Beyond relying on irrationality, many economists explain long swings in exchange rates as "bubbles." Following the contemporary approach, these bubble trajectories are the nonfundamental solutions of REH models. These models presume that when forming their forecasts, market participants somehow collectively agree to form their forecasts according to one of the infinite fully predetermined bubble paths. As we discussed in the previous chapter, bubble models represent an even further retreat from the research program of basing explanations of aggregate outcomes on individual foundations. In this chapter, we argue that these models are also inconsistent with the pattern of long swings that we actually observe in currency markets.

7.1. Exchange Rates and Macroeconomic Fundamentals: The Futile Search for a Fully Predetermined Relationship

Over the past three decades, international macroeconomists have been confronting their conventional models of the exchange rate with time-series

---

1. For an excellent textbook treatment of the calibration methodology in the context of international macroeconomics, see Mark (2001).

data. With few exceptions, this literature is based on testing the reduced-form predictions of models with linear structures. Researchers estimate exchange rate relationships with fixed coefficients that are attached to unchanging sets of causal variables. In many studies, economists search for a single linear relationship between the exchange rate and macroeconomic fundamentals over periods lasting even longer than two or three decades.

7.1.1. Is a Linear Relationship in the Data?

The first exchange rate studies to test the reduced-form predictions of REH models were conducted in the 1970s. The reduced forms implied by the Frenkel (1976) and Bilson (1978a,b) flexible-price monetary model (the FB model), the Dornbusch (1976) and Frankel (1979) sticky-price monetary model (the DF model), and the Hooper and Morton (1982) sticky-price hybrid model (the HM model) are encompassed in the following equation:

$$S_t = \beta_0 + \beta_1 \left(M_t - M_t^* \right) + \beta_2 \left(Y_t - Y_t^* \right) + \beta_3 \left(i_t - i_t^* \right)$$
$$+ \beta_4 \left(\pi_t - \pi_t^* \right) + \beta_5 \left(TB_t - TB_t^* \right) + \epsilon_t, \tag{7.1}$$

where π_t and TB_t denote, respectively, the expected secular rate of domestic inflation and the cumulative domestic trade balance, and all other variables are defined as in equation (6.9).[2] We note that equation (7.1) also encompasses the reduced forms of the intertemporal monetary models of Stockman (1980) and Lucas (1982), which relate the exchange rate to a stable function of money and income.

The results of the empirical studies of the 1970s, which examined several U.S. dollar and nondollar exchange rates, were quite favorable to conventional exchange rate models. Using in-sample regression analysis and monthly and quarterly data, researchers found that macroeconomic fundamentals entered regression equations significantly, with coefficients whose signs were consistent with their models.[3] Many of the studies found that the magnitude of the estimated coefficient on money was insignificantly different from unity. This finding was particularly important, because it was an indication of the long-run neutrality of money—one of the core predictions of both New Keynesian and New Classical macroeconomics.

---

2. Hooper and Morton (1982) allow for a risk premium in an otherwise standard sticky-price monetary model. We follow Meese and Rogoff (1983) and specify the Hooper and Morton model with cumulative trade balances instead of cumulative deviations of current account balances from trend as in the original study. Table 15.1 in chapter 15 summarizes the sign predictions on the β coefficients that are implied by the REH models.

3. See, for example, Frenkel (1976), Bilson (1978a,b), Hodrick (1978), Frankel (1979), and Hooper and Morton (1982). For a review article, see Levich (1985).

A key feature of all of these studies, however, is that their sample periods necessarily excluded the late 1970s and beyond. When researchers updated their samples to include at least the late 1970s, the stellar results of the earlier studies disappeared. Researchers found a lack of co-integrating relationships[4] and parameter estimates that were either insignificant or significant and of the wrong sign.[5]

As poor as the in-sample regression results are, the findings most often cited as illustrating the empirical failure of conventional exchange rate models are those reported in Meese and Rogoff (1983). This study examines the out-of-sample fit of the three exchange rate models captured in equation (7.1), as well as several univariate and multivariate time-series models using monthly data for the German mark, British pound, and Japanese yen markets.

Meese and Rogoff's out-of-sample fit analysis is based on a sample period that began in March 1973 and ended in June 1981. Parameter estimates of all models are first computed for an initialization period that ran until November 1976 using ordinary least squares. The in-sample parameter estimates of the structural models are then combined with the actual out-of-sample future values of the explanatory variables to generate "forecasts" of the exchange rate at the 1-, 6-, and 12-month horizons beyond November 1976. Additional forecasts are generated by updating the in-sample estimation period one observation at a time and computing forecasts at all three time horizons after each update. Although Meese and Rogoff's use of rolling regressions allows the coefficients of the structural models to change over the forecasting period, their experiment does not drop any observations from the beginning of the in-sample estimation period as new observations are added. They also measure forecasting performance by averaging together the errors generated by each model over the entire forecasting period, from December 1976 through June 1981. The aim of such an experiment is to test the forecasting performance of fully predetermined models with invariant (linear) structures. With such models, additional observations lead to better estimates of the underlying parameters, which are presumed to be fixed.

Meese and Rogoff's main finding is that none of the structural models examined are able to outperform the simple random walk model at any forecasting horizon. This finding suggests that very little is known about what moves exchange rates over the short and medium runs. Even if economists could somehow obtain information on the actual future realizations of the explanatory variables, the ability to forecast on the basis of conventional ex-

    4. See Meese (1986), Meese and Rogoff (1988), and Meese and Rose (1991).

    5. See Dornbusch (1980), Frankel (1983, 1984), Backus (1984), and Boothe and Glassman (1987).

change rate models would be no better than if economists were to rely on flipping a coin.

This finding, however, is hardly surprising. If, as we argue throughout this book, the relationship between the exchange rate and macroeconomic fundamentals varies over time, then mixing observations from subperiods in which different relationships drive the exchange rate is likely to generate large errors. Indeed, in Goldberg and Frydman (1996b), we incorporate this temporal instability into the Meese and Rogoff forecasting experiment without prespecifying it fully. We find, contrary to Meese and Rogoff, that the structural models outperform the random walk model by considerable margins, but only if the analysis takes into account the structural instability of the relationship between the exchange rate and macroeconomic fundamentals.[6]

There have been numerous attempts to overturn the Meese and Rogoff finding, but, except for our study, they all presume that economists should continue to search for a fully predetermined model. Consequently, these studies have had little success.[7] Cheung et al. (2005), for example, investigate the out-of-sample forecasting performance of the DF model, as well as several more recent models.[8] As with most of the literature, the authors presume that their models are temporally stable. They examine two out-of-sample forecasting periods during the 1980s and 1990s and forecasting performance over 1-, 4-, and 20-quarter horizons. They also examine a large number of exchange rates, involving five U.S. dollar and five nondollar rates. Their main finding is that the more recent exchange rate models are unable to outperform the older DF model, let alone the random walk, at all forecasting horizons.[9]

Some studies find particular subperiods of floating in which structural models outperform the random walk model.[10] But the results are "fragile, in the sense that it is generally hard to replicate the superior forecasting performance for alternative periods and alternative currencies" (Sarno and Taylor, 2002, p. 135).

---

6. We discuss these results in chapter 15.

7. For reviews of this literature, see Frankel and Rose (1995) and Sarno and Taylor (2002).

8. The authors consider a PPP model, the DF model, a DF model that includes a Balassa-Samuelson effect, a composite specification motivated by the behavioral equilibrium exchange rate model of Clark and MacDonald (1999) and the Natrex model of Stein (1995), and a specification based on uncovered interest rate parity (UIP).

9. The authors find that an error-correction specification based on PPP and the older sticky-price monetary model can predict the direction of change of the exchange rate for some currencies at the longer forecasting horizon of four years. We return to this finding in section 7.3.

10. See, for example, Woo (1985), Finn (1986), Somanath (1986), and MacDonald and Taylor (1993, 1994).

The failure of linear conventional exchange rate models, with their fixed sets of fundamentals and coefficients, to explain short- and medium-run movements in the exchange rate both in sample and out of sample has led many researchers to conclude that "exchange rates are moved largely by factors other than the obvious, observable, macroeconomic fundamentals" (Dornbusch and Frankel, 1995, p. 16). Obstfeld and Rogoff (2000) refer to these findings as the "exchange rate disconnect puzzle."[11]

7.1.2. Widespread Temporal Instability

The widely held view among international macroeconomists that exchange rates are disconnected from macroeconomic fundamentals over the short and medium runs is rather remarkable. To arrive at this view, they have had to ignore their own empirical findings that macroeconomic fundamentals do matter for exchange rates. The findings of the empirical studies of the 1970s clearly indicate that for subperiods spanning the middle of the decade, exchange-rate movements correlated with the fundamental variables implied by the monetary models in ways that were consistent with the sign predictions of those models. Indeed, it would be difficult to improve on these studies' empirical success. That these results disappeared when researchers updated their samples to include the late 1970s and 1980s should not be interpreted as an indication that macroeconomic fundamentals do not matter for exchange rates. Rather, the obvious conclusion to draw is that the relationship between the exchange rate and macroeconomic fundamentals is temporally unstable.

The temporal instability of empirical exchange rate models can also be seen in more recent empirical studies, which use more powerful statistical methods for estimating linear co-integrating relationships and expanded theoretical specifications of the monetary model. MacDonald and Taylor (1994), Cushman et al. (1996), and MacDonald and Marsh (1997) all find significant co-integrating relationships. The first and last of these studies also find that the monetary model dominates the random walk in out-of-sample forecasting. However, using similar methodologies but different sample periods, other researchers find a lack of co-integrating relationships,[12] as

11. Obstfeld and Rogoff (2000) also include as part of the exchange rate disconnect puzzle the failure of the monetary models to explain large estimates of the half-lives of PPP deviations (see Rogoff, 1996) and the much higher volatility of floating-rate regimes relative to fixed-rate regimes (see Baxter and Stockman, 1989; Flood and Rose, 1995, 2002). These anomalies are referred to as the "PPP puzzle" and the "exchange rate regime puzzle," respectively. For an IKE analysis of the PPP puzzle see Frydman, Goldberg, and Juselius (2007).

12. See Baillie and Pecchenino (1991), Chinn and Meese (1995), and Papell (1997).

well as an inability on the part of the monetary models to outperform the random walk in out-of-sample forecasting.[13]

There are also several studies in the literature that formally test the temporal stability of linear exchange rate models. All find clear evidence of temporal instability.[14] As Richard Meese remarks, "the most menacing empirical regularity that confronts exchange rate modelers is the failure of the current generation of empirical exchange rate models to provide stable results across subperiods of the modern floating rate period" (Meese, 1986, p. 365).

7.1.3. Is a Fully-Predetermined Nonlinear Relationship in the Data?

The results of the empirical exchange rate studies suggest that macro-economic fundamentals matter, but in a way that is not stable over time. Reviewing the empirical record, Richard Meese concludes that

> the set of explanatory variables most correlated with exchange rate move-ments depends on the sample period analyzed. For example, most re-cently researchers have shifted focus from the real interest differentials (the focus of the early 1980s) to U.S. budget and current account deficits (the focus from the mid-1980s to the present). The current account was also an important explanatory variable in the late 1970s. (Meese, 1990, p. 126)

This observation is exactly what one would expect in capitalist economies, with their intermittent changes in forecasting strategies and social context. In Goldberg and Frydman (1996a, 2001), and in chapter 15, we estimate a piecewise linear co-integrating relationship for the German mark–U.S. dollar exchange rate based on an IKE version of the monetary model. A piecewise linear relationship can be viewed as an approximation to a fully predetermined nonlinear model. But, in contrast to the contemporary approach, we do not suppose that the nonlinearity in the data can be fully prespecified. Consequently, we prespecify neither the points of structural change nor the particular fundamental variables that might be relevant in each linear piece or subperiod of floating. We find not only that the temporal instability of linear exchange rate relationships is widespread and occurs in

---

13. See Chinn and Meese (1995) and Cheung, Chinn, and Pascal (2005).

14. See, for example, Boughton (1987), Meese and Rogoff (1988), and Goldberg and Frydman (1996a,b, 2001).

every decade of floating, but that, as Meese emphasized, this instability takes on a striking form: different sets of fundamentals matter for exchange rates during different subperiods of floating.

Our findings also suggest that the timing of the structural change or the set of macroeconomic fundamentals that matter for exchange rate movements depends, in part, on historical events, such as the appointment of a new Federal Reserve chairman or international policy coordination.[15] Attempts to prespecify fully the nonlinearity between the exchange rate and macroeconomic fundamentals, therefore, are tantamount to a presumption that economists can fully prespecify the timing and consequences of such historical events. This view that a fully predetermined nonlinear model is unlikely to capture adequately the timing and nature of the temporal instability of exchange rate relationships is borne out by Frömmel et al. (2005). This study allows for a fully prespecified, piecewise linear exchange rate process based on the DF model.[16] The authors use a two-state Markov-switching procedure to estimate two different regimes and transitions between these regimes. The results are not favorable for the DF model.

7.2. The Exchange Rate Disconnect Puzzle: An Artifact of the Contemporary Approach

The methodology of the contemporary approach has led economists to ignore the evidence that macroeconomic fundamentals matter for exchange rates in the short and medium runs. Because they insist on fully predetermined representations of individual behavior and aggregate outcomes, contemporary economists consider only exchange rate relationships in which fundamentals matter in fully prespecified ways. This methodology has generated countless studies trying to find fully predetermined, mostly linear, relationships between the exchange rate and macroeconomic fundamentals.

Not finding such relationships in the data, contemporary economists have come to a striking conclusion: exchange rates and macroeconomic

15. In Goldberg and Frydman (1996b), we find points of structural change that are proximate to the appointment of Paul Volcker in October 1979 and the Plaza Accord in September 1985. See chapter 15.

16. There are also studies that incorporate random coefficient techniques into their analysis. For example, see Alexander and Thomas (1987), Wolf (1987), and Schinasi and Swamy (1989). As with other contemporary models, these studies fully predetermine the stochastic variation of parameter values, typically around fixed means. These studies are not designed, therefore, to deal with the kind of temporal instability that we find in the data: different sets of fundamentals matter during different time periods.

fundamentals are not connected over the short and medium runs. The fact that their own results indicate that fundamentals do indeed matter, although not in a fully predetermined way, reveals that the exchange-rate disconnect puzzle is merely an artifact of the flawed methodology of the contemporary approach.

7.3. Macroeconomic Fundamentals over Long Horizons: Self-Limiting Long Swings

In addition to uncovering evidence that macroeconomic fundamentals matter for the exchange rate over the short and medium runs, contemporary economists have also found considerable evidence that fundamentals matter over the long run. Much of this research estimates a fully predetermined univariate model of the real exchange rate and tests whether this price has a tendency to revert to the mean, that is, to readjust to a constant level over long time horizons. If so, it would imply that PPP serves as an anchor around which the long swings in nominal exchange rates revolve.

Compelling evidence of mean reversion in real exchange rates during floating-rate regimes is provided by studies that estimate a fully predetermined nonlinear model that allows the speed of adjustment to PPP to depend on the magnitude of the deviation from PPP.[17] To motivate this nonlinear adjustment of PPP deviations, these studies usually appeal to exchange rate models that incorporate transactions costs.[18] In these models, commodity arbitrage works to push the exchange rate and goods prices back to PPP, but only if deviations from PPP are large enough to compensate arbitragers for their transactions costs.

A popular specification in the literature is the exponential smooth transition autoregressive (ESTAR) model of Granger and Teräsvirta (1993), which can be written as:

$$\Delta Q_t = \alpha + \rho Q_{t-1} + \left\{\alpha^* + \rho^* Q_{t-1}\right\} \Phi\left(Q_{t-d} - \mu\right) + \varepsilon_t, \qquad (7.2)$$

17. Real exchange rate studies that allow for nonlinear adjustment include Michael et al. (1997), Taylor et al. (2001), Kilian and Taylor (2003), and Basci and Caner (2005). Studies that assume linear adjustment usually find mixed results when the analysis is confined to floating-rate periods. For review articles of the long-run PPP literature, see Rogoff (1996) and Taylor and Taylor (2004).

18. See, for example, Dumas (1992), Sercu et al. (1995), and Obstfeld and Taylor (1997). Obstfeld and Rogoff (2000), however, argue that although "trade costs must constitute an essential element" in resolving the exchange rate disconnect puzzle, economists need "a much richer framework featuring imperfect competition plus sticky prices and/or wages, as in . . . new open economy macroeconomics." In the next section, we argue that these NOEM models also have difficulty explaining the empirical record.

where Q_t denotes the log of the real exchange rate at time t, Δ is the first-difference operator, $\Phi\left(Q_{t-d} - \mu\right)$ is a transition function, μ is the level of the real exchange rate that is consistent with PPP, d is a delay parameter, ε_t is a white noise error, and autoregressive terms ΔQ_{t-j} have been omitted for convenience. The transition function is assumed to take on the exponential form:

$$\Phi\left(Q_{t-d} - \mu\right) = 1 - e^{-\theta^2\left(Q_{t-d}-\mu\right)^2},$$

which implies that Φ is bounded between zero and unity such that $\Phi(0) = 0$ and $\lim_{x \to \pm\infty} \Phi(x) = 1$.

The key parameters of the model are ρ and ρ^*. If Φ were always equal to zero, then, with $\rho = 0$, Q_t would have a unit root and there would be no tendency for the real exchange rate to adjust back to its PPP level, μ. However, as Q_{t-d} deviates from μ, the bracketed term in equation (7.2) exerts its influence, and it is the sum of the parameters $\rho' = \rho + \Phi\rho^*$ that determines the tendency of the real exchange rate to revert to the mean. If $\rho^* < 0$, then the real exchange rate does revert to the mean, and this tendency strengthens as deviations from PPP grow. Taylor et al. (2001), for example, report highly significant parameter estimates that are consistent with $\rho = 0$ and a ρ^* considerably less than zero for all four U.S. dollar exchange rates examined.[19] They thus find clear evidence that small deviations from PPP are characterized by little mean reversion, whereas large deviations are associated with a strong tendency to adjust back to PPP.

By estimating the ESTAR model in equation (7.2) with constant parameters, researchers assume a fully predetermined nonlinear model. Although they find results consistent with nonlinear mean reversion, these results are far from sufficient for showing that the univariate exchange rate process can be fully prespecified.[20] In our view, these results should be interpreted as shedding light on the qualitative nature of exchange rate fluctuations: although exchange rates often move persistently away from PPP levels for extended periods of time, these swings are self-limiting. Eventually, sustained countermovements occur in which exchange rates move persistently back to PPP. The self-limiting nature of exchange rate swings indicates that macroeconomic fundamentals matter for exchange rates over long time horizons.

19. This study examined the British pound, German mark, French franc, and Japanese yen exchange rates against the U.S. dollar using monthly data over a sample period from January 1973 through December 1996.

20. Taylor and Peel (2000) provide evidence that deviations from PPP-based monetary fundamentals follow a similar nonlinear process. Mark (1995), Mark and Choi (1997), Kilian and Taylor (2003), and Cheung et al. (2005) find that deviations from PPP and PPP-based monetary fundamentals have predictive power, but only over horizons greater than three or four years.

Figure 7.1   DM/$ Exchange Rate: 1973–98

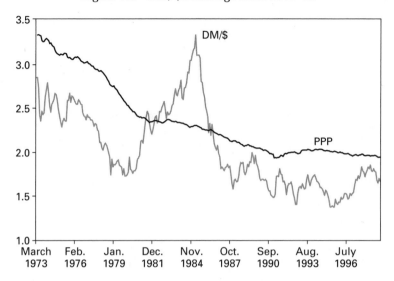

But it does not necessarily indicate that fundamentals matter in a fully pre-determined way.

A key feature of the long-swings process in asset markets is that it is highly irregular. This irregularity is evident in figures 7.1, 7.2, and 7.3, where we plot the values of the German mark (DM), British pound (BP), and Japanese yen (JY), respectively, against the U.S. dollar ($), along with estimates of their corresponding PPP exchange rates.[21]

In every decade of floating and in each currency market, the exchange rate moved persistently away from PPP for extended periods of time, leading to large misalignments. Consistent with the results of the nonlinear studies, the figures show that the exchange rate did not move away from PPP without bound. Eventually, it experienced persistent countermovements back to this benchmark.

But the three figures also show that the duration of the exchange rate swings and the points at which sustained countermovements occurred varied considerably in each market. In some cases, the swings away lasted two years, whereas in others they lasted four years, for example, the DM/$ swings

21. The PPP exchange rates in figures 7.1–7.3 are based on the *Big Mac* PPP exchange rates reported in the April 1990 issue of *The Economist* magazine (which were 1.96, 0.64, and 168 for the mark, pound, and yen, respectively) and consumer price index (CPI) inflation rate differentials from the *International Financial Statistics* of the International Monetary Fund (IMF).

Figure 7.2   BP/$ Exchange Rate: 1973–2005

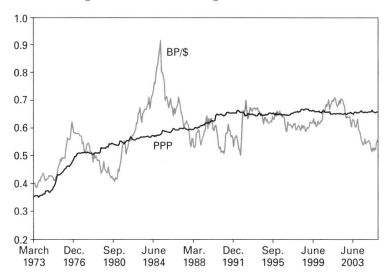

Figure 7.3   JY/$ Exchange Rate: 1973–2005

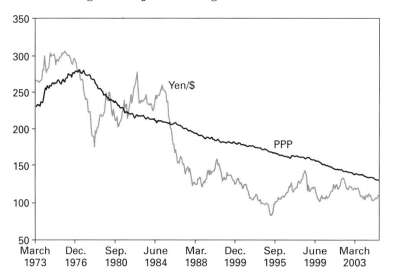

Figure 7.4   Standard & Poor's 500 Stock Price: 1881–2005

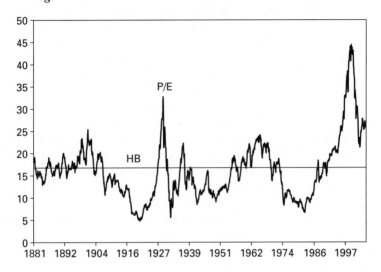

during 1985–86 and 1981–85, respectively. Some swings away led to misalignments of more than 20 percent before a sustained countermovement occurred, but for others, sustained countermovements did not set in until the misalignments were as high as 60 percent, for example, the BP/$ swings that occurred from 1977–80 and 1981–85, respectively.

Figure 7.4 shows that the tendency of asset prices to exhibit long swings that revolve around historical benchmark levels is not a phenomenon peculiar to foreign exchange markets; such behavior is a feature of asset markets in which prices are freely determined by the forces of supply and demand. The figure plots the price of the Standard & Poor's 500 basket of stocks relative to its underlying earnings (labeled P/E in the figure).[22] Long swings that revolve around a historical average price-earnings ratio (labeled HB in the figure) of 16 are quite evident.[23] The irregularity of these swings is also clear in the figure.

22. Figure 7.4 is based on data from Shiller (2000), which are updated on his web site: www.econ.yale.edu/~shiller.

23. Researchers have found that long swings in stock prices away from levels consistent with historical averages of standard valuation ratios are bounded. They have also found that deviations from such historical averages have predictive power regarding future stock prices over longer time horizons. See Shiller (1981) and Campbell and Shiller (1988, 1998).

The non-routine nature of the forecasting process and unforeseen shifts in the social context imply that any invariant nonlinear model of the exchange rate will experience parameter instability.[24] But, as long as the large swings away from PPP are self-limiting, we would expect estimates of a fully predetermined univariate ESTAR model to indicate that mean reversion of real exchange rates is greater for large deviations from PPP.

It is important to point out that researchers' reliance on transactions costs and commodity arbitrage to motivate their nonlinear models of PPP deviations is odd in markets where it is widely known that more than 95 percent of the volume stems from asset flows. Indeed, the key insight of the asset market approach to exchange rates that was developed in the 1970s is that exchange rates are determined by the demand for and supply of assets, not goods. Moreover, transaction costs, even if they are embedded in a richer NOEM framework, do not provide an explanation for why asset prices often move persistently away from benchmark levels for extended periods of time or for the timing and nature of the instability of exchange rate relationships. In the next two sections, we examine the inability of the contemporary approach, with its fully predetermined representations, to provide reasonable explanations of the long-swings behavior of floating exchange rates.

7.4. Can REH Models Explain Long Swings in Exchange Rates?

The long swings depicted in figures 7.1–7.4 are difficult to explain with conventional models. Conventional economists construct two types of monetary models to explain deviations of nominal exchange rates from PPP levels: flexible-price and sticky-price models.[25] But the conventional approach instructs an economist not only to fully predetermine his models, but to use REH, which renders representations of individual forecasting behavior derivative of the other components of his model. Consequently, to explain long swings in the exchange rate, an economist must rely on "action" in these other components, that is, in tastes and technology, such policy variables as money supply, or bubbles.

---

24. We are unaware of any attempt to examine the temporal stability of the ESTAR or other nonlinear models of the exchange rate.

25. Economists also construct barter models of real resource allocation to explain long-run (for example, decade-to-decade) changes in real exchange rates. The classic model in this literature is attributable to Balassa (1964) and Samuelson (1964). For a review of this literature, see Froot and Rogoff (1995).

7.4.1. Tastes, Technology, and Flexible Prices: Permanent Deviations

Conventional flexible-price monetary models assume that all prices, including goods prices and wages, adjust instantaneously to their equilibrium levels.[26] These models imply that deviations from PPP are largely permanent and arise because of "real disturbances to supplies and demands for goods [which] cause changes in relative prices, including the real exchange rate" (Stockman, 1987, p. 12). To explain long swings, these models require that shifts in preferences and technology be not only big enough, but occur mainly in one direction for periods lasting one, two, or more years, which are then followed by systematic shifts in the opposite direction. Such frequent and persistent swings in tastes and technology, however, are not plausible. In discussing the failure of this class of models to explain the large exchange rate swings of the 1980s, Dornbusch argued, "the events were too large and the reversal too sharp and complete to allude to mystical shifts in tastes and technology" (Dornbusch, 1989, p. 415).

When confronted with the exchange rate dynamics depicted in figures 7.1–7.3, most conventional economists invoke some type of sticky-price monetary model, in which goods prices and/or wages adjust only sluggishly over time to their long-run equilibrium levels. Although these models do generate temporary deviations of exchange rates from PPP levels following jumps in money supply, they are difficult to reconcile with long swings.

7.4.2. Policy and Sticky Prices: Temporary Deviations versus Long Swings

The contemporary sticky-price approach to exchange rates has its origins in the 1970s, when Dornbusch (1976) incorporated the assumptions of REH and sticky goods prices into the seminal open-economy framework of Fleming (1962) and Mundell (1963). Dornbusch showed that these assumptions implied a key result: nominal and real exchange rates could overshoot their long-run equilibrium (PPP) levels in the short run because of unanticipated one-time changes in money supply.[27] Dornbusch's "overshooting model," as it is called, quickly became the field's workhorse, for it provided a simple and reasonable explanation for the much greater volatility of nominal and real exchange rates compared to relative goods prices that characterize

---

26. The seminal articles in this literature are Stockman (1980) and Lucas (1982). See also Helpman (1981) and Svensson (1985). These models can be seen as generalizations of the older flexible-price monetary models of Frenkel (1976) and Bilson (1978a,b), which assume REH but rely on ad hoc specifications based on Cagan (1956) to represent aggregate money demand.

27. Frankel (1979) extended the model to show that unanticipated changes in money growth rates could also lead to short-run overshooting of exchange rates from PPP levels.

floating-rate regimes. However, although the overshooting model offers an explanation of the greater volatility of exchange rates, it is largely inconsistent with the long-swings behavior captured in figures 7.1–7.3. The problem stems from the assumption of REH, which instructs an economist to tie his representation of individual forecasting behavior rigidly to the other components of his model.

As was still common in the 1970s, these other components consisted of aggregate equations that appealed only loosely to individual foundations. A two-country, discrete-time version of these components can be written as:

$$M_{r_t} = P_{r_t} + \phi Y_{r_t} - \lambda i_{r_t} \qquad (7.3)$$

$$E(S_{t+1}|X_t) - S_t = i_{r_t} \qquad (7.4)$$

$$P_{r_{t+1}} - P_{r_t} = \delta \left(S_t - P_{r_t} - \bar{Q} \right), \qquad (7.5)$$

where a subscript r denotes a domestic value relative to its foreign counterpart, $\bar{Q}$ denotes the log of the goods-market clearing level of the real exchange rate, which is assumed to be constant, and all other variables are defined as in chapter 6. Equation (7.3) is the relative equilibrium condition for the domestic and foreign money markets. For simplicity, we follow Dornbusch (1976) and assume that M_t and Y_t are exogenous and not expected to change from their current levels; for example, they both follow random walks.[28] Equation (7.4) is uncovered interest parity, which represents equilibrium in the foreign exchange market under the assumptions that domestic and foreign assets are perfect substitutes, capital is perfectly mobile, and expectations are homogeneous.[29] Equation (7.5) represents the adjustment of relative goods prices as a positive function of the relative excess demand for goods, which is assumed to depend positively on the real exchange rate. A domestic currency depreciation, for example, makes domestic goods cheaper relative to foreign goods, causing excess demand for the former and excess supply of the latter. These disequilibria, then,

28. Dornbusch (1976) also examines a version of the model in which income is determined by demand. In this case, the exchange rate may not overshoot its PPP level when money supply changes.

29. The assumption of homogeneous expectations is not merely a simplification in models in which UIP is assumed to characterize equilibrium in the foreign exchange market. Although homogeneous expectations in a model that also assumes perfect asset substitutability and perfect capital mobility implies that equilibrium is characterized by UIP, this would not be the case were one to assume that expectations are heterogeneous. The assumptions of perfect asset substitutability and perfect capital mobility, together with heterogeneous expectations, implies that market participants would want to take positions in foreign exchange of unlimited size whenever they perceive a profit opportunity. Consequently, under these assumptions, there is no equilibrium exchange rate that would balance the supply of and demand for foreign exchange.

trigger a process in which over time, goods prices adjust back toward their equilibrium (PPP) levels.

The imposition of REH leads to the following well-known representation of individual forecasting behavior:

$$E(S_{t+1}^{\text{RE}}|X_t) - S_t = \theta \left(\bar{S}_t^{\text{PPP}} - S_t \right), \tag{7.6}$$

where $\bar{S}^{\text{PPP}}$ denotes the PPP exchange rate when goods prices are at their equilibrium levels and θ is one minus the stable root of the system, so that $0 < \theta < 1$. The REH forecasting rule in equation (7.6) ties the prediction of the future change in the exchange rate rigidly to the PPP exchange rate: it predicts a return of the exchange rate back to PPP at the constant rate of θ whenever a gap appears between these two variables. This result follows directly from the assumption in equation (7.5) that the adjustment of goods prices always involves movements back to PPP, as well as from the coupling of REH representations of individual forecasts to the other components of the model.

By design, the predictions represented by equation (7.6) at the individual level are identical to those implied at the aggregate level. An unanticipated monetary shock causes an immediate jump in the exchange rate away from PPP by some prespecified magnitude. But the REH solution of the model implies that whenever such deviations occur, the exchange rate moves persistently back over time to its PPP level.

Persistent movements away from PPP can arise in the model as a result of a sequence of monetary shocks that happen to be of the same sign. But such an explanation is not plausible, given that swings in floating exchange rates often last for several years.[30] The overshooting model, therefore, offers an explanation of temporary deviations from PPP, but not of persistent swings away from it. In discussing the failure of their overshooting model, "and indeed with the more general rational expectations approach," to explain the persistent appreciation of the U.S. dollar during the first half of the 1980s, Dornbusch and Frankel argued that

> it does not explain well the shorter-term [long-swings] dynamics. In the first place, the entire increase in the real interest rate differential and in the value of the dollar should have occurred in one (or two or three) big jumps. . . . Yet the appreciation in fact took place month-by-month, over four years. (Dornbusch and Frankel, 1995, p. 16)

---

30. As with the flexible-price monetary model, persistent and permanent deviations from PPP can also arise in the overshooting model as a result of real shocks to $\bar{Q}$ that are systematically of the same sign. But, as we pointed out in the context of the flexible-price model, such explanations are also not plausible.

In the past decade or so, the warning of Dornbusch and Frankel and others—that REH does not adequately represent forecasting behavior in real world markets—was ignored. Instead, much effort has been devoted to generalizing the sticky-price REH framework of Dornbusch (1976) to include complete intertemporal microfoundations.

7.4.2.1. *Disregarding the Flaws of REH:*
New Open Economy Macroeconomics

NOEM models provide richer frameworks for incorporating nominal rigidities than do closed-economy models. They assume imperfect competition in product or factor markets, thereby enabling the explicit analysis of pricing decisions.[31] As in closed-economy macroeconomics, nominal rigidities are "rigorously assumed" in NOEM models by appealing to menu costs (à la Akerlof and Yellen, 1985, and Mankiw, 1985) and staggered wage setting (à la Taylor, 1979a,b, and Calvo, 1983a,b).[32] Many of the NOEM models make use of the traditional producer-currency pricing (PCP) assumption common to traditional Mundell-Fleming type models. They emphasize the expenditure-switching role of exchange rate movements, in which goods prices are rigid in producers' currencies and there is complete exchange rate pass-through. In these models, the law of one price in tradables holds, which has led researchers who model deviations from PPP to rely on the presence of nontradables.[33]

Although NOEM models have had some success in matching moments, their ability to explain persistent swings away from PPP and the timing and nature of the instability of exchange rate relations is as limited as the original overshooting model.[34] But Engel (1999), Chari et al. (2002), and others present evidence showing that fluctuations in real exchange rates stem largely from deviations from the law of one price in tradables. This evi-

31. The seminal work in this literature is Obstfeld and Rogoff (1995, 1996, 1998, 2000a). See also Svensson and Wijnbergen (1989) and Betts and Devereux (1996, 2000). For textbook treatments, see Obstfeld and Rogoff (1996), Mark (2001), and Sarno and Taylor (2002). For a review article, see Lane (2001).

32. We follow Dornbusch and use the term "rigorously assume" to denote "the current fashion of intoducing ad hocery at a lower level, and then deriving its implications rigorously" (Dornbusch, 1989, p. 412).

33. See for example, Obstfeld and Rogoff (1996, 2000a) and Hau (2000). Hau allows for price discrimination across countries in his model. But the law of one price in tradables still holds in equilibrium, owing to a linear specification of production.

34. In quantitative studies, NOEM models have been shown to generate not only short-run variability of nominal and real exchange rates that matches the data, in contrast to many flexible-price models, but also much higher variability of exchange rates over relative prices. See, for example, Hau (2000), Kollmann (2001), and Benigno (2004).

dence has motivated a number of researchers to assume what is called "local currency pricing" (LCP) as an alternative way to permit deviations from PPP in NOEM models.[35] With LCP, goods prices are rigid in the buyers' currencies and there is zero exchange rate pass-through.[36] The LCP assumption, therefore, in contrast to PCP, implies that currency depreciations can lead to improvement rather than deterioration in a country's terms of trade.

Regardless of whether NOEM models rely on the presence of nontradables or LCP to model deviations from PPP, exchange rate overshooting of PPP values, as in Dornbusch (1976), is possible.[37] However, these models rely on REH to represent individual forecasting behavior.[38] As with Dornbusch (1976), therefore, representations of exchange rate expectations are tied rigidly to their goods-market clearing levels: any deviation of the exchange rate from PPP leads to the expectation of a gradual return at a prespecified rate. Consequently, in these models, the exchange rate moves persistently back to its PPP level following unanticipated monetary shocks. Thus, NOEM models, too, offer an explanation of temporary deviations, but not of persistent swings away, from PPP.

7.5. REH Bubble Models and the Pattern of Long Swings in Real World Markets

Many REH models, including the monetary models of the preceding section, imply not only a stable equilibrium price function based on macroeconomic fundamentals but also an infinite number of possible unstable price functions according to which the asset price diverges from its fundamental value over time. The failure of the fundamental solutions of REH

---

35. See, for example, Betts and Devereux (2000), Chari et al. (2000), Kollmann (2001), and Benigno (2004). These models build on the pricing-to-market theory of Dornbusch (1987) and Krugman (1987a).

36. Whether the PCP or the LCP assumption best characterizes the data is an open question in the literature. For evidence and arguments in favor of PCP, see Obstfeld and Rogoff (2000a) and Obstfeld (2002). For additional evidence that consumer prices are unresponsive to exchange rate fluctuations, see Engel (1993, 2000), Engel and Rogers (1996, 2001), and Parsley and Wei (2001).

37. In these models, the consumption elasticity of money demand must be below unity for exchange rate overshooting. See Obstfeld and Rogoff (1996) and Betts and Devereux (2000). Despite the similar overshooting result, NOEM models based on PCP and LCP have very different implications not only for the terms of trade but also for the co-movements of consumption and income across countries. Moreover, these models have very different implications for the choice between fixed- and floating-rate regimes.

38. Exceptions here include Devereux and Engel (2002) and Kollmann (2005), which model deviations from UIP as resulting from conditionally biased exchange-rate expectations. These models build on Jeanne and Rose (2002), which relies on a monetary model without complete intertemporal microfoundations.

models to explain the long swings in asset markets motivated economists to consider the unstable bubble trajectories of REH models as a way to shed light on asset price movements.[39]

In the foreign exchange market, REH bubbles are routinely advanced as one of the leading explanations of long swings.[40] Researchers have relied on the bubble solutions implied by the overshooting model of Dornbusch (1976).[41] But, as we show in this section, these REH bubble models are inconsistent with the kind of swings that actually occur in currency markets.

In previous chapters, we advanced several arguments to explain why REH models rest on flawed individual foundations, and why they are best interpreted as capturing grossly irrational behavior. The validity of these arguments does not depend on whether one assumes away their unstable time paths. Indeed, allowing for the indeterminacy that is inherent in many REH models renders a behavioral interpretation of REH representations even more problematic: each jump of an asset price to a bubble path in these models presumes collective agreement on the part of all individuals on the particular bubble path—of which the number of possibilities is infinite. It is difficult to fathom how such coordination of beliefs in a market setting might materialize.

Beyond resting on flawed foundations, REH bubble models of the exchange rate are inconsistent with the empirical record. The fully pre-determined bubble paths generated by these models are difficult to recon-cile with the long-lasting, but partial, reversals that occur during most large swings away from benchmark values.

Figure 7.5 is based on daily data for the DM/$ nominal exchange rate. It focuses on the period from January 3, 1983, to March 15, 1985. Over this period, the DM/$ exchange rate rose from 2.37 to 3.40, im-plying a dollar appreciation of 44 percent. There are two key features of this nominal exchange rate swing. First, it involves persistent movements away from PPP. At a rate of 2.37, the dollar was, by most accounts, consid-ered to be overvalued relative to PPP in 1983.[42] Second, the swing away from PPP involves several extended subperiods in which the exchange rate moves persistently, but partially, back to PPP. For example, on January 9,

39. For the incompatability of stable REH solutions with swings in stock and bond markets, see Shiller (1978, 1979, 1981, 1990).

40. See, for example, Frankel (1985), Evans (1986), Krugman (1986), Meese (1986), MacDon-ald and Taylor (1993), and Sarno and Taylor (1999, 2002).

41. The flexible-price monetary model does generate bubbles involving a steadily rising or falling nominal exchange rate. But, along each of these trajectories, PPP holds continuously. These bubbles, therefore, do not provide an explanation of the long swings in figures 7.1–7.3.

42. See, for example, Frankel (1985) and Krugman (1986). The exchange rate swing in figure 7.5 led both authors to consider the REH bubble view as an explanation.

Figure 7.5   DM/$ Swing: 1983–85

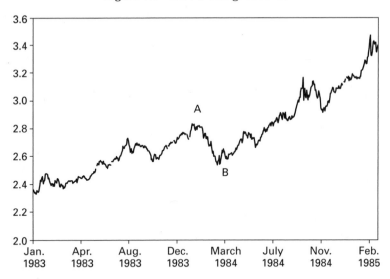

1984, the market entered a period lasting roughly nine weeks during which the price of the dollar steadily fell from 2.84 to 2.55 (points A and B in the figure). The value of the dollar fell in eight of the nine weeks during this period. The sticky-price monetary model is capable of generating bubble trajectories along which the exchange rate moves persistently away from PPP. But it is difficult to reconcile this model with the kind of swings depicted in figure 7.5.

This point is illustrated in the phase diagram shown in figure 7.6, which is based on the overshooting model of Dornbusch (1976). The figure highlights one bubble trajectory.[43] Suppose the market finds itself on this path and that at point A the bubble bursts. According to the prespecified bubble process of Blanchard and Watson, the system immediately jumps back to its intrinsic fundamental value. But goods prices are sticky. Consequently, the fundamental value to which the exchange rate jumps is given by point B on the saddle path, labeled DD in the diagram. It is easily shown that at point B, the nominal exchange rate is below its PPP level.

This implication of the model, which involves a quick fall in the exchange rate to a level below PPP, is at odds with the sustained but partial reversals that occur in most swings, such as during 1983–85. The Blanchard

43. The trajectories in the diagram depict expected values. For an explanation of this phase diagram, see any graduate textbook on international macroeconomics, for example, Obstfeld and Rogoff (1996).

Figure 7.6   Overshooting Model Phase Diagram

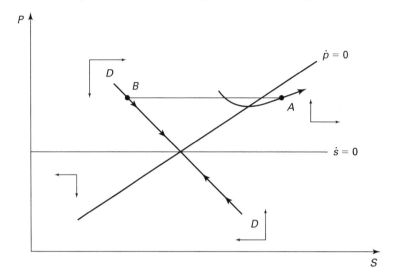

and Watson bubble process could be generalized to enable a jump to a new bubble path when the current bubble bursts, but such an extension would provide no help to the REH bubble view of swings. It is clear from figure 7.5 that there is no prespecified bubble path to which the system could jump that would imply a sustained depreciation of the dollar.[44] Thus, to reconcile the REH bubble view with the empirical record, one would have to argue that individuals somehow expect a rising exchange rate during extended subperiods in which the exchange rate systematically moves in the opposite direction.

7.6. Lost Fundamentals and Forsaken Rationality: Behavioral Models

The inability of conventional exchange rate models to explain long swings in exchange rates, together with regression results that seem to imply that macroeconomic fundamentals are unimportant over the short and medium runs, have prompted economists to construct behavioral models in which swings away from PPP are unrelated to macroeconomic fundamentals. They have also constructed models in which, although the exchange rate depends

---

44. This feature of the model follows from the sticky-price assumption, which implies that interest rates, and thus the expected change in the exchange rate, are fixed at a point in time.

on macroeconomic fundamentals, systematic misinterpretation of news on the part of market participants can lead to persistent movements away from PPP.

7.6.1. Fully Prespecifying the Use of Technical Trading Rules

A popular explanation of exchange rate swings is based on models that involve what economists call "momentum" or "feedback" traders: individuals whose trading rules extrapolate in some way from past price trends. The seminal study in this literature is Frankel and Froot (1987), whose model of fundamentalists and chartists we examined in chapter 6. Studies that build on the Frankel and Froot model to explain exchange rate movements include Goodhart (1988), De Grauwe et al. (1993, 2006), Brock and Hommes (1998), Kilian and Taylor (2001), and De Grauwe and Grimaldi (2005a,b, 2006).[45] In these models, swings away from PPP occur because the weight of the market subscribing to a chartist rule gradually increases.

There is much evidence that over shorter forecast horizons (hours, days, and weeks) the use of technical (chartist) trading rules, which largely fall into the category of momentum or trend-following rules, is widespread not only in currency markets, but in all major asset markets.[46] For example, in their survey of dealers in the London interbank market, Allen and Taylor (1990) and Taylor and Allen (1992) find that roughly 90 percent of respondents use technical trading rules to some extent in forming their forecasts at the shorter forecast horizons.[47] Indeed, the major software packages on which market participants rely for price quotations (for example, Reuters and Knight Ridder) all provide access to the most popular technical trading indicators at the touch of a few computer keys.

The Frankel and Froot model, however, presumes that the use of technical trading rules is grossly irrational. As we showed in chapter 6, although their fully predetermined representation of forecasting behavior allows for a gradual switching between a fixed fundamental model and a fixed chartist model, they attribute to individuals one fixed overarching forecasting rule. The interpretation that such forecasting rules presume grossly irrational behavior is particularly transparent in the case of the Frankel and Froot model.

45. For the stock market, see DeLong et al. (1990a) and Hong and Stein (1999).

46. For a discussion of the most popular technical trading rules used in both currency and stock markets, as well as an analysis of their profitability over different forecasting horizons, see Schulmeister (1987, 2006, 2007) and Schulmeister and Goldberg (1989).

47. Similar evidence of the use of technical trading rules based on surveys of market participants is also reported in Lui and Mole (1998) for the interbank market in Hong Kong; Cheung and Wong (1999, 2000) for markets in Hong Kong, Tokyo, and Singapore; Cheung and Chinn (2001) for the U.S. interbank market; and Cheung et al. (1999) for the London market.

In this model, with sticky prices, the representation of individual forecasts can be written as:

$$E^i(S_{t+1}|X_t^i) - S_t = \omega_t \theta \left(S_t^{PPP} - S_t \right),\qquad(7.7)$$

where ω_t, as before, denotes the weight attached to the prediction of the fundamentalist rule. This forecasting rule, which is based on the Dornbusch (1976) model, predicts a return to PPP at every point in time at a prespecified rate. Despite this rule, however, the exchange rate moves persistently away from PPP in the model as ω_t gradually falls. Thus, the representation of forecasting behavior in the Frankel and Froot model implies not only systematic forecasting errors along any bubble trajectory, but forecasts that systematically predict incorrectly the direction of change of the exchange rate.

7.6.2. Fully Prespecifying Bias in Forecasting

The implication of gross irrationality also characterizes behavioral models of asset price fluctuations that attribute to market participants systematically biased forecasts of the causal variables driving prices. The exchange rate model of Gourinchas and Tornell (2004), for example, attributes to a representative individual a forecasting rule that systematically underpredicts the degree of persistence of interest rate shocks by some prespecified magnitude relative to the level of persistence assumed in the aggregate model. This assumption, in turn, implies that individuals' exchange rate forecasts in the model underreact to an interest rate shock, thereby causing the resulting change in the exchange rate to be smaller than would occur under REH.[48]

In response to an interest rate shock, the Gourinchas and Tornell model produces what Eichenbaum and Evans (1995) call a "delayed overshooting effect": a persistent swing in the exchange rate that rises above its long-run equilibrium level, followed by a gradual return.[49] Using a monthly data set that includes survey data from the *Financial Times Currency Forecaster* on eurocurrency interest rate forecasts, Gourinchas and Tornell estimate a linear model with a fixed underreaction parameter. They assume, therefore, that market participants underreact to news in exactly the same way over their

---

48. For related studies that model underreaction to news in the stock market, see Barberis et al. (1998) and Cecchetti et al. (2000).

49. The Gourinchas and Tornell (2004) model also attempts to explain the forward discount anomaly. We question this attempt in the next chapter.

entire sample period, which runs from August 1986 through October 1995. They interpret their regression results as strong evidence that market participants systematically underreact to news about interest rate movements. They also find that their estimate of the fixed underreaction parameter implies a delayed overshooting effect for six exchange rates ranging from 2 to 13 months in duration.[50]

Forecasting the interest rate is, arguably, as difficult as forecasting the exchange rate. To be sure, there may be particular episodes in the markets during which interest rate and exchange rate forecasts, in some average sense, could be reasonably characterized as biased. But such episodes, if they last long enough, provide powerful incentives for market participants to discover them and, once they do, to revise their forecasting strategies in ways that alter the nature of any bias. We would expect, therefore, that there would be some time periods in which forecasts could be characterized as underpredicting price movements and other periods characterized by overprediction. When such time periods might begin and how long they might last is, however, unpredictable.

As Eugene Fama has observed, "Apparent over-reaction to information is about as common as under-reaction, and post-event continuation of pre-event abnormal returns is about as frequent as post-event reversal" (Fama, 1998, p. 283). Contrary to Fama's findings, Gourinchas and Tornell presume that individuals misperceive interest rate shocks and underpredict the magnitude of exchange rate changes in the same way *endlessly*.[51] Thus, as with Frankel and Froot (1986), the Gourinchas and Tornell (2004) model is best interpreted as representing grossly irrational behavior.

---

50. The six U.S. dollar exchange rates examined in their analysis include the five used in Eichenbaum and Evans (1995)—the BP, DM, French franc, Italian lira, and JY—plus the Canadian dollar.

51. As is common in contemporary economics, Gourinchas and Tornell do not test for structural change in their model.

8 "Anomalous" Returns on Foreign Exchange

Is It Really Irrationality?

> What is surprising is the widespread finding that realized exchange rate changes tend to be, if anything, in the opposite direction to that predicted by the forward premium. If taken literally, [this] finding . . . is startling. It suggests that one can make predictable profits by betting against the forward rate.
>
> MAURICE OBSTFELD AND KENNETH ROGOFF,
> *Foundations of International Macroeconomics*, p. 589

> There is no positive evidence that the forward discount's bias is due to risk. . . . Survey data on exchange rate expectations suggest that the bias is entirely due to expectational errors. . . . Taken as a whole, the evidence suggests that explanations which allow for the possibility of market inefficiency should be seriously investigated.
>
> KENNETH FROOT AND RICHARD H. THALER,
> "Anomalies: Foreign Exchange,"
> *Journal of Economic Perspectives*, p. 190

Beyond their inability to account for exchange rate fluctuations, conventional exchange rate models encounter difficulty in explaining the behavior of foreign exchange returns. By imposing REH and uncovered interest rate parity (UIP), the monetary models of the 1970s imply that the ex post one-period-ahead return on foreign exchange should be uncorrelated with all current and past information on returns and the causal variables that an economist includes in his representation of forecasting behavior. Researchers have found, however, that ex post returns in many currency markets are persistent. Moreover, dozens of studies report significantly negative estimates of the slope coefficient in regressions of the future change in the spot exchange rate on the forward premium. This finding, called the "forward discount anomaly," suggests that the forward rate is a biased predictor of future changes in the exchange rate and that ex post returns are negatively correlated with the forward premium.

There are three possible explanations for this behavior: (1) REH holds and there is a market premium that is correlated with macroeconomic variables, such as the forward premium; (2) the market premium is constant, and perhaps zero, and REH fails, in that market participants' forecast errors vary systematically with macroeconomic variables; or (3) both UIP and REH fail.[1] The literature has focused its efforts on the first two explanations.

In pursuing the first explanation, conventional economists replace UIP's assumption of risk neutrality with risk aversion in representing the preferences of market participants. In their models, individuals require a premium for holding the relatively riskier currency to compensate them for their aversion to risk. However, when based on the usual specification of risk-averse preferences, researchers find that their REH risk-premium models are grossly inconsistent with the behavior of returns on foreign exchange.[2] The fundamentals implied by these models—asset supplies, consumption, or money and income—are not variable enough to explain the behavior of returns without implausibly large estimates of the degree of risk aversion. Moreover, these models are unable to explain the sign reversals in regression estimates of the expected return on foreign exchange.

REH instructs economists to represent individual forecasting behavior as derivative of the other components of their models. Thus, when REH models based on the usual specification of risk-averse preferences were found to fail, conventional economists were led to search for alternative representations of preferences.[3] But empirical research provides "no positive evidence that the forward discount's bias is due to risk" (Froot and Thaler, 1990, p. 190).

Given their lack of autonomous microfoundations and the incompatibility of risk-averse preferences with experimental evidence, these empirical difficulties of conventional models are hardly surprising. However, economists have not concluded that REH and risk aversion are inadequate assumptions for representing the compensation for risk in asset markets. Instead, they have interpreted their empirical findings as indications that outcomes in the foreign exchange market are driven by irrational behavior and that "market inefficiency should be seriously investigated" (Froot and Thaler, 1990, p. 190). Moreover, the literature has concluded that market participants are not only irrational, but absurdly so. Supposedly, "one can make predictable profits" (Obstfeld and Rogoff, 1996, p. 589) in the foreign exchange market by following a rule as simple as betting against the forward

---

1. Forecast errors under REH can be persistent and correlated with the forward premium in small samples if market participants are assumed to either learn about a one-time switch in the process driving the exchange rate (Lewis, 1989a,b) or place probability on a switch that differs from the frequency of such switches in the econometrician's sample (Kaminsky, 1993; Evans and Lewis, 1995). Such REH-based learning and "peso-problem" explanations, however, are generally recognized to be unable to account for the behavior of foreign exchange returns. See Engel (1996).

2. For excellent review articles, see Lewis (1995) and Engel (1996). See also below.

3. For example, see Backus et al. (1993), Sibert (1996), and Bekaert et al. (1997).

rate, and yet, remarkably, market participants, for some unexplained reason, do not exploit this opportunity.

In this chapter, we examine the behavior of ex post returns on foreign exchange using a monthly data set for the German mark–U.S. dollar (DM/\$), British pound–U.S. dollar (BP/\$), and Japanese yen–U.S. dollar (JY/\$) markets. We regress the future change in the spot rate on the forward premium, which we refer to as the Bilson (1981) and Fama (1984) (BF) regression, and reproduce the standard result of negative estimates of the slope coefficient. We then discuss the two main avenues that contemporary economists have pursued in attempting to explain the behavior of foreign exchange returns: an REH risk premium or irrationality.

One would not expect the slope coefficient in a BF regression to be stable over time in a world in which market participants revise their forecasting strategies and the social context changes in ways that cannot be fully foreseen by anyone. Indeed, there are several well-known studies in the literature that provide evidence of such instability. However, most economists in the field ignore this evidence and continue to interpret their fixed-parameter estimates from BF regressions as indications of a negative bias—and thus of obvious and unexploited profit opportunities. As with the evidence of unstable exchange rate relations that we discussed in chapter 7, the practice of considering only fully prespecified, mostly invariant relationships has led contemporary economists to ignore their own findings.

We formally test whether the slope coefficient in our BF regressions is stable across the three major subperiods of our sample—the 1970s, 1980s, and 1990s—for all three markets. We find strong rejections of this conjecture. In chapter 13, we extend our structural-change analysis and find temporal instability within these major subperiods. Our analysis indicates that forward-rate predictions can be negatively biased, positively biased, unbiased, and devoid of predictive content during time periods of considerable duration. As with the exchange-rate-disconnect puzzle, therefore, the forward-discount "anomaly" is merely another artifact of the contemporary approach's insistence on constructing fully predetermined models.

8.1. The Record on Foreign Exchange Returns

The ex post return on a pure long position in foreign exchange held one period, R_{t+1}, can be written as:[4]

---

4. To take a pure long position in foreign exchange for one period, which requires no money down at time t, an individual would borrow, say, one unit of domestic currency at time t at the rate i_t. She would then immediately sell this domestic currency in the spot market at $\frac{1}{s_t}$ and lend

$$R_{t+1} = \Delta S_{t+1} + i_t^* - i_t, \tag{8.1}$$

where $\Delta S_{t+1} = S_{t+1} - s_t$ and i is defined as in previous chapters.[5] To model this return, economists assume that the exchange rate adjusts to equilibrate demand and supply. Whether individual preferences are represented as risk neutral or risk averse, or are based on prospect theory, equilibrium in the foreign exchange market under perfect capital mobility can be written as

$$\hat{r}_{t|t+1} = \widehat{pr}_{t|t+1}, \tag{8.2}$$

where $\hat{r}_{t|t+1}$ and $\widehat{pr}_{t|t+1}$ represent aggregates of all market participants' point forecasts of R_{t+1} and the premiums that they require to hold open positions in foreign exchange, conditional on their time t forecasting strategies and information sets, respectively.

The monetary models of the 1970s use REH to represent an individual's forecasting behavior and so equate $\hat{r}_{t|t+1}$ to the conditional expectation of R_{t+1} implied by these models. They also represent individual preferences as risk neutral, which implies that $\widehat{pr}_{t|t+1} = 0$. The assumptions of REH and UIP thus lead to the conclusion that the ex post return has a conditional mean of zero and is uncorrelated with the causal variables that an economist includes in his representation.

There has been much research investigating whether the joint hypothesis of UIP and REH is consistent with the data. Figures 8.1 through 8.3 plot the realized ex post monthly returns on holding foreign exchange (U.S. dollars) in the BP/\$, DM/\$, and JY/\$ markets over the modern period of floating rates.[6]

The data show that ex post returns vary widely over this period, between +150 percent and −150 percent on a per annum basis for all three currencies. The figures also suggest that foreign exchange returns are persistent. For example, R_{t+1} tends to be negative from 1976 through 1979 and generally positive from 1980 through 1985 for all three currencies. Hansen and

---

$\frac{1}{s_t}$ units of foreign currency at i_t^*. At the end of one period, our individual would sell $\frac{1}{s_t}(1 + i_t^*)$ units of foreign exchange spot at S_{t+1}. The total future return on her long position would be $\frac{S_{t+1}}{s_t}(1 + i_t^*) - (1 + i_t)$. Taking the present value and log approximations yields equation (8.1). To take a pure short position in foreign exchange, one would borrow foreign currency and lend domestic currency. It is straightforward to show that the return on this short position is given by $-R_{t+1}$. We note that forward contracts can also be used to take pure long and short positions in foreign exchange.

5. This return is often referred to as an excess return because $S_{t+1} - s_t + i_t^*$ is the return on holding foreign assets and i_t is the return on domestic assets in domestic currency.

6. To measure the ex post monthly return, we use data on the spot and one-month forward exchange rates from Data Resources, Inc. As long as covered interest rate parity holds, $R_{t+1} = S_{t+1} - f_t$, where f_t denotes the log of the forward exchange rate. Our sample spans the period from May 1973 through February 1997.

Figure 8.1   Actual Return: BP/$

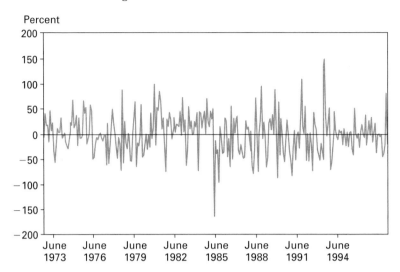

Figure 8.2   Actual Return: DM/$

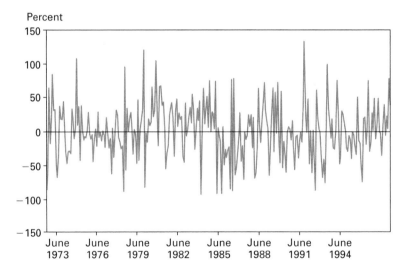

Figure 8.3   Actual Return: JY/$

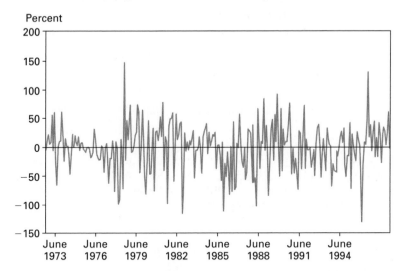

Hodrick (1980) and Cumby and Obstfeld (1981) formally test for persistence in actual returns in several markets, including those for the DM/$, BP/$, and JY/$, and reject the null hypothesis of no persistence in all cases.

Much of the research that tests UIP and REH has been based on the BF regression:

$$\triangle S_{t+1} = \alpha + \beta fp_t + u_{t+1}, \tag{8.3}$$

where $fp_t = f_t - s_t$ is the forward premium, f_t is the log of the forward exchange rate, and u_{t+1} is an error term. Under the null hypothesis of UIP and REH, $\alpha = 0$, $\beta = 1$, and u_{t+1} has a conditional mean of zero.

To see this, we write the equilibrium condition in equation (8.2) as

$$\triangle S_{t+1} = \widehat{pr}_{t|t+1} - fp_t + u_{t+1}, \tag{8.4}$$

where $u_{t+1} = \triangle S_{t+1} - \triangle \widehat{S}_{t|t+1}$ is the forecast error implied by an economist's representation of the market's conditional forecast of $\triangle S_{t+1}$. Thus, the projection of $\triangle S_{t+1}$ on fp_t in equation (8.3) can be expressed as

$$E\left(\triangle S_{t+1}|fp_t\right) = E\left(\widehat{pr}_{t|t+1}|fp_t\right) + fp_t + E\left(u_{t+1}|fp_t\right). \tag{8.5}$$

Table 8.1   The BF Regression: Full-Sample Estimates[a]

Currency	Sample period	$\hat{\alpha}$	$\hat{\beta}$	R^2
DM	May 1973–February 1997	−0.002	−0.52	.002
		(0.002)	(0.72)	
BP	May 1973–February 1997	0.005***	**−1.52****	.016
		(0.002)	(0.71)	
JY	January 1975–February 1997	−0.007***	**−3.97*****	.025
		(0.002)	(1.52)	

[a] Standard errors are in parentheses. ** and *** indicate significance from zero at the 5 and 1 percent levels, respectively. Bold numbers for $\hat{\beta}$ indicate significance from one at the 5 percent level. DM, BP, and JY denote the German mark, British pound, and Japanese yen markets, respectively.

If UIP and REH both hold, then $E\left(\widehat{pr}_{t|t+1}|fp_t\right) = E\left(u_{t+1}|fp_t\right) = 0$, thereby implying that $\alpha = 0$ and $\beta = 1$. In this case, the forward premium is an unbiased predictor of the future spot rate.

In table 8.1, we report OLS estimates of the BF regression under the assumption that its parameters are constant. For the full sample, we find estimates of β that are significantly less than one when based on the *t*-statistic in all three cases and significantly less than zero in the pound and yen markets. These results are typical of the results found in the literature. Froot and Thaler (1990) report that the average of the full-sample point estimates of β in 75 published articles is −0.88. Thus, the results of much empirical study seem to suggest that the ex post return on foreign exchange in many markets is correlated not only with its past values but also with the forward premium.[7]

8.2. An REH Risk Premium?

Conventional international macroeconomists have constructed several types of risk-premium models of foreign exchange returns, including portfolio-balance models (Solnik, 1974; Kouri, 1978; Kouri and De Macedo, 1978; Dornbusch, 1983b) and intertemporal consumption-based asset-pricing models (Lucas, 1982; Svensson, 1985). We discuss the portfolio balance model and its failure to explain the behavior of foreign exchange returns in chapter 12. In this section, we focus on the failure of consumption-based asset-pricing models.

---

7. $\beta \neq 1$ implies a correlation between R_{t+1} and fp_t, since $R_{t+1} = \alpha + (\beta - 1)\left(fp_t - s_t\right) + u_{t+1}$.

8.2.1. Inability to Explain Variability

We sketched such a model in the appendix to chapter 6. One of the Euler equations implied by this model, which governs the equilibrium real return on any asset, is given by

$$\frac{1}{p_t C_t^\phi} = (1 + i_t)\, \beta E\left[\frac{1}{P_{t+1} C_{t+1}^\phi} \mid x_t \right], \tag{8.6}$$

where, given the CRRA utility function, $C^{-\phi}$ is the marginal utility of consumption.[8] In equilibrium, the utility derived from a unit of domestic currency in period t, $\frac{1}{p_t C_t^\phi}$, must equal the discounted, expected utility from lending this domestic currency for one period and consuming the proceeds in period $t + 1$: $(1 + i_t)\, \beta E\left[\frac{1}{P_{t+1} C_{t+1}^\phi} \mid x_t \right]$. But a pure long position in foreign exchange requires no money down in period t. According to the model, therefore, the expected utility from such positions must be zero in equilibrium, thereby implying:

$$E\left[\frac{(f_t - S_{t+1})}{P_{t+1}} \left(\frac{C_t}{C_{t+1}} \right)^\phi \mid x_t \right] = 0. \tag{8.7}$$

Mark (1985) was the earliest study to test the implications of equation (8.7), and his results are typical of those reported by later researchers. Mark estimates ϕ jointly for the DM/\$, BP/\$, Dutch guilder/\$, and Canadian dollar/\$ markets using a generalized method of moments estimator, with the forward premium and its lags as instrumental variables. He rejects the overidentifying restrictions implied by the model. He also reports estimates of ϕ above 40, which are implausibly high.[9] These estimates, however, are found to be insignificantly different from zero.

The problem with the model can be seen by imposing the usual assumption that variables are lognormally distributed and rewriting equation (8.7) as:

$$\hat{r}_{t|t+1} = \phi\, Cov_t\left(C_{t+1}, S_{t+1} \mid x_t \right), \tag{8.8}$$

---

8. We recall that, unless otherwise indicated, lower-case letters denote realizations of time t variables and not, as is customary in the literature, log values.

9. Krugman (1981) suggests that a plausible value for ϕ is 2, while Mehra and Prescott (1985), who also find a high ϕ when estimating the intertemporal asset-pricing model in the equity market, argue that a value above 10 is unreasonable.

where $Cov_t\left(C_{t+1},\ S_{t+1}\mid x_t\right)$ is the conditional covariance between log values of C_{t+1} and S_{t+1}.[10] By imposing REH, an economist ties his representation of forecasting behavior rigidly to the other components of his model, which in the setup here implies that $\hat{r}_{t|t+1}$ depends on individuals' degree of risk aversion and the co-variation between consumption and the spot exchange rate. But C is simply not variable enough. Consequently, the high variation in actual returns forces ϕ to be implausibly high.

Other studies based on longer sample periods, additional exchange rates, and expanded utility specifications have found similar results.[11] In reviewing the empirical record, Charles Engel concludes that consumption is "not variable enough to explain the high variance of ex ante returns from foreign exchange without implausibly large estimates of the coefficient of relative risk aversion" (Engel, 1996, p. 155).[12]

8.2.2. An Inability to Explain Sign Reversals

There is another dimension along which REH risk-premium models fail to provide reasonable explanations of the data. Researchers find that regression-based estimates of expected returns on foreign exchange experience frequent sign reversals over the modern period of floating rates.[13]

In principle, the conditional covariance $Cov_t\left(C_{t+1},\ S_{t+1}\mid x_t\right)$ may change sign as new realizations of x_t emerge. Mark and Wu (1998) test the prediction of the model that positive (negative) values of $\hat{r}_{t|t+1}$ should be associated with a positive (negative) $Cov_t\left(C_{t+1},\ S_{t+1}\mid x_t\right)$. To place the model in the best possible light, Mark and Wu assume habit persistence and choose a relative degree of risk aversion equal to 7. The authors find a tendency for $\hat{r}_t > 0$ when $Cov_t\left(C_{t+1},\ S_{t+1}\mid x_t\right) < 0$.

---

10. Equation (8.8) follows much of the literature and omits the Jensen's inequality term $\frac{1}{2} Var_t(S_{t+1}) - Cov_t(S_{t+1}, P_{t+1})$. This term is widely recognized to be small and unable to account for the behavior of returns. See Engel (1996).

11. See, for example, Modjtahedi (1991), Kaminsky and Peruga (1990), and Backus et al. (1993).

12. Implausibly large estimates of ϕ also emerge from studies that use money and income data rather than consumption data.

13. With negative estimates of the slope coefficient and a zero intercept, the expected return implied by the BF regression switches sign every time the forward premium switches sign. Lewis (1995) shows, for example, that the fitted values from the BF regression for the DM/\$ and JY/\$ markets change sign many times in a sample that begins in 1975 and ends in 1989. Mark and Wu (1998) and Mark (2001) find similar behavior using the fitted values from a bivariate vector error-correction model of the change in the exchange rate and the forward premium for the same markets plus the BP/\$ market.

8.3. Is Irrationality the Answer?

The empirical failure of REH risk-premium models has led many economists to the view that the market premium is constant and that foreign
exchange returns are driven by decisions of market participants who are
"irrational." This perspective has motivated some of them to construct fully
predetermined models in which UIP holds and market participants systematically mispredict foreign exchange returns.

8.3.1. *Ignoring Systematic Forecast Errors*

Mark and Wu (1998), for example, construct a model along the lines of
DeLong et al. (1990b), in which the REH forecasting rule is attributed to
"fully informed" individuals and another fixed forecasting rule is attributed
to noise traders. Noise traders are assumed to believe, erroneously, that
returns depend on factors other than fp_t, which leads them to form forecasts
of R_{t+1} that are systematically distorted. In this model, the number of traders
who are fully informed and those who hold distorted beliefs is fixed. The
Gourinchas and Tornell (2004) model also attempts to explain returns in
currency markets on the basis of irrational behavior. As we discussed in
chapter 7, this model presumes that all market participants systematically
underpredict the degree of persistence of interest-rate shocks.

In both of these models, the return on foreign exchange is persistent
and, under a range of parameter values, negatively correlated with the
forward premium, thereby implying a negative slope coefficient in the
BF regression. However, by fully predetermining their representations of
individual behavior, both models imply that market participants are not only
irrational, but grossly irrational. Although a rule as simple as betting against
the forward premium would generate profits in these models, individuals
are presumed to ignore this possibility and adhere to their fixed non-REH
forecasting rules in perpetuity.

8.3.2. *Evidence from Ex Ante Data*

Empirical studies that make use of survey data to measure expected returns
seem to support the view that market participants are grossly irrational.
The seminal studies in this literature are Frankel and Froot (1987) and
Froot and Frankel (1989).[14] Froot and Frankel's survey data are from the
Economist, American Express Banking Corporation (AMEX), and Money
Market Services International (MMSI). The data consist of the median

14. See also Taylor (1988), MacDonald and Torrance (1988), Ito (1990), and Liu and Maddala
(1992). For a review of this literature, see Takagi (1991).

of participants' forecasts at various horizons for several exchange rates, including the DM/\$, BP/\$, and JY/\$.[15]

Using the survey data to measure $\Delta \widehat{S}_{t+1}$, Froot and Frankel (1989) run the following regression:

$$\Delta \widehat{S}_{t|t+1} = \alpha' + \beta' fp_t + v_{t+1}, \qquad (8.9)$$

where v_{t+1} is an error term that captures measurement error.[16] Under the null hypothesis that the market premium, $\widehat{pr}_{t|t+1} = \Delta \widehat{S}_{t+1} - fp_t$, is equal to some constant, say, c, then $\alpha' = c$ and $\beta' = 1$.

In seven of the nine cases that Froot and Frankel examine, they find estimates of the slope coefficient that are statistically indistinguishable from unity under the assumption that the parameters in equation (8.9) are constant.[17] They also report a significant intercept in every case. Thus, the ex ante data seem to suggest that the market premium is constant. This conclusion, in turn, implies that the observed correlation between ex post returns and the forward premium is entirely due to systematic forecast errors.[18]

In table 8.2, we report full-sample estimates of the regression in equation (8.9) using survey data from MMSI.[19] We find that the full-sample estimate of the slope coefficient for the DM/\$ market is insignificantly different from unity, which is consistent with Frankel and Froot's (1989) findings. We also find that the intercept of this regression is insignificant, suggesting that the

15. The MMSI data are monthly and consist of one- and three-month forecasts for the DM/\$, BP/\$, JY/\$, and Swiss franc/\$ exchange rates. The *Economist* data are biannual and consist of three-, six-, and twelve-month forecasts for these four exchange rates plus the French franc/\$, whereas the AMEX survey was conducted every six weeks for the six- and twelve-month forecast horizons.

16. The surveys ask respondents for point forecasts of S_{t+1} rather than for forecasts of the future rate of change of the spot rate. Moreover, for the MMSI and *Economist* surveys, participants are allowed to respond by phone throughout the day of the survey, whereas for the AMEX survey, participants respond by mail over a period of up to a month. To construct an observation on $\Delta \widehat{S}_{t|t+1}$, however, Froot and Frankel must use one spot rate at a particular time on a particular day, which is not, in general, the spot rate respondents used in forming their point forecasts of S_{t+1}. Nevertheless, there is no reason to believe that the measurement error is systematic.

17. Froot and Frankel pool the data across all currencies at each forecast horizon for each survey. This method gives rise to seven regressions. (See footnote 15.) They pool the data across all currencies and forecast horizons for the *Economist* and AMEX data as well, giving rise to two more regressions.

18. Froot and Frankel provide evidence that the forecast errors implied by the survey data are correlated with the forward premium. However, as with the regression in equation (8.9), they make no allowance for the possibility that this relationship may be unstable. In chapter 13, we find that this relationship is indeed unstable and discuss the implications of this finding for market efficiency.

19. Our data consist of one-month forecasts for the DM/\$, BP/\$, and JY/\$ exchange rates over a sample that runs from December 1982 through February 1997. Unfortunately, MMSI no longer exists, leaving us unable to update our sample.

Table 8.2 Survey Data: Full-Sample Estimates[a]

Currency	Sample period	$\hat{\alpha}$	$\hat{\beta}$	R^2
DM	December 1983–February 1997	1.25	1.11*	.084
		(0.98)	(0.28)	
BP	December 1983–February 1997	4.372***	−.207**	.002
		(1.433)	(0.381)	
JY	December 1983–February 1997	−2.025	**−0.554**	.008
		(1.496)	(0.470)	

[a] Standard errors are in parentheses. ** and *** indicate significance from zero at the 5 and 1 percent levels, respectively. Bold numbers for $\hat{\beta}$ indicate significance from one at the 5 percent level. DM, BP, and JY denote the German mark, British pound, and Japanese yen markets, respectively.

market premium is not only constant, but zero. However, unlike Frankel and Froot, we find estimates of the slope coefficient that are significantly less than one for the BP/\$ and JY/\$ markets, indicating the presence of a time-varying risk premium. But these results, like those of Froot and Frankel (1989), are misleading: in a world of imperfect knowledge, we would not expect regressions based on equation (8.9) to be temporally stable.

Given the definition of the premium, the projection in equation (8.9) implies that

$$E\left(\widehat{pr}_{t|t+1}|fp_t\right) = E\left(\Delta\widehat{S}_{t|t+1}|fp_t\right) - fp_t. \qquad (8.10)$$

Thus, changes in the relationship between market participants' forecasts of ΔS_{t+1} and the causal factors that enter their forecasting strategies will, in general, cause instability in the relationship between the market premium and the forward premium, as long as the forward premium is either among the causal factors or correlated with them. Moreover, instability would also follow from changes in the social context that cause the process driving fp to change.

Table 8.3 reports estimates of regressions based on equation (8.9) using the MMSI survey data for three subperiods in the 1980s and 1990s. We find that estimates of the slope coefficient are not unity, as suggested by the results of Froot and Frankel (1989) or our results for the DM/\$ market when based on the entire sample. Rather, the slope coefficient is at times negative, positive and less than one, insignificantly different from one, and greater than one. In almost every case, the null hypothesis of no structural change can be rejected with very low p-values.

Table 8.3   **Survey Data: Subsample Estimates**[a]

Currency	Sample period[b]	$\hat{\alpha}$	$\hat{\beta}$	R^2	Structural change test[c]
DM	December 1982–December 1984	−9.298	**−1.94**	.077	198.46
	(December 1989)	(6.789)	(1.43)		(.00)
	January 1985–December 1989	−9.41	**−0.81**	.004	151.15
	(December 1994)	(5.06)	(1.69)		(.00)
	January 1990–December 1993	−6.85**	**2.95***	.267	134.09
	(February 1997)	(2.97)	(0.72)		(.00)
BP	December 1982–December 1984	4.95**	−0.23	.001	162.65
	(December 1989)	(1.96)	(1.43)		(.00)
	January 1985–December 1989	17.21***	**5.28**	.212	75.01
	(December 1994)	(5.22)	(1.34)		(.09)
	January 1990–December 1993	13.50	**−1.35**	.049	28.58
	(February 1997)	(4.78)	(0.87)		(.87)
JY	December 1982–December 1984	10.352**	**−2.354**	.140	272.71
	(December 1989)	(4.610)	(1.216)		(.00)
	January 1985–December 1989	−5.775	0.535	.003	68.460
	(December 1994)	(4.155)	(1.342)		(.210)
	January 1990–December 1993	−2.931	3.673**	.087	249.82
	(February 1997)	(1.849)	(1.757)		(.00)

[a] Standard errors for $\hat{\alpha}$ and $\hat{\beta}$ are in parentheses. ** and *** indicate significance from zero at the 5 and 1 percent levels, respectively. Bold numbers for $\hat{\beta}$ indicate significance from one at the 5 percent level. DM, BP, and JY denote the German mark, British pound, and Japanese yen markets, respectively.
[b] Dates in parentheses indicate the end of the forecast period used for the structural change test reported in the last column of the table. In each case, the forecast period begins on the first month after the in-sample period.
[c] Forecast χ^2 test of Hendry (1980), p-values are in parentheses.

These results indicate that the premium in currency markets is not constant. Moreover, they indicate that the relationship between this premium and macroeconomic variables, such as the forward premium, is temporally unstable. Thus, any empirically relevant model of the premium must be consistent with this instability.

8.4. The Forward-Discount "Anomaly": Another Artifact of the Contemporary Approach

The foreign exchange market is the largest financial market in the world, with an estimated daily volume close to two trillion U.S. dollars. The stakes in this market, as in any other large asset market, are extremely high. Financial institutions, which hire the bulk of the participants who move the markets, pay large sums of money to attract the best and the brightest. Is it really possible that these individuals can make money by following a rule as simple as one based on estimates of the BF regression, and that they do not recognize this opportunity?

It is clear from equations (8.5) and (8.10) that instability in the relationship between market participants' forecasts of ΔS_{t+1} and the forward premium will cause instability in the BF regression. Table 8.4 reports estimates of the BF regression for the 1970s, 1980s and 1990s.

As with the regression in equation (8.9), we find that estimates of the slope coefficient differ considerably across the three major subperiods. In four of the six cases, we reject the null hypothesis of no structural change with very low p values. Bekaert and Hodrick (1993), Lewis (1995), Engel (1996), and Mark and Wu (1998) also find very different estimates of β when they split their samples into the 1970s and 1980s. Bekaert and Hodrick (1993) formally test for structural change and reject the no-break null hypothesis at very low significance levels.

In chapter 13, we extend our structural-change analysis and find temporal instability within the subperiods examined in table 8.4. The results show that forward-rate predictions are at times negatively biased, positively biased, unbiased, and devoid of predictive content during periods of considerable duration. Thus, betting against the forward rate may be profitable during some periods but not others. Moreover, because β is sometimes positive and sometimes negative, regression estimates based on equation (8.3) are likely to be profitable only if one is able to predict in advance the timing and nature of the structural change. We show, unsurprisingly, that trading rules based on betting against forward-rate predictions do not deliver significant profits over the modern period of floating in the DM/\$, BP/\$, and JY/\$ markets. Devising a profitable trading strategy in currency markets, it turns out, is considerably more difficult than preprogramming a rule based on the BF regression. These results lead us to rethink the implications of market efficiency for outcomes in financial markets.

Table 8.4   BF Regression: Subsample Estimates and Temporal Instability[a]

Currency	Sample period[b]	$\hat{\alpha}$	$\hat{\beta}$	R^2	Structural change test[c]
DM	May 1973–December 1979	−0.340	0.85	.003	174.33
	(December 1989)	(0.577)	(2.02)		(.00)
	January 1980–December 1989	−1.794**	**−5.57**	.062	122.32
	(February 1997	(0.886)	(2.81)		(.00)
	January 1990–February 1997)	−0.057	−0.16	.000	—
		(0.355)	(1.52)		
BP	May 1973–December 1979	−0.170	−0.04)	.000	190.63
	(December 1989)	(0.539)	(1.12)		(.00)
	January 1980–December 1989	−0.908**	**−4.49****	.106	92.72
	(February 1997)	(0.323)	(1.114)		(.24)
	January 1990–February 1997	0.280	1.20	.006	—
		(0.416)	(1.86)		
JY	May 1973–December 1979	−0.054	1.63	.033	177.60
	(December 1989)	(0.326)	(1.09)		(.00)
	January 1980–December 1989	−1.305***	**−6.41****	.047	67.57
	(February 1997)	(0.496)	(2.95)		(.90)
	January 1990–February 1997	−0.277	**−7.16**	.043	—
		(0.331)	(3.77)		

[a] Standard errors for $\hat{\alpha}$ and $\hat{\beta}$ are in parentheses. ** and *** indicate significance from zero at the 5 and 1 percent levels, respectively. Bold numbers for $\hat{\beta}$ indicate significance from one at the 5 percent level. DM, BP, and JY denote the German mark, British pound, and Japanese yen markets, respectively.

[b] Dates in parentheses indicate the end of the forecast period used for the structural change test reported in the last column of the table. In each case, the forecast period begins on the first month after the in-sample period.

[c] Forecast χ^2 test of Hendry (1980), p-values are in parentheses. — indicates last subperiod of sample.

PART III

Imperfect Knowledge Economics of Exchange Rates and Risk

9 Modeling Preferences in Asset Markets

Experimental Evidence and Imperfect Knowledge

Like extant approaches, IKE constructs its models of aggregate outcomes on individual foundations. These foundations consist of representations of an individual's preferences over alternative uses of resources, her constraints, and her forecasts of future outcomes that are relevant to her well-being. IKE also imposes qualitative conditions on its representations at an initial arbitrary point in time. But, in sharp contrast to the contemporary approach, IKE does not fully prespecify how its representations of an individual's decision making change between an initial point in time and all other points in time. In this and the following chapter we develop representations of preferences and forecasting strategies that will serve as the building blocks of our IKE models of individual behavior and aggregate outcomes in the foreign exchange market.

Conventional representations of preferences are based on a set of a priori assumptions that economists suppose characterize how rational individuals rank the alternative uses of resources available to them. One of these assumptions, which underpins the vast majority of representations of portfolio-allocation decisions, is risk aversion. To represent the preferences of risk-averse investors, economists use a class of parametric functions, such as the one employed in the appendix to chapter 6, that relate an individual's utility to her level of wealth. To specify preferences over gambles that can result in one of a number of uncertain outcomes, conventional economists have relied on the *expected utility hypothesis* (von Neumann and Morgenstern, 1944): the utility of a gamble is equal to the expected value of the utilities of the single outcomes that comprise the gamble.[1] There is, however, much research showing that

> the deviations of actual behavior from the normative model [based on expected utility theory] are too widespread to be ignored, too systematic to be dismissed as a random error, and too fundamental to be accommodated by relaxing the normative system. (Tversky and Kahneman, 1986, p. S252)

The gross empirical failure of risk-averse preferences and the expected utility hypothesis led Kahneman and Tversky (1979) and Tversky and Kahneman (1992) to develop prospect theory, which summarizes their findings on how individuals actually choose among gambles with uncertain outcomes in laboratory experiments. Tversky and Kahneman formalize these findings with three assumptions. One supposes that an individual's utility depends on the change in an individual's wealth or some other outcome variable (gain or loss), relative to some reference point, rather than on the level of her final wealth per se. Prospect theory also assumes that individuals are loss averse: they are more sensitive to a loss than to a gain of the same magnitude. Finally, this alternative theory assumes that an individual's utility depends nonlinearly on the magnitudes of gains and losses—it is concave in the domain of gains and convex in the domain of losses. Tversky and Kahneman (1992) formalize these assumptions with a parametric specification of an individual's utility function.

Prospect theory represents preferences over gambles with prospective utilities, which are defined as weighted sums of the values of the single outcomes that make up the gambles. Kahneman and Tversky (1979) present experimental evidence that these weights, which they call "decision weights," are nonlinear functions of true probabilities. Because the true probabilities are perfectly known to subjects in an experimental setting, the distinction between decision weights and true probabilities can be inferred from subjects' choices among the gambles presented to them by the experimenter. On the basis of their experimental data, Tversky and Kahneman (1992) estimate a nonlinear function relating the decision weights to true probabilities.

As compelling as Kahneman and Tversky's experimental evidence is concerning the properties of the utility function, its nonlinearity poses several difficulties for using prospect theory to model both individual be-

---

1. To distinguish between preferences over gambles that result in one of two or more uncertain outcomes and preferences over single outcomes comprising a gamble, we refer to the latter as the "utilities of single outcomes."

havior and aggregate outcomes. Extant behavioral finance models typically sidestep these difficulties by disregarding Kahneman and Tversky's empirical finding of diminishing sensitivity: they constrain the utility function to be linear over gains and losses.[2] We show in this chapter, however, that this linear "simplification" is actually quite costly: it implies that an individual would want to take a position of unlimited size whenever she perceives a profit opportunity, thereby ruling out a well-defined equilibrium.

Kahneman and Tversky (1979) present experimental evidence indicating that the utility function is not only nonlinear, but that its curvature in the domain of losses may be greater than in the domain of gains. The latter observation leads us to propose a modification of Tversky and Kahneman's (1992) utility function that implies a positive relationship between the degree of loss aversion and the size of the stake. This feature of the utility function, which we call *endogenous loss aversion,* enables us to model limits to speculation, and thereby derive a well-defined equilibrium, on the basis of prospect theory.

By contrast, to model limits to speculation, which are usually called "limits to arbitrage," Barberis et al. (2001), as well as other behavioral finance theorists, rely on a utility function that embodies both risk aversion and loss aversion. This reliance on risk aversion in recent behavioral finance models is puzzling in view of the fact that its rejection in favor of loss aversion has come to be viewed as one of the key findings in behavioral economics.

Beyond jettisoning risk aversion, our formulation of preferences differs from extant behavioral finance models in two important respects. Because the size of the speculative position depends on an individual's forecast, which we only partially prespecify, the degree of loss aversion, and thus the representation of preferences, is also only partially predetermined in our model. Moreover, our formulation of the utility function is linear in single gains and losses but nonlinear in the position size. We show that, in contrast to extant specifications, our alternative is consistent with Kahneman and Tversky's empirical findings.

Our formulation of the utility function for single outcomes also enables us to address an important problem that is inherent in any application of prospect theory. To derive implications of prospect theory–based models and confront them with time-series data on asset prices, an economist must relate prospective utilities, which are decision-weighted sums, to some causal variables.[3] However, as Kahneman and Tversky (1979, pp. 288–289)

2. For example, see Barberis et al. (2001).

3. The linearization of the utility function, which we mentioned above, sidesteps this problem: it replaces prospective utilities with linear functions of expected values. An alternative approach is taken by Benartzi and Thaler (1995), who develop a model of the premium on U.S. stocks over

have pointed out: "in the typical situation of choice, where the probabilities of outcomes are not explicitly given[,] . . . the decision weights may be affected by other considerations, such as ambiguity or vagueness." They cite Ellsberg (1961) and Fellner (1965), who used the terms *ambiguity* and *vagueness* to refer to factors that cannot be represented adequately with specific parametric functions of probabilities. These additional factors and other considerations that arise from the imperfection of knowledge is what distinguishes decision making in real world markets from that in experimental settings where the experimenter conveys to his subjects the true probability distribution of payoffs.

Disregarding the distinction between decision-weighted sums and expected values of prospects may be unavoidable. But we have argued that, in representing an individual's behavior, regardless of whether an economist uses prospect theory or any other specification of utility, an economist should not presume that he can fully prespecify the way she makes and revises her decisions. Consequently, in modeling preferences over gambles with uncertain outcomes, we replace the decision-weighted sums that are involved in the definition of prospective utilities with IKE representations of an individual's forecasts of the return and potential loss from holding speculative positions. In this way, we do not disregard the importance of ambiguity and vagueness in how individuals make decisions in real world markets. We call our alternative approach to representing preferences over gambles "endogenous prospect theory."

Our use of endogenous prospect theory to model an individual's speculative decision leads to a key result: all speculators require a minimum return—a premium—to commit capital to speculating in the foreign exchange market. We show that this premium depends positively on an individual's forecast of the potential loss from speculation.

Extant approaches model an individual's premium on the basis of risk-averse preferences and fully predetermined, predominantly REH, representations of individual forecasts. By contrast, the premium that we derive recognizes that the main risk that individuals face in real world markets stems from the inherent imperfection of knowledge. Echoing Knight's (1921) distinction between uncertainty and risk, we call the premium implied by our IKE model of the speculative decision an *individual uncertainty premium*.

---

bonds in which decision weights are computed using Tversky and Kahneman's (1992) experimentally based weighting function of probabilities. However, as we point out in section 9.3.1, this approach not only disregards the inapplicability of experimentally based weighting functions in real world settings, but is also unsuitable in modeling how individual behavior and aggregate outcomes change over time.

9.1. Prospect Theory and Speculative Decisions

Kahneman and Tversky specify an individual's preferences over alternative allocations of her resources in terms of gains and losses in wealth relative to some reference point. We begin by defining these terms in the context of the foreign exchange market.

9.1.1. Basic Setup

We assume that there are two countries, A and B, and two types of non-monetary assets, A and B bonds. Bonds of types A and B are denominated in country-A currency (to be referred to as the "domestic currency") and country-B currency, respectively. The riskless nominal returns on these bonds from time t to $t + 1$ are denoted by i_t^A and i_t^B, respectively. There are no barriers to short selling, implying that both domestic and foreign individuals can issue A and B bonds (that is, borrow domestic and foreign currency, respectively) without limit.

As before, we use log approximations to define the ex post nominal return on a pure long position in foreign exchange held one period, R_{t+1}^L:

$$R_{t+1}^L = S_{t+1} - s_t + i_t^B - i_t^A, \tag{9.1}$$

where s_t denotes the log level of the spot rate at time t.[4] Analogously, the ex post nominal return on a pure short position in foreign exchange held one period is given by:

$$R_{t+1}^S = s_t - S_{t+1} + i_t^A - i_t^B. \tag{9.2}$$

The speculative decision problems faced by country-A and country-B wealth holders are identical. Consequently, we develop our analysis from the point of view of country-A individuals.

Following prospect theory, we assume that the carriers of value are gains and losses in wealth relative to some reference level. Using log approximations, we can write the change in wealth relative to some reference level as:

$$\begin{aligned} \Delta W_{t+1}^i &= W_{t+1}^i - \Gamma_t^i \\ &= W_t^i \left[a_t^i R_{t+1} + \left(1 + i_t^A - p_t \right) \right] - \Gamma_t^i, \end{aligned} \tag{9.3}$$

---

4. See footnote 4 in chapter 8 for how an individual would take a pure long or short position in foreign exchange.

where W_t^i denotes an individual's nonmonetary real wealth at time t, a_t^i denotes an individual's portfolio share of B bonds at time t, p_t is the non-stochastic domestic rate of inflation, Γ_t^i denotes an individual's reference level, and the random variable R_{t+1} is the one-period-ahead return on a pure long position in foreign exchange, as well as the excess real return on B bonds relative to A bonds.[5] Whenever $\Delta W_{t+1}^i > 0$ ($\Delta W_{t+1}^i < 0$), an individual is said to experience a gain (a loss).

The definitions of a gain and loss in equation (9.3) leave open the specification of the reference level. In general, each individual chooses her own reference level. But neither prospect theory nor available experimental evidence provides guidance as to how an economist should represent an individual's reference level.[6] Nevertheless, there seems to be a natural reference level in the context of a decision to speculate: the level of wealth an individual would obtain were she to stay out of the market.

We attribute this reference level to each individual in defining losses and gains from participation in foreign exchange speculation:[7]

$$\Gamma_t^i = W_t^i \left(1 + i_t^A - p_t \right) \quad \text{for all } i \text{ and } t. \tag{9.4}$$

Substitution of equation (9.4) into equation (9.3) yields the following expression for the change in an individual's wealth relative to her reference level:

$$\Delta W_{t+1}^i = a_t^i W_t^i R_{t+1}. \tag{9.5}$$

A positive realization of R_{t+1}, which we denote by r_{t+1}^+, leads to a gain for an individual who holds a long position (that is, $a_t^i > 0$) and a loss if she holds a short position (that is, $a_t^i < 0$).[8] A negative realization of R_{t+1}, which we

---

5. For a domestic wealth holder, the real return on B and A bonds is $S_{t+1} - s_t + i_t^A - p_t$ and $i_t^A - p_t$, respectively, where we assume that domestic individuals use only domestic prices to deflate nominal values. We note that $W_{t+1}^i = W_t^i [a_t^i(S_{t+1} - s_t + i_t^B - p_t) + (1 - a_t^i)(i_t^A - p_t)] = W_t^i [a_t^i R_{t+1} + (1 + i_t^A - p_t)]$. Because exchange rates are considerably more volatile than goods prices, the assumption of a nonstochastic inflation rate is common in the portfolio-balance literature. See, for example, Krugman (1981), Frankel (1982), and Dornbusch (1983b).

6. Kahneman and Tversky (1979) conclude on the basis of experimental evidence that the choice of a reference level depends on idiosyncratic factors, such as individual perceptions and interpretations of the outcomes offered by a gamble. See Ang et al. (2004) for an extensive discussion of the difficulties inherent in modeling the reference level in the context of prospect theory.

7. Other studies that use this reference level in applying prospect theory to modeling asset prices include Barberis and Huang (2001) and Barberis et al. (2001).

8. We note that for a domestic individual to hold a short position in foreign exchange, she must hold A bonds in excess of the value of her total wealth, $\left(1 - a_t^i \right) > 1$. She does so by borrowing foreign exchange at i_t^B (that is, by issuing B bonds), selling this foreign exchange spot for domestic currency, and using the proceeds to buy A bonds.

denote by r_{t+1}^{-}, leads to the converse. It is common to refer to individuals with long and short positions as "bulls" and "bears," respectively.

9.1.2. Utility Function

It is useful to refer to each possible value of ΔW_{t+1}^{i} as a prospect.[9] Kahneman and Tversky's formulation of prospect theory postulates that risky prospects are evaluated by a utility function that has the following three basic characteristics:[10]

Reference Dependence *"The carriers of [utility] are gains and losses defined relative to a reference point."*

Loss Aversion *The disutility from losses exceeds the utility from gains of the same magnitude for all values of gains and losses. As Tversky and Kahneman put it, "losses loom larger than corresponding gains."*

Diminishing Sensitivity *"The marginal utility of both gains and losses decreases with their size." Equivalently, the utility function is concave in the domain of gains and convex in the domain of losses.*

Tversky and Kahneman (1992) propose the following utility function embodying these three characteristics to represent the preferences of loss averse individuals:

$$V(\Delta W) = \begin{cases} (\Delta W)^{\alpha} & \text{if } \Delta W > 0 \\ -\lambda(-\Delta W)^{\beta} & \text{if } \Delta W < 0, \end{cases} \qquad (9.6)$$

where $V(\cdot)$ is defined over gains and losses in wealth relative to a reference level, λ is a constant, and for convenience we suppress the indices i and t. In the context of our setup for the foreign exchange market, the utility function in equation (9.6) takes the following form:

$$V(\Delta W) = \begin{cases} (W \,|ar^{g}|)^{\alpha} & \text{if } \Delta W > 0 \\ -\lambda(W \,|ar^{l}|)^{\beta} & \text{if } \Delta W < 0, \end{cases} \qquad (9.7)$$

where[11]

9. By contrast, Kahneman and Tversky refer to a prospect as all possible values of ΔW_{t+1}^{i} and their probabilities.

10. See Tversky and Kahneman (1991, pp. 1039–40).

11. Note that postive (negative) values of R_{t+1} imply a gain (loss) on long positions and a loss (gain) on short positions. It is convenient, however, to define gains and losses on both long and short positions as positive and negative values, respectively.

$$a > 0, \; r^g = r^+_{t+1}, \; r^l = r^-_{t+1} \quad \text{for a bull} \tag{9.8}$$

$$a < 0, \; r^g = -r^-_{t+1}, \; r^l = -r^+_{t+1} \quad \text{for a bear.}$$

Diminishing sensitivity implies that the utility function in equation (9.7) is concave over gains and convex over losses; that is, $\alpha < 1$ and $\beta < 1$. Researchers using equation (9.7) often constrain the utility function to be linear over gains and losses, that is, they constrain $\alpha = \beta = 1$. Under this assumption, the degree of loss aversion—defined as the ratio of the disutility from losses over the utility from gains of the same magnitude, which we denote by Λ—is equal to the constant λ. In this case, the function in equation (9.6) is said to embody loss aversion if $\lambda > 1$. We also note that equation (9.6) can be rewritten as $V(\Delta W) = (W \, |ar^g|)^\alpha - \lambda (W \, |ar^l|)^{\beta - \alpha} (W \, |ar^l|)^\alpha$, from which it follows that:

$$\Lambda = \lambda (|\Delta W|)^{\beta - \alpha}. \tag{9.9}$$

More generally, then, the degree of loss aversion is given by the constant λ as long as the curvatures in the domains of gains and losses are equal, that is, $\alpha = \beta$.

9.1.3. Preferences over Gambles

In addition to the utility function over single outcomes, any theory of choice in uncertain situations, regardless of whether it is based on prospect theory or embodies risk aversion, must represent preferences over gambles, each of which may result in one of two or more potential outcomes.

9.1.3.1. Experimentally Based Representations

To represent preferences over gambles, Kahneman and Tversky (1979) and Tversky and Kahneman (1992) report on laboratory experiments in which a subject was asked to choose among J gambles. In such a setting, an experimenter conveys to a subject the true values of the potential payoffs, which consist of K^+_j potential gains, $\mathcal{G}_j = \{r^g_{j,k} > 0, \, k = 1, \ldots K^+_j\}$, and K^-_j potential losses, $\mathcal{L}_j = \{r^l_{j,k} < 0, \, k = 1, \ldots K^-_j\}, j = 1 \ldots J$. The union of these sets, $\mathcal{R}_j = \mathcal{G}_j \cup \mathcal{L}_j$, constitutes the set of $K_j = K^+_j + K^-_j$ potential returns from choosing gamble j. Moreover, the experimenter also informs the subject about the true probabilities associated with each potential gain or loss comprising the gamble j, $\mathcal{P}_j = \{p_{j,k}, \, k = 1, \ldots K_j\}$, where for each j, $\sum_k p_{j,k} = 1$.

Using this experimental setup, Kahneman and Tversky represent the utility that an individual attaches to a gamble with a weighted sum of the values of the single outcomes making up a gamble. Using the original formulation of the utility function in equation (9.6), we can express the prospective utility choosing gamble j as:

$$PU_j = \sum_{k}^{K^+} \pi_{j,k}^g \left(r_{j,k}^g\right)^\alpha - \lambda \sum_{k}^{K^-} \pi_{j,k}^l \left(-r_{j,k}^l\right)^\beta, \tag{9.10}$$

where $\pi_{j,k}$ denotes the weight that individuals attach to the utility of each prospect.

9.1.3.2. *Preferences over Gambles in Financial Markets*

Gambles in financial markets differ in several important respects from those in a laboratory setting. To begin with, the structure of payoffs in a typical laboratory experiment, the pair of sets $(\mathcal{R}_j, \mathcal{P}_j)$, can differ in an arbitrary way among the gambles that comprise the experiment. In contrast, the payoffs comprising alternative gambles in the foreign exchange market are all multiples of the return from taking a unit position in foreign exchange.

To express this observation more formally, let the pair of sets $(\mathcal{R}, \mathcal{P})$ denote the probability distribution of the return on a unit position. We also note from equation (9.5) that the total return from taking a position of size $W|a|$ in foreign exchange is a multiple of the return on a unit position. Thus, the probability distribution of payoffs from gamble j is characterized by a pair of sets $(W|a_j|\mathcal{R}, \mathcal{P})$, where the set $W|a_j|\mathcal{R}$ is composed of all elements of $\mathcal{R}$ multiplied by the position size $W|a_j|$. In this setup, for a given probability distribution of the return on a unit position, $(\mathcal{R}, \mathcal{P})$, the choice among the alternative gambles faced by an individual is tantamount to the choice of a position size.

In contrast to experimental subjects, participants in real world markets do not know the true probability distribution of payoffs. Thus, to represent their decisions, an economist must represent market participants' forecasting strategies and their revisions over time. Let the pair of sets $(\widehat{\mathcal{R}}_{t|t+1}, \widehat{\mathcal{P}}_{t|t+1})$ denote the probability distribution of the return on *a unit position* at time $t+1$ that is implied by an economist's representation of forecasting behavior, conditional on the realizations of the causal variables that it includes at time t. Then, using the original formulation of the utility function in equation (9.7), as well as equation (9.8) and equation (9.10), we define an individual's prospective utility of a gamble involving a long position of size $W_t|a_t|$ as:

$$PU_t^L = \left(a_t W_t\right)^\alpha \sum_{k}^{K^+} \hat{\pi}_{t|t+1,k}^+ \left(\hat{r}_{t|t+1,k}^+\right)^\alpha - \lambda \left(a_t W_t\right)^\beta \sum_{k}^{K^-} \hat{\pi}_{t|t+1,k}^- \left(-\hat{r}_{t|t+1,k}^-\right)^\beta,$$

$$\tag{9.11}$$

where $\hat{r}^+_{t|t+1,k}$ and $\hat{r}^-_{t|t+1,k}$ denote the kth positive and negative values that make up an economist's representation of an individual's forecast of R_{t+1}, that is, the positive and negative values in $\widehat{\mathcal{R}}_{t|t+1}$, respectively, and $\hat{\pi}^+_{t|t+1,k}$ and $\hat{\pi}^-_{t|t+1,k}$ denote an economist's representation of the kth decision weights associated with $\hat{r}^+_{t|t+1,k}$ and $\hat{r}^-_{t|t+1,k}$, respectively.[12]

In contrast to a long position, the set of potential gains (losses) from a unit short position consists of the negative (positive) values in $\widehat{\mathcal{R}}_{t|t+1}$. Thus, the prospective utility from a short position in foreign exchange $(a_t < 0)$ is:

$$PU^s_t = \left(-a_t W_t\right)^\alpha \sum_k^{K^-} \hat{\pi}^-_{t|t+1,k} \left(-\hat{r}^-_{t|t+1,k}\right)^\alpha$$

$$- \lambda \left(-a_t W_t\right)^\beta \sum_k^{K^+} \hat{\pi}^+_{t|t+1,k} \left(\hat{r}^+_{t|t+1,k}\right)^\beta. \tag{9.12}$$

As we noted above, Kahneman and Tversky represent decision weights as nonlinear functions of true probabilities. However, Kahneman and Tversky pointed out that their experimentally estimated decision weights may not be applicable in nonexperimental settings: in addition to probabilities, decision weights may be affected by other factors that cannot be adequately represented with fully predetermined functions of probabilities. Thus, in addition to the difficulties of representing forecasting behavior, which are common to modeling choices under uncertainty, the use of prospect theory to represent preferences over gambles in real world markets also requires that an economist represent decision weights.

Before we examine how the literature has dealt with this problem and put forth our own alternative, we derive the implications of the original formulation of prospect theory for an individual's choice over gambles whose prospective utilities are given in equations (9.11) and (9.12).

9.1.4. No Limits to Speculation

Given a representation of an individual's forecasting behavior, which implies values of the potential prospects $\hat{r}^+_{t|t+1,k}$ and $\hat{r}^-_{t|t+1,k}$, as well as a representation of her decision weights $\hat{\pi}_{t|t+1,k}$, and the value of her wealth at time t, the choice among gambles is tantamount to the choice of the position

---

12. Tversky and Kahneman (1992) presented prospect theory for a finite set of prospects. We follow them here by assuming that the set of potential prospects on a unit position, $\widehat{\mathcal{R}}_{t|t+1}$, is finite.

size a_t that maximizes her prospective utility. We note that the prospective utilities PU_t^L and PU_t^S are defined only for $a_t \geq 0$ and $a_t \leq 0$, respectively. Thus, this representation of an individual's decision problem involves solving two constrained maximization problems, one for long positions using equation (9.11) and one for short positions using equation (9.12). An economist would then attribute to an individual the solution—long, short, or no participation—that delivers the greatest prospective utility.

It is clear from the way a_t enters the expressions for the prospective utilities in equations (9.11) and (9.12) that the existence of a finite solution for position size depends on the relationship between the curvatures in the domains of gains α and losses β. To streamline our discussion of this solution, we rewrite the expressions for prospective utilities in equations (9.11) and (9.12) as:

$$PU_t^L = (a_t W_t)^\alpha P[\widehat{\mathcal{G}}_{t|t+1}^L; \alpha] + \lambda (a_t W_t)^\beta P[\widehat{\mathcal{L}}_{t|t+1}^L; \beta] \qquad (9.13)$$

$$PU_t^S = (a_t W_t)^\alpha P[\widehat{\mathcal{G}}_{t|t+1}^S; \alpha] + \lambda (a_t W_t)^\beta P[\widehat{\mathcal{L}}_{t|t+1}^S; \beta], \qquad (9.14)$$

where we refer to $P[\widehat{\mathcal{G}}_{t|t+1}^L; \alpha]$ ($P[\widehat{\mathcal{G}}_{t|t+1}^S; \alpha]$) and $P[\widehat{\mathcal{L}}_{t|t+1}^L; \beta]$ ($P[\widehat{\mathcal{L}}_{t|t+1}^S; \beta]$) as the prospective gain and loss on a unit long (short) position, respectively. We also define the prospective return $P[\widehat{\mathcal{R}}_{t|t+1}^L; \alpha, \beta]$ ($P[\widehat{\mathcal{R}}_{t|t+1}^S; \alpha, \beta]$) on a unit long (short) position as:

$$P[\widehat{\mathcal{R}}_{t|t+1}^L; \alpha, \beta] = P[\widehat{\mathcal{G}}_{t|t+1}^L; \alpha] + P[\widehat{\mathcal{L}}_{t|t+1}^L; \beta]$$

$$= \sum_k^{K^+} \hat{\pi}_{t|t+1,k}^+ \left(\hat{r}_{t|t+1,k}^+\right)^\alpha - \sum_k^{K^-} \hat{\pi}_{t|t+1,k}^- \left(-\hat{r}_{t|t+1,k}^-\right)^\beta \qquad (9.15)$$

$$P[\widehat{\mathcal{R}}_{t|t+1}^S; \alpha, \beta] = P[\widehat{\mathcal{G}}_{t|t+1}^S; \alpha] + P[\widehat{\mathcal{L}}_{t|t+1}^S; \beta]$$

$$= \sum_k^{K^-} \hat{\pi}_{t|t+1,k}^- \left(-\hat{r}_{t|t+1,k}^-\right)^\alpha - \sum_k^{K^+} \hat{\pi}_{t|t+1,k}^+ \left(\hat{r}_{t|t+1,k}^+\right)^\beta. \qquad (9.16)$$

As we discuss more extensively in section (9.3), the behavioral finance literature has set $\alpha = \beta = 1$. This restriction is a special case of the constraint that the curvature of the utility function is the same in the domains of gains and losses; that is, $\alpha = \beta$. Under this constraint, we can rewrite the prospective utilities in equations (9.13) and (9.14) in terms of the prospective return and prospective loss on a unit position in foreign exchange:

$$PU_t^{\mathrm{L}} = \left(a_t W_t\right)^{\alpha} \left[P[\widehat{\mathcal{R}}_{t|t+1}^{\mathrm{L}}; \alpha, \alpha] - (1-\lambda) P[\widehat{\mathcal{L}}_{t|t+1}^{\mathrm{L}}; \alpha] \right] \qquad (9.17)$$

$$PU_t^{\mathrm{S}} = \left(a_t W_t\right)^{\alpha} \left[P[\widehat{\mathcal{R}}_{t|t+1}^{\mathrm{S}}; \alpha, \alpha] - (1-\lambda) P[\widehat{\mathcal{L}}_{t|t+1}^{\mathrm{S}}; \alpha] \right]. \qquad (9.18)$$

Expressions (9.17) and (9.18) imply an unambiguous decision rule for choosing whether to speculate:[13]

- Stay out of the market when $P[\widehat{\mathcal{R}}_{t|t+1}^{\mathrm{L}}; \alpha, \alpha] \leq (1-\lambda) P[\widehat{\mathcal{L}}_{t|t+1}^{\mathrm{L}}; \alpha]$ and $P[\widehat{\mathcal{R}}_{t|t+1}^{\mathrm{S}}; \alpha, \alpha] \leq (1-\lambda) P[\widehat{\mathcal{L}}_{t|t+1}^{\mathrm{S}}; \alpha]$;

- Hold a long position in foreign exchange when $P[\widehat{\mathcal{R}}_{t|t+1}^{\mathrm{L}}; \alpha, \alpha] > (1-\lambda) P[\widehat{\mathcal{L}}_{t|t+1}^{\mathrm{L}}; \alpha]$ (that is, $PU_t^{\mathrm{L}} > 0$); or

- Hold a short position in foreign exchange when $P[\widehat{\mathcal{R}}_{t|t+1}^{\mathrm{S}}; \alpha, \alpha] > (1-\lambda) P[\widehat{\mathcal{L}}_{t|t+1}^{\mathrm{S}}; \alpha]$ (that is, $PU_t^{\mathrm{S}} > 0$).

However, if either PU_t^{L} or PU_t^{S} is positive, equations (9.17) and (9.18) imply no limit to the size of the speculative position that maximizes utility. For example, suppose that $P[\widehat{\mathcal{R}}_{t|t+1}^{\mathrm{L}}; \alpha, \alpha] > (1-\lambda) P[\widehat{\mathcal{L}}_{t|t+1}^{\mathrm{L}}; \alpha]$, so that a unit long position would be expected to raise the prospective utility attributed to an individual. It is clear from equation (9.17) that, for this prospective return and loss on a unit position, every unit increase in position size increases an individual's prospective utility.[14] Thus, an individual would not only decide to take a long position, but she would want to take a long position of unlimited size.[15]

This result rules out a well-defined equilibrium in any market where the asset is in positive supply or individuals' forecasts are heterogeneous. As

---

13. Note that for $\alpha = \beta$, the definitions of the prospective return and loss in equations (9.15) and (9.16) imply that if $P[\widehat{\mathcal{R}}_{t|t+1}^{\mathrm{L}}; \alpha, \alpha] > (1-\lambda) P[\widehat{\mathcal{L}}_{t|t+1}^{\mathrm{L}}; \beta]$, then $P[\widehat{\mathcal{R}}_{t|t+1}^{\mathrm{S}}; \alpha, \alpha] < (1-\lambda) P[\widehat{\mathcal{L}}_{t|t+1}^{\mathrm{S}}; \beta]$, and vice versa.

14. In chapter 11, we examine the use of risk-averse preferences to represent an individual's speculative decision problem. Comparison of equations (9.17) and (9.18) with the risk-averse utility function in equation (11.2) in chapter 11 makes clear that the prospective return and prospective loss on a unit position play roles similar to those played by representations of an individual's expected return and conditional variance under risk aversion.

15. This result is based on the assumption that the reference point attributed to individuals is the level of wealth they would receive were they to stay out of the market. However, even if individual reference levels are not given by equation (9.4), the value function in equation (9.7) with $\alpha = \beta$ does not, in general, imply limits to speculation. Ang et al. (2004) prove that under an arbitary reference level, the maximization of expected utility over all prospects yields a finite position size if the expected values of the gains and losses on long and short positions satisfy special restrictions. For a related analysis see Gomes (2005).

we discussed in the introduction, other asset market studies using prospect theory sidestep this problem by embedding the assumption of loss aversion into an otherwise standard utility function that implies risk aversion. This practice in behavioral finance is difficult to justify in view of the findings by Kahneman and Tversky and many others that risk-averse preferences fail to capture adequately decision making under uncertainty.

9.2. Endogenous Loss Aversion and Limits to Speculation

We now show that limits to speculation can be modeled solely on the basis of prospect theory.

9.2.1. *Endogenous Degree of Loss Aversion*

The experimental evidence of Kahneman and Tversky and others is consistent with a utility function whose curvature in the domain of losses is greater than in the domain of gains, that is, $\beta > \alpha$. With this assumption, for a given r^l, the degree of loss aversion implied by equations (9.9) and (9.7) increases with the size of the stake:

$$\Lambda = \lambda(W \left|ar^l\right|)^{\beta-\alpha}, \tag{9.19}$$

where $W|a|$ and r^l are the position size and the loss on a unit position, respectively. Because the position size is chosen by an individual, we refer to the formulation of the utility function in equation (9.7) under $\beta > \alpha$ as embodying an "endogenous degree of loss aversion."

9.2.2. *Endogenous Loss Aversion*

Constraining $\beta > \alpha$ introduces the possibility that the original Kahneman and Tversky utility function may not be compatible with the core assumption of loss aversion: with $\beta > \alpha$, there is a range of small values for the position size $W \left|a\right|$ within which an individual would prefer losses over gains, that is; $\Lambda = \lambda(W \left|ar^l\right|)^{\beta-\alpha} < 1$.

To ensure that our formulation of preferences implies loss aversion at all position sizes, even when $\beta > \alpha$, we introduce a simple modification to Kahneman and Tversky's original formulation in equation (9.6). We modify the specification for the degree of loss aversion to be:

$$\Lambda = \lambda_1 + \lambda_2^1(W \left|ar^l\right|)^{\beta-\alpha}, \tag{9.20}$$

where $\lambda_1 > 1$ and $\lambda_2^1 > 0$ are constant preference parameters. Because $\lambda_1 > 1$, equation (9.20) implies that $\Lambda > 1$ for all values of a.

It readily follows that, with the specification of endogenous loss aversion in equation (9.20), the utility function is:

$$V(\Delta W) = \begin{cases} (W \,|ar^g|)^\alpha & \text{if } \Delta W > 0 \\ -\lambda_1 (W \,|ar^l|)^\alpha - \lambda_2^1 (W \,|ar^l|)^\beta & \text{if } \Delta W < 0. \end{cases} \tag{9.21}$$

We note that this utility function satisfies the three assumptions of the original formulation of prospect theory that we listed in section 9.1.2. Moreover, as we show below, the positive relationship between the degree of loss aversion and position size ensures that prospect theory implies limits to speculation.[16] For this reason, we explicitly augment the three assumptions of the original formulation of prospect theory with the following assumption:

Endogenous Loss Aversion *The degree of loss aversion increases with the size of the speculative position.*

9.2.3. Position Size

The modified utility function in equation (9.21) implies the following prospective utilities for long and short positions:

$$PU_t^{\text{L}} = \left(a_t W_t\right)^\alpha P[\widehat{\mathcal{G}}_{t|t+1}^{\text{L}}; \alpha] + \lambda_1 \left(a_t W_t\right)^\alpha P[\widehat{\mathcal{L}}_{t|t+1}^{\text{L}}; \alpha]$$

$$+ \lambda_2^1 \left(a_t W_t\right)^\beta P[\widehat{\mathcal{L}}_{t|t+1}^{\text{L}}; \beta] \tag{9.22}$$

$$PU_t^{\text{S}} = \left(-a_t W_t\right)^\alpha P[\widehat{\mathcal{G}}_{t|t+1}^{\text{S}}; \alpha] + \lambda_1 \left(-a_t W_t\right)^\alpha P[\widehat{\mathcal{L}}_{t|t+1}^{\text{S}}; \alpha]$$

$$+ \lambda_2^1 \left(-a_t W_t\right)^\beta P[\widehat{\mathcal{L}}_{t|t+1}^{\text{S}}; \beta]. \tag{9.23}$$

These specifications of prospective utility are concave in an individual's position size under the constraint that $\beta > \alpha$. Consequently, the utility function in equation (9.21) implies that individuals would limit the size of their speculative positions whenever they perceive an opportunity for gain. As we show in the appendix to this chapter, the position sizes that would maximize the prospective utilities in equations (9.22) and (9.23) are given by:

16. We are unaware of any experimental evidence demonstrating directly a positive relationship between the degree of loss aversion and the size of the stake. But as emphasized by Myron Scholes in his presentation delivered at the conference on "Derivatives 2003: Reports from the Frontiers," Stern School of Business, New York University, New York, January 31, 2003, such a relationship accords well with how participants in real world markets actually behave.

$$a_t^L = \frac{W^{-1} \left(\frac{\alpha}{\lambda_2^{\frac{1}{\beta}} \beta} \right)^{\frac{1}{\beta - \alpha}}}{\left\{ -P[\widehat{\mathcal{L}}^L; \beta] \right\}^{\frac{1}{\beta - \alpha}}} \left\{ P[\widehat{\mathcal{R}}^L; \alpha, \alpha] - (1 - \lambda_1) P[\widehat{\mathcal{L}}^L; \alpha] \right\}^{\frac{1}{\beta - \alpha}} \qquad (9.24)$$

$$-a_t^S = \frac{W^{-1} \left(\frac{\alpha}{\lambda_2^{\frac{1}{\beta}} \beta} \right)^{\frac{1}{\beta - \alpha}}}{\left\{ -P[\widehat{\mathcal{L}}^S; \beta] \right\}^{\frac{1}{\beta - \alpha}}} \left\{ P[\widehat{\mathcal{R}}^S; \alpha, \alpha] - (1 - \lambda_1) P[\widehat{\mathcal{L}}^S; \alpha] \right\}^{\frac{1}{\beta - \alpha}}. \qquad (9.25)$$

where, for ease of notation, we have suppressed the subscript $t|t + 1$ in the expressions.

In deriving these representations, we have imposed the constraints $a_t^L \geq 0$ and $a_t^S \leq 0$. The Kuhn-Tucker conditions imply that when $P[\mathcal{R}^L; \alpha, \alpha] - (1 - \lambda_1) P[\mathcal{L}^L; \alpha] < 0$, $a_t^L = 0$, and when $P[\mathcal{R}^S; \alpha, \alpha] - (1 - \lambda_1) P[\mathcal{L}^S; \alpha] > 0$, $a_t^S = 0$. Moreover, as we noted in footnote 13, whenever $a_t^L > 0$, $a_t^S = 0$ and vice versa.

Given that the coefficients in front of the bracketed terms in equations (9.24) and (9.25) are positive, these representations for position size imply the following decision rule:

- Stay out of the market when $P[\widehat{\mathcal{R}}^L_{t|t+1}; \alpha, \alpha] \leq (1 - \lambda_1) P[\widehat{\mathcal{L}}^L_{t|t+1}; \alpha]$ and $P[\widehat{\mathcal{R}}^S_{t|t+1}; \alpha, \alpha] \leq (1 - \lambda_1) P[\widehat{\mathcal{L}}^S_{t|t+1}; \alpha]$;

- Hold a long position in foreign exchange of size $a^L W_t$ when $P[\widehat{\mathcal{R}}^L_{t|t+1}; \alpha, \alpha] > (1 - \lambda_1) P[\widehat{\mathcal{L}}^L_{t|t+1}; \alpha]$; or

- Hold a short position in foreign exchange of size $-a^S W_t$ when $P[\widehat{\mathcal{R}}^S_{t|t+1}; \alpha, \alpha] > (1 - \lambda_1) P[\widehat{\mathcal{L}}^S_{t|t+1}; \alpha]$.

This decision rule reveals three important implications of endogenous loss aversion for representations of speculative behavior. First, once an individual perceives an opportunity for gain and enters the market, she takes a position of limited size. This feature of the representation stems from endogenous loss aversion, which implies that prospective utility is concave in position size.

Second, λ_1, which represents an individual's degree of loss aversion at $a = 0$, and the prospective loss may be large enough so that, although the prospective return $P[\widehat{\mathcal{R}}^L_{t|t+1}; \alpha, \alpha]$ or $P[\widehat{\mathcal{R}}^S_{t|t+1}; \alpha, \alpha]$ may be positive, an economist's representation implies that an individual nonetheless decides to stay out of the market.

Finally, endogenous loss aversion gives rise to a new specification of the premium on speculative positions. The utility function in equation (9.21) implies that speculators require a prospective return in excess of a minimum positive value to take open positions in foreign exchange. The representations in equations (9.24) and (9.25) show that the minimum return an individual requires for taking a long or short position can be represented as the following simple function of her prospective potential loss on a unit position and the loss-aversion parameter $\lambda_1 > 1$:[17]

$$\widehat{up}_t^{\text{L}} = \left(1 - \lambda_1\right) P[\widehat{\mathcal{L}}_{t|t+1}^{\text{L}}; \alpha] > 0 \tag{9.26}$$

$$\widehat{up}_t^{\text{S}} = \left(1 - \lambda_1\right) P[\widehat{\mathcal{L}}_{t|t+1}^{\text{S}}; \alpha] > 0. \tag{9.27}$$

We note that setting $\lambda_1 = 0$ and $\lambda_2^1 = \lambda$ in equations (9.24) and (9.25) yields the solutions for the size of the long and short positions that are implied by the original Tversky and Kahneman's (1992) utility function. Thus, for $\beta > \alpha$, the original formulation in equation (9.7) also implies limits to speculation. However, as we show in the appendix to this chapter, in contrast to the possibility of nonparticipation that is implied by our modification in equation (9.21), the original utility function in equation (9.7) implies that individuals take open positions in foreign exchange as long as they forecast a nonzero prospective return.[18]

9.3. Experimental Evidence and Behavioral Finance Models

The representations that we constructed on the basis of prospect theory in the previous section relate an individual's position size and premium to her prospective return and prospective loss, $P[\widehat{\mathcal{R}}_{t|t+1}; \alpha, \alpha]$ and $P[\widehat{\mathcal{L}}_{t|t+1}; \alpha]$, respectively. Therefore, for such representations to explain how an individual revises the size of her speculative position and how these revisions translate into movements of aggregate outcomes—the exchange rate and the premium on open positions in foreign exchange—an economist must model how an individual revises her prospective return and loss. Only then can a model based on prospect theory be confronted with time-series data.

The prospective return and loss are nonlinear functions of the values of future returns—potential gains and/or losses—that are implied by an econ-

---

17. We note that these minimum returns, which are required for participation in the market, are the same as those with the value function in equation (9.7) with $\alpha = \beta$. See equations (9.17) and (9.18). But in that case, whenever an individual's prospective return exceeded the minimum positive value, she would want to take a position of unlimited size.

18. The reason for this result is that, when $\beta > \alpha$, the original specification in equation (9.7) violates the assumption of loss aversion at small position sizes.

omist's representation of forecasting behavior. Moreover, $P[\widehat{\mathcal{R}}_{t|t+1}; \alpha, \alpha]$ and $P[\widehat{\mathcal{L}}_{t|t+1}; \alpha]$ depend on representations of decision weights. But as Kahneman and Tversky point out, these weights depend on factors that are inherently related to the necessity for market participants to cope with imperfect knowledge when revising their decisions. In applying prospect theory, however, behavioral finance models fully prespecify the way participants in financial markets decide on the allocation of their wealth to speculative assets. They have done so in two ways.

9.3.1. Using the Unconditional Distribution of Returns

Benartzi and Thaler (1995) use prospect theory to model the premium on equity holdings in the U.S. stock market. To estimate the probability distribution of prospects, they presume that the unconditional distribution of ex post monthly returns on holding the Standard & Poor's 500 basket of stocks is time invariant during 1926–90. Given this assumption, they construct a distribution of returns during that period. Moreover, Benartzi and Thaler represent market participants' forecasting behavior during the entire period 1926–90 with the simulated distribution of ex post returns. This procedure allows them to construct a representation of single prospects and their associated probabilities. Disregarding Kahneman and Tversky's doubts concerning the adequacy of their experimentally based weighting function when representing behavior in real world markets, Benartzi and Thaler use this function to construct decision weights. These weights, together with the simulated values for single prospects, enable them to compute one value for the prospective utility for the entire period 1926–90.

Beyond assuming that one distribution characterizes stock returns over 70 years, Benartzi and Thaler's approach has limited applicability. It is not useful in testing economic models, which attempt to explain such aggregate outcomes as asset prices and the premium in terms of some set of causal variables over time.

9.3.2. Using the Conditional Distribution of Returns: Reducing Prospective to Expected Values

Typically, extant behavioral finance models of prices in the stock market represent an individual's prospective return and loss in terms of some causal variables by reducing these prospective values to the expected values implied by their representations of forecasting behavior. They do so by assuming that

- The utility function in equation (9.6) is linear in gains and losses;[19] and

- The decision weights attached to the single prospects are equal to the conditional probabilities associated with those prospects.

Setting $\alpha = \beta = 1$ in equation (9.7) reduces prospective utility to a linear relationship in the $\hat{r}^+_{t|t+1,k}$ and $\hat{r}^-_{t|t+1,k}$ implied by an economist's representation of forecasting behavior. For example, the prospective utility on a long position in equation (9.17) becomes the following linear function of single prospects:

$$
PU^{\mathrm{L}}_t = \left(a_t W_t\right)\left[\sum_k^K \hat{\pi}_{t|t+1,k}\hat{r}_{t|t+1,k} - (1-\lambda)\sum_k^{K^-} \hat{\pi}^-_{t|t+1,k}\hat{r}^-_{t|t+1,k} \right]
$$

$$
= \left(a_t W_t\right)\left[\widehat{\Pi}(\hat{r}) - (1-\lambda)\widehat{\Pi}(\hat{r}^-) \right], \tag{9.28}
$$

where $\widehat{\Pi}(\cdot)$ denotes the decision-weighted sums of prospects.

Imposing linearity over gains and losses does not violate loss aversion: for $\alpha = \beta = 1$, loss aversion is implied by $\lambda > 1$. However, it is inconsistent with diminishing sensitivity, which is among the main assumptions that underpin prospect theory. Moreover, linearity is problematic not only because it violates diminishing sensitivity. As we showed above, assuming $\alpha = \beta = 1$ in equation (9.7) implies no limits to speculation.

It is unclear how to distinguish decision weights from probabilities in real world markets, in which neither participants nor economists have access to true probabilities. Recognizing this difficulty, behavioral finance theorists have replaced decision weights with the probabilities implied by their fully predetermined representations of forecasting behavior. For example, Barberis et al. (2001) use REH to represent an individual's forecasts, although they could have employed any of the extant non-REH representations. This assumption enables them to express prospective utility, such as in equation (9.28), in terms of the expected return $\hat{r}^{\mathrm{L}}_{t|t+1}$, and loss $\hat{l}^{\mathrm{L}}_{t|t+1}$ implied by their representation of forecasting behavior:

$$
PU^{\mathrm{L}}_t = \left(a_t W_t\right)\left[\sum_k^K \hat{p}_{t|t+1,k}\hat{r}_{t|t+1,k} - (1-\lambda)\sum_k^{K^-} \hat{p}^-_{t|t+1,k}\hat{r}^-_{t|t+1,k} \right]
$$

$$
= \left(a_t W_t\right)\left[\hat{r}^{\mathrm{L,\,FP}}_{t|t+1,k} - (1-\lambda_1)\hat{l}^{\mathrm{L,\,FP}}_{t|t+1} \right], \tag{9.29}
$$

19. For example, Barberis et al. (2001) set $\alpha = \beta = 1$ in equation (9.6).

where the $\hat{p}_{t|t+1,k}$ and $\hat{p}^-_{t|t+1,k}$ are the probabilities associated with their corresponding prospects.

The extant approaches relate representations of an individual's forecasts $\hat{r}^L_{t|t+1}$ and $\hat{l}^L_{t|t+1}$ to some set of causal factors in a fully predetermined way. Thus, once an economist expresses prospective values as a function of expected values, such as in equation (9.29), his representation of forecasting behavior enables him to relate prospective values to a set of causal factors and thereby examine the implications of models based on prospect theory for change on the individual and aggregate levels.

Replacing decision-weighted sums in equation (9.28) with representations of forecasts of the return and loss in equation (9.29) may indeed be unavoidable in a nonexperimental setting. The reliance on fully predetermined representations, however, disregards the dependence of decision weights on such factors as "ambiguity" or "vagueness," which arise from the importance of the imperfection of knowledge in real world markets.

9.4. Moving beyond Behavioral Finance Models

In this section, we develop an alternative specification of the utility function over single prospects that implies that prospective utility can be expressed as a linear function of single prospects, as in equation (9.28). In contrast to extant specifications, we obtain this representation without imposing linearity in terms of the position size. We show that our alternative is consistent with Kahneman and Tversky's experimental findings. It is also consistent with endogenous loss aversion and thus, it implies limits to speculation.

9.4.1. Modifying the Utility Function

To motivate our alternative, we recall that, by setting $\alpha = \beta = 1$ in equation (9.7), extant behavioral models express the prospective gain and loss on a unit position as linear in both single prospects and the position size. However, we note from equation (9.28) that obtaining a representation in terms of decision-weighted sums of $\hat{r}_{t|t+1,k}$ only requires that the utility function in equation (9.21) be linear in single prospects. This observation leads us to formulate the following utility function in the context of our setup for the foreign exchange market:

$$V(\Delta W) = \begin{cases} (W\,|a|)^\alpha\,|r^g| & \text{if } \Delta W > 0 \\ -\lambda_1(W\,|a|)^\alpha\,|r^l| - \lambda_2^2(W\,|a|)^\beta\,|r^l| & \text{if } \Delta W < 0, \end{cases} \quad (9.30)$$

where $\lambda_1 > 1$, $\lambda_2^2 > 0$, a is positive for a bull and negative for a bear, and $r^g > 0$ and $r^l < 0$ are defined in equation (9.8).

The degree of loss aversion implied by equation (9.30) takes an analogous form to equation (9.20):

$$\Lambda = \lambda_1 + \lambda_2^2 (W \, |a|)^{\beta - \alpha}. \qquad (9.31)$$

We note that for $\beta > \alpha$, the expression for Λ in equation (9.31) embodies the assumption of endogenous loss aversion

In contrast to the linear utility function used in extant behavioral finance models, our alternative utility function in equation (9.30) is consistent with Kahneman and Tversky's finding of diminishing sensitivity. We recall from section 9.1.3.2 that gambles in our setup differ only by the position size, so that the differential of the total loss is $dL = Wr^l d \, |a|$ and $\frac{dV}{dL} = \frac{\partial V}{\partial L} \frac{1}{Wr^l}$. For example, for a bull, we have:

$$\frac{d^2 V(\Delta W)}{dL d(-L)} = -\frac{\alpha(\alpha - 1)\lambda_1 \, (Wa)^{\alpha - 2} + \beta(\beta - 1)\lambda_2^2 \, (Wa)^{\beta - 2}}{r^l} < 0, \quad (9.32)$$

where the inequality follows from $\alpha < 1$ and $\beta < 1$, and $r^l < 0$. Analogously for gains, G, equation (9.30) implies diminishing sensitivity; that is, $\frac{d^2 V(\Delta W)}{d^2 G} = \frac{\alpha(\alpha - 1)(Wa)^{\alpha - 2}(\alpha - 1)}{r^g} < 0$. Thus, as the original Tversky and Kahneman (1992) function in equation (9.7), our modified specification in equation (9.30) is concave for gains and convex for losses.

9.4.2. Position Size

Although the utility function in equation (9.30) is nonlinear in position size, prospective utilities are linear in single prospects:

$$PU_t^L = \left(a_t W_t \right)^\alpha \left[\widehat{\Pi}(\hat{r}) - (1 - \lambda)\widehat{\Pi}(\hat{r}^-) \right] + \lambda_2^2 \left(a_t W_t \right)^\beta \widehat{\Pi}(\hat{r}^-) \qquad (9.33)$$

$$PU_t^S = \left(-a_t W_t \right)^\alpha \left[\widehat{\Pi}(\hat{r}) - (1 - \lambda)\widehat{\Pi}(-\hat{r}^+) \right] + \lambda_2^2 \left(a_t W_t \right)^\beta \widehat{\Pi}(-\hat{r}^+), \quad (9.34)$$

where the decision-weighted sums are defined in equation (9.28). This concavity of prospective utilities in the position size implies that if an individual were to enter the market, she would want to take a position of limited size:

$$a_t^L = \frac{(W)^{-1} \left(\dfrac{\alpha}{\lambda_2^2 \beta} \right)^{\frac{1}{\beta - \alpha}}}{\left(-\widehat{\Pi}(\hat{r}^-) \right)^{\frac{1}{\beta - \alpha}}} \left[\widehat{\Pi}(\hat{r}) - (1 - \lambda_1)\widehat{\Pi}(\hat{r}^-) \right]^{\frac{1}{\beta - \alpha}} \qquad (9.35)$$

$$-a_t^{\mathrm{s}} = \frac{(W)^{-1}\left(\frac{\alpha}{\lambda_2^2\beta}\right)^{\frac{1}{\beta-\alpha}}}{\left(-\widehat{\Pi}(-\hat{r}^+)\right)^{\frac{1}{\beta-\alpha}}}\left[\widehat{\Pi}(\hat{r}) - (1-\lambda_1^i)\widehat{\Pi}(-\hat{r}^+)\right]^{\frac{1}{\beta-\alpha}}. \qquad (9.36)$$

9.4.3. Prospect Theory and Heterogeneity of Forecasts

We note that if an economist were to impose the representative-individual assumption, so that market participants' forecasts were represented as homogenous, he would only need to represent the decision-weighted sums $\widehat{\Pi}(\cdot)$ in terms of the expected values $\hat{r}_{t|t+1}$ and $\hat{l}_{t|t+1}$ defined in equation (9.29). We note, however, that if an economist wanted to allow for heterogeneity of forecasts, the nonlinearity of equations (9.35) and (9.36) in $\widehat{\Pi}(\cdot)$ would, in general, render it impossible to examine the implications of the model on the aggregate level in terms of a representation of an aggregate of market participants' forecasts.

For example, suppose that an economist were to represent $\widehat{\Pi}(\cdot)$ in terms of their expected-value counterparts, $\hat{r}_{t+1}$ and $\hat{l}_{t+1}$ and that the heterogeneity of forecasts was characterized in terms of a representative bull and a representative bear. The net demand for foreign exchange would be $aW = a^{\mathrm{L}}W^{\mathrm{L}} + a^{\mathrm{S}}W^{\mathrm{S}}$. Defining $\omega^i = \frac{W^i}{W}$, where $i = \mathrm{L}$ or S, and $W = W^{\mathrm{L}} + W^{\mathrm{S}}$, it is customary to define the aggregate (net) demand, as a proportion of total market wealth, as $a = a^{\mathrm{L}}\omega^{\mathrm{L}} + a^{\mathrm{S}}\omega^{\mathrm{S}}$. Using equations (9.35) and (9.36) we have:[20]

$$a_t = \left(\frac{\alpha}{\lambda_2^2\beta}\right)^{\frac{1}{\beta-\alpha}}\left\{\begin{array}{l}\dfrac{\omega^{\mathrm{L}}}{\left(-\hat{l}_{t|t+1}^{\mathrm{L}}\right)^{\frac{1}{\beta-\alpha}}}\left[\hat{r}_{t|t+1}^{\mathrm{L}} - (1-\lambda_1)\hat{l}_{t|t+1}^{\mathrm{L}}\right]^{\frac{1}{\beta-\alpha}} \\[3ex] -\dfrac{\omega^{\mathrm{S}}}{\left(-\hat{l}_{t|t+1}^{\mathrm{S}}\right)^{\frac{1}{\beta-\alpha}}}\left[\hat{r}_{t|t+1}^{\mathrm{S}} - (1-\lambda_1)\hat{l}_{t|t+1}^{\mathrm{S}}\right]^{\frac{1}{\beta-\alpha}}\end{array}\right\}. \qquad (9.37)$$

Thus, the implications of the model on the aggregate level depend on the magnitude of the revisions of a bull's and a bear's forecasts, which would need to be separately represented in terms of some set of causal variables. Consequently, the behavior of the aggregates, such as a, cannot, in

---

20. For an example of the use of such wealth-weighted averages in the analysis of equilibrium in the foreign exchange market, see Dornbusch (1983b). We note that the specification of weights we use in our example omits the possibility that under prospect theory, some individuals may not participate in the foreign exchange market at time t. See chapter 10 for a more complete definition of equilibrium in the foreign exchange market with our formulation of prospect theory.

general, be analyzed in terms of representations of the aggregate forecasts
$\hat{r}_{t|t+1} = \omega^{\mathrm{L}} \hat{r}_{t|t+1}^{\mathrm{L}} - \omega^{\mathrm{S}} \hat{r}_{t|t+1}^{\mathrm{S}}$ and $\hat{l}_{t|t+1} = \omega^{\mathrm{L}} \hat{l}_{t|t+1}^{\mathrm{L}} - \omega^{\mathrm{S}} \hat{l}_{t|t+1}^{\mathrm{S}}.$[21]

9.5. IKE Representations of Preferences in Asset Markets: Individual Uncertainty Premiums

By imposing linearity in their utility functions, extant behavioral finance models assume away the aggregation problem. As we noted in the previous section, the cost of such a constraint is an inconsistency with Kahneman and Tversky's findings on the curvature of the utility function and a reliance on empirically rejected risk-averse specifications of preferences in modeling individual behavior and aggregate outcomes.

As we show in chapters 11 and 12, allowing for heterogeneity of market participants' forecasts in our prospect theory–based model is crucial for understanding the behavior of the equilibrium premium in asset markets. However, the foregoing difficulty of analyzing models of aggregate outcomes that involve heterogenous forecasts indicates that we need to modify further the specification of the utility function in equation (9.30).

9.5.1. The Utility Function Once Again

Expressions (9.35) and (9.36) suggest a modification of the utility function that would be sufficient to solve the aggregation problem:

$$V(\Delta W) = \begin{cases} (W\,|a|)^{\alpha}\,|r^g| & \text{if } \Delta W > 0 \\ -\lambda_1 (W\,|a|)^{\alpha}\,|r^l| - \dfrac{\lambda_2^3}{-\widehat{\Pi}(\hat{r}^l)}(W\,|a|)^{\alpha+1}\,|r^l| & \text{if } \Delta W < 0, \end{cases} \tag{9.38}$$

where $\lambda_1 > 1$ and $\lambda_2^3 > 0$ denote preference parameters, which are constants, and $-\widehat{\Pi}(\hat{r}^l)$, which is defined in equation (9.33), is implied by an economist's representation of the decision weights and the conditional probability distribution of R_{t+1}. We note again that in representing an individual's decision concerning the position size, an economist treats $-\widehat{\Pi}(\hat{r}^l)$ as given.

The degree of loss aversion implied by equation (9.38) takes an analogous form to equation (9.31). For example, for a bull, the utility function in equation (9.38) implies that:

$$\Lambda = \lambda_1 + \frac{\lambda_2^3}{-\widehat{\Pi}(\hat{r}^-)} W\,|a|\,. \tag{9.39}$$

---

21. We recall for convenience that $\hat{r}_{t+1}^{\mathrm{s}}$ and $\hat{l}_{t+1}^{\mathrm{s}}$ are defined as positive and negative values, respectively (see equation (9.8)). Consequently, $\hat{r}_{t+1}^{\mathrm{s}}$ and $\hat{l}_{t+1}^{\mathrm{s}}$ enter with negative signs into the definition of the aggregates $\hat{r}_{t+1}$ and $\hat{l}_{t+1}$. See footnote 11 for further remarks on this point.

Because $\lambda_1 > 1$, $\lambda_2^3 > 0$, and $-\widehat{\Pi}(\hat{r}^-) > 0$, the utility function in equation (9.38) is consistent with both the assumptions of loss aversion and endogenous loss aversion; that is $\Lambda > 1$ and $\frac{d\Lambda}{d|a|} > 0$. Moreover, substituting $\beta = \alpha + 1$ and $\lambda_2^2 = \frac{\lambda_2^3}{-\widehat{\Pi}(\hat{r}^-)}$ into equation (9.32) implies that:

$$\frac{d^2 V(\Delta W)}{dLd(-L)} = (a)^{\alpha-2}\,(A + Ba), \qquad (9.40)$$

where $A = -\frac{\alpha(\alpha-1)\lambda_1 W^{\alpha-2}}{r^l} < 0$ and $B = -\frac{(\alpha+1)\alpha\lambda_2^2 W^{\alpha-1}}{\left(-\widehat{\Pi}(\hat{r}^-)\right)r^l} > 0$. Thus, the utility function in equation (9.38) embodies diminishing sensitivity, $\frac{d^2 V^l}{dLd(-L)} < 0$, for all magnitudes of the position size $a < \frac{-A}{B}$, and increasing sensitivity, $\frac{d^2 V^l}{dLd(-L)} > 0$, for $a > \frac{-A}{B}$. We refer to this property of the utility function as "endogenous sensitivity."

Endogenous Sensitivity *The marginal value of both gains and losses decreases with position size, except when the size of the position becomes large, at which point the marginal value of losses increases with position size.*

We note that diminishing sensitivity in the domain of losses implies that, on the margin, an individual becomes more willing to gamble as the magnitude of her potential losses increases. Tversky and Kahneman (1991) assume this behavior throughout the entire domain of losses. However, in discussing their experimental results in Kahneman and Tversky (1979), they recognize that the curvature of the utility function in the domain of losses may depend on the magnitude of the potential loss: although diminishing sensitivity is typical for smaller gambles, individual preferences may be characterized by increasing sensitivity for larger gambles. As Kahneman and Tversky put it:

> The difference between a loss of 100 and a loss of 200 appears greater than the difference between a loss of 1,100 and a loss of 1,200, *unless the larger loss is intolerable* . . . thus we hypothesize that the utility function for changes of wealth . . . is often [but not always] convex [in the domain of losses]. (Kahneman and Tversky, 1979, p. 278, emphasis added)

9.5.2. Position Size

Substituting $\beta = \alpha + 1$ and $\lambda_2^2 = \frac{\lambda_2^3}{\left(-\widehat{\Pi}(\hat{r}^-)\right)}$ into equations (9.35) and (9.36) immediately implies that the following representations maximize the prospective utility in equation (9.38):

$$a_t^{\text{L}} = \frac{\alpha}{\lambda_2^3(\alpha + 1)W} \left[\widehat{\Pi}(\hat{r}) - (1 - \lambda_1)\widehat{\Pi}(\hat{r}^-) \right] \tag{9.41}$$

$$-a_t^{\text{S}} = \frac{\alpha}{\lambda_2^3(\alpha + 1)W} \left[\widehat{\Pi}(\hat{r}) - (1 - \lambda_1)\widehat{\Pi}(-\hat{r}^+) \right]. \tag{9.42}$$

9.5.3. IKE Representation of the Position Size and an Individual Uncertainty Premium

To examine the implications of the representations in equations (9.41) and (9.42) for the way individuals revise their speculative positions and what the implications of such revisions are for the movement in the exchange rate and equilibrium premium, an economist must relate the decision-weighted sums to some causal variables.

As we discussed above, in view of the importance of imperfect knowledge in nonexperimental settings, it is not clear how economists could build a distinction between the decision weights that are attached to the values of single prospects and the likelihoods of those prospects into models of behavior in real world markets. But we have also argued that in representing behavior, the economist should not presume that he can fully prespecify the way individuals revise their decisions. Consequently, in modeling preferences over gambles with uncertain outcomes, we replace the decision-weighted sums that are involved in the definition of prospective utilities with partially predetermined expected values. Using IKE to represent an individual's forecasts of the return and potential unit loss from holding speculative positions and their revisions yields:

$$a^{\text{L}} = \frac{1}{W\lambda_2} \left[\hat{r}_{t|t+1}^{\text{L,IKE}} - (1 - \lambda_1)\hat{l}_{t|t+1}^{\text{L,IKE}} \right] \tag{9.43}$$

$$-a^{\text{S}} = \frac{1}{W\lambda_2} \left[\hat{r}_{t|t+1}^{\text{S,IKE}} - (1 - \lambda_1)\hat{l}_{t|t+1}^{\text{S,IKE}} \right], \tag{9.44}$$

where to simplify notation, we define the preference parameter $\lambda_2 = \frac{\lambda_2^3(1+\alpha)}{\alpha}$ and we use the superscript IKE to distinguish IKE representations from their fully predetermined counterparts.[22]

These representations show that our modification of the utility function in equation (9.38) preserves the key implications of the specification of the

---

22. For our formulation of partially predetermining restrictions that define IKE representations of the point forecast of the return and potential unit loss from speculation, see the next chapter. See also chapter 4 for a simple algebraic example of IKE restrictions.

original utility function in equation (9.21), which assumes loss aversion at all position sizes ($\lambda_1 > 1$) and endogenous loss aversion ($\beta > \alpha$):

- An individual's assessment of the expected loss on a unit position and her degree of loss aversion may be large enough so that although she may forecast the rate of return from speculation to be positive, she nonetheless decides to stay out of the market.

- The representation of the minimum return that an individual requires for taking a long or short position is a function of her expected loss on a unit position and the loss-aversion parameter $\lambda_1 > 1$. Analogously to equations (9.26) and (9.27), the premiums on long and short positions are given by:

$$\widehat{up}^{\mathrm{L}}_{t+1} = \left(1 - \lambda_1\right) \hat{l}^{\mathrm{L,\,IKE}}_{t|t+1} > 0 \qquad (9.45)$$

$$\widehat{up}^{\mathrm{S}}_{t+1} = \left(1 - \lambda_1\right) \hat{l}^{\mathrm{S,\,IKE}}_{t|t+1} > 0. \qquad (9.46)$$

As we discussed in the introduction to this chapter, we refer to $\widehat{up}^{\mathrm{L}}_{t+1}$ and $\widehat{up}^{\mathrm{S}}_{t+1}$ as uncertainty premiums for taking long and short positions in foreign exchange, respectively.

Finally, we note that equations (9.43) and (9.44) show that our reformulation of the utility function offers a solution to the aggregation problem for heterogenous forecasts. In the context of our example in the previous section, the utility function in equation (9.38) implies that aggregate demand in equation (9.37) can be related to representations of aggregates of market participants' expected return and loss:

$$a_t = \frac{1}{\lambda_2} \left[\hat{r}_{t|t+1} + (1 - \lambda_1)\hat{l}_{t|t+1} \right],$$

where $\hat{r}_{t|t+1} = \omega^{\mathrm{L}}\hat{r}^{\mathrm{L}}_{t|t+1} - \omega^{\mathrm{S}}\hat{r}^{\mathrm{S}}_{t|t+1}$ and $\hat{l}_{t|t+1} = \omega^{\mathrm{L}}\hat{l}^{\mathrm{L}}_{t|t+1} - \omega^{\mathrm{S}}\hat{l}^{\mathrm{S}}_{t|t+1}$. Thus, once an economist represents the change in $\hat{r}_{t|t+1}$ and $\hat{l}_{t|t+1}$, he can analyze the implications of prospect theory for the movements of aggregate outcomes, such as asset prices or the equilibrium premium.

9.6. Imperfect Knowledge and Preferences over Gambles: Endogenous Prospect Theory

In this chapter we developed an alternative formulation of the utility function that is consistent with Kahneman and Tversky's experimental findings and yet enables an economist to express the implications of prospect theory in terms of representations of forecasting behavior and to model limits to speculation. To examine the implications of preferences over gambles defined in this chapter for the movement of aggregate outcomes in a world of imperfect knowledge, we also proposed that IKE representations of market participants' forecasts be used to examine change in prospective utilities on the individual and aggregate levels. We refer to our modification of prospect theory as *endogenous prospect theory*, which we summarize with the following set of assumptions:

Utility function

- **Reference dependence:**

  The carriers of value are gains and losses defined relative to a reference point.

- **Loss aversion:**

  The disutility from losses exceeds the utility from gains of the same magnitude for all values of gains and losses.

- **Endogenous loss aversion:**

  For bets involving equal magnitudes of gains and losses on a unit position, the degree of loss aversion increases with the size of the speculative position.

- **Endogenous sensitivity:**

  The marginal value of both gains and losses decreases with position size, except when the size of losses becomes large, at which point the marginal value of losses increases with position size.

Preferences over gambles

- **IKE Representations of change in prospective values:**

  Models that aim to represent individual decision making in non-experimental settings should not fully prespecify revisions of prospective values.

Appendix 9.A:
Limits to Speculation under Endogenous Loss Aversion

Representations for the position size that maximizes prospective utility takes the same form for both short and long positions. Consequently, we need only differentiate PU_t^L, defined in equation (9.22), with respect to the position size a_t^L:

$$\frac{\partial PU^L}{\partial a^L} = \alpha \, (W)^\alpha \, P[\widehat{\mathcal{G}}^L; \alpha] \, (a)^{\alpha-1} - \lambda_1 \alpha \, (W)^\alpha \left\{ -P[\widehat{\mathcal{L}}^L; \alpha] \right\} (a)^{\alpha-1}$$

$$- \lambda_2^1 \beta \, (W)^\beta \left\{ -P[\widehat{\mathcal{L}}^L; \beta] \right\} (a)^{\beta-1}, \tag{9.47}$$

where for ease of notation we suppress the superscript i and the time subscripts t and $t+1$.

Setting $\frac{\partial PU^L}{\partial a^L} = 0$ and using the definition of the prospective return in equation (9.15) implies the following representation for the size of a long position:

$$a^L = \frac{W^{-1} \left(\frac{\alpha}{\lambda_2^1 \beta} \right)^{\frac{1}{\beta-\alpha}}}{\left\{ -P[\widehat{\mathcal{L}}^L; \beta] \right\}^{\frac{1}{\beta-\alpha}}} \left\{ P[\widehat{\mathcal{R}}^L; \alpha, \alpha] - (1 - \lambda_1) P[\widehat{\mathcal{L}}^L; \alpha] \right\}^{\frac{1}{\beta-\alpha}}, \tag{9.48}$$

where a^L is constrained to be nonnegative. Analogously, for bears, we have:

$$-a^S = \frac{W^{-1} \left(\frac{\alpha}{\lambda_2^1 \beta} \right)^{\frac{1}{\beta-\alpha}}}{\left\{ -P[\widehat{\mathcal{L}}^S; \beta] \right\}^{\frac{1}{\beta-\alpha}}} \left\{ P[\widehat{\mathcal{R}}^S; \alpha, \alpha] - (1 - \lambda_1) P[\widehat{\mathcal{L}}^S; \alpha] \right\}^{\frac{1}{\beta-\alpha}}, \tag{9.49}$$

where a^S is constrained to be nonpositive.[23]

Setting $\lambda_1 = 0$ in equations (9.48) and (9.49) reduces these expressions to position sizes that are implied by the original Kahneman and Tversky's utility function in equation (9.7). Moreover, for $\lambda_1 = 0$, both PU_t^L and PU_t^L are positive when evaluated at their maxima a^L and $-a^S$. This conclusion follows by setting $\lambda_1 = 0$ and substituting the resulting expressions for a^L and a^S into equations (9.22) and (9.23), respectively:

$$PU_t^L = \left(a_t^L W_t^i \right)^\alpha P[\widehat{\mathcal{G}}^L; \alpha] \left(1 - \frac{\alpha}{\beta} \right)$$

$$PU_t^S = \left(a_t^S W_t^i \right)^\alpha P[\widehat{\mathcal{G}}^S; \alpha] \left(1 - \frac{\alpha}{\beta} \right).$$

23. Given that $\alpha < \beta$, equation (9.47) is concave in the position size. Thus, a^L in equation (9.48) and $-a^S$ in equation (9.49) maximize the prospective utility from a long and a short position, respectively.

Since $\alpha < \beta$, $P[\widehat{\mathcal{G}}^{\mathrm{L}}; \alpha] > 0$, and $P[\widehat{\mathcal{G}}^{\mathrm{S}}; \alpha] > 0$, both PU_t^{L} and PU_t^{S} are positive. Thus, an individual will always hold an open position in foreign exchange: she will hold a long (short) position if

$$P[\widehat{\mathcal{G}}^{\mathrm{L}}; \alpha] > P[\widehat{\mathcal{G}}^{\mathrm{S}}; \alpha] \left(P[\widehat{\mathcal{G}}^{\mathrm{L}}; \alpha] < P[\widehat{\mathcal{G}}^{\mathrm{S}}; \alpha] \right).$$

10 Modeling Individual Forecasting Strategies and Their Revisions

We have related an individual's decisions on whether to speculate in an asset market and, if so, how much capital to place at risk, to her point forecasts of the future return and the potential unit loss that may result from holding a speculative position. We represented these forecasts as the mean and expected value of the loss part of a probability distribution for the future return. The objective of the present chapter is to formulate the partially predetermining restrictions that we use in subsequent chapters to represent an individual's forecasting strategy and its revisions.

The set of restrictions that we use depends on the context that we want to model. In chapter 15, for example, we construct an IKE model of the exchange rate to help us examine whether movements in this price are related to macroeconomic fundamentals over the modern floating-rate period. To represent an individual's forecast of the future return in terms of a set of macroeconomic fundamentals at every point in time, we make use of TCEH proposed by Frydman and Phelps (1990). TCEH is based on the idea that economists' models summarize their qualitative insights concerning the causal mechanism underpinning market outcomes and that, presumably, these insights are shared by market participants. Economists usually have several models of an aggregate outcome. Thus, TCEH representations of forecasting behavior make use of several economic models, rather than relying on just one. One of the problems with implementing TCEH is that economists' models themselves involve market participants' forecasts. Without specifications for these forecasts, economists' models do not imply even a qualitative relationship between the outcome variable and any causal variable. We show how this problem can be addressed while recognizing that individuals must cope with imperfect knowledge.

An IKE model allows for the possibility, however, that, over time, not only do the causal variables change, but individuals may revise their forecasting strategies. Consequently, imposing TCEH restrictions at every point in time is insufficient to imply even a qualitative relationship between changes in the exchange rate and any one of the causal variables in the model. For example, suppose an economist uses TCEH to restrict the parameter that he attaches to money supply to be positive in his representation of an individual's forecast of the future exchange rate. Over time, money supply could rise and the individual's forecast could nonetheless fall even if the values of the other variables that enter the model do not change. This scenario could occur if the parameter for money, although remaining positive at every point in time, were to fall simultaneously.

Strikingly, although the TCEH restrictions do not constrain change in our representations sufficiently, such strong assumptions are often not needed to account for outcomes in real world markets. For many of the results that we derive in subsequent chapters, we do not prespecify a set of potential causal variables and their influences in representing an individual's forecasting strategy.[1] Rather, we impose only partially predetermining restrictions on how our representations can change over time.

In motivating our IKE restrictions, we rely on the premise that the way a market participant forecasts the future depends to a large extent on her social context, which includes conventions and the historical record on market outcomes and government policy. Because economists and other social scientists share the social context with market participants, their knowledge and intuitions concerning this context may help in modeling forecasting behavior.[2] We also make use of empirical findings from psychology and economics to motivate some of our partially predetermining restrictions.

In our model of exchange rate swings, we use a well-known finding in psychology that individuals often revise their beliefs in a conservative way. What constitutes conservative behavior depends on the context being modeled. Our formulation takes conservative behavior to imply that an individual's forecast of the future exchange rate is "not too different" from the forecast that she would have had if she did not revise her forecasting strategy. Our conservative restrictions do not constrain the set of causal variables or how these variables might matter for an individual's forecast. Moreover, by imposing only qualitative constraints on change, our model is consistent with countless transition paths that characterize how an individual's forecast of the future exchange rate develops over time. Nevertheless, we show in

---

1. We do, however, assume that individual forecasting strategies depend on the current exchange rate.

2. See chapter 2 for a discussion of Weber's reliance on the social context for understanding "rational" behavior at the time of the emergence of capitalism.

chapter 14 that as long as revisions of individuals' forecasting strategies are conservative, then not only can long swings in the exchange rate away from PPP arise in the model, but movements in macroeconomic fundamentals may be the primary factor driving such swings.

In our model of the premium on foreign exchange, we build on an insight of Keynes (1936) that social conventions and benchmark levels play a key role in how market participants forecast potential losses from speculative positions in asset markets. Our model makes use of two partially predetermining restrictions—one for market participants who hold long positions (bulls) and another for those who hold short positions (bears). These restrictions capture the idea that, as the asset price, for example, increases further above its perceived benchmark level, bulls (bears) become more concerned (less concerned) about a movement back to the historical benchmark level (about continuation of the swing away) and raise (lower) their forecasts of the potential unit loss. As with the conservative restrictions that we use to model exchange rate swings, our gap restrictions require an economist to prespecify neither the potential set of causal variables that underpin change in outcomes nor the influences of these variables in his representation. Nevertheless, these restrictions constrain change in our model sufficiently to derive implications that can be confronted with the data.

10.1. Theories Consistent Expectations Hypothesis

TCEH explores the possibility that because economists share the social context with market participants, the qualitative features of economists' models may be useful in representing an individual's forecasting strategy. To fix ideas, we suppose that a model for the exchange rate involves an individual's point forecast of the future exchange rate. Typically, an economist would represent this forecast as the mean of some probability distribution, $S^{i,\mathrm{RP}}_{t|t+1}$, conditional on a set of causal variables, X^i_t. Denoting the mean of this distribution by $\hat{S}^{i,\mathrm{RP}}_{t|t+1}$, we express it as a linear function:

$$\hat{S}^{i,\mathrm{RP}}_{t|t+1} = E[S^{i,\mathrm{RP}}_{t|t+1}] = \hat{\beta}^i_t X^i_t, \tag{10.1}$$

where, for convenience, we assume that the representation does not depend on the current exchange rate.[3]

Based on a specification of preferences, constraints, and some objective function an economist derives the so-called "semi-reduced" form of a model for aggregate outcomes. We suppose that the semi-reduced form of one such

---

3. Below and in chapter 15, we allow for $\hat{S}^{i,\mathrm{RP}}_{t|t+1}$ to depend on the exchange rate S_t.

model for the exchange rate is given by:

$$S_t^{(1)} = \beta^{(1)} X_t^{(1)} + \theta^{(1)} \hat{S}_{t|t+1}^{RP}, \tag{10.2}$$

where $X_t^{(1)}$ is the set of causal variables that appear in the representation of preferences and constraints, the parameters $(\beta^{(1)}, \theta^{(1)})$ are functions of the parameters used in specifying individual preferences and the processes governing the causal variables, and $\hat{S}_{t|t+1}^{RP}$ is an aggregate of individuals' forecasts of the exchange rate.[4] Without loss of generality, we constrain the sign of $\theta^{(1)}$ to be positive.[5] We also follow the usual practice and assume that the parameters of the semi-reduced form are invariant over time. The superscript (1) underscores the fact that the particular model in equation (10.2) is only one of many models of the exchange rate that an economist could construct.

An economist would usually use REH, which constrains the set of causal variables that enter his representation of individual forecasting behavior to those that appear in the one semi-reduced form that he has derived, that is, $X^i = X^{(1)}$ for all i. REH also constrains the set of parameters that are attached to these variables in this simple setup to be functions of $\beta^{(1)}$ and $\theta^{(1)}$. The REH representation of the aggregate forecast can be written as:

$$\hat{S}_{t|t+1}^{RE(1)} = \hat{\beta}^{RE(1)} X_t^{(1)}, \tag{10.3}$$

where $\hat{\beta}^{(1)} = f^{(1)}(\beta^{(1)}, \theta^{(1)})$.[6] We note that, in this typical setup, REH constrains $\hat{\beta}^{RE(1)}$ to be unchanging over time.

10.1.1. Qualitative Features and a Plurality of Models

By contrast, TCEH does not ignore the pluralism of models in economics. Like all other IKE models it allows for change in its representations of individual forecasting behavior and, moreover, it only partially prespecifies this change.

TCEH constrains its representations at each point in time to be consistent with the qualitative features of a set of extant models. There are two problems with formulating such constraints. First, how does one discern the

4. For an example of the derivation of a semi-reduced form such as in equation (10.2), see the appendix to chapter 6.

5. Typically, in models of asset markets, such as the ones considered throughout this book, the parameter attached to the forecast in the semi-reduced form is positive. If this parameter were negative, its sign could always be reversed by reversing the signs of the parameters of the represention of the forecasting strategy, defined in equation (10.3).

6. For examples, see chapters 3 and 6.

qualitative features of even one model if they depend on a specification of forecasting behavior? And second, how can the qualitative features of several models, which may in some cases conflict, be combined to represent an individual's forecasting behavior?

To uncover the qualitative features of one of the extant models, we propose a simple procedure: we impose constraints on our representation of an individual's point forecast of the exchange rate so that the aggregate model necessarily implies the same qualitative features concerning the causal mechanism underpinning the conditional mean of exchange rate.

In terms of model 1, we specify an average of individuals' forecasts in terms of the causal variables that appear in the semi-reduced form:

$$\hat{S}_{t|t+1}^{\text{RP}(1)} = \hat{\beta}_t^{(1)} X_t^{(1)}. \tag{10.4}$$

Using this form and shifting equation (10.2) forward yields the aggregate model at $t + 1$:

$$S_{t+1}^{(1)} = \left(\beta^{(1)} + \theta^{(1)}\hat{\beta}_{t+1}^{(1)}\right) X_{t+1}^{(1)}. \tag{10.5}$$

To compare the qualitative features of the representation in equation (10.4) with those of the aggregate model, we need to express equation (10.5) in terms of information at time t. We thus need to represent how the causal variables evolve over time. A common practice is to assume random walks with drift.[7] This assumption implies the following aggregate model:

$$S_{t+1}^{(1)} = \left(\beta^{(1)} + \theta^{(1)}\hat{\beta}_{t+1}^{(1)}\right) X_t^{(1)} + \epsilon_{t+1}, \tag{10.6}$$

where $X_t^{(1)}$ is assumed to include drift terms and ϵ_{t+1} is an error term.

It is clear that the qualitative features of the aggregate model in equation (10.6) would be the same as those that are implied by the specification of an individual's forecast in equation (10.4) only if the signs of $\hat{\beta}_t^{(1)}$ and $\left(\beta^{(1)} + \theta^{(1)}\hat{\beta}_{t+1}^{(1)}\right)$ were the same. In our example, with $\theta^{(1)} > 0$, setting the signs of the parameters in $\hat{\beta}_t^{(1)}$ to be equal to those in $\beta^{(1)}$ at each point in time indeed ensures that the qualitative features of equations (10.6) and (10.4) are the same.[8]

---

7. This procedure would deliver different qualitative restrictions on the forecasting behavior if the causal variables were assumed to follow other processes.

8. It is possible that one or more of the parameters of the semi-reduced form have ambiguous signs. In this case, the reduced-form model would not imply a clear qualitative prediction concerning how the corresponding causal variables influenced the exchange rate.

This procedure implies that the qualitative features of model 1 in equation (10.6) consist of the causal variables that may be important for forecasting the future exchange rate—those in $X_t^{(1)}$—and the signs of the reduced-form parameters in equation (10.6) ($\beta^{(1)} + \theta^{(1)}\hat{\beta}_{t+1}^{(1)}$), which by construction are the same as those in $\beta^{(1)}$.

Although TCEH recognizes that economists' models might be useful in representing forecasting strategies, it also acknowledges that there exists a pluralism of economic models. It does so by using the qualitative features from a set of economic models to constrain its representations of individual behavior. Thus, to implement TCEH, an economist must restrict the set of extant models that he will use in his analysis. For example, in chapter 15, we make use of a class of three monetary models of the exchange rate.

To highlight the steps involved in the formulation of a TCEH representation, we suppose that the set of models chosen by an economist consists of model 1 and a second model, the semi-reduced form of which is:

$$S_t^{(2)} = \beta^{(2)} X_t^{(2)} + \theta^{(2)} \hat{S}_{t|t+1}^{\mathrm{RP}}, \tag{10.7}$$

where, in general, $X_t^{(2)}$ contains some causal variables that are not included in $X_t^{(1)}$ and the values of the parameters in $\beta^{(2)}$ and $\theta^{(2)}$ differ from those in $\beta^{(1)}$ and $\theta^{(1)}$. Using the same procedure as before to uncover the qualitative features of the model, we have:

$$S_{t+1}^{(2)} = \left(\beta^{(2)} + \theta^{(2)}\hat{\beta}_{t+1}^{(2)}\right) X_t^{(2)} + \epsilon_{t+1}, \tag{10.8}$$

where we impose a set of sign restrictions on the $\hat{\beta}^{(2)}$ parameters so that the signs of the parameters in $\hat{\beta}_t^{(2)}$ and $\left(\beta^{(2)} + \theta^{(2)}\hat{\beta}_{t+1}^{(2)}\right)$ are the same. Consequently, the qualitative features of model 2 consist of the causal variables in $X_t^{(2)}$ and the signs of the reduced-form parameters in equation (10.8), which, by construction, are the same as those in $\beta^{(2)}$.

10.1.2. TCEH Representations

The partially predetermining restrictions that TCEH imposes on its representations of individual forecasting behavior take into account the qualitative features of all extant models considered by an economist. In our example, it first restricts the composition of the causal variables that *might* enter the representation of forecasting behavior to the union of the variables involved in both models, $X_t^i = \left[X_t^{(1)} \ X_t^{(2)}\right]$, that is:

$$\hat{S}^{i,\text{TCE}}_{t|t+1} = \hat{\beta}^i_t \left[X^{(1)}_t \ X^{(2)}_t \right].$$
(10.9)

In general, TCEH recognizes that only a subset of the causal variables in equation (10.9) may be needed to adequately represent an individual's forecasting behavior during a particular subperiod; that is, some of the parameters in $\hat{\beta}^i_t$ may be zero. This subset may include only some of the variables implied by any one model. TCEH also allows for the possibility that the set of causal variables that are needed to represent forecasting behavior may change from one subperiod to another. Moreover, it prespecifies neither the timing of this change nor which variables may be relevant in any period of time.[9]

However, if a causal variable does enter an economist's representation of forecasting behavior, TCEH constrains it to do so either with a parameter whose sign is consistent with the set of extant models chosen by the economist or with a parameter that is unrestricted.

There are two cases in which TCEH imposes qualitative restrictions on the parameters of its representation of forecasting behavior. It does so if there are causal variables that either enter more than one of the extant models with parameters whose signs agree across those models or that enter only one of the extant models. In both cases, TCEH would restrict the signs of the parameters of its representation to be the same as those of the corresponding parameters of the extant models.

However, if there are variables that enter more than one model, but with parameter values that differ in sign, then the set of extant models that is considered by the economist does not convey unambiguous qualitative information about how these variables influence the outcome variable. In this case, we assign the same importance to the qualitative features of all extant models. Consequently, TCEH does not restrict the signs of the corresponding parameters in its representation of forecasting behavior.

We note that this procedure is only one way to address the problem of how an economist could use the qualitative information conveyed by a set of models when this information involves conflicting features. Alternatively, an economist could adopt a criterion for combining the qualitative features of his models that makes use of extra-model considerations. For example, his intuition and/or empirical evidence may lead him to place greater weight

---

9. This freedom has an important implication for the empirical analysis of TCEH, and more generally IKE, models. See chapter 15.

on the qualitative features of one extant model over another.[10] In our view, one method does not appear to be superior to another.[11]

To illustrate how TCEH formulates its qualitative restrictions, suppose that at time t, the set of causal variables that is used by an economist to represent forecasting behavior (those that enter with non-zero parameters) consists of four variables $X_t = (X_{1,t}, X_{2,t}, X_{3,t}, X_{4,t})$. We express the representation in equation (10.9) as:

$$\hat{S}^{i,\text{TCE}}_{t|t+1} = \hat{\beta}_{1,t} X_{1,t} + \hat{\beta}_{2,t} X_{2,t} + \hat{\beta}_{3,t} X_{1,t} + \hat{\beta}_{4,t} X_{2,t}. \qquad (10.10)$$

Let the first two variables enter both of the models in equations (10.6) and (10.8), that is, $X_{1,t} = X^{(1)}_{1,t} = X^{(2)}_{1,t}$ and $X_{2,t} = X^{(1)}_{2,t} = X^{(2)}_{2,t}$. Moreover, let the other two variables enter only one of the models: for example, suppose that $X_{3,t} = X^{(1)}_{3,t}$ from model 1 and $X_{4,t} = X^{(2)}_{3,t}$ from model 2. Thus, we rewrite the semi-reduced forms in equations (10.2) and (10.7) as:

$$S^{(1)}_t = \beta^{(1)}_1 X_{1,t} + \beta^{(1)}_2 X_{2,t} + \beta^{(1)}_3 X_{3,t} + \theta^{(1)} \hat{S}^{\text{RP}}_{t|t+1}$$

$$S^{(2)}_t = \beta^{(2)}_1 X_{1,t} + \beta^{(2)}_2 X_{2,t} + \beta^{(2)}_3 X_{4,t} + \theta^{(2)} \hat{S}^{\text{RP}}_{t|t+1},$$

where, for convenience, we assume that all of the β parameters in these equations have unambiguous signs.

The restrictions on the parameters in equation (10.10) that TCEH imposes can now be written as:

$$\text{sign}(\hat{\beta}_{k,t}) = \begin{cases} \text{sign}(\beta^{(1)}_k) & \text{if } \text{sign}(\beta^{(1)}_k) = \text{sign}(\beta^{(2)}_k) \\ \text{unrestricted} & \text{if } \text{sign}(\beta^{(1)}_k) \neq \text{sign}(\beta^{(2)}_k) \end{cases} \quad \text{for all } t \text{ and } k$$

$$\text{sign}(\hat{\beta}_{3,t}) = \text{sign}(\beta^{(1)}_3); \quad \text{sign}(\hat{\beta}_{4,t}) = \text{sign}(\beta^{(2)}_3) \quad \text{for all } t. \qquad (10.11)$$

10.1.3. Price Level Effect

In representing individual behavior in some of our IKE models, we presume that, in addition to a set of causal variables, forecasts of the future exchange

---

10. Such criteria could also be used in uncovering the qualitative features of one extant model in cases where some of the parameters of the semi-reduced form are ambiguous in sign.

11. The empirical findings of chapter 15, however, reveal that, regardless of the method an economist uses to deal with a conflict between extant models, relying solely on them to represent individual forecasts has serious limitations. We find that some of our empirical results are difficult to interpret within the context of the class of monetray models that we consider unless additional considerations—for example, changes in institutions—are included in the analysis.

rate depend on the current exchange rate at every point in time:

$$\hat{S}^{i,\text{IKE}}_{t|t+1} = \hat{\beta}^{i'}_t X^i_t + \rho_t S_t. \tag{10.12}$$

While IKE can accommodate the possibility that the influence of S_t on an individual's forecast may change from one point in time to another, we impose the following partially predetermining constraint on ρ_t:

$$0 < \rho_t < 1 \quad \text{for all } t. \tag{10.13}$$

This restriction implies that, if the forecasting strategy and the causal variables were to remain unchanged while the exchange rate rose or fell, the forecast in equation (10.12) would move in the same direction as the change in the exchange rate but by less than one-for-one.

Motivation for this restriction comes from our use of TCEH to uncover the qualitative features of two sticky-price monetary models. We find that, if the restriction in equation (10.13) is imposed on these models, then the resulting aggregate models imply the same qualitative relationship between the current exchange rate and its future values.

Such a restriction is common in many asset market models. Typically, these models are invariant, so that, as the asset price changes over time in these models, an individual's forecast necessarily changes in the same direction but less than one-for-one. This implication underlies the usual downward-sloping feature of the demand curve in these models.

However, once an economist recognizes that an individual may revise her forecasting strategy when the exchange rate or any other causal factor changes, the analysis is very different. For example, in an IKE model, the imposition of the price level restriction at every point in time does not ensure that an individual's forecast changes in the same direction as the exchange rate while holding the causal variables X^i constant.[12] Thus, to ensure such behavior in an IKE model, regardless of whether the model relies on the price level restriction, we need to constrain revisions of forecasting strategies with a separate partially predetermining restriction.[13]

10.2. IKE Representations of Revisions: An Overview

Although the partially predetermining TCEH and price level restrictions are weaker than the fully predetermining restrictions of contemporary models,

---

12. For example, suppose the exchange rate rises between $t - 1$ and t. If, over this period, ρ were to fall, but continued to satisfy the price level restriction at both points in time, the change in an individual's forecast could be negative.

13. For a simple example of such a model, see chapter 4.

they are still rather audacious. They require that an economist prespecify the set of relevant variables for—and their influences on—individual behavior and aggregate outcomes. Based on theoretical and empirical considerations, an economist may feel reasonably confident that his representations of an individual's exchange rate forecast should include the current exchange rate. But deciding on which causal variables may be relevant in accounting for behavior is much less clear.

Fortunately, many of the results that we derive in this book do not involve any particular assumptions about which causal variables individuals might use at any particular point in time to forecast the future or how these causal variables might matter. Rather, our results stem from the use of qualitative restrictions on representations of how individuals revise their forecasting strategies over time.

An IKE model represents the revision of an individual's forecasting strategy at each point in time as a transition between any one of the conditional probability distributions for R_{t+1} that is consistent with its partially predetermining restrictions. These partially predetermined probabilistic representations of change imply countless forecast transition paths.[14] Nevertheless, because these transition paths all have certain features in common, an IKE model delivers implications that can be confronted with empirical evidence.

10.3. Trend Restriction

As in many fully predetermined models, we need to constrain how an individual's exchange rate forecast changes as the exchange rate varies to ensure stability in our models. A change in an individual's exchange rate forecast, in general, stems either from new realizations of the causal variables and the exchange rate or from a revision in her forecasting strategy. We represent the total change in this forecast, which we denote by $\mathcal{D}\hat{S}_{t|t+1}^{i,\text{IKE}}$, as:

$$\mathcal{D}\hat{S}_{t|t+1}^{i,\text{IKE}} = \hat{\beta}_{t-1}^{i}\Delta X_t^i + \left(\hat{\rho}_{t-1}^i \Delta S_t + \Delta\hat{\beta}_t^i X_t^i + \Delta\hat{\rho}_t^i S_t\right)$$

$$= \hat{\beta}_{t-1}^i \Delta X_t^i + \mathcal{D}^S \hat{S}_{t|t+1}^{i,\text{IKE}}, \tag{10.14}$$

where $\mathcal{D}^S\hat{S}_{t|t+1}^{i,\text{IKE}}$ denotes the partial change in an individual's exchange rate forecast that arises solely because of changes in her forecasting strategy and/or the exchange rate and Δ denotes the first difference operator. The "$\mathcal{D}$" notation reflects the fact that with IKE, a change in $\hat{S}_{t|t+1}^{i,\text{IKE}}$ may result from

---

14. See chapter 4 for the definitions of a partially predetermined probabilistic representation of change and a forecast transition path.

a change in the structure of this representation and not just from variation in the exchange rate.[15]

To guarantee stability in our models, we impose the following trend restriction on all of our representations of how an individual revises her forecasting strategy of R_{t+1}:

$$0 < \frac{\mathcal{D}^S \hat{S}_{t|t+1}^{i,\text{IKE}}}{\Delta S_t} < 1. \tag{10.15}$$

To clarify how this partially predetermining restriction constrains our representations, we suppose that, between $t-1$ and t, the exchange rate rises while the causal variables remain unchanged. In general, the rise in the exchange rate will lead an individual to revise her forecasting strategy. We represent this revision as a transition to any conditional probability distribution for R_{t+1} at time t that is consistent with the trend restriction in equation (10.15). This restriction constrains the set of possible postchange distributions to those whose conditional means presume that the individual's forecast of the future exchange rate rises, but less so than the rise in the exchange rate.[16]

We note that, because the trend restriction constrains only the partial change in $\hat{S}_{t|t+1}^{i,\text{IKE}}$, it does not preclude the possibility that an individual may revise her forecast down if the rise in the exchange rate is accompanied by changes in the causal variables that influence $\hat{S}_{t|t+1}^{i,\text{IKE}}$. We also note that equation (10.15) places no constraint on what variables, beyond the exchange rate, may be needed to represent an individual's forecasting strategy or how these variables may influence her forecast.

By imposing only a qualitative condition on change, this restriction is compatible with innumerable possible revisions of an individual's forecasting strategy at each point in time. It is consistent, therefore, with countless transition paths that characterize how an individual's forecasting strategy develops over time. Each of these paths is based on a particular sequence of transitions between conditional probability distributions that satisfy equation (10.15). In an IKE model, the representation of an individual's forecasting behavior over any extended period of time would be given by any one of these forecast transition paths. Nevertheless, all of the transition paths that

---

15. The $\mathcal{D}$ and $\mathcal{D}^S$ operators serve roles that are analogous to the total and partial differentials, which, in general, do not exist when both the arguments and the structure of the representation change.

16. We assume that the values of the exchange rate and the interest rates are known to individuals at time t. Thus, constraining the conditional mean of $R_{t+1} = S_{t+1} - s_t - fp_t$ is tantamount to constraining the conditional mean of S_{t+1}, where S_t and fp_t denote the exchange rate and forward premium, respectively.

are consistent with equation (10.15) share a common feature: the partial change in an individual's forecast of the exchange rate, $D^S \hat{S}_{t|t+1}^{i,\text{IKE}}$, between any two adjacent points in time is in the same direction as the change in S but is less than one-for-one. It is this feature of our representations of individual forecasting behavior that is important for ensuring stability in our models.

Beyond theoretical considerations, motivation for the trend restriction also comes from empirical observation. There is much evidence from the market microstructure literature that trend-following technical trading rules are widely used in all financial markets. Such rules extrapolate recent price movements to determine whether a long or short position in the market should be taken or, if the individual is already in the market, whether her position should be maintained.[17]

The study of Frankel and Froot (1987), which uses survey data on actual exchange rate forecasts, also provides evidence that individuals' forecasts extrapolate the most recent price movement.[18] They also find evidence that although market participants' forecasts increase with the current exchange rate, they do so less than one-for-one.

10.4. Conservative Revisions

In many contemporary models of the exchange rate, the key variable driving change is the aggregate of individual forecasts of the future exchange rate. This is also the case in our IKE model of exchange rate swings. One of the restrictions that we use to model revisions of individual forecasting strategies is consistent with a well-documented phenomenon in psychology called conservatism. Edwards (1968) and other psychologists have found that individuals can be slow to change their beliefs in the face of new evidence. Shleifer (2000, p. 127) summarizes this finding as:

> [When one] benchmarks a subject's reaction to new evidence against that of an idealized rational Bayesian in which the true normative value of a piece of evidence is well defined . . . experiments [reveal that] individuals update their posteriors in the right direction, but by too little relative to the rational Bayesian benchmark. . . . A conventional first approximation to the data would say that it takes anywhere from two to

17. See section 7.6.1 in chapter 7 for references.

18. For a discussion of these data, see chapter 8. See also DeBondt (1993), who finds strong evidence of extrapolative behavior using both investor surveys and classroom experiments.

five observations to do one observation's worth of work in inducing the subject to change his opinions.[19]

What constitutes conservative behavior depends on the context being modeled. For example, in their fully predetermined model of investor sentiment in security markets, Barberis et al. (1998) formulate conservative behavior as underreaction to separate earnings announcements. By contrast, our formulation implies that an individual behaves conservatively when a revision of her forecasting strategy, ceteris paribus, leads to a new forecast that is not too different from the forecast that she would have formed had she not revised her strategy. But conservative behavior is not universal: what qualifies as "not too different" in our model of swings in chapter 14 depends on whether we assume that goods prices are fully flexible or adjust to their equilibrium values only sluggishly.

Beyond findings in psychology, motivation for our formulation of conservatism comes from the structural change findings that we report in chapter 15. These findings indicate that the relationship between the exchange rate and macroeconomic fundamentals is characterized by relatively stable parameters over subperiods of the modern period of floating currencies.

To illustrate how we formulate a conservative restriction, we express the total change in an individual's exchange rate forecast as:

$$\mathcal{D}\hat{S}^{i,\text{IKE}}_{t|t+1} = \hat{\beta}^{i'}_{t-1}\Delta X^i_t + \Delta\hat{\beta}^{i'}_t X^i_t = \Delta^U\hat{S}^{i,\text{IKE}}_{t|t+1} + \mathcal{D}^R\hat{S}^{i,\text{IKE}}_{t|t+1}, \qquad (10.16)$$

where $\mathcal{D}^R\hat{S}^{i,\text{IKE}}_{t|t+1}$ denotes the partial change in an individual's forecast that occurs only because of a revision of her forecasting strategy at time t, and $\Delta^U\hat{S}^{i,\text{IKE}}_{t|t+1}$ denotes the change in $\hat{S}^{i,\text{IKE}}_{t|t+1}$ that would occur between $t-1$ and t if the individual's forecasting strategy were unchanged and only new realizations of the causal variables led her to revise her forecast.[20] A simple conservative restriction can be written as:

$$\left|\mathcal{D}^R\hat{S}^{i,\text{IKE}}_{t|t+1}\right| < \hat{\beta}^i_{t-1}\left|E\left[\Delta X^i_t|X^i_{t-1}\right]\right|, \qquad (10.17)$$

19. We note that because of imperfect knowledge, "the true normative value of a piece of evidence" is *not* so "well defined" in the context of our model. As such, the magnitude of the updating found by Edwards (1968) most likely overstates the magnitude of the updating that would occur with imperfect knowledge.

20. The conservative restrictions that we use to model long swings in the exchange rate are imposed on the component of our representations of forecasting behavior that does not depend on the exchange rate. We thus abstract from the influence of changes in the exchange rate in equation (10.16).

where $|\cdot|$ denotes absolute value and $E[\Delta X_t^i | X_{t-1}^i]$ is a conditional expectation.[21] This restriction, as with the trend restriction, constrains the conditional probability distribution of R_{t+1} that is used at time t relative to the distribution at $t-1$. It constrains the postchange distribution to be one that implies that the new exchange rate forecast is not too different, as defined by equation (10.17), from the one that would obtain at t were an individual to leave her forecasting strategy unchanged.

The conservative restriction in equation (10.17) constrains neither the set of causal variables that may enter an economist's representation of forecasting behavior nor how these variables may matter. Because this restriction constrains only the change in the point forecast, it does not rule out substantial revisions of forecasting strategies. Moreover, the conservative restriction does not imply that the magnitude of the change in an individual's forecast between any two adjacent points in time must be small. If changes in the causal variables are large, then the change in $\hat{S}_{t|t+1}^{i,\text{IKE}}$ may also be large.

As before, our representation of an individual's forecasting strategy and its revisions is given by any one of myriad forecast transition paths. Because all such paths are consistent with equation (10.17), they all share a common feature: the direction of change of $\hat{S}_{t|t+1}^{i,\text{IKE}}$ between any two adjacent points in time is, on average, determined by movements of the causal variables. It is this feature of our representation of individual forecasting behavior that is important in generating exchange rate swings that depend on macroeconomic fundamentals.

We should also emphasize that we do not prespecify when conservative restrictions might be satisfied in our model. Instead, we examine the implications of imposing them over some limited period of time. Although they may often be consistent with how market participants revise their forecasting strategies in real world markets, conservative restrictions eventually become inadequate as characterizations of behavior. Indeed, we argue that, if the gap from PPP grows large enough, revisions in forecasting strategies will become nonconservative. This assumption is important for generating sustained countermovements in the exchange rate back to its historical benchmark. Because we do not prespecify when forecasting behavior may be conservative in our models, we do not prespecify when protracted exchange rate swings away from PPP might begin or end.[22]

21. If we assume that goods prices and interest rates do not vary, then the conservative condition in equation (10.17) would ensure that movements in the causal variables themselves would lead to exchange rate swings. More generally, however, more involved conservative restrictions are needed for swings. See chapter 14.

22. This feature of the model is crucial for avoiding Lucas's modeling inconsistency problem. See chapter 14.

10.5. Revisions of the Expected Unit Loss

We show in the next chapter that equilibrium in the foreign exchange market under endogenous prospect theory equates the aggregate of market participants' forecasts of the return on holding foreign exchange to the market premium. The market premium is based on representations of individuals' uncertainty premiums, which, as we showed in the previous chapter, depend on their forecasts of the potential unit loss. To derive implications from any of our IKE models, therefore, we must impose restrictions on our representations of how an individual revises this forecast.

We recall from chapter 9 that the expected unit loss is represented at time t as:

$$\hat{l}_{t|t+1}^{i,\mathrm{L}}\left(z_t\right) = E_t^i[R_{t+1} < 0|z_t^i] < 0 \tag{10.18}$$

if the individual is a bull or as

$$\hat{l}_{t|t+1}^{i,\mathrm{S}}\left(z_t\right) = -E_t^i[R_{t+1} > 0|z_t^i] < 0 \tag{10.19}$$

if she is a bear, where z_t^i consists of current and past values of the exchange rate and some set of causal variables that represent the factors that an individual uses when forming her forecasts of the potential unit loss.[23] As in chapter 9, we define losses for both bulls and bears as negative values.

In general, when a market participant revises her forecast of the return on foreign exchange at time t, either because of a revision in her forecasting strategy or because of new realizations of the causal variables, she revises her forecast of the potential unit loss. We represent the total change in this forecast between $t - 1$ and t as:

$$\mathcal{D}\hat{l}_{t|t+1}^{i} = \hat{l}_{t|t+1}^{i}\left(z_t\right) - \hat{l}_{t-1|t}^{i}\left(z_{t-1}\right). \tag{10.20}$$

Our IKE model of the market premium, which we call the "gap plus model," is based on two sets of qualitative restrictions that constrain how changes in the exchange rate and causal variables influence $\mathcal{D}\hat{l}_{t|t+1}^{i}$. One set of restrictions appeals to an insight put forth by Keynes (1936). Keynes understood that, although asset prices have a tendency to move persistently away from historical benchmark levels for protracted periods of time, they eventually undergo, at unpredictable moments, sustained countermovements back to these benchmark levels.[24] He recognized that this feature of

---

23. For ease of notation, we drop the superscript IKE. It is convenient to express the conditional forecasts in equations (10.18) and (10.20) in terms of the realizations of the variables in z_t^i.

24. For evidence that asset prices exhibit long swings that revolve around historical benchmark levels, see chapter 7 and references therein.

the social context is key to understanding how participants in asset markets form their forecasts. In discussing the question of why a market participant might hold cash rather than interest-bearing bonds, Keynes argued that

> [the demand for cash] will not have a definitive quantitative relation to a given rate of interest of r; what matters is not the *absolute* level of r but the degree of its divergence from what is considered a fairly *safe* level of r, having regard to those calculations of probability which are being relied on. (Keynes, 1936, p. 201)

A historical benchmark is, of course, specific to each asset market. Each individual arrives at her own determination of the benchmark value and so, in general, these assessments will differ among individuals. However, there are a few general characteristics of a benchmark that are important for our analysis and that are explicit in Keynes's discussion of the notion of a "safe level of r":

1. The benchmark varies less than the observed asset price, as, for example, is the case for individual benchmarks based on averages of past prices.

2. "Unless reasons are believed to exist why future experience will be very different from past experience" (Keynes, 1936, p. 202), market participants are likely to use some notion of a historical benchmark level in forming their forecasts of future prices.

3. Market participants' perceptions of the historical benchmark level are based on convention and the historical record. For example, some measure of PPP has long been widely used by market participants and economists in the foreign exchange market, while in equity markets, much attention is given to historical averages of price-equity ratios.

This understanding of the importance of the historical benchmark suggests that an individual's expected loss from holding a speculative position in an asset depends on her evaluation of the gap between the expected asset price and the historical benchmark. If an individual were a bull and an asset price were to rise above its perceived benchmark, then her concern about a capital loss, which would result if the price were to revert back subsequently to its benchmark level, would tend to increase. However, if she were a bear, then her concern about a capital loss, which would result if the price were to continue to move away from the benchmark, would tend to fall.

To formalize this insight in the context of the foreign exchange market, we suppose that the causal variables that an individual uses to form her forecast of the potential unit loss influence this forecast indirectly through their effect on her evaluation of the gap, which we define as:

$$\widehat{gap}_t^i\left(z_t\right) = \hat{s}_{t|t+1}^i\left(z_t\right) - \hat{s}_t^{\mathrm{HB}i}\left(z_t\right), \tag{10.21}$$

where $\hat{s}_t^{\mathrm{HB}i}(z_t)$ denotes an individual's assessment at time t of the historical benchmark exchange rate.[25] We also suppose that the causal variables may have a direct influence on $\hat{l}_{t|t+1}^i$ beyond their impact on $\widehat{gap}_t^i(z_t)$. We thus express our representation of an individual's forecast of the potential unit loss as:

$$\hat{l}_{t|t+1}^i(z_t) = \hat{l}_{t|t+1}^i\left(\widehat{gap}_t^i(z_t)\right) + \left[\hat{l}_{t|t+1}^i(z_t) - \hat{l}_{t|t+1}^i\left(\widehat{gap}_t^i(z_t)\right)\right]$$

and the total change in this forecast between adjacent points in time as:

$$\mathcal{D}\hat{l}_{t|t+1}^i = \mathcal{D}^G\hat{l}_{t|t+1}^i + \bar{\mathcal{D}}^G\hat{l}_{t|t+1}^i, \tag{10.22}$$

where $\mathcal{D}^G$ denotes the partial change in $\hat{l}^i$ that is solely due to the influence of the causal variables on $\widehat{gap}^i$ and $\bar{\mathcal{D}}^G$ denotes the partial change in $\hat{l}^i$ that is due to a change in the causal variables in addition to any impact that this change may have on $\hat{l}^i$ through $\widehat{gap}_t^i$.

To model revisions of an individual's forecasting strategy in terms of the causal variables, we impose qualitative restrictions on $\mathcal{D}^G\hat{l}_{t|t+1}^i$ and $\bar{\mathcal{D}}^G\hat{l}_{t|t+1}^i$.

10.5.1. Gap Restrictions

The restrictions that we impose on $\mathcal{D}^G\hat{l}_{t|t+1}^i$ depend on whether an individual is a bull or a bear:

$$\frac{\mathcal{D}^G\hat{l}_{t|t+1}^L}{\mathcal{D}\widehat{gap}_t^L} < 0 \text{ or } \frac{\mathcal{D}^G\hat{l}_{t|t+1}^S}{\mathcal{D}\widehat{gap}_t^S} > 0. \tag{10.23}$$

To illustrate how these gap restrictions constrain our representations of individual forecasting behavior, we consider the case $\mathcal{D}\hat{l}_{t|t+1}^i = \mathcal{D}^G\hat{l}_{t|t+1}^i$. For concreteness, we also suppose that both s_{t-1} and $\hat{s}_{t-1|t}^i$ lie above $\hat{s}_t^{\mathrm{HB}i}$.

Consider now the impact of movements in the exchange rate and the causal factors on an individual's expected loss. To fix ideas, we suppose that these movements are associated with a revision of her forecasting strategy at time t and an increase in her point forecast of the future exchange rate further above her assessment of the historical benchmark, that is, $\mathcal{D}\widehat{gap}_t^i > 0$. In a similar fashion as before, we represent the individual's revised forecasting strategy with any conditional probability distribution for R_{t+1} that is consistent with the gap restrictions in equation (10.23). The moments of each one of these postchange distributions imply that,

---

25. The gap can also be defined in terms of the exchange rate at time t, rather than the forecast of the future exchange rate, or some weighted average of the two. See Frydman and Goldberg (2003). The conclusions of our analysis are not affected by either of these specifications of the gap variable.

relative to time $t - 1$, the magnitude of a bull's (bear's) expected loss $-\hat{l}^i_{t|t+1}$ increases (decreases).

All individuals understand that the exchange rate undergoes long swings and thus, may move away from its perceived benchmark level for an extended time before reverting back. The problem, of course, is that no one can be certain of when a swing in the exchange rate will end. If an individual is a bull, she believes that s will continue to move away from its benchmark value over the ensuing time period.[26] The rise in her $\hat{s}^i_{t|t+1}$ implies, ceteris paribus, that she expects a greater return from holding a long position in foreign exchange. Simultaneously, however, we hypothesize that the rise in $\widehat{gap}^i_t$ leads her to become more concerned about a countermovement back to the benchmark and a capital loss. The gap restriction for a bull in equation (10.23) captures this idea by constraining the probability distribution that is used to represent her forecasting strategy at time t to be one that involves a higher value of $-\hat{l}^i_{t|t+1}$.

If an individual is a bear, she believes that the exchange rate will undergo a movement back to its benchmark value over the ensuing time period. The rise in her $\hat{s}^i_{t|t+1}$ implies, ceteris paribus, that she expects a smaller return from holding a short position in foreign exchange. Simultaneously, however, we hypothesize that the rise in $\widehat{gap}^i_t$ leads her to become less concerned about a continuation of the swing away from the benchmark and a capital loss. The gap restriction for a bear in equation (10.23) accounts for this idea by constraining the probability distribution that is used to represent her forecasting strategy at time t to be one that involves a smaller value of $-\hat{l}^i_{t|t+1}$.

We note that, as with the trend and conservative restrictions, the gap restrictions place no constraints on the set of causal variables that may enter an economist's representation of forecasting behavior or how these variables may matter at any point in time.

10.5.2. Cumulative Current Account Restriction

Beyond influencing how an individual revises her expected unit loss indirectly through a gap effect, one or more of the causal factors may have a direct influence. The exchange rate literature suggests that a country's current account balance and international financial position may play such a role.

---

26. We are ignoring the possibility that the interest rate differential could be so large that an individual could be a bull without expecting a rise in the exchange rate. In this case, the rise in her forecast would still imply a greater expected return from holding a long position.

The historical record on currency crises indicates that although large negative exchange rate movements can occur for many different reasons, such movements are often associated with weakness in a country's current account and international financial position.[27] The studies of Sachs (1981, 1982) find that for large countries, years that involve current account deficits tend to be associated with real exchange rate depreciations. Indeed, the prediction that sustained current account deficits lead to a depreciating currency is one of the main qualitative implications of the portfolio-balance models of Kouri (1976) and others. This theory has led international macro-economists to argue that the recent deterioration of the U.S. current account and buildup of international debt imply that, over the medium-run, the dollar will have to depreciate considerably relative to the euro and yen.[28]

These empirical and theoretical considerations suggest that sustained or growing weakness in a country's current account and international financial position may have a direct influence on how market participants forecast the potential unit loss from speculative positions in currency markets. More specifically, beyond any possible indirect effect through the gap, we hypothesize that such weakness on the part of the foreign country may lead bulls to become more concerned about the possibility of a fall in the exchange rate and a capital loss. Conversely, for a bear, who speculates on the belief of a fall in the exchange rate, the concern over a capital loss may decline.

To illustrate how other causal variables might influence revisions of the expected loss, we suppose that the cumulative sum of past bilateral current account balances, which we denote by CCA_t, influences $\bar{\mathcal{D}}\hat{l}^i_{t|t+1}$ directly.[29] We constrain this influence with the following partially predetermining restrictions for a bull and bear, respectively:

$$\frac{\bar{\mathcal{D}}^G \hat{l}^L_{t|t+1}}{\Delta CCA_t} < 0 \quad \text{or} \quad \frac{\bar{\mathcal{D}}^G \hat{l}^S_{t|t+1}}{\Delta CCA_t} > 0, \tag{10.24}$$

27. The empirical literature has defined a currency crisis as a large negative movement in a country's exchange rate, regardless of whether this movement is associated with the abandonment of a pegged-rate regime. See, for example, Frankel and Rose (1995) and Milesi-Ferretti and Razin (2000).

28. For example, see Blanchard et al. (2005), Obstfeld and Rogoff (2005), and Roubini (2006).

29. Other causal variables may be needed to model $\bar{\mathcal{D}}^G \hat{l}^i_{t|t+1}$. For example, the currency crisis literature suggests that for developing countries, such variables as foreign direct investment and public sector debt may be important.

where $CCA_t > 0$ signifies a cumulative current account surplus (deficit) for the domestic (foreign) country.

10.5.3. Forecast Transition Paths

By imposing only qualitative conditions on changes in our representations of individual forecasting behavior, the gap and cumulative current account restrictions are consistent with countless possible transition paths that characterize how an individual's forecasting strategy develops over time. All of these forecast transition paths have in common that changes in the magnitude of a bull's (bear's) expected loss between any two adjacent points in time are positively (negatively) related to changes in her evaluation of the gap and the cumulative current account. It is this feature of our representation of individual forecasting behavior, and the heterogeneity among individuals' forecasting strategies—the existence of bulls and bears—that are important in modeling the market premium on foreign exchange.

11 Bulls and Bears in Equilibrium

Uncertainty-Adjusted Uncovered Interest Parity

As we discussed in chapter 9, there is much experimental evidence indicating that the expected utility hypothesis and risk-averse preferences provide an inadequate foundation on which to represent the decisions of individuals who are faced with uncertain outcomes. Moreover, REH and other fully predetermined models are flawed on epistemological grounds. It is therefore unsurprising that models based on risk-averse preferences and REH are grossly inconsistent with the empirical record on exchange rates and the market premium.

In this chapter, we develop a new momentary equilibrium condition for the exchange rate and premium on foreign exchange, which we refer to as *uncertainty-adjusted uncovered interest parity* (UAUIP). This condition is based on a partial-equilibrium, two-period, utility-maximization setup, as in extant short-run portfolio balance models of exchange rate determination.[1] But we replace the conventional assumptions of risk aversion and expected utility theory with a specification of preferences based on the endogenous prospect theory that we developed in chapter 9. We also jettison REH and rely on IKE representations of forecasting behavior that we developed in chapter 10.

To set the stage for UAUIP, we sketch a conventional short-run portfolio balance model.[2] Momentary equilibrium in this model implies that risk-adjusted expected returns on domestic and foreign assets are equal. This

---

1. See, for example, Dooley and Isard (1982), Frankel (1983, 1984), and Dornbusch (1983b).

2. By "short-run," we mean that goods prices, outputs, and intial asset holdings are taken as exogenous.

condition, which we refer to as *risk-adjusted uncovered interest parity* (RAUIP), involves an equilibrium premium on foreign exchange that is a function of asset supplies, the conditional variance of end-of-period wealth, and the degree of risk aversion. Momentary equilibrium under endogenous prospect theory is also characterized by an equality between the adjusted expected returns on domestic and foreign assets. As with RAUIP, the premium implied by UAUIP is a function of asset supplies. By contrast, instead of the conditional variance and the degree of risk aversion, this premium depends on market participants' forecasts of the potential losses from speculation and their degree of loss aversion.

Portfolio balance models typically assume homogeneous expectations concerning the future return on an open position and its conditional variance. We show that RAUIP is also well defined under the assumption that, in equilibrium, some market participants—bulls—bet on an appreciation of the exchange rate, while others—bears—bet on a depreciation. However, even if we allow for heterogeneity of expectations in a traditional portfolio balance model, it still fails to explain the empirical record on foreign exchange returns. By contrast, the distinction between bulls and bears plays a key role in the ability of our IKE model of the premium to explain the behavior of returns in the foreign exchange market, particularly their frequent sign reversals.

Moreover, unlike the behavioral approach, IKE represents diversity among forecasting strategies without appealing to irrationality on the part of market participants. As in real world markets, heterogeneity of forecasts in any IKE model stems from attempts by profit-seeking—or more broadly, purposeful—individuals to cope with imperfect knowledge of market outcomes.

Under IKE, UAUIP represents the relationship between the causal factors and the exchange rate or market premium as transitions between partially predetermined momentary equilibria for the exchange rate. We conclude the chapter by examining how our partially predetermined restrictions on representations of forecasting behavior imply an IKE analog of stability in our model: were a disequilibrium to arise, the equilibration process would lead the exchange rate to move toward one of the partially predetermined equilibria.

11.1. Momentary Equilibrium in the Foreign Exchange Market

Momentary equilibrium in the foreign exchange market is defined by a balance between the demand for and supply of foreign exchange. In deriving the condition for momentary equilibrium, we assume that equilibrium in both the domestic and foreign money markets is determined independently of both the spot-rate process and the level of wealth, and that domestic (foreign) money is held only by domestic (foreign) wealth holders.[3] The first assumption implies that equilibrium in the foreign exchange market can be modeled in terms of domestic (foreign) individuals' decisions concerning how to divide their nonmonetary wealth between A and B bonds. The second assumption ensures that whenever a domestic (foreign) individual changes her holdings of B (A) bonds, which are priced only in B (A) currency, she will buy or sell foreign (domestic) currency.

With these assumptions, momentary equilibrium in the foreign exchange market can be written as:

$$\sum_i \left(B_t^{d^i} - B_t^i \right) = B_t^d - B_t = 0, \tag{11.1}$$

where $B_t^{d^i}$ denotes an individual's demand for B bonds at time t, B_t^i denotes her holdings of B bonds entering time t (that is, at time $t - h$, where h denotes an infinitesimally small interval of time), and B_t^d and B_t denote the total demand for and supply of B bonds at time t, respectively. In each period t, an individual decides how much of her nonmonetary wealth she will hold in B bonds. If this demand exceeds (falls short of) the B bonds she holds entering the period, she will purchase (sell) $B_t^{d^i} - B_t^i$ of B bonds. To do so, she will purchase foreign exchange of equal value. In equilibrium, the individual demands and supplies of foreign exchange sum to zero.

11.2. Equilibrium under Risk Aversion

11.2.1. An Individual's Decision

Traditional portfolio balance models represent an individual's portfolio decision in the context of a two-period setup: the portfolio share in any period is chosen to maximize next period's expected utility. Risk-averse preferences are typically assumed to depend positively on the conditional mean $\hat{\mu}_{t|t+1}^w$ of the next period's wealth and negatively on its conditional variance $\hat{v}_{t|t+1}^w$, which are implied by an economist's representation of an individual's forecasting behavior.[4] We follow the portfolio balance literature by using the following utility function:

---

3. Branson and Henderson (1985, p. 754) include these assumptions in their "basic asset market specification."

4. Although the two-period setup is more restrictive than the intertemporal optimizing framework, Giovannini and Jorin (1989) show that it is consistent with intertemporal optimization if the elasticity of intertemporal substitution is set equal to unity.

$$U = U\left(\hat{\mu}^w_{t|t+1}, \hat{v}^w_{t|t+1}\right) \quad \frac{\partial U}{\partial \hat{\mu}^w_{t|t+1}} > 0 \text{ and } \frac{\partial U}{\partial \hat{v}^w_{t|t+1}} < 0, \quad (11.2)$$

where, to simplify notation, we suppress the superscript i indicating that the utility function and the conditional moments in equation (11.2) refer to an individual.

We recall that next period's wealth is given by $W_{t+1} = W_t[a_t R_{t+1} + \left(1 + i^j_t - p^j_t\right)]$, where $j = A, B$ and a_t, R_{t+1}, i^j_t, and p^j_t are defined as in equation (9.3). It follows that the portfolio share that maximizes utility in equation (11.2) is:

$$a_t = \frac{\hat{r}_{t|t+1}}{\rho \hat{v}^{\triangle s}_{t|t+1}} + d, \quad (11.3)$$

where $\hat{r}_{t|t+1}$ (as before) and $\hat{v}^{\triangle s}_{t|t+1}$ denote realizations of the conditional mean of R_{t+1} and variance of $\triangle S_{t+1} = S_{t+1} - s_t$, respectively, that are implied by an economist's representation; ρ denotes the coefficient of relative risk aversion implied by equation (11.2); and d denotes the minimum-variance portfolio. Equation (11.3) assumes that the rates of domestic and foreign inflation are deterministic, implying that $\hat{v}^w_{t|t+1} = \hat{v}^{\triangle s}_{t|t+1}$. We also assume that domestic (foreign) individuals use only domestic (foreign) prices to deflate nominal values. These two assumptions imply that the minimum- (zero-)variance portfolio for domestic and foreign individuals contains bonds issued only by their respective countries; that is, $d = 0$ ($d = 1$) for domestic (foreign) individuals.[5]

A domestic wealth holder, therefore, holds an open position in foreign exchange (that is, she is exposed to exchange rate risk) when $a_t \neq 0$, whereas a foreign wealth holder holds an open position when $a_t \neq 1$. The solution in equation (11.3) implies that both domestic and foreign individuals want to hold a long (short) position in foreign exchange of size $(a_t - d)W_t(-[a_t - d]W_t)$ whenever $\hat{r}_{t|t+1} > 0$ ($\hat{r}_{t|t+1} < 0$) and no position when $\hat{r}_{t|t+1} = 0$.[6] Moreover, the size of an individual's open position increases with the size of her forecast of the return and decreases with her degree of risk aversion and her perception of the risk involved, as measured by $\hat{v}^{\triangle s}_{t|t+1}$.

5. Lewis (1995) and Engel (1996) also use these assumptions. See footnote 6 in chapter 9 for additional references and for the motivation behind the assumption of deterministic inflation rates.

6. A domestic (foreign) individual holds a long position in foreign exchange when $a_t > 0$ ($a_t > 1$) and a short position when $a_t < 0$ ($a_t < 1$). For convenience, we set the domestic and foreign price levels at time t equal to one. Thus, $(a_t - d) W_t$ denotes an individual's position size in both real and nominal terms.

11.2.2. Risk-Adjusted UIP

11.2.2.1. Homogeneous Preferences and Forecasts

The literature typically assumes that market participants' forecasts and preferences are homogenous. Under this assumption, the equilibrium condition in equation (11.1) and the representation of an individuals' optimal portfolio share in equation (11.3) lead to the following expression for momentary equilibrium in the foreign exchange market:

$$\hat{r}_{t|t+1} = \widehat{rp}_{t|t+1}, \tag{11.4}$$

where

$$\widehat{rp}_{t|t+1} = \rho\hat{v}^{\Delta s}_{t|t+1}IFP_t. \tag{11.5}$$

$\hat{r}_{t|t+1}$ and $\hat{v}^{\Delta s}_{t|t+1}$ are the moments implied by an economist's representation of the common forecasting strategy, $IFP_t = \frac{B^A_t - A^B_t/s_t}{W_t}$, B^A_t and A^B_t denote the total values of B and A bonds entering period t that are held by country A and country B wealth holders, respectively, and $W_t = \Sigma W^i_t$ is the total non-monetary wealth in countries A and B.

The IFP_t term is the international financial position of country A relative to country B, expressed as a proportion of total market wealth. If $IFP_t > 0$, for example, country A is a net creditor to country B. IFP_t determines the net long position in foreign exchange (short position if $IFP_t < 0$) that must be held by the market at time t.[7]

Equation (11.4), which we call RAUIP, implies that equilibrium in the foreign exchange market occurs when the aggregate, risk-adjusted, expected returns on foreign and domestic bonds are equal; that is, when $\hat{s}_{t|t+1} - s_t + i^B_t = i^A_t + rp_t$. Momentary equilibrium in the foreign exchange market is associated with a positive (negative) risk premium on foreign exchange whenever the market must hold a net long (short) position in foreign exchange, that is, when $IFP_t > 0$ ($IFP_t < 0$). This equilibrium risk premium depends positively on individuals' degree of risk aversion, ρ, their assessment of the riskiness of holding open positions, $\hat{v}^{\Delta s}_{t|t+1}$, and the size of the net long positions that must be held, IFP_t.

---

7. B^A_t, which includes both inside and outside B bonds, represents the aggregate long position held by country A wealth holders in excess of any short positions at time t. Similarly, A^B_t, which includes both inside and outside A bonds, represents the aggregate short position held by country B wealth holders in excess of any long positions at time t.

11.2.2.2. *Heterogeneous Forecasts*

The distinction between bulls and bears plays an important role in the model of the equilibrium premium based on endogenous prospect theory. By contrast, regardless of whether forecasts are homogeneous or heterogeneous, the implications of RAUIP are grossly inconsistent with the behavior of returns in currency markets, particularly with their frequent sign reversals.

To characterize RAUIP in terms of the expectations of bulls and bears, we make two simplifying assumptions. First, we note that, although the forecasts of bulls and bears are ipso facto heterogeneous, there is no reason to suppose that the degree of risk aversion differs between these two groups. This assumption enables us to express RAUIP in equation (11.5) as:

$$\frac{W_t^{\mathrm{L}}}{W_t}\hat{r}_{t|t+1}^{\mathrm{L}} - \frac{W_t^{\mathrm{S}}}{W_t}\hat{r}_{t|t+1}^{\mathrm{S}} = \rho\hat{v}_{t|t+1}^{\triangle s}\mathit{IFP}_t, \tag{11.6}$$

where $W_t^{\mathrm{L}} = \Sigma^{N_t^{\mathrm{L}}} W_t^i$ and $W_t^{\mathrm{S}} = \Sigma^{N_t^{\mathrm{S}}} W_t^i$ is the total of wealth of the N_t^{L} and N_t^{S} bulls and bears, respectively;

$$\hat{v}_{t|t+1}^{\triangle s} = \frac{1}{\displaystyle\sum \frac{W_t^i}{W_t\hat{v}_{t|t+1}^{\triangle s,i}}}$$

$$\hat{r}_{t|t+1}^{\mathrm{L}} = \sum^{N_t^{\mathrm{L}}} \omega_t^{\mathrm{L}i}\hat{r}_{t|t+1}^{\mathrm{L}i} = \hat{s}_{t|t+1}^{\mathrm{L}} - s_t - \mathit{fp}_t$$

$$\hat{r}_{t|t+1}^{\mathrm{S}} = \sum^{N_t^{\mathrm{S}}} \omega_t^{\mathrm{S}i}\hat{r}_{t|t+1}^{\mathrm{S}i} = \mathit{fp}_t - s_t - \hat{s}_{t|t+1}^{\mathrm{S}}$$

$$\omega_t^{\mathrm{L}i} = \frac{W_t^{\mathrm{L}i}\hat{v}_{t|t+1}^{\triangle s,\mathrm{L}}}{W_t^{\mathrm{L}}\hat{v}_{t|t+1}^{\triangle s,\mathrm{L}i}}$$

$$\omega_t^{\mathrm{S}i} = \frac{W_t^{\mathrm{S}i}\hat{v}_{t|t+1}^{\triangle s,\mathrm{S}}}{W_t^{\mathrm{S}}\hat{v}_{t|t+1}^{\triangle s,\mathrm{S}i}},$$

and fp_t is the forward premium.

Although the total wealth of the group of bulls and bears as a proportion of total nonmonetary wealth, $\frac{W_t^{\mathrm{L}}}{W_t}$ and $\frac{W_t^{\mathrm{S}}}{W_t}$, respectively, may vary over time, we follow other asset market models that allow for heterogeneous forecasts in assuming that these wealth shares are constant.[8] Moreover, because there

---

8. See, for example, DeLong et al. (1990b) and Mark and Wu (1998).

is no reason to suppose that the total wealth of the bulls is systematically greater or smaller than that of the bears, we set these shares equal to 1/2. This assumption allows us to write:

$$\frac{1}{2}\left(\hat{r}^{\text{L}}_{t|t+1} - \hat{r}^{\text{s}}_{t|t+1}\right) = \rho \hat{v}^{\Delta s}_{t|t+1} I\!FP_t, \tag{11.7}$$

where RAUIP in equation (11.4) can be expressed in terms of an aggregate of the returns that the bulls expect to receive from taking long positions, $\hat{r}^{\text{L}}_{t+1}$, minus an aggregate of the returns that the bears expect to receive from taking short positions, $\hat{r}^{\text{s}}_{t+1}$.

In equilibrium, both the bulls and bears expect to receive an excess return from holding open positions in the foreign exchange market. As before, the algebraic sign of $I\!FP_t$ determines the sign of $\hat{r}_{t|t+1}$ and whether the market holds a net long or short position in foreign exchange. If, for example, $I\!FP_t > 0$ in equilibrium, the bulls must expect a return from speculation that is larger than that of the bears, to compensate them for the risk of holding a larger open position in total.

Thus, regardless of whether forecasts are homogeneous or heterogeneous, RAUIP implies that the sign of the equilibrium premium on foreign exchange depends only on the sign of the international financial position between the domestic and foreign countries, $I\!FP_t$. Consequently, a sign reversal in $\widehat{rp}_{t|t+1}$ can occur only if the value of $I\!FP_t$ switches sign. Shifts in the international financial position between countries, however, occur much too infrequently to explain the sign reversals in estimates of expected returns.[9]

11.2.3. Equilibrium Price Function in a Fully Predetermined Model

Contemporary economists construct fully predetermined models, and the vast majority of these have time-invariant structures. In such models, the conditional probability distributions used in representing individual forecasts and aggregate outcomes are also time invariant: different values of the conditioning set of variables are associated with mechanistic revisions of the conditional mean and higher moments.[10]

Typically, portfolio balance models assume that the conditional variance $\hat{v}^{\Delta s}_{t|t+1}$ is independent of the exchange rate.[11] To represent how market

9. For references, see the next chapter.

10. In chapter 6, we showed that mechanistic revisions characterize fully predetermined models even if their structures are allowed to change.

11. Empirical researchers have modeled changes in $\hat{v}^{\Delta s}_{t|t+1}$ in a fully predetermined way either by asuming an ARCH process (for example, Mark, 1988; Engel and Rodrigues, 1989) or by relating

participants update their point forecasts of next period's return, $\hat{r}_{t|t+1}$, the literature assumes REH.[12] With these assumptions, RAUIP implies an equilibrium price function—a one-to-one mapping between the equilibrium exchange rate and the set of causal variables that are implied by the model.[13] Consequently, the dynamics of the exchange rate and market premium are represented as movements along a given equilibrium price function that arise from changes in the causal variables.

11.3. Uncertainty-Adjusted UIP

As in the portfolio balance model, a country-B wealth holder under endogenous prospect theory holds a long position in foreign exchange when the value of her B bonds exceeds her wealth ($a_t - 1 > 0$) and a short position when she holds A bonds ($a_t - 1 < 0$). Consequently, the solutions for the optimal portfolio shares for country-A bulls and bears in chapter 9 (equations (9.43) and (9.44)) imply analogous representations for country-B wealth holders:

$$a_t^{\text{L}} - 1 = \frac{\hat{r}_{t|t+1}^{\text{L}} - \left(1 - \lambda_1\right)\hat{l}_{t|t+1}^{\text{L}}}{\lambda_2} \tag{11.8}$$

$$-\left(a_t^{\text{s}} - 1\right) = \frac{\hat{r}_{t|t+1}^{\text{s}} - \left(1 - \lambda_1\right)\hat{l}_{t|t+1}^{\text{s}}}{\lambda_2}, \tag{11.9}$$

where $a_t^{\text{L}} - 1$ and $a_t^{\text{s}} - 1$ are constrained to be nonnegative and nonpositive, respectively. As in our derivation of RAUIP, we ignore in this chapter differences in the preference parameters, λ_1 and λ_2, between bulls and bears.[14]

We now substitute the optimal position sizes for country-A and country-B wealth holders into the definition of momentary equilibrium in equation (11.1). In doing so, we must recognize that the optimal solutions in equations (11.8) and (11.9) and from chapter 9 only apply to those wealth holders for whom $\hat{r}_{t|t+1}^{\text{L}} - \left(1 - \lambda_1\right)\hat{l}_{t|t+1}^{\text{L}} > 0$ or $\hat{r}_{t|t+1}^{\text{s}} - \left(1 - \lambda_1\right)\hat{l}_{t|t+1}^{\text{s}} > 0$. The other

---

$\hat{v}_{t|t+1}^{\Delta s}$ to macroeconomic variables, such as money supply and oil prices (see Engel and Rodrigues, 1989).

12. Researchers have explored the implications of adaptive and static expectations in portfolio balance models that are based on postulated asset demands instead of explict utility maximization. See Kouri (1976) and Branson and Henderson (1985).

13. A complete model of the exchange rate would involve specifications for relative interest rates, goods prices, and the international financial position. See chapters 14 and 15.

14. In the next chapter, we consider the so-called "house money effect" of Thaler and Johnson (1990), which suppposes that there is a systematic difference between the degree of loss aversion of bulls and bears.

N_t^O wealth holders stay out of the market; that is, they set $a_t = 0$ if they are from country A and $a_t = 1$ if they are from country B. This nonparticipation result leads to the following expression for momentary equilibrium:

$$\tfrac{1}{2}\left(\hat{r}^{\mathrm{L}}_{t|t+1} - \hat{r}^{\mathrm{S}}_{t|t+1}\right) = \tfrac{1}{2}\left(1 - \lambda_1\right)\left(\hat{l}^{\mathrm{L}}_{t|t+1} - \hat{l}^{\mathrm{S}}_{t|t+1}\right) \tag{11.10}$$

$$+ \lambda_2 \sum_{i=1}^{N_t^{\mathrm{L}} \cup N_t^{\mathrm{S}} \cup N_t^O} \left[I_t^i\left(\frac{W_t^i}{W_t^{\mathrm{M}}}\right) - \frac{B_t^i}{W_t^{\mathrm{M}}} \right],$$

where I_t^i is an indicator variable that equals 0 (1) if an individual is from country A (country B), $W_t^{\mathrm{M}} = \sum^{N_t^{\mathrm{L}} + N_t^{\mathrm{S}}} W_t^i$ denotes the real wealth of all individuals who take an open position at time t, and, for convenience, we set the domestic and foreign price levels at time t equal to one.[15] As before, because there is no reason to suppose that the total wealth of the bulls is systematically greater or smaller than that of the bears, we set their wealth shares equal to 1/2. The aggregate of the forecasts of the return and potential unit loss for bulls and bears are defined analogously to equation (11.7).

Equation (11.10) can be written as an equality between the aggregate forecast of the return on holding foreign exchange and the market premium:

$$\hat{r}_{t|t+1} = \widehat{pr}_{t|t+1}, \tag{11.11}$$

where

$$\hat{r}_{t|t+1} = \tfrac{1}{2}\left(\hat{r}^{\mathrm{L}}_{t|t+1} - \hat{r}^{\mathrm{S}}_{t|t+1}\right) \tag{11.12}$$

$$\widehat{pr}_{t|t+1} = \widehat{up}_{t|t+1} + \lambda_2 IFP_t \tag{11.13}$$

$$\widehat{up}_{t|t+1} = \frac{1}{2}\left(\widehat{up}^{\mathrm{L}}_{t|t+1} - \widehat{up}^{\mathrm{S}}_{t|t+1}\right) = \tfrac{1}{2}\left(1 - \lambda_1\right)\left(\hat{l}^{\mathrm{L}}_{t|t+1} - \hat{l}^{\mathrm{S}}_{t|t+1}\right), \tag{11.14}$$

IFP_t is defined in terms of W_t^{M}, and $\widehat{up}_{t|t+1}$ is the aggregate uncertainty premium.

Equation (11.11), or UAUIP, represents the equilibrium in the foreign exchange market as an equality between the aggregate uncertainty-adjusted expected returns on foreign and domestic bonds; that is, $\hat{s}_{t|t+1} - s_t + i_t^B = i_t^A + pr_t$. Alternatively, as with RAUIP, equilibrium prevails when the net

---

15. We note that country-A individuals who decide to stay out of the market at time t may be holding B bonds entering period t. Thus, the summation in equation (11.10) must include all country-A and country-B individuals who are out of the market at time t.

demand for long positions in foreign exchange as a proportion of total market wealth, $\frac{\hat{r}_{t|t+1} - \widehat{up}_{t|t+1}}{\lambda_2}$, equals the net supply of long positions as a proportion of total market wealth, IFP_t.

The key difference between UAUIP in equation (11.11) and RAUIP in equation (11.4) is in the specification of the equilibrium premium. Both specifications depend on the net long position that must be held by the market, IFP_t. But instead of the conditional variance $\hat{v}_{t|t+1}^{\triangle s}$, the other main determinant of the equilibrium premium under endogenous prospect theory is an aggregate uncertainty premium. Equation (11.14) shows that $\widehat{up}_{t|t+1}$ depends on the difference between the uncertainty premium of the bulls minus the uncertainty premium of the bears. These two terms, in turn, represent aggregations involving the bulls' and bears' forecasts of the potential unit loss from speculation.

In equilibrium, each market participant expects to receive a return in excess of her uncertainty premium for holding an open position in the foreign exchange market. In the aggregate, the side of the market that forecasts a greater excess return depends on the algebraic sign of IFP_t. If, for example, $IFP_t > 0$ in equilibrium, the bulls' forecast of the excess return from speculation must be larger than that of the bears to compensate the former for holding a larger open position in total; that is, $(\hat{r}_{t|t+1}^{\mathrm{L}} - \widehat{up}_{t|t+1}^{\mathrm{L}}) > (\hat{r}_{t|t+1}^{\mathrm{s}} - \widehat{up}_{t|t+1}^{\mathrm{s}})$.

11.3.1. *Homogeneous versus Heterogeneous Forecasts*

Unlike RAUIP, the implications of the representation for the premium in equation (11.13) depend on whether forecasts are represented as homogeneous or heterogeneous. Under homogeneous forecasts, market participants are either all bulls or all bears. In this case, the algebraic sign of the equilibrium premium, as with RAUIP, must be the same as the sign of IFP_t. If IFP_t is positive (negative) in equilibrium, then all individuals are bulls (bears) and the equilibrium uncertainty premium is positive (negative); that is, $\widehat{up}_{t|t+1} = \widehat{up}_{t|t+1}^{\mathrm{L}} > 0$ $(\widehat{up}_{t|t+1} = -\widehat{up}_{t|t+1}^{\mathrm{s}} < 0)$. Consequently, $\widehat{pr}_{t|t+1}$ is positive (negative); sign reversals can occur only if IFP_t switches sign.

Under the assumption of heterogeneous forecasts, however, the algebraic sign of the equilibrium uncertainty premium is not constrained to be the same as that for IFP_t, but instead depends on which side of the market requires a greater uncertainty premium to speculate in foreign exchange. The answer to this question, in turn, depends on which group's forecast of the potential unit loss from holding open positions is larger. It is clear from equations (11.13) and (11.14) that the possibility of sign reversals in $\widehat{up}_{t|t+1}$ implies the possibility of sign reversals in $\widehat{pr}_{t|t+1}$ without such reversals in IFP_t. In the next chapter, we show that this feature of UAUIP, which stems from heterogeneity of forecasts, enables us to explain the frequency of sign reversals in foreign exchange returns that models based on risk-averse preferences have found anomalous.

11.3.2. Equilibration in a Partially Predetermined Model

We now show how UAUIP serves as an equilibrium condition for the spot exchange rate under IKE. We assume that the market is in equilibrium at some time t and analyze how a change in one of the causal variables creates a disequilibrium in the market and how the resulting adjustment of the exchange rate eliminates this disequilibrium.

IKE models forecasting behavior with partially predetermined probabilistic representations, which in the present setup involve countless conditional probability distributions for R_{t+1} at every point in time.[16] The two aspects of these conditional probability distributions that are important for the analysis are their mean and expected unit loss. For bulls

$$\hat{r}_{t|t+1}^{\mathrm{L,IKE}} = E_t^{\mathrm{L,IKE}}\left[R_{t+1}|s_t, x_t^{\mathrm{L}}\right] = E_t^{\mathrm{L,IKE}}\left[S_{t+1}|s_t, x_t^{\mathrm{L}}\right] - s_t - f\!p_t$$

$$\hat{l}_{t|t+1}^{\mathrm{L}} = E_t^{\mathrm{L,IKE}}\left[R_{t+1} < 0|s_t, x_t^{\mathrm{L}}\right],$$

whereas for bears

$$\hat{r}_{t|t+1}^{\mathrm{S,IKE}} = -E_t^{\mathrm{S,IKE}}\left[R_{t+1}|s_t, x_t^{\mathrm{S}}\right] = f\!p_t + s_t - E_t^{\mathrm{L,IKE}}\left[S_{t+1}|s_t, x_t^{\mathrm{S}}\right]$$

$$\hat{l}_{t|t+1}^{\mathrm{S}} = -E_t^{\mathrm{S,IKE}}\left[R_{t+1} > 0|s_t, x_t^{\mathrm{S}}\right].$$

The variables x_t^{L} and x_t^{S} represent the sets of causal factors used by the group of bulls and bears, respectively, to form forecasts. We recall that the superscript IKE indicates that these representations are only partially predetermined: the conditional probability distribution used to represent an individual's forecasting strategy at time t is any one of the distributions implying a change between $t - 1$ and t that satisfies the IKE restrictions of the model.

As in chapter 5, however, we are interested in the properties of any of the partially predetermined demand paths that are generated in the model at a point in time, where we assume that the causal variables remain unchanged as the market price adjusts in a disequilibrium situation. To model revisions of the forecasting strategies that underpin the demand paths, we make use of the IKE gap and trend restrictions:

$$\frac{\mathcal{D}\hat{l}_{t|t+1}^{i,\mathrm{IKE}}}{\mathcal{D}\widehat{gap}_t^{i,\mathrm{IKE}}} < 0 \text{ for a bull}$$

---

16. For the definition of partially predetermind probabilistic representations, see chapter 4.

$$\frac{\mathcal{D}\hat{t}^{i,\text{IKE}}_{t|t+1}}{\mathcal{D}\widehat{gap}^{i,\text{IKE}}_t} > 0 \text{ for a bear} \tag{11.15}$$

$$0 < \frac{\mathcal{D}\hat{s}^{i,\text{IKE}}_{t|t+1}}{\Delta s_t} < 1, \tag{11.16}$$

which are assumed to hold for any change in $\widehat{gap}^{i,\text{IKE}}_t$ and s_t that occurs in the model between adjacent points in time.[17]

We express equilibrium in the foreign exchange market as an equality between the net demand for long positions $D^L_t = \frac{\hat{r}^{\text{IKE}}_{t|t+1} - \widehat{up}^{\text{IKE}}_{t|t+1}}{\lambda_2}$ and the net supply that must be held, $S^L_t = IFP_t$. As in chapter 5, this equality allows us to treat the supply side of the market as fully predetermined. We follow the portfolio balance literature and consider the baseline case in which $\frac{\partial IFP_t}{\partial s_t} > 0$.[18] This assumption leads to the upward-sloping supply curve in figure 11.1.

We suppose that at some initial point in time, $t = 1$, the market is in equilibrium at point ip in figure 11.1. We also suppose that changes in the causal variables between $t = 1$ and $t = 2$ lead the group of bulls and bears to increase their forecasts of the future spot rate; that is, both $\hat{s}^{\text{L,IKE}}_{t|t+1}$ and $\hat{s}^{\text{S,IKE}}_{t|t+1}$ rise, while their assessments of the historical benchmark and the forward premium remain unchanged. These revisions lead bulls to raise their forecasts of the return from holding long positions, $\hat{r}^{\text{L,IKE}}_{t|t+1} = \hat{s}^{\text{L,IKE}}_{t|t+1} - s_t - fp_t$, while for bears, $\hat{r}^{\text{S,IKE}}_{t|t+1} = s_t + fp_t - \hat{s}^{\text{S,IKE}}_{t|t+1}$ falls.

If the speculative decision depended only on an individual's expected return, bulls would want to increase the size of their long positions, while bears would want to decrease the size of their short positions. But the rise in $\hat{s}^{\text{L,IKE}}_{t|t+1}$ and $\hat{s}^{\text{S,IKE}}_{t|t+1}$ also leads bulls and bears to revise upward their assessments of the gap. Our IKE representations presume, therefore, that the revisions of market participants' forecasting strategies are associated with revisions in their forecasts of the potential unit loss from holding open positions in foreign exchange. The IKE gap restriction for the bulls assumes that, as they revise $\widehat{gap}^{\text{L,IKE}}_t$ upward, they become more concerned about the possibility of a capital loss, which is represented as an increase in $-\hat{t}^{\text{L,IKE}}_{t|t+1}$. This, in turn, leads them to require a higher uncertainty premium, which restrains their desire to increase their long positions caused by the rise in $\hat{r}^{\text{L,IKE}}_{t|t+1}$. As for

---

17. See chapter 10.

18. When a country holds a negative position in foreign assets—that is, either $B^A_t < 0$ or $A^B_t < 0$—then $\frac{\partial IFP_t}{\partial s_t}$ may be negative. In this case, the supply curve is downward sloping, and there is the possibility of instability in the model. See Martin and Mason (1979), Henderson and Rogoff (1982), and Branson and Henderson (1985).

Figure 11.1 Equilibration in an IKE Model of the Foreign Exchange Market

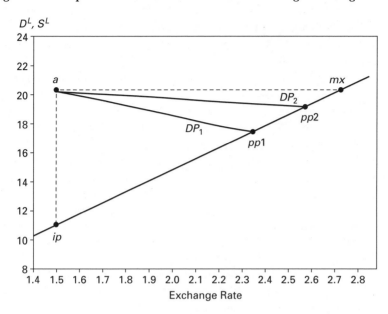

the bears, the gap restriction assumes that, as they revise $\widehat{gap}_t^{S,\,IKE}$ upward, they become less concerned about the possibility of a capital loss; that is, $-\hat{l}_{t|t+1}^{S,\,IKE}$ falls in the model. This fall, in turn, leads them to require a smaller uncertainty premium, which restrains their desire to reduce their short positions.

In general, both bulls and bears may revise their forecasting strategies in ways that imply either an increase or decrease in their forecasts of the excess return from holding open positions in the market; that is, both $\hat{r}_{t|t+1}^{L,\,IKE} - \widehat{up}_{t|t+1}^{L,\,IKE}$ and $\hat{r}_{t|t+1}^{S,\,IKE} - \widehat{up}_{t|t+1}^{S,\,IKE}$ may rise or fall. However, it is natural to assume that, unless the size of the gap is large, an individual's revision of her expected loss does not completely reduce her willingness to change her position size in the direction implied by the change in her expected return.[19] With this assumption, the upward revisions of $\hat{s}_{t|t+1}^{L,\,IKE}$ and $\hat{s}_{t|t+1}^{S,\,IKE}$ lead bulls to revise upward and bears to revise downward their forecasts of the excess return. These reactions, in turn, create an excess demand for foreign exchange, which we depict as a movement to point a in figure 11.1.[20]

---

19. If we were to assume that an individual's expected loss rises more than her expected return, the market would be characterized by an excess supply. In this case, price would fall in the model to reequilibrate the market.

20. Our IKE model does not prespecify the magnitudes by which the bulls and bears revise their forecasts. Thus, it does not prespecify the magintude of the excess demand at point a.

Consider first the bulls as s_t rises. The trend restriction presumes that they revise upward their forecast of the future spot rate. The assumption that $\hat{s}^{L,IKE}_{t|t+1}$ changes less than one-for-one with s ensures stability in the model. [21] The rise in $\hat{s}^{L,IKE}_{t|t+1}$ also leads to an increase in the bulls' expected gap, which causes them to raise their forecasts of the potential unit loss. Consequently, $\hat{r}^{L,IKE}_{t|t+1}$ falls and $\widehat{up}^{L,IKE}_{t|t+1}$ rises, and both of these revisions lead bulls to reduce their demand for long positions.

Our representation of the bears' forecasting behavior presumes that the rise in s_t causes them to increase $\hat{s}^{S,IKE}_{t|t+1}$ and lower $\widehat{up}^{S,IKE}_{t|t+1}$. The rise in s_t, therefore, causes the net demand for long positions in the market, D^L_t, to decline. Consequently, the gap and trend restrictions imply that all of the partially predetermined demand paths in the model are downward sloping. Figure 11.1 provides two examples, which we denote by DP_1 and DP_2. In this figure, ip is the initial point and mx is the maximum equilibrium point consistent with the partially predetermining restrictions in equations (11.15) and (11.16).

As in chapter 5, with an upward-sloping supply curve, the rise in the market price causes excess demand in the model to decline. Although the model does not prespecify the precise equilibrium position to which the market will adjust, it does imply that some equilibrium will be reached. The model also implies that the new equilibrium will be associated with a higher exchange rate.[22] Moreover, because the rise in both $\hat{s}^{IKE}_{t|t+1}$ and s_t cause the bulls to increase and the bears to decrease their uncertainty premium, the equilibrium uncertainty premium will also be higher. This increase, together with a larger IFP_t, leads to a higher equilibrium premium on foreign exchange. We note that if $\widehat{pr}^{IKE}_{t|t+1}$ were negative at the initial equilibrium point ip in figure 11.1, then its rise may be associated with a change to a positive value.

11.3.3. Partially Predetermined Transitions between Momentary Equilibria

The UAUIP condition together with the IKE restrictions in equations (11.15) and (11.16) imply that changes in the causal variables lead to equilibrium movements in the exchange rate and market premium. This implication also holds with the fully predetermined RAUIP condition in the

---

21. This assumption also ensures stability in the portfolio balance model for the typical case in which $\frac{\partial IFP_t}{\partial s_t} > 0$.

22. If we had assumed that the revisions of forecasting strategies that resulted from the increase in x from $t=1$ to $t=2$ created an excess supply in the market, then, because all demand-transition paths slope downward in the model, a resulting fall in the spot rate would reequilibrate the market.

preceding section, which models the causal mechanism as movements along a given equilibrium price function. However, the partially predetermined UAUIP condition represents the relationship between the causal factors and the exchange rate or market premium as transitions between partially predetermined equilibrium price functions.

Because the barriers to the flow of capital across national borders are minimal in many currency markets, international macroeconomists typically assume that these markets adjust instantaneously to reach equilibrium at each point in time. This assumption leads us to view the time-series data on the exchange rate and market premium as transitions between partially predetermined equilibrium points.

12 IKE of the Premium on Foreign Exchange

Theory and Evidence

The short-run portfolio balance model that we sketched in the last chapter relates the equilibrium premium on foreign exchange to an individual's degree of risk aversion, a country's international financial position, and the conditional variance of the spot exchange rate: $\widehat{rp}_{t|t+1} = \rho \widehat{v}^{\triangle s}_{t|t+1} IFP_t$. To confront this model with empirical evidence, contemporary economists often presume that the expected return and variance are adequately represented by the moments of some invariant distribution, typically one that is implied by REH. As with the intertemporal asset pricing model that we discussed in chapter 8, empirical investigators have found that ρ would have to be unreasonably large to reconcile the portfolio balance model (RAUIP) with the data. The problem is that its fundamentals—asset supplies and the conditional variance—do not vary enough.[1]

Adhering steadfastly to REH, and thus ruling out an autonomous role for expectations, conventional economists have responded to the failure of risk-premium models by developing alternative specifications of preferences. A widely cited recent study that pursues this line of research in the

---

1. Lewis (1995), for example, estimates that the standard deviation of the monthly ex ante return is 9 percent in the $/DM market and 11 percent in the BP/$ and JY/$ markets. She also reports that the standard deviation of measures of outside bonds and relative wealth positions is about 1–3 percent per year. Engel and Rodrigues (1989) find that during 1979, which was the period of the largest variation in the conditional variances, movements in the variance among six developed countries lie in a range of 0.3 percent per year.

equity market is Barberis et al. (2001).[2] To generate a more volatile premium on equity in their model, the authors assume that an individual is both risk and loss averse. They also assume that an individual's degree of loss aversion varies over time according to what has been dubbed the "house-money effect": individuals become less (more) loss averse when they incur gains (losses) on their speculative positions.[3] Relying on the calibration methodology, Barberis et al. find that their model can generate an equity premium whose mean, volatility, and cross correlations "match" with the first and second moments of the historical data.

Calibration involves a comparison of the moments of the observed data, as if they came from one invariant distribution, with the moments from the computer simulation of the model's output. Such exercises necessarily require that an economist fully prespecify the causal mechanism. Although a fully predetermined model may look good when its computer-simulated moments are compared with the presumably invariant moments of the observed data, its implications may be grossly inconsistent with the causal mechanism that underpins the actual time path of the variable of interest, such as the market premium.[4]

Calibration exercises typically do not involve an explicit comparison of alternative explanations of economic phenomena. In contrast, we formulate two IKE models that have competing predictions concerning the qualitative relationship between the equilibrium premium on foreign exchange and the aggregate gap from PPP. One of the models incorporates a house money effect into its specification of preferences. We show that this model, which we call the house money model, implies that the premium on foreign exchange moves in the opposite direction over time to the movements of the aggregate gap from PPP. The other IKE model is based on the gap and cumulative current account restrictions that we motivated in chapter 10. In contrast to the house money model, our alternative gap plus model implies that the market premium and the gap move, ceteris paribus, in the same direction over time.

2. Other studies in the equity market include Epstein and Zin (1989, 1990), Abel (1990), Constantinides (1990), and Campbell and Cochrane (1999). For studies in the foreign exchange market, see footnote 11 in chapter 8.

3. Barberis et al. (2001) appeal to experimental evidence indicating that prior outcomes are related to an individual's willingness to take on risk. See Thaler and Johnson (1990) and Gertner (1993).

4. One example of this problem is provided by calibration analyses of NOEM models. Researchers find that the moments generated by NOEM models in calibration exercises "match" those of the observed exchange rate. As we pointed out in chapter 7, however, these models are unable to explain the actual time path of the exchange rate, which often involves a persistent movement away from PPP.

Beyond formulating an explicit alternative explanation of the premium, our approach to testing alternative IKE models of the premium does not presume that the time-series data come from an invariant probability distribution. In confronting the house money and gap plus models with time-series data, we allow for the possibility that the magnitudes of the gap, cumulative current account, and house money effects might vary over time. Moreover, our empirical analysis recognizes that the timing of and thresholds at which these effects might change cannot be prespecified fully.

We find that the house money model can be rejected in favor of the gap plus model. Our results also provide some indication that the cumulative current account has influenced the premium in the major currency markets, particularly in the 1990s when the U.S. current account markedly deteriorated.

Beyond accounting for the time path of the premium on foreign exchange, the gap plus model provides an explanation of another aspect of the empirical record that extant models have found "anomalous." As we discussed in chapter 8, this premium changes sign too frequently and at moments in time that appear puzzling when viewed through the prism of extant risk-premium models. We showed in chapter 11 that, regardless of whether forecasts are homogeneous or heterogeneous, the portfolio balance models imply that a sign reversal in the market premium will occur only if the international financial position between countries, IFP_t, switches sign. Shifts in IFP_t, however, occur much too infrequently to explain the sign reversals in estimates of expected returns.

By contrast, IKE's focus on the imperfection of knowledge gives rise to a diversity of views. We show that this diversity—particularly a distinction between bulls and bears—plays a key role in the gap plus model's ability to explain the frequency of sign reversals in the equilibrium premium. Under the assumption of heterogeneous forecasts, the algebraic sign of the equilibrium premium is not constrained to be the same as that for IFP_t, but rather, also depends on which side of the market requires a greater uncertainty premium to speculate in foreign exchange. We show that this implication is consistent with the frequency of sign reversals that is observed in the data.

12.1. An IKE House Money Model: Time-Varying Preferences

A simple way to incorporate a house money effect into a model that is based on endogenous prospect theory is to assume that an increase in the spot exchange rate, s_t, which leads to gains for bulls and losses for bears, causes bulls to decrease and bears to increase their degree of loss aversion.

This connection between exchange rate movements and gains and losses motivates the following partially predetermining house money restrictions on changes in the degree of loss aversion λ_1 for the groups of bulls and bears:

$$\frac{\mathcal{D}\lambda_1^{\text{L}}}{\Delta s} < 0 \quad \text{for the bulls} \tag{12.1}$$

$$\frac{\mathcal{D}\lambda_1^{\text{S}}}{\Delta s} > 0 \quad \text{for the bears,} \tag{12.2}$$

where the $\mathcal{D}$ and Δ operators denote the total change between adjacent points in time.[5] We recall from chapter 10 that $\mathcal{D}$ is not a total differential: with IKE, a change in λ_1^{L} may result from a change in the relationship between λ_1 and s and not just from a change in the exchange rate.

To see the implications of these restrictions for the behavior of the equilibrium premium under endogenous prospect theory, we express UAUIP as:

$$\widehat{r}_{t|t+1} = \widehat{pr}_{t|t+1}. \tag{12.3}$$

The market premium depends on the expected loss and the degrees of loss aversion of bulls and bears:

$$\widehat{pr}_{t|t+1} = \tfrac{1}{2}\left[\left(1 - \lambda_1^{\text{L}}\right)\widehat{l}_{t|t+1}^{\text{L}} - \left(1 - \lambda_1^{\text{S}}\right)\widehat{l}_{t|t+1}^{\text{S}}\right] + \lambda_2 \mathit{IFP}_t. \tag{12.4}$$

We now consider a change in the causal variables from one time period to another. Such changes, in general, lead market participants to revise their forecasts of the return and unit loss from holding open positions. However, to contrast the implications of the house money restrictions with those of the gap restrictions, we assume that all revisions of forecasting strategies involve no change in the expected loss for both bulls and bears.[6] We also set $\Delta \mathit{IFP} = 0$, which allows us to focus exclusively on the equilibrium uncertainty premium as the main determinant of the return on foreign exchange. As we mentioned at the start of the chapter, there is much evidence in the literature indicating that the co-variation between a country's international financial position and the return on foreign exchange is negligible. Indeed,

---

5. The restrictions in equations (12.1) and (12.2) assume that individuals view the gain or loss incurred at each time period separately from the gains or losses in all other time periods. By contrast, the specification used by Barberis et al. (2001) assumes that an individual's degree of loss aversion depends on the cumulative gain or loss from the initial time period. Adding in such a complication would not alter our main conclusions.

6. Alternatively, we could have assumed that changes in the expected loss of the bulls and bears are consistent with negative gap effects—bulls decrease and bears increase the size of their expected loss as the gap increases—without affecting our conclusions.

if this co-variation were larger, the standard models of the risk premium might be more successful in explaining foreign exchange returns.

With these assumptions, we can write the total change in equation (12.4) between any two adjacent points in time as:

$$\mathcal{D}\widehat{pr}_{t|t+1} = -\frac{1}{2}\left[\hat{l}^{\mathrm{L}}_{t|t+1}\frac{\mathcal{D}\lambda^{\mathrm{L}}_1}{\Delta s_t}\Delta s_t - \hat{l}^{\mathrm{S}}_{t|t+1}\frac{\mathcal{D}\lambda^{\mathrm{S}}_1}{\Delta s_t}\Delta s_t\right]. \tag{12.5}$$

Plugging in the equilibrium spot exchange rate, $\Delta s_t = \mathcal{D}\hat{s}_{t|t+1} - \Delta fp_t - \mathcal{D}\widehat{pr}_{t|t+1}$, leads to the following expression for the total change in the equilibrium premium on foreign exchange:

$$\mathcal{D}\widehat{pr}_{t|t+1} = A_t\left(\mathcal{D}\hat{s}_{t|t+1} - \Delta fp_t\right), \tag{12.6}$$

where

$$A_t = \frac{-\frac{1}{2}\left(\hat{l}^{\mathrm{L}}_{t|t+1}\frac{\mathcal{D}\lambda^{\mathrm{L}}_1}{\Delta s_t} - \hat{l}^{\mathrm{S}}_{t|t+1}\frac{\mathcal{D}\lambda^{\mathrm{S}}_1}{\Delta s_t}\right)}{1 - \frac{1}{2}\left(\hat{l}^{\mathrm{L}}_{t|t+1}\frac{\mathcal{D}\lambda^{\mathrm{L}}_1}{\Delta s_t} - \hat{l}^{\mathrm{S}}_{t|t+1}\frac{\mathcal{D}\lambda^{\mathrm{S}}_1}{\Delta s_t}\right)},$$

and fp_t denotes the forward premium.

We show in the appendix that constraining all partially predetermined demand paths that are generated in the model to be downward sloping, which is a sufficient condition for stability in the model, implies that the denominator of A_t takes on only positive values.[7] Moreover, we know that the numerator of A_t is negative, given the house money restrictions in equations (12.1) and (12.2), and the fact that $\hat{l}^{\mathrm{L}}_{t|t+1}$ and $\hat{l}^{\mathrm{S}}_{t|t+1}$ are both less than zero. Consequently, $A_t < 0$. According to the house money model, therefore, the direction of change of the ex ante equilibrium premium on foreign exchange between any two consecutive time periods is determined by the relative value of $\mathcal{D}\hat{s}_{t|t+1}$ and Δfp_t.

The survey data that we used in chapter 8 reveals that the monthly change in the market's forecast of the future exchange rate is, with very few exceptions, greater in magnitude than the change in the forward premium.[8] This finding motivates us to assume that $\left|\mathcal{D}\hat{s}_{t|t+1}\right| > \left|fp_t\right|$ between any two consecutive time periods.

We thus obtain the main testable *qualitative* implication of the house money model:

---

7. See chapter 5 for the definition of a partially predetermined demand path.

8. When based on the monthly survey data from MMSI and pooling observations across all three currencies studied, the size of $\Delta\hat{s}_{t|t+1}$ is greater than the size of Δfp_t for 505 of 510 observations.

- The equilibrium premium on foreign exchange and the market's forecast of the future spot exchange rate change in opposite directions between any two consecutive time periods.

The intuition behind this result is straightforward. A higher $\hat{s}_{t|t+1}$, for example, creates an excess demand for foreign exchange, which bids up the exchange rate and creates a gain for bulls and a loss for bears. With the house money restrictions, bulls lower and bears raise their degree of loss aversion. The resulting fall in the uncertainty premium for the bulls and rise for the bears leads to a lower equilibrium premium.

12.2. An IKE Gap Plus Model: Autonomous Revisions in Forecasting Strategies

IKE represents revisions of forecasting strategies as partially predetermined transitions across conditional probability distributions. To model revisions of the uncertainty premium, we impose the gap and current account restrictions on these transitions. Our restrictions presume that as a market participant revises her forecasting strategy, she considers only those strategies that imply a particular movement in her expected loss.

We recall from equation (10.23) that the gap restrictions for bulls and bears are:

$$\frac{\mathcal{D}^{G}\hat{l}^{\mathrm{L}}_{t|t+1}}{\mathcal{D}\widehat{gap}^{\mathrm{L}}_{t|t+1}} < 0 \text{ and } \frac{\mathcal{D}^{G}\hat{l}^{\mathrm{s}}_{t|t+1}}{\mathcal{D}\widehat{gap}^{\mathrm{s}}_{t|t+1}} > 0, \tag{12.7}$$

where $\mathcal{D}^{G}\hat{l}^{\mathrm{L}}_{t|t+1}$ and $\mathcal{D}^{G}\hat{l}^{\mathrm{s}}_{t|t+1}$ denote the partial changes in the bulls' and bears' expected loss between $t-1$ and t, respectively, that are due solely to the influence of the causal variables and the exchange rate on bulls' and bears' evaluations of the gap. Beyond these indirect effects, changes in the causal variables may have a direct effect on an individual's expected loss. In chapter 10, we provided motivation for the current account as one such variable. We represented its direct effect with the following current account restrictions for bulls and bears:

$$\frac{\bar{\mathcal{D}}^{G}\hat{l}^{\mathrm{L}}_{t|t+1}}{\Delta CCA_{t}} < 0 \text{ and } \frac{\bar{\mathcal{D}}^{G}\hat{l}^{\mathrm{s}}_{t|t+1}}{\Delta CCA_{t}} > 0, \tag{12.8}$$

where $\bar{\mathcal{D}}^{G}\hat{l}^{\mathrm{L}}_{t|t+1}$ and $\bar{\mathcal{D}}^{G}\hat{l}^{\mathrm{s}}_{t|t+1}$ denote the partial change in the bulls' and bears' expected loss between $t-1$ and t, respectively, that is due to a change in the cumulative current account (CCA) in excess of any indirect impact that this change may have on individuals' expected losses through the gap variable.

To contrast the implications of the gap plus model with those of the house money model, we assume that the preference parameter λ_1 for bulls and bears is the same and does not vary over time. Consequently, the total change in the equilibrium premium that results from a change in the values of the causal variables, the exchange rate, and revisions of forecasting strategies can be written as:

$$
\mathcal{D}\widehat{pr}_{t|t+1} = \tfrac{1}{2}\left(1-\lambda_1\right)\left[\frac{\mathcal{D}^G\hat{\imath}^{\mathrm{L}}_{t|t+1}}{\mathcal{D}\widehat{gap}^{\mathrm{L}}_{t|t+1}}\frac{\mathcal{D}\hat{s}^{\mathrm{L}}_{t|t+1}}{\mathcal{D}\hat{s}_{t|t+1}} - \frac{\mathcal{D}^G\hat{\imath}^{\mathrm{S}}_{t|t+1}}{\mathcal{D}\widehat{gap}^{\mathrm{S}}_{t|t+1}}\frac{\mathcal{D}\hat{s}^{\mathrm{S}}_{t|t+1}}{\mathcal{D}\hat{s}_{t|t+1}}\right]\mathcal{D}\hat{s}_{t|t+1}
$$
$$
+ \tfrac{1}{2}\left(1-\lambda_1\right)\left[\frac{\bar{\mathcal{D}}^G\hat{\imath}^{\mathrm{L}}_{t|t+1}}{\Delta CCA_t} - \frac{\bar{\mathcal{D}}^G\hat{\imath}^{\mathrm{S}}_{t|t+1}}{\Delta CCA_t}\right]\Delta CCA_t,
$$

(12.9)

where we assume, for convenience, that changes in $\widehat{gap}^{\mathrm{L}}_{t|t+1}$ and $\widehat{gap}^{\mathrm{S}}_{t|t+1}$ stem solely from changes in $\hat{s}^{\mathrm{L}}_{t|t+1}$ and $\hat{s}^{\mathrm{S}}_{t|t+1}$, respectively. We thus set $\frac{\mathcal{D}\widehat{gap}^{\mathrm{L}}_{t|t+1}}{\mathcal{D}\hat{s}^{\mathrm{L}}_{t|t+1}} = \frac{\mathcal{D}\widehat{gap}^{\mathrm{S}}_{t|t+1}}{\mathcal{D}\hat{s}^{\mathrm{S}}_{t|t+1}} = 1$ in equation (12.9).

We first consider a change in $\widehat{pr}_{t|t+1}$ due solely to the indirect effect of the causal variables and the exchange rate on $\hat{s}_{t|t+1}$. Using the gap restrictions in equation (12.7) and recalling that $\left(1-\lambda_1\right) < 0$, equation (12.9) shows that if $\hat{s}^{\mathrm{L}}_{t|t+1}$ and $\hat{s}^{\mathrm{S}}_{t|t+1}$ were to always change in the same direction— that is, $\frac{\mathcal{D}\hat{s}^{\mathrm{L}}_{t|t+1}}{\mathcal{D}\hat{s}_{t|t+1}}$ and $\frac{\mathcal{D}\hat{s}^{\mathrm{S}}_{t|t+1}}{\mathcal{D}\hat{s}_{t|t+1}}$ were both positive or negative—the equilibrium premium would always move in the same direction as $\hat{s}_{t|t+1}$, and thus, in the same direction as $\widehat{gap}_{t|t+1}$. In other words, if there were no direct effect, we would expect to see a positive relationship between movements in $\widehat{pr}_{t|t+1}$ and $\widehat{gap}_{t|t+1}$ over time.

However, changes in the causal variables and the exchange rate may be associated with movements in $\hat{s}^{\mathrm{L}}_{t|t+1}$ and $\hat{s}^{\mathrm{S}}_{t|t+1}$ that are in opposite directions. For example, suppose that a rise in $\hat{s}_{t|t+1}$ is associated with an increase in $\hat{s}^{\mathrm{L}}_{t|t+1}$ and a decrease in $\hat{s}^{\mathrm{S}}_{t|t+1}$. In this case, the gap restrictions imply that the group of bulls and bears raise their expected loss: the higher $\widehat{gap}^{\mathrm{L}}_{t|t+1}$ and lower $\widehat{gap}^{\mathrm{S}}_{t|t+1}$ lead bulls and bears to become more concerned about an exchange rate movement in the wrong direction. This concern, in turn, leads to an increase in the uncertainty premiums of the bulls and bears, that is, in both $\widehat{up}^{\mathrm{L}}_{t|t+1}$ and $\widehat{up}^{\mathrm{S}}_{t|t+1}$, respectively. And since $\widehat{pr}_{t|t+1}$ depends on the relative values of $\widehat{up}^{\mathrm{L}}_{t|t+1}$ and $\widehat{up}^{\mathrm{S}}_{t|t+1}$, the equilibrium premium, in general, could rise or fall.

This aggregation problem is typical of models with heterogeneous individuals. It seems plausible, however, that if the bulls revise their assessment of the gap by a greater (smaller) magnitude compared with the bears, then they would also tend to revise their forecasts of the unit loss by a greater (smaller) magnitude. Formally, we write these relative gap restrictions as:

$$\left|\mathcal{D}\widehat{gap}^{\mathrm{L}}_{t|t+1}\right| > \left|\mathcal{D}\widehat{gap}^{\mathrm{S}}_{t|t+1}\right| \Rightarrow \left|\mathcal{D}\hat{l}^{\mathrm{L}}_{t|t+1}\right| > \left|\mathcal{D}\hat{l}^{\mathrm{S}}_{t|t+1}\right|$$

$$\left|\mathcal{D}\widehat{gap}^{\mathrm{L}}_{t|t+1}\right| < \left|\mathcal{D}\widehat{gap}^{\mathrm{S}}_{t|t+1}\right| \Rightarrow \left|\mathcal{D}\hat{l}^{\mathrm{L}}_{t|t+1}\right| < \left|\mathcal{D}\hat{l}^{\mathrm{S}}_{t|t+1}\right|,$$

(12.10)

where $|\cdot|$ denotes absolute value. We show in the appendix that under these relative gap restrictions, the first bracketed term in equation (12.9) is unambiguously negative. Consequently, the gap plus model implies that movements in the aggregate gap lead to movements in the equilibrium premium in the same direction.

Beyond allowing the causal variables to influence an individual's expected loss indirectly through a gap effect, the gap plus model also allows for the cumulative current account to have a direct effect on the premium. However, unlike the gap effect, we do not need an aggregation condition to obtain an unambiguous prediction from the model. Changes in the cumulative current account are assumed to be observable by both bulls and bears. Thus, their direct effect on the representation of bulls' and bears' expected losses follows immediately from the current account restrictions in expression (12.8):

$$\left[\frac{\mathcal{D}\hat{l}^{\mathrm{L}}_{t|t+1}}{\Delta CCA_t} - \frac{\mathcal{D}\hat{l}^{\mathrm{S}}_{t|t+1}}{\Delta CCA_t}\right] < 0.$$

We thus obtain the main testable qualitative implications of the gap plus model:

- A movement in the aggregate gap between any two consecutive points in time leads to a change in the equilibrium premium in the same direction.

- Beyond its indirect effect through the aggregate gap, a change in the cumulative current account between any two consecutive time periods leads the equilibrium premium to change in the same direction.

12.3. Confronting the Gap Plus and House Money Models with Time-Series Data

To confront the predictions of the house money model with those of the gap plus model, we use the MMSI survey data and one-month forward rates from Data Resources, Inc., to construct a measure of the equilibrium premium $\widehat{pr}_{t|t+1}$. We also use the *Big Mac* PPP as a measure of the historical benchmark, as we did in chapters 7 and 8.

Our analysis assumes that the magnitude of the monthly change in the market's forecast of the future spot exchange rate is greater than that in the aggregate assessment of the historical benchmark during most time periods.[9] This assumption implies that the gap plus and house money models generate opposite predictions concerning the qualitative nature of the partial relationship between $\widehat{pr}_{t|t+1}$ and $\widehat{gap}_{t|t+1}$: the former implies a positive connection, whereas the latter implies a negative one.

It is possible that the premium on foreign exchange depends on a house money effect, as well as on gap and cumulative current account effects. In our statistical analysis, therefore, we consider two sets of hypotheses:

H_0: *ceteris paribus*, $\widehat{pr}_{t|t+1}$ and $\widehat{gap}_{t|t+1}$ change in opposite directions between two consecutive points in time or their movements are unrelated.

H_A: *ceteris paribus*, $\widehat{pr}_{t|t+1}$ and $\widehat{gap}_{t|t+1}$ change in the same direction between two consecutive time periods.

The null hypothesis here assumes that either the house money effect dominates any possible gap effect, or that these two effects are of the same magnitude. The alternative hypothesis is that the gap effect dominates any potential house money effect.

The second set of hypotheses concern the partial relationship between the cumulative current account and the premium:

H_0: *ceteris paribus*, $\widehat{pr}_{t|t+1}$ and CCA_t change in opposite directions between two consecutive time periods or their movements are unrelated.

H_A: *ceteris paribus*, $\widehat{pr}_{t|t+1}$ and CCA_t change in the same direction between the two consecutive time periods.

It is useful to begin our empirical analysis with a graphical look at the data. Figures 12.1–12.3 plot our measures of $\widehat{pr}_{t|t+1}$ and $\widehat{gap}_{t|t+1}$ for the BP/\$, DM/\$, and JY/\$ markets. The time plots reveal a consistent story. There is a clear tendency for $\widehat{pr}_{t|t+1}$ to change in the same direction as $\widehat{gap}_{t|t+1}$ during the 1980s in all three markets. The figures show that the overvalued currency tends to be associated with a positive premium: the bulls required a greater premium than did the bears to hold open positions in the overvalued dollar

---

9. The MMSI survey data provide strong support for this assumption. When we combine the 170 observations for the BP/\$, DM/\$, and JY/\$ markets, we find that the magnitude of the change in $\hat{s}_{t|t+1}$ is greater than that for our PPP-based measure of the historical benchmark, $\hat{s}_{t|t+1}^{HB}$, in 470 of 510 observations.

Figure 12.1   Excess Returns and the Gap: The BP/$ Market

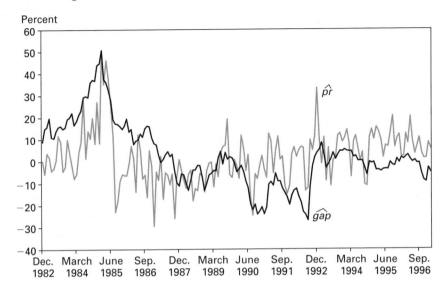

Figure 12.2   Excess Returns and the Gap: The DM/$ Market

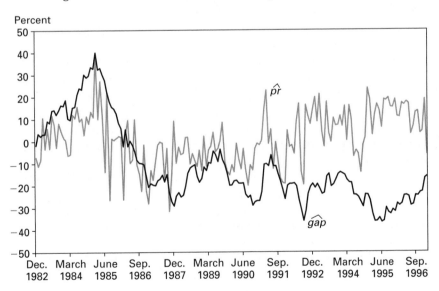

Figure 12.3   Excess Returns and the Gap: The JY/$ Market

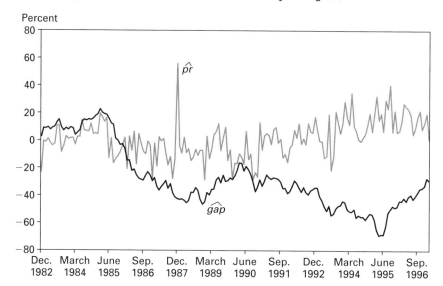

during 1983–85, whereas the bears required a higher premium to hold open positions in the overvalued mark during 1987–89. This behavior suggests that the value of the market premium associated with a $\widehat{gap}_{t|t+1} = 0$ was close to zero during the 1980s.

During the 1990s, all three markets are characterized by a gradual rise in $\widehat{pr}_{t|t+1}$. Though less pronounced than in the 1980s, a positive relationship between monthly changes in $\widehat{pr}_{t|t+1}$ and $\widehat{gap}_{t|t+1}$ is discernible for the BP/$, DM/$, and, to a lesser extent, JY/$ markets.

Table 12.1 provides additional evidence of the positive relationship between monthly changes in $\widehat{pr}_{t|t+1}$ and $\widehat{gap}_{t|t+1}$. It contains descriptive statistics on the ratio of the number of observations for which the premium and the gap move in the same direction to the number of observations for which they move in opposite directions.

These "success ratio" statistics are strongly in favor of the gap effect: the number of observations for which $\widehat{pr}_{t|t+1}$ and $\widehat{gap}_{t|t+1}$ move in the same direction is more than 50 percent greater than the observations for which these variables move in opposite directions.[10] The table also suggests that the strength of the gap effect may depend on the size of the

---

10. The standard contingency table test also rejects the null hypothesis of no relationship between the change in the premium and the gap in favor of a positive one. However, this test can only be treated as suggestive, because its test statistic is not distributed as χ^2 for the time-series data we have here, which are serially correlated.

Table 12.1 Aggregate Gap and Market Premium Qualitative Relationship

| | | Success ratio[b] | | |
| | | --- | --- | --- |
Currency	Gap threshold[a]	December 1982–February 1997	December 1982–December 1989	January 1990–February 1997
BP	0	1.27	1.15	1.36
	5	1.46	1.35	1.67
DM	0	1.66	1.55	1.74
	5	1.74	1.70	1.93
JY	0	1.83	1.71	1.93
	5	1.83	1.70	1.93

[a] Size of aggregate gap in percent below which observations are excluded.

[b] Ratio of monthly observations for which the gap and market premium move in the same direction over the number of observations for which they move in opposite directions.

gap. This relationship is particularly apparent for the BP and DM markets; for example, if we exclude the observations for which $\widehat{gap}_{t|t+1} < 5$ percent, the ratio of observations in favor of the gap effect increases for the BP and DM in all subperiods.

The time plots in figures 12.1–12.3 and the descriptive statistics in table 12.1 suggest that, although the degree of loss aversion may change in a way that is consistent with a house money effect, the behavior of the equilibrium premium in currency markets is consistent with a dominant gap effect.

The time plots also suggest that factors other than the assessment of the gap were important for the premium in the 1990s. UAUIP implies that, in addition to the aggregate uncertainty premium, the international financial position between countries, as a percentage of total market wealth, influences the equilibrium premium on foreign exchange: a greater supply of dollar long positions (a higher IFP_t) in equilibrium implies a higher $\widehat{pr}_{t|t+1}$. Data on the bilateral financial positions between countries as a percentage of total market wealth are not available. However, bilateral current account balances for the United Kingdom, Germany, and Japan vis-à-vis the United States, which we report in figures 12.4–12.6, suggest a marked improvement of the international financial positions of these countries in the 1990s.[11]

We note that the improvement of the German and Japanese current accounts accelerated at the beginning of the 1990s, precisely when the expected returns in these markets began their gradual rise. Moreover, the

11. Our current account data for Japan and United Kingdom are from the U.S. Bureau of Economic Analysis and data for Germany are from the German Bundesbank.

Figure 12.4   Bilateral Current Account: United Kingdom and United States

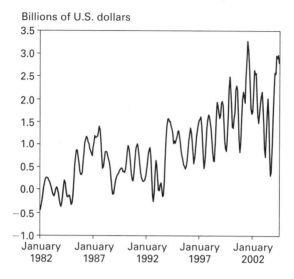

Figure 12.5   Bilateral Current Account: Germany and United States

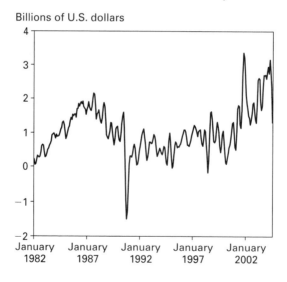

Figure 12.6   Bilateral Current Account: Japan and United States

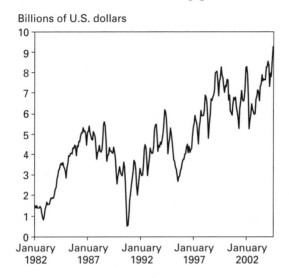

large improvement of the current account in the United Kingdom, which occurred later than in the other two countries, also coincided closely with the gradual shifting up of the expected return in this market.

Beyond their positive impact on *IFP* in the 1990s, the improving current account balances for the United Kingdom, Germany, and Japan may have influenced the aggregate uncertainty premium through their effect on market participants' expected losses. We allow for this influence indirectly through the gap effect and directly with the cumulative current account restrictions in equation (12.8).

12.3.1. Allowing for Structural Change

One of the key implications of IKE is that empirical researchers need to allow for temporal instability in estimating causal relationships without fully prespecifying the timing or nature of this instability. Consequently, in testing the house money model against our gap plus alternative, we allow for the possibility that the magnitudes of the relationships between $\hat{l}_{t|t+1}$ on the one hand and $\widehat{gap}_{t|t+1}$ and CCA_t on the other might vary over our sample at points in time and in ways that cannot be prespecified fully.

There is another important channel through which temporal instability can arise in an empirical model. In real world markets, market participants' forecasts often rely on factors that an economist excludes from his model, either because he is unaware of these factors or because he is unable to obtain data on them. A regression model would be structurally unstable if the correlations between the included and excluded variables change over the sample.

To allow for this type of temporal instability in our empirical analysis, we suppose that the relationship between $\widehat{pr}_{t|t+1}$, $\widehat{gap}_{t|t+1}$, and CCA_t is approximately piecewise linear. Each linear piece in the data corresponds to a subperiod in which the relationship between the bulls' and bears' expected losses and $\widehat{gap}_{t|t+1}$ and CCA_t, at least in the aggregate, can be approximated with constant parameters. Such a subperiod of relative parameter stability could arise because market participants in the aggregate change their forecasting strategies little over the subperiod or, if their forecasting strategies do change considerably, such revisions involve little change in the way $\hat{l}_{t|t+1}$ is related to $\widehat{gap}_{t|t+1}$ and CCA_t.

When each subperiod of relative parameter constancy might begin and end cannot be prespecified. Moreover, the causal factors that are relevant for market participants in forming their forecasts may change from one subperiod to another. For example, the cumulative current account may be important for forecasted losses during the 1990s, but not during the 1980s, as suggested by figures 12.1–12.3.[12] Consequently, we rely on recursive procedures that allow us to test for the likelihood of structural change without fully prespecifying its timing or nature.

To model each subperiod of relative parameter constancy in the data, we use an autoregressive distributive lag (ADL) specification of order two:

$$\widehat{pr}_t = b_0 + \sum_{i=1}^{2} b_{1i}\widehat{pr}_{t-i} + \sum_{i=0}^{2} \left(b_{2i}\widehat{gap}_{t-i} + b_{3i}CCA_{t-i}\right) + \epsilon_t, \quad (12.11)$$

where we have simplified the subscripts for convenience. The dynamic specification in equation (12.11) enables us to deal with the problem of unit roots.[13]

To determine when each linear piece in the data begins and ends, we use a combination of the cusum test of Brown et al. (1975) and the forecast χ^2 test of Hendry (1980). We begin with the cusum test, which uses an initialization period to estimate the ADL in equation (12.11) using ordinary least squares and then rolls the regression forward through the sample one observation at a time, computing a residual for each recursion. Under the null hypothesis of no structural change, the cumulative sum of scaled residuals—the cusum—is expected to behave like a random walk. However,

---

12. In chapter 15, we show that this type of structural change is crucial for understanding the shifting relationship between the exchange rate and macroeconomic fundamentals.

13. We find that two lags are sufficient to obtain white-noise residuals. For an excellent treatment of how to model relationships involving unit-root variables, see Hendry and Juselius (2000, 2001).

Figure 12.7 Cusum Test Gap Plus Model: DM/$

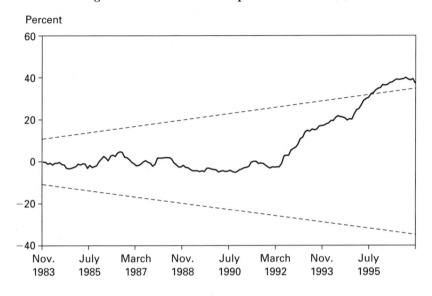

if there is a structural break, the cusum will begin to grow persistently in one direction or another from the point of the break, eventually crossing one of the bounds that the random walk would not be expected to cross.

Figure 12.7 plots the cusum for the DM/$ market when based on the full sample, which begins in December 1982 and ends in February 1997. The dotted lines in the figure provide the 5 percent confidence bands for the test. As can be seen, the cusum grows beyond the upper band at the beginning of 1995, which indicates that a point of structural change occurred prior to this date. But, even though this procedure provides a test for structural change, it does not produce a precise date for the location of the break point.

However, we know that the point of the break is proximate to the point in time at which the cusum starts to grow steadily away from the zero line. We thus take the date immediately after the cusum crosses the zero line and begins to grow in one direction, eventually crossing one of the confidence bounds for the first time, as the point of structural change.[14] In figure 12.7, this date is June 1992. To test whether June 1992 is indeed the first observation of a new subperiod of relative parameter constancy, we use the forecast χ^2 statistic. This statistic indicates a break between May and June of 1992 with a p-value that is nearly zero.

---

14. In chapter 15, we use a combination of the cusum test and the Quandt ratio technique (Quandt, 1960). We find that this alternative approach produces results that are similar to those produced by the approach we use here.

Because there may be additional break points in the data, we re-run the cusum test for the two subsamples implied by the first break, that is, December 1982–May 1992 and June 1992–February 1997.[15] This test does not detect additional break points in our sample. Consequently, to test the house money model against the gap plus model for the DM/$ market, we estimate one ADL model for each of our two subperiods of "statistical parameter constancy."

When applied to the JY/$ market over the entire sample, the cusum test does not reject the null hypothesis of no structural change. We thus estimate an ADL model for the full sample. However, a plot of the cusum (not shown) reveals that this statistic steadily grows beginning in 1991 and just misses crossing the 10 percent upper band by the end of the sample. This finding leads us to test for a break point using the forecast χ^2 statistic in January 1991. We find that we can reject the null hypothesis of no structural change with a *p*-value of zero. Consequently, we also estimate separate ADL models for the implied subperiods of statistical parameter stability.

The cusum test also does not find points of structural change when based on the entire sample for the BP/$ market. We thus estimate an ADL model for the full sample. But figures 12.1–12.3 indicate that the relationship between $\widehat{pr}_{t|t+1}$ and $\widehat{gap}_{t|t+1}$ changes between 1980s and 1990s. We also note that the break points that were found for the DM/$ and JY/$ markets match closely with the points at which the cumulative current account balances in these markets begin their steep rises. We suspect, therefore, that there may be a break point in the BP/$ market between December 1992 and January 1993, which is when this market undergoes a steep rise in CCA_t. When based on the forecast χ^2 statistic, we find that the null hypothesis of no structural change can be rejected with a *p*-value that is nearly zero. Consequently, we also estimate separate ADL models for the implied subperiods of statistical parameter constancy.

12.3.2. *Testing the House Money Model Against the Gap Plus Model*

To clarify the connection between our theoretical models of the premium and the empirical specification in equation (12.11), we express the ADL in error-correction form:

$$\Delta\widehat{pr}_t = \alpha_1\Delta\widehat{pr}_{t-1} + \sum_{i=0}^{1}\left(\alpha_{2i}\Delta\widehat{gap}_{t-i} + \alpha_{3i}\Delta CCA_t\right) + \alpha_4 ECT_{t-2} + \varepsilon_t,$$

$$(12.12)$$

15. It is necesaary to test for structural change in the first subsample because the cusum test scales the recursive residuals by the standard error of the regression based on the entire sample. Consequently, it is possible for the cusum test to indicate a break prior to May 1992 when based on a subsample that ends in May 1992.

where the error-correction term is:

$$ECT_{t-2} = \beta_0 + \beta_1\widehat{gap}_{t-2} + \beta_2 CCA_{t-2} - \widehat{pr}_{t-2}, \qquad (12.13)$$

and $\alpha_1 = b_{11} - 1$, $\alpha_{20} = b_{20}$, $\alpha_{21} = b_{20} + b_{21}$, $\alpha_{30} = b_{30}$, $\alpha_{31} = b_{30} + b_{31}$, $\alpha_4 = 1 - b_{11} + b_{12}$, $\beta_0 = b_0/\alpha_4$, $\beta_1 = (b_{20} + b_{11} + b_{12})/\alpha_4$, $\beta_2 = (b_{30} + b_{31} + b_{32})/\alpha_4$.

The house money and gap plus models of the equilibrium premium relate the one-period change in $\widehat{pr}$ to the contemporaneous change in $\widehat{gap}$. The error-correction specification in equation (12.12) captures this contemporaneous relationship with the first-difference terms. We are interested in the combined effect of these terms on the market premium. We thus solve equation (12.12) for the static relationship that is implied by that equation:

$$\Delta\widehat{pr}_t = \gamma_0 + \gamma_1\Delta\widehat{gap}_t + \gamma_2\Delta CCA_t - \gamma_3 ECT_{t-2} + \varepsilon_t, \qquad (12.14)$$

where $\gamma_0 = \alpha_0/(1 - \alpha_1)$, $\gamma_1 = (\alpha_{20} + \alpha_{21})/(1 - \alpha_1)$, $\gamma_2 = (\alpha_{30} + \alpha_{31})/(1 - \alpha_1)$, and $\gamma_3 = \alpha_4/(1 - \alpha_1)$. The house money model implies that $\gamma_1 < 0$, whereas the gap plus model implies $\gamma_1 > 0$.

Beyond its contemporaneous effect, the error-correction specification in (12.14) also allows $\widehat{gap}$ to influence the one-period change in the market premium through the error-correction term. This term provides for a relationship among the levels of $\widehat{pr}$, $\widehat{gap}$, and CCA. If $\gamma_3 > 0$, then the market has a tendency to move toward this relationship over time. For example, suppose that ECT_{t-2} takes on positive values in some period; that is, market participants in the aggregate expect a premium on foreign exchange that is too low compared to the level implied by $\beta_0 + \beta_1\widehat{gap}_{t-2} + \beta_2 CCA_{t-2}$. Consequently, the premium that market participants expect will tend to rise over subsequent periods.

A higher $\hat{s}_{t|t+1}$ (and thus a higher $\widehat{gap}_t$) implies a higher exchange rate, ceteris paribus, leading to gains for bulls and losses for bears. The house money model, therefore, implies that if the levels relationship is relevant (that is, $\gamma_3 > 0$), then β_1 should be negative. By contrast, the gap restrictions imply that β_1 should be positive.

The error-correction specification in equation (12.12) also allows CCA to influence the one-period change in the premium through two channels. The current account restrictions imply that $\gamma_2 > 0$ and $\beta_2 > 0$. However, data on bilateral current account balances are available only quarterly. We thus interpolated these data to obtain monthly series. It is unlikely, therefore, that the contemporaneous ΔCCA terms will enter the estimated error-correction model in equation (12.14) significantly: market participants do not observe the monthly changes implied by our interpolation and thus cannot react in a contemporaneous way. Thus, we would expect that, if the cumulative current account balance influences how market participants forecast potential losses, this effect would be captured by the error-correction term, ECT_{t-2}.

Table 12.2 Gap Plus Model Error-Correction Specification[a]

Currency	Sample period	γ_1	γ_3	R^2	Durbin-Watson statistic
DM	December 1982–February 1997	1.10***	−.28***	.50	2.12
		(.16)	(.04)		
	December 1982–May 1992	1.33***	−.51***	.66	2.05
		(.14)	(.05)		
	June 1992–February 1997	.71***	−.38***	.51	1.99
		(.28)	(.08)		
BP	December 1982–February 1997	.84***	−.33**	.41	2.01
		(.15)	(.04)		
	December 1982–December 1992	.92***	−.37***	.45	1.98
		(.16)	(.05)		
	January 1993–February 1997	.93***	−.49***	.53	1.98
		(.32)	(.07)		
JY	December 1982–February 1997	.84***	−.29***	.45	2.03
		(.19)	(.04)		
	December 1982–December 1990	.83**	−.44***	.54	1.95
		(.23)	(.06)		
	January 1991–February 1997	2.12***	−.62***	.51	2.00
		(.26)	(.08)		

[a] Regression estimates based on the error-correction specification in equation (12.14). Insignificant cumulative current account terms deleted from the short-run component of model. Standard errors are in parentheses. ** and *** indicate significance from zero at the 5 and 1 percent levels. DM, BP, and JY denote the German mark, British pound, and Japanese yen markets, respectively.

Table 12.2 reports results for the static relationship in equation (12.14), which are based on estimates of the error-correction model in equation (12.12). As expected, the ΔCCA terms in the estimated error-correction models are insignificant for all currencies and all subperiods. We thus drop these terms from the models.

Table 12.2 shows that we are able to reject the null hypothesis, at the 1 percent level, that either the house money effects dominate the gap effects or they are of equal magnitude. For all currencies and all subperiods, we find that the contemporaneous relationship between $\widehat{pr}_t$ and $\widehat{gap}_t$ is positive. If the house money considerations influence market participants' behavior, they are completely dominated by the gap effects.

Table 12.2 also shows that the error-correction term enters the model significantly for all currencies and all subperiods. Moreover, estimates of γ_1 and γ_3 reveal that the contemporaneous influence of changes in $\widehat{gap}$ on the market premium is twice or more the size of the influence of ECT. Thus, although we find (in table 12.3) some evidence that movements in CCA influence the market premium through ECT, the dominant influence on monthly changes in $\widehat{pr}_t$ stems from changes in $\widehat{gap}_t$.

Table 12.3   Gap Plus Model Error-Correction Term[a]

Currency	Sample period	β_1	β_2	Wald statistic
DM	December 1982–February 1997	.29*	.10	.16
		(.15)	(.06)	
	December 1982–May 1992	.43***	.05	.00
		(.07)	(.03)	
	June 1992–February 1997	−.24	.02	.64
		(.29)	(.18)	
BP	December 1982–February 1997	.56***	.24	.00
		(.10)	(.05)	
	December 1982–December 1992	.99***	.67***	.00
		(.18)	(.15)	
	January 1993–February 1997	.67	.22*	.88
		(.67)	(.12)	
JY	December 1982–February 1997	.19	.04**	.05
		(.16)	(.02)	
	December 1982–December 1990	.13	−.03	.00
		(.13)	(.02)	
	January 1991–February 1997	−.34	.04	.06
		(.25)	(.03)	

[a] Regression estimates based on the error-correction term in equation (12.13). Insignificant cumulative current account terms are deleted from the short-run component of model. Standard errors are in parentheses. *, **, and *** indicate significance from zero at the 10, 5, and 1 percent levels, respectively. DM, BP, and JY denote the German mark, British pound and Japanese yen markets, respectively.

The results for the error-correction term are reported in table 12.3, which are based on estimates of the ADL in equation (12.11). We find that, when $\widehat{gap}$ enters the error-correction term significantly, it does so with a positive coefficient, thereby lending further support to the gap plus model. We also find that the cumulative current account also enters the error-correction term positively in five of the six subperiods examined, although significantly so only for the BP market. These results, together with the finding that $\gamma_3 > 0$, provide some indication that movements in *CCA* influence how market participants revise their forecasts of the potential losses.

12.4. The Gap Plus Model and the Frequency of Sign Reversals

In discussing the implications of endogenous prospect theory in chapter 11, we pointed out that the potential for the equilibrium premium on foreign exchange to undergo sign reversals is greater under the assumption of heterogeneous forecasts than under homogeneous forecasts. For convenience, we recall UAUIP:

$$\widehat{pr}_{t|t+1} = \widehat{up}_{t|t+1} + \lambda_2 IFP_t. \tag{12.15}$$

Under heterogeneous forecasts, the algebraic signs of the equilibrium uncertainty premium and IFP_t can differ. It is clear that movements of $\widehat{up}_{t|t+1}$ can be associated with a sign reversal in $\widehat{pr}_{t|t+1}$.

Fluctuations in the equilibrium return depend on new realizations of the causal variables and the exchange rate, and on how market participants revise their forecasting strategies. In any one period, the change in $\widehat{pr}_{t|t+1}$ may involve a sign reversal. But it is clear that as the magnitude of $\widehat{pr}_{t|t+1}$ becomes larger, the changes in the causal variables, the exchange rate, and forecasting strategies that would lead to a sign reversal would also have to be larger. In general, therefore, we would expect that the frequency of sign reversals would become smaller as the magnitude of $\widehat{pr}_{t|t+1}$ becomes large.

UAUIP implies a large equilibrium premium when one side of the market, either the bulls or the bears, forecasts a large potential unit loss from speculation while the other side does not—$\widehat{up}_{t|t+1} = \frac{1}{2}(1 - \lambda_1)(\hat{l}^{L}_{t|t+1} - \hat{l}^{S}_{t|t+1})$ is large in size—and the net supply of long positions, IFP_t, is either small in size or reinforces the impact of $\widehat{up}_{t|t+1}$. Alternatively, a large equilibrium premium will prevail when the magnitude of IFP_t is large and the magnitude of $\widehat{up}_{t|t+1}$ is either small or reinforces the impact of IFP_t.

As we mentioned above, data on IFP_t are not available. However, figures 12.4–12.6 are suggestive that the size of IFP_t may have been small in the 1980s and large and positive during the 1990s for all three countries considered. Thus, if we could qualitatively relate the size of $\widehat{up}_{t|t+1}$ to some observable variables, we would be able to test the implications of UAUIP for the frequency of sign reversals in our sample.

The gap and cumulative current account restrictions in equations (12.7), (12.8), and (12.10) imply that $\widehat{pr}_{t|t+1}$ moves positively with $\widehat{gap}_{t|t+1}$ and CCA_t. This tendency, in turn, would seem to imply that, when the size of $\widehat{gap}_{t|t+1}$ and CCA_t are large, the size of the aggregate uncertainty premium is also large. But this is not necessarily the case because our IKE restrictions constrain only the changes in $\widehat{pr}_{t|t+1}$ and not the magnitudes of these changes between consecutive time periods.

For example, suppose that the changes in $\widehat{gap}_{t|t+1}$ over τ successive time periods alternate between positive and negative values, while CCA_t remains constant. Also suppose that, over these τ periods, the positive changes in $\widehat{gap}_{t|t+1}$ are larger in magnitude than the negative changes, so that $\widehat{gap}_{t|t+1}$ increases from a small positive value to a much larger value. Although the gap restrictions imply that $\widehat{gap}_{t|t+1}$ and $\widehat{up}_{t|t+1}$ move in the same direction, it is possible that the positive changes in $\widehat{gap}_{t|t+1}$, though larger, are associated with changes in $\widehat{up}_{t|t+1}$ that are of the same magnitude as those associated with negative changes in $\widehat{gap}_{t|t+1}$. In this case, $\widehat{up}_{t|t+1}$ would remain unchanged despite $\widehat{gap}_{t|t+1}$ having risen over the τ periods.

Under what conditions would we expect a large $\widehat{gap}_{t|t+1}$ in magnitude to be associated with a large $\widehat{up}_{t|t+1}$ in magnitude? To clarify this issue, suppose that CCA_t is either small in magnitude or its effect on $\widehat{up}_{t|t+1}$ reinforces that of $\widehat{gap}_{t|t+1}$. It is then reasonable to suppose that if $\widehat{gap}_{t|t+1}$ were above (below) some positive (negative) threshold value, the bulls (bears) would be much more concerned than the bears (bulls) about an exchange rate movement in the wrong direction. This greater concern would, in turn, imply a large positive (negative) $\widehat{up}_{t|t+1}$. During the 1980s, the size of CCA_t was relatively small for all three markets. We thus suppose that, during this decade, there was a threshold above and below $\widehat{gap}_{t|t+1} = 0$ such that a gap beyond this threshold was associated with a large magnitude of $\widehat{up}_{t|t+1}$.

With this assumption, the gap plus model generates a testable prediction concerning the frequency of sign reversals in $\widehat{pr}_{t|t+1}$ during the 1980s. If we divide the observations for $\widehat{pr}_{t|t+1}$ into two groups—those associated with a $\widehat{gap}_{t|t+1}$ that is large in size (above some threshold) and those associated with a $\widehat{gap}_{t|t+1}$ that is small in size—we should find that the frequency of sign reversals is smaller for the observations associated with a large $\widehat{gap}_{t|t+1}$.

As for the 1990s, the gap plus model does not generate a clear prediction. Figures 12.1–12.3 show that during this decade, when CCA_t is large in all three markets, $\widehat{gap}_{t|t+1}$ is mostly negative and also large in size. During this decade, then, the impact of the gap effect on the equilibrium premium is opposite to that of CCA_t. The gap plus model, however, implies nothing about which effect, if any, might dominate. Thus, it is consistent with an equilibrium premium that is either large or small in size, and thus, with a low or high frequency of sign reversals during 1990s.

To test the prediction of the gap plus model concerning sign reversals for the 1980s, we need an empirical standard of "large." Figures 12.1–12.3 show that $\widehat{gap}_{t|t+1}$ varies over a wide range, from a high of 50 percent for the JY market to a low of -30 percent for the DM and BP markets. With no obvious standard available, we examine the implications of three definitions: 5, 10, and 20 percent. For each market, we tally the number of observations for which $\widehat{gap}_{t|t+1}$ is below the threshold and the number of observations for which it is above. We also compute the number of sign reversals in $\widehat{pr}_{t|t+1}$ that occur between two consecutive time periods as a proportion of the total number of observations in each group.[16] Table 12.4 reports these results and provides a Z statistic for a difference in means test.

At the lowest threshold of 5 percent, the results are consistent with the prediction of the gap plus model: the proportion of sign reversals that are associated with observations for $\widehat{gap}_{t|t+1}$ that are larger than 5 percent is more than 2 times (1.5 times) the proportion associated with a $\widehat{gap}_{t|t+1}$ smaller than this threshold for the DM (JY) market. For the DM market, this factor is significant with a very low p-value. For the BP market, the proportions associated with a large and small $\widehat{gap}_{t|t+1}$ are inconsistent with the gap plus model, although this difference is not significant.

As we increase the value of the threshold, however, the results indicate support for the gap plus model in all three markets. The proportion of sign reversals associated with a large $\widehat{gap}_{t|t+1}$ relative to the proportion associated with a small $\widehat{gap}_{t|t+1}$ falls for the BP market each time the threshold is increased. With a threshold of 20 percent, the proportion associated with a large $\widehat{gap}_{t|t+1}$ is significantly smaller, with a very low p-value. For the JY market, the smaller proportion of sign reversals that is associated with a $\widehat{gap}_{t|t+1}$ above the 10 percent (20 percent) threshold is significant at the .05 (.08) level, and for the DM market this proportion remains significant at low p-values.

The ability of the IKE gap plus model to explain sign reversals in the premium on foreign exchange stands in sharp contrast to the failure of REH risk-premium models to shed light on this feature of the data.

---

16. Observations that straddle the threshold from below and above are included in the below-threshold proportion. Including them in the above-threshold proportion does not change our results.

Table 12.4   Sign Reversals in the Market Premium: 1980s

		Threshold on aggregate gap					
		5 percent		10 percent		20 percent	
Currency[a]	*Statistics*[b]	*Larger*	*Smaller*	*Larger*	*Smaller*	*Larger*	*Smaller*
BP	Obs	44	39	33	50	15	68
	P	.27	.26	.21	.29	0	.32
	Z	−.17 (.57)		.91 (.18)		5.70 (.00)	
DM	Obs	54	29	31	52	18	65
	P	.22	.55	.16	.44	.17	.38
	Z	3.04 (.00)		2.94 (.00)		2.05 (.02)	
JY	Obs	76	7	67	16	34	49
	P	.37	.57	.34	.56	.29	.45
	Z	1.04 (.15)		1.60 (.05)		1.47 (.08)	

[a] DM, BP, and JY denote the German mark, British pound, and Japanese yen markets, respectively.
[b] Obs denotes the number of observations for which the magnitude of the aggregate gap is either larger or smaller than the threshold. P is the proportion of observations above and below a threshold (5, 10, or 20 percent) that are associated with a sign reversal in the market premium. Z is a Z-statistic for a difference in means test, where numbers in parentheses are *p*-values.

12.5. Avoiding the Presumption of Gross Irrationality

The risk-premium models of Mark and Wu (1998) and Gourinchas and Tornell (2004) attribute forecasting strategies to market participants whose predictions deviate systematically from those of the aggregate models. These models thus presume that market participants are grossly irrational. The gap plus model, however, provides an explanation of the premium in the foreign exchange market without the presumption of gross irrationality.

The gap plus model avoids a modeling inconsistency by relying on partially predetermining restrictions and by representing different aspects of the causal mechanism on the individual and aggregate levels. The model implies that the equilibrium premium depends positively on the aggregate gap. Our representations on the individual level, however, involve qualitative predictions concerning a different aspect of the causal mechanism, namely, the expected loss from holding a speculative position.

Appendix 12.A

12.A.1. Downward-Sloping Demand Paths in the House Money Model

The net demand for long positions in foreign exchange is given by $D_t^{\mathrm{L}} = \frac{\hat{r}_{t+1} - \widehat{up}_t}{\lambda_2}$. Thus, constraining all demand-transition paths to be downward sloping implies:

$$\frac{\mathcal{D}\hat{s}_{t|t+1}}{\Delta s_t} - 1 + \tfrac{1}{2}\left(\hat{l}_{t|t+1}^{\mathrm{L}}\frac{\mathcal{D}\lambda_1^{\mathrm{L}}}{\Delta s_t} - \hat{l}_{t|t+1}^{\mathrm{S}}\frac{\mathcal{D}\lambda_1^{\mathrm{S}}}{\Delta s_t}\right) < 0.$$

Given that $\frac{\mathcal{D}\hat{s}_{t|t+1}}{\Delta s_t} > 0$ from the trend restriction, $1 - \tfrac{1}{2}\left(\hat{l}_{t|t+1}^{\mathrm{L}}\frac{\mathcal{D}\lambda_1^{\mathrm{L}}}{\Delta s_t} - \hat{l}_{t|t+1}^{\mathrm{S}}\frac{\mathcal{D}\lambda_1^{\mathrm{S}}}{\Delta s_t}\right)$ must be positive to ensure that all demand-transition paths are downward sloping.

12.A.2. The Relative Gap Restrictions and the Total Change in the Premium

We express the total change in $\widehat{pr}_{t|t+1}$ as:

$$\mathcal{D}\widehat{pr}_{t|t+1} = \tfrac{1}{2}\left(1 - \lambda_1\right)\left[\frac{\mathcal{D}\hat{l}_{t|t+1}^{\mathrm{L}}}{\mathcal{D}\hat{s}_{t|t+1}} - \frac{\mathcal{D}\hat{l}_{t|t+1}^{\mathrm{S}}}{\mathcal{D}\hat{s}_{t|t+1}}\right]\mathcal{D}\hat{s}_{t|t+1}.$$

Without loss of generality, suppose that $\mathcal{D}\hat{s}_{t|t+1} > 0$. We know that if $\hat{s}_{t|t+1}^{\mathrm{L}}$ and $\hat{s}_{t|t+1}^{\mathrm{S}}$ both rise, then $\mathcal{D}\widehat{pr}_{t|t+1} > 0$. Thus, we need to show that the relative gap restrictions imply that if $\hat{s}_{t|t+1}^{\mathrm{L}}$ and $\hat{s}_{t|t+1}^{\mathrm{S}}$ move in opposite directions, while $\hat{s}_{t|t+1}$ rises, $\widehat{pr}_{t|t+1}$ will still rise.

From the definition of the aggregate $\hat{s}_{t|t+1}$, we know that:

$$\mathcal{D}\hat{s}_{t|t+1}^{j} = 2\mathcal{D}\hat{s}_{t|t+1} - \mathcal{D}\hat{s}_{t|t+1}^{j}\quad j = \mathrm{L}, \mathrm{s}.$$

It follows that the side of the market that revises its forecast of the future exchange rate in the same direction as $\hat{s}_{t|t+1}$ must have the larger revision. Again, without loss of generality, suppose that $\hat{s}_{t|t+1}^{\mathrm{L}}$ rises while $\hat{s}_{t|t+1}^{\mathrm{S}}$ falls, thereby implying that $\mathcal{D}\hat{s}_{t|t+1}^{\mathrm{L}} > -\mathcal{D}\hat{s}_{t|t+1}^{\mathrm{S}}$. According to the relative gap restrictions, then, $\left|\mathcal{D}\hat{l}_{t|t+1}^{\mathrm{L}}\right| > \left|\mathcal{D}\hat{l}_{t|t+1}^{\mathrm{S}}\right|$. Consequently, $\left|\frac{\mathcal{D}\hat{l}_{t|t+1}^{\mathrm{L}}}{\mathcal{D}\hat{s}_{t|t+1}}\right| > \left|\frac{\mathcal{D}\hat{l}_{t|t+1}^{\mathrm{S}}}{\mathcal{D}\hat{s}_{t|t+1}}\right|$, thereby implying that $\mathcal{D}\widehat{pr}_{t|t+1} > 0$.

13 The Forward Discount "Anomaly"

The Peril of Fully Prespecifying Market Efficiency

In the absence of a risk or uncertainty premium, the equilibrium in the foreign exchange market implies that the one-period-ahead change in the spot rate and the forward premium move one-for-one, that is, the slope coefficient in the Bilson (1981) and Fama (1984) (BF) regression should be unity. As we discussed in chapter 8, however, many studies have reported that this slope coefficient not only differs from unity but is significantly negative.

Adhering to the contemporary approach, the vast majority of economists, including Bilson and Fama themselves, have estimated the BF regression under the maintained hypothesis that the relationship between the change in the spot rate and the forward premium is unchanging over time. If such invariance were to be consistent with the data, estimates of the parameters of the BF regression would become more reliable as the sample period is lengthened. Consequently, researchers have relied on samples that span three decades of floating exchange rates without allowing for the possibility of structural change. The results of these empirical investigations led to the consensus that the future change in the spot rate co-varies negatively with the forward premium.

Economists have engaged in an intensive effort to find an REH model of the risk premium that would rationalize the belief in a negative slope coefficient. Unable to find such a model that is empirically relevant, economists attributed their findings to a correlation between the aggregate forecast error and the forward premium. This correlation has been interpreted as "irrationality" on the part of market participants because "it suggests that one can make predictable profits by betting against the forward rate" (Obst-feld and Rogoff, 1996, p. 589). This apparent forward discount "anomaly"—that these profits remain unexploited—has become one of the major puzzles in the international finance literature.

In this chapter, we show that the belief in a negative slope coefficient in the BF regression appears to be an artifact of the contemporary approach's search for a fully predetermined—in this case, invariant—relationship be-tween the change in the exchange rate and the forward premium. By con-trast, IKE suggests that this relationship is unstable over time, which is indeed what we find. As reported in chapter 7, the value of the slope co-efficient is sometimes positive, sometimes insignificantly different from one and zero, and sometimes negative.

We make use of our IKE gap plus model of the premium and argue that estimates of the slope coefficient result from coincidental trends in the mar-ket premium and the forward premium. The gap plus model implies that when the gap effect dominates all other effects, swings in the exchange rate will be associated with swings in the market premium in the same direction. In general, the forward premium does not have to move persistently during such periods of swings. However, if the forward premium does so, the co-incidence of the trends in the market premium and the forward premium may result in a value of the slope coefficient in the BF regression that differs from unity.

To examine this possibility, we consider the most pronounced exchange rate swings in the 1970s and 1980s, during which the forward premium also happened to move persistently. We find that the value of the slope coefficient during the swings in the 1970s is significantly greater than unity, whereas for those in the 1980s it is significantly negative for all three currencies studied (DM, BP, JY). We find that the gap plus model is consistent with these results and that the market premium plays a role in the observed instability in the BF regression.

There is, therefore, no systematic correlation between the market pre-mium and the forward premium. Moreover, this correlation changes sign from one subperiod to another. These findings suggest that fixed rules based on estimates of the BF regression are unlikely to provide profitable ways to speculate in currency markets. To be profitable, one would have to deter-mine, at each point in time, how much of the recent history should be used in estimating the BF regression and anticipate when its parameters will un-dergo change.

Successful speculation in currency markets, therefore, is not as simple as the international financial literature suggests. Indeed, we show in this chapter that predictable profits cannot be made by simply betting against the forward rate. While the rule delivers profits in some subperiods for some currencies, it stops being profitable at times that cannot be fully predetermined. We also show that, even at those occasional times when the rule delivers profits, they are not large enough to provide reasonable compensation for uncertainty.

Of course, it is impossible to prove that there is no fixed rule that can deliver profits systematically, whether based on the BF regression or some other fully predetermined model. The results in this chapter, however, show that relying on fully predetermined models to examine efficiency of markets is likely to lead to misleading conclusions.

13.1. Bilson-Fama Regression and the Forward Discount "Anomaly"

It is useful to summarize briefly our discussion of the literature on the BF regression from chapter 8. This regression is based on:

$$\Delta s_{t+1} = \alpha + \beta f p_t + v_t, \tag{13.1}$$

where Δs_{t+1} and $f p_t$ denote the one-period ahead change in the spot exchange rate and forward premium, respectively, and v_t is an error term.

The condition for momentary equilibrium in the foreign exchange market is

$$\widehat{r}_{t|t+1} = \Delta \widehat{s}_{t|t+1} - f p_t = \widehat{pr}_{t|t+1}, \tag{13.2}$$

which implies that

$$\Delta s_{t+1} = f p_t + \widehat{pr}_{t|t+1} + v_{t|t+1}, \tag{13.3}$$

where $\widehat{pr}_{t|t+1}$, $\widehat{r}_{t|t+1}$, and $\Delta \widehat{s}_{t|t+1}$ denote representations of the market premium, aggregate expected return on holding foreign exchange, and the aggregate forecast of Δs_{t+1}, respectively, and $v_{t|t+1} = \Delta s_{t+1} - \Delta \widehat{s}_{t|t+1}$ is the aggregate forecast error. Thus, if market participants are risk neutral and the aggregate forecast error is uncorrelated with the forward premium, then equilibrium in the foreign exchange market implies that $\alpha = 0$ and $\beta = 1$. Alternatively, if $\beta \neq 1$, then either $E_t[\widehat{pr}_{t|t+1}|f p_t] \neq 0$ and/or $E_t[v_{t|t+1}|f p_t] \neq 0$, where we use the subscript on $E_t[\cdot]$ to allow for the possibility that expectations may be based on different probability distributions at different times.

Following the contemporary approach, most economists, including both Bilson and Fama, have estimated the BF regression in equation (13.1) while maintaining the hypothesis that the relationship between Δs_{t+1} and

fp_t is unchanging over time. The results of these empirical investigations led to the consensus that $\beta < 0$.[1]

13.2. Structural Instability of the BF Regression and the Gap Plus Model

In real world markets, however, one should not presume that the parameters of the BF regression are unchanging over time. As table 8.4 in chapter 8 shows, the BF regression is indeed structurally unstable between the decades of the 1970s, 1980s, and 1990s.[2] For all three currencies considered, $\hat{\beta}$ is positive and insignificantly different from one and zero for the 1970s and, with the exception of the JY, for the 1990s as well. During the 1980s, however, $\hat{\beta}$ is negative and significantly so for all three currencies. These structural change results show that the negative $\hat{\beta}$ obtained when using the full sample is driven by the data for the 1980s.

The instability of the BF regression suggests that, if the compensation for risk or uncertainty plays an important role in underpinning returns in currency markets, then the relationship between the market premium and the forward premium should itself be structurally unstable. As we report in table 8.3 in chapter 8, regressions of $\widehat{pr}_{t|t+1}$ on fp_t show that such instability is indeed the case. This finding, in turn, suggests that the gap plus model may shed light on the unstable nature of the BF regression.

The gap plus model relates movements of the market premium to movements of the aggregate gap, $\widehat{gap}_{t|t+1} = \hat{s}_{t|t+1} - \hat{s}_t^{HB}$ and the cumulative current account CCA_t, where we recall that the superscript HB refers to the historical benchmark level. In general, market participants' forecasts of the future exchange rate, and therefore the aggregate gap, may depend on the forward premium. But we would not expect this relationship to be systematic: the correlation between $\widehat{pr}_{t|t+1}$ and fp_t, if any, is likely to depend on the time period examined.

The gap plus model predicts that time periods that are characterized by a persistent swing in the exchange rate in one direction and a dominant gap effect should also be characterized by a persistent swing in the market premium in the same direction. Figures 12.1–12.3 in chapter 12 show that this prediction holds for the swings in the 1980s. Thus, if during such swings, the forward premium also happens to move persistently in one direction or

---

1. Table 8.1 of chapter 8 reproduces the standard estimate of a negative estimate of the slope coefficient in the BF regression when based on more than two decades of floating rates.

2. See section 8.4 in chapter 8 for the few studies that have looked for and found structural instability in the BF regression.

Figure 13.1   DM/$ Exchange Rate

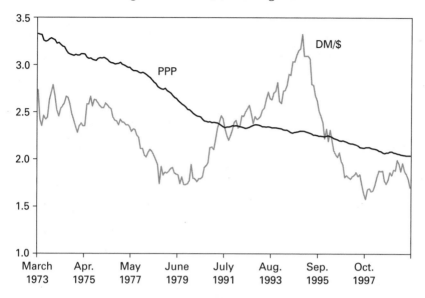

the other, the market premium and the forward premium will appear to be correlated with each other. If, although coincidental, this correlation is sufficiently strong, it would cause the value of the slope coefficient in the BF regression to depart from unity.

This reasoning leads us to consider estimates of the BF regression for time periods in which a swing in $\widehat{gap}_{t|t+1}$ is clearly discernible and in which the gap effect is likely to dominate all other effects.[3] Consequently, we focus our attention on the 1970s and 1980s. We also restrict our analysis to the most pronounced exchange rate swing away from PPP in each of the first two decades, when the gap effect is likely to be most dominant.

Consider first the DM/$ exchange rate, which is plotted in figure 13.1 along with its PPP value. The figure shows that the most pronounced exchange rate swing away from PPP in the 1970s occurs between November 1975 and October 1978 and in the 1980s between June 1982 and February 1985. The gap plus model implies that during these subperiods, the market premium should also be trending. If the forward premium also happens to

---

3. A more complete analysis would also look at swings in other subperiods. Moreover, the observed pattern of positive and negative values of the slope coefficient could also be due to the transient correlation between the forecast errors and the forward premium.

Figure 13.2   DM/$ Forward Premium

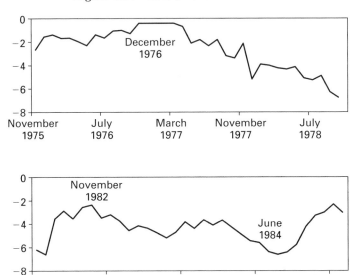

be trending in the same (opposite) direction in each of these subperiods, then we would expect β to be greater (less) than unity.

Figure 13.2 plots the forward premium in the two subperiods involving the most pronounced exchange rate swings. The figure shows that a clear trend in *fp* arises in both subperiods, but only after the exchange rate swing in each subperiod begins. For the 1970s subperiod, the trend in *fp* begins in December 1976, and for the 1980s, it begins in November 1982. Moreover, for the latter subperiod, the trend in *fp* abruptly changes direction in June 1984, prior to the end of the exchange rate swing. Consequently, we estimate the BF regression for the two subperiods—December 1975–October 1978 and November 1982–June 1984—in which the exchange rate swings are associated with clear trends in the forward premium.

According to the gap plus model, a swing in the exchange rate is associated with a swing in the market premium in the same direction. But the trend in *fp* happens to be in the same direction as the exchange rate swing in the 1970s, whereas it is in the opposite direction for the swing in the 1980s. Thus, the gap plus model implies that β should be greater than unity during the first subperiod and less than unity during the second subperiod.

Table 13.1 reports the results of the BF regressions for our two subperiods. Despite the small sample sizes, the estimates of β are large in magnitude and significantly different from unity in the 1970s and 1980s. Moreover, as implied by the gap plus model, the DM/$ exchange rate swing

Table 13.1 **BF Regression: Major Swings**[a]

Currency	Time period	β Swing	β Postswing[b]	χ^2 test[c]
BP	June 1975–September 1976[d]	3.59***	−2.99*	.00
		(1.17)	(1.00)	
	March 1983–June 1984	−13.02*	−15.42***	.00
		(7.16)	(5.09)	
DM	December 1976–September 1978[d]	5.13***	−.27	.00
		(1.62)	(1.58)	
	November 1982–June 1984	−19.80**	−11.56	.00
		(8.33)	(9.05)	
JY	May 1977–September 1984[b]	12.46***	−6.30*	.00
		(4.31)	(3.22)	
	January 1983–June 1984	−22.29**	−17.06	.00
		(10.28	(11.33)	

[a] Standard errors are in parentheses. *, **, and *** indicate significance from zero at the 10, 5, and 1 percent level. BP, DM, and JY denote the British pound, German mark, and Japanese yen markets, respectively.
[b] Postswing subperiods are 24 months in length.
[c] p-values of forecast χ^2 statistic of Hendry (1979).
[d] Insignificant constant was deleted from regression.

in the 1970s is associated with $\beta > 1$, while the swing in the 1980s is associated with $\beta < 1$.

A similar picture emerges when we consider the BP/\$ and JY/\$ markets. Figures 13.3 and 13.5 plot the BP/\$ and JY/\$ exchange rates along with their PPP levels, respectively, while figures 13.4 and 13.6 plot the forward premium during the subperiods involving the most pronounced exchange rate swing away from PPP.

The figures show a similar pattern to the one found in figures 13.1 and 13.2—for both the BP/\$ and JY/\$ markets, the forward premium and the exchange rate trend in the same direction during 1970s subperiod and in opposite directions during the 1980s.[4] Thus, as with the DM/\$ market,

4. The subperiods involving the most pronounced exchange rate swing are February 1975–October 1976 and June 1982–February 1985 for the BP/\$ and May 1977–October 1978 and May 1981–February 1985 for the JY/\$. The subperiods involving both swings in the exchange rate and forward premium are June 1975–October 1976 and March 1983–June 1984 for the BP/\$ and May 1977–September 1978 and January 1983–June 1984 for the JY/\$.

Figure 13.3   BP/$ Exchange Rate

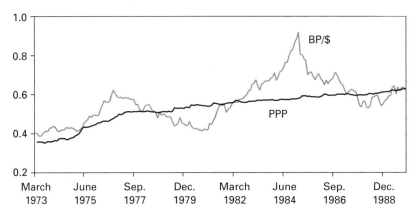

Figure 13.4   BP/$ Forward Premium

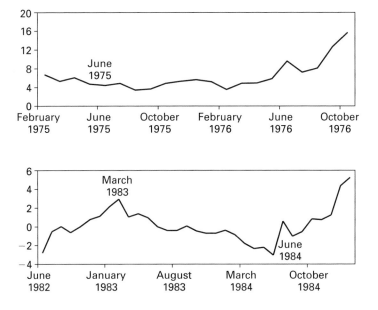

the gap plus model implies that β should be greater than unity during the subperiods in the 1970s and less than unity during those in the 1980s.

The results for these markets are also reported in table 13.1. As implied by the gap plus model, they show the same pattern of deviations of β from unity as that for the DM/$ market: for both the BP/$ and JY/$ markets, the

Figure 13.5 JY/$ Exchange Rate

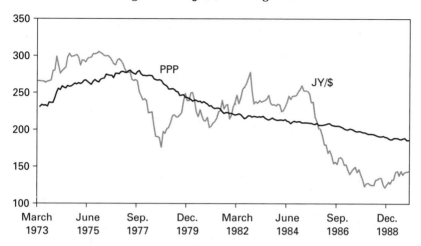

estimates of β are large in magnitude and significantly different from one. Moreover, $\beta > 1$ for the subperiods in the 1970s and $\beta < 1$ for those of the 1980s.

There are studies that have attempted to connect a negative β to the long swings in the exchange rate.[5] However, the results in table 13.1 for all three currencies lead to the conclusion that exchange rate swings can result in both positive (and greater than one) and negative values of the slope coefficient in the BF regression.

The gap plus model of the market premium implies that the correlation between Δs_{t+1} and fp_t should change at times and in ways that cannot be fully prespecified. This instability is clearly the case here, as the value of β changes when the swing in the exchange rate and/or trend in the forward premium disappears or changes direction. The last column of table 13.1 presents evidence on this point. It shows that there is a structural break at the end of each of the subperiods considered in the table at p-values that are nearly zero. Moreover, the divergence of β from unity in the postswing subperiods either loses its significance or changes its sign. These results indicate that the temporal instability of the BF regression is connected with the long-swings behavior of the exchange rate and the coincidental trend in the forward premium. Taken as a whole, the results in table 13.1 suggest that movements in the market premium play a significant role in determining the value of β in any one time period.

5. See Engel and Hamilton (1990), Bekaert and Hodrick (1993), Kaminsky (1993), and Evans and Lewis (1995).

Figure 13.6   JY/$ Forward Premium

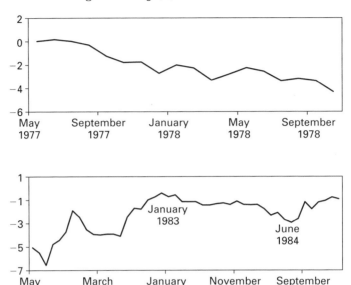

13.3. BF Regression and Market Efficiency

The finding that the correlation between the market premium and the forward premium is not only unsystematic but changes sign from one subperiod to another suggests that fixed rules based on estimates of the BF regression are unlikely to provide profitable ways to speculate in currency markets. To be profitable, one would have to determine, at each point in time, how much of the recent history should be used in estimating the BF regression and anticipate when its parameters will undergo change. The results of the preceding section indicate that such a task would involve forecasting whether recent trends in the exchange rate *and* the forward premium will continue. We now show that the widespread belief that one can make predictable profits by betting against the forward rate is specious.

13.3.1. Betting against the Forward Rate

A rule based on systematically betting against the forward rate implies that, whenever the forward premium is positive (negative), the change in the spot exchange rate over the coming period will be negative (positive), that is, that the domestic currency will appreciate (depreciate).[6] To capitalize on this prediction at each point in time, one would buy (sell) domestic currency forward at the current rate of $1/f_t$ and then sell (buy) domestic currency at the spot rate prevailing one period later, $1/s_{t+1}$; where f_t denotes the forward exchange rate.

To compute the return each period from using this forward-rate rule, we assume that our fictitious trader can transact at the prices prevailing in the interbank market for foreign exchange. To account for the costs associated with transacting in this market, we compute the one-period return on long and short positions in the forward market as:

$$g_t^L = 1 - \frac{s_{t+1}^a}{f_t^b} \quad \text{and} \quad g_t^S = \frac{s_{t+1}^b}{f_t^a} - 1, \tag{13.4}$$

where the superscripts b and a denote a bid and asked price for foreign currency, respectively. Our data are monthly and come from Data Resources, Inc.

Table 13.2 reports the mean monthly return that would have been earned if a trader used the forward-rate rule to take open positions in the BP/\$, DM/\$, and JY/\$ markets over the entire sample period, as well as during the three separate subperiods, the 1970s, 1980s, and 1990s. The table also reports the success rate for this trading rule—the number of individual months the rule produces a positive return over the total number of observations.

The results show that contrary to the prevailing view in the literature, we cannot reject the hypothesis that the mean return from betting against the forward-rate prediction is zero in every market for the full sample when based on the 5 percent significance level. If we are willing to accept a significance level of 10 percent, then this hypothesis can be rejected only for the BP/\$ market.

Consider further the results for the BP/\$ market. The success rate indicates that the forward-rate rule has some ability to predict the direction of change of the spot exchange rate over the full sample. However, the results for the separate subperiods indicate that this predictive ability stems from the experience of the 1980s. During this decade, the mean return from using the forward-rate rule is positive and significantly different from zero and the success rate of 58 percent is borderline significant at the 10 percent level. This profitability is borne out in figure 13.7, which plots the separate monthly profits generated by the forward-rate rule.

---

6. The exchange rate is defined as the domestic currency price of foreign exchange.

Table 13.2 **Performance of the Forward-Rate Rule: 1970s and 1980s**[a]

Currency	Time period	Mean return	Success rate[b]
BP	May 1973–February 1997	.36*	.57**
		(.20)	
	May 1973–December 1979	−.00	.56
		(.32)	
	January 1980–December 1989	.74**	.58*
		(.32)	
	January 1990–February 1997	.00	.54
		(.36)	
DM	May 1973–February 1997	.10	.52
		(.20)	
	May 1973–December 1979	−.27	.41*
		(.35)	
	January 1980–December 1989	.28	.56
		(.34)	
	January 1990–February 1997	.18	.55
		(.35)	
JY	May 1973–February 1997	.24	.60***
		(.20)	
	May 1973–December 1979	−.10	.54
		(.34)	
	January 1980–December 1989	.02	.60**
		(.31)	
	January 1990–February 1997	.67*	.67**
		(.35)	

[a] Standard errors are in parentheses. *, **, and *** indicate significance from zero at the 10, 5, and 1 percent levels, respectively. BP, DM, and JY denote the British pound, German mark, and Japanese yen markets, respectively.
[b] Proportion of positive monthly returns in sample.

But this result is exactly what one would expect, *ex post,* from the negative estimate of β that was found for the 1980s. The problem, of course, is that to exploit the implied negative correlation between the change in the spot rate and forward premium in the 1980s, one would have needed to know,

Figure 13.7   Profits, BP Market: 1980s

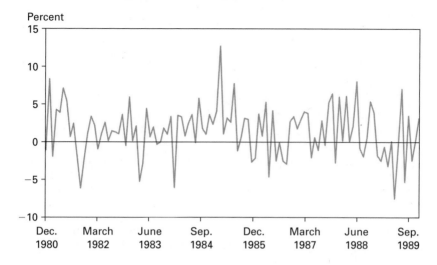

ex ante, that the 1980s would be characterized by extraordinary exchange rate and interest rate swings.

Indeed, the 1970s and 1990s are not characterized by a significantly negative estimates of β. Consequently, the forward-rate rule shows no ability to deliver profits during these decades in the BP/$ market. This failure is illustrated by the time plots of the monthly profits generated by this rule in the 1970s and 1990s shown in figures 13.8 and 13.9, respectively.

The subsample results for the DM/$ market show that the forward-rate rule has no ability to generate positive returns even in the 1980s. Indeed, the success rate shows that, were one to have bet with the forward rate, rather than against it, one would have earned profits during this period.

As for the JY/$ market, the odds ratio shows that the forward-rate rule has predictive ability over the entire sample and in the 1980s and 1990s. These results suggest that although the mean return is insignificantly different from zero for the entire sample, a rule of betting against the forward rate may have been profitable in the JY/$ market over our sample. But these results can hardly be viewed as support for the usual claim that profits can be made by betting against the forward rate. To exploit any predictive ability that this rule might have had in the JY/$ market, a trader would need to have known, ex ante, that she should have speculated in this market and not the other two.

Figure 13.8   Profits, BP Market: 1970s

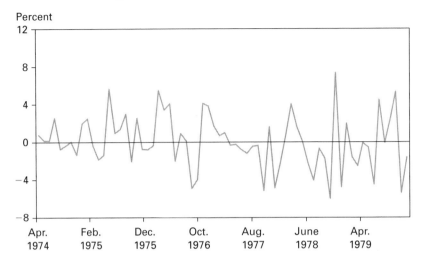

Figure 13.9   Profits, BP Market: 1900s

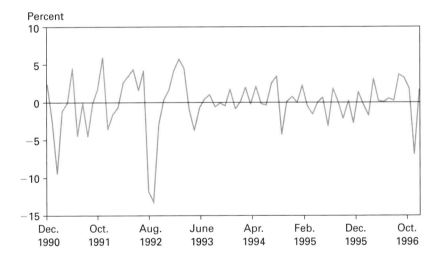

13.3.2. Market Efficiency

We thus find that predictable profits cannot be made by merely betting against the forward rate. This finding may be startling to some, given the extensive literature that has developed over more than two decades trying to explain the belief in such predictable profits. But it surely comes as no surprise to the participants in the interbank currency markets, who spend enormous sums of money attempting to forecast future exchange rate movements.

Of course, it is impossible to prove that there is no fixed rule that can deliver profits systematically, whether based on the BF regression or some other metric. But the argument that we have made in part I concerning the importance of non-routine behavior for outcomes in real world markets, together with the empirical results that we presented in this and other chapters, suggest that it would be extremely difficult to find a profitable trading strategy that could be "put on a computer and run."[7]

Suppose one discovered such a rule. Would such a discovery imply that the foreign exchange market was inefficient? The answer is clearly no. To reject the hypothesis that this, or any other, market is efficient, one would need to show that this rule generates a mean return that is significantly greater than the market premium.

For example, suppose the results for the 1980s concerning the profitability of the forward-rate rule in the BP/\$ market had been obtained for all three currencies considered over the entire sample. This is the market and subperiod that generates the highest mean return in table 13.2. Given this mean return and its standard error, however, a market premium greater than .1 percent on a monthly basis is all that would be required to accept the null hypothesis of market efficiency. Our empirical results and those of other studies, therefore, provide no support for the view that currency markets are inefficient.

---

7. We examined the profitability of a fixed ex ante rule based on recursively rolling the BF regression through our sample. As we expected, the profitability of this rolling-regression rule depends on the sample period examined. In general, the rule produces significantly positive returns only in the 1980s.

14 Imperfect Knowledge and Long Swings in the Exchange Rate

International macroeconomists plausibly presume that market participants' forecasts concerning the return from holding foreign exchange is the primary factor that underpins exchange rate movements. They have also presumed that these forecasts are based on macroeconomic fundamentals and that they are formed in largely rational, reasonable ways. But the use of REH to represent rational forecasting strategies and their revisions has made it difficult to construct models that deliver plausible explanations of the salient features of the empirical record. One of the "anomalous" features is the tendency of floating exchange rates to undergo protracted swings away from PPP. To explain these swings, conventional flexible-price monetary models must rely on implausibly large and persistent real shocks. The sticky-price monetary models, for their part, can only account for one-time deviations from PPP. This limitation has led economists to construct sticky-price monetary models in which long swings in the exchange rate result from the decisions of market participants who either somehow all agree to follow "REH bubbles" that are fully prespecified or are "irrational" in deciding on their holding of speculative positions.[1]

We show in this chapter that, once we jettison REH in favor of IKE representations of forecasting behavior, exchange rate swings away from PPP can arise in a traditional monetary model. This result holds true even if we assume that goods prices are fully flexible and that individuals' forecasts are based solely on macroeconomic fundamentals. To represent revisions of forecasting strategies, we appeal to the findings in

---

1. See chapters 6 and 7.

psychology that we discussed in chapter 10. These findings suggest that individuals tend to revise their beliefs slowly in the face of new evidence. We make use of a set of restrictions that constrain revisions of forecasting strategies to reinforce the movement of the real exchange rate that would arise in the model in the absence of such revisions. What counts as conservative or reinforcing behavior depends on the size of the expected movements of the causal variables and whether goods prices are assumed to be fully flexible or to adjust to their equilibrium values only sluggishly.

The conservative and reinforcing restrictions that we impose on our representations of forecasting behavior constrain neither the set of causal variables nor how these variables might matter for an individual's forecast. Yet our model implies that any subperiod of floating currencies that is characterized by (1) conservative and/or reinforcing forecasting behavior and by (2) macroeconomic fundamentals that tend to move persistently in one direction will also be characterized by a persistent movement of the exchange rate either toward or away from PPP. If the movement of the exchange rate is initially toward PPP and the subperiod of conservative or reinforcing forecasting behavior endures, then eventually, the exchange rate will shoot through this benchmark level and begin trending away from PPP from the other side. And because our model presumes imperfect knowledge, it generates such exchange rate behavior without the presumption of gross irrationality.[2] Strikingly, we find that the restrictions on forecasting behavior that are needed for macroeconomic fundamentals to be the primary factor driving exchange rate swings away from PPP in the model are *more stringent* when goods prices are assumed to be sticky rather than flexible.

Findings by psychologists suggest that conservative forecasting behavior may characterize revisions of forecasting strategies over extended periods of time. Although we do not assume that this regularity characterizes behavior at every point in time, as long as it persists, our model implies that the exchange rate will move persistently away from or toward PPP.

Our model of swings does not fully prespecify how long forecast behavior may be adequately characterized as conservative or reinforcing or how long the policy environment may remain unchanged. We assume, however,

---

2. Frydman, Goldberg, and Juselius (2007) use the IKE monetary model of this chapter to reexamine the PPP puzzle of Rogoff (1996). The model implies that nominal and real exchange rates can be approximated as $I(2)$ processes, even though goods prices may adjust quickly to equilibrium levels. It also implies that the real exchange rate and real interest rate differential, while nonstationary separately, should be cointegrated. Frydman, Goldberg, and Juselius (2007) provide empirical support for these predictions. They also find that goods prices mean revert to equilibirum levels with an average half life of 2 months.

that these representations will cease to be adequate if the gap between the exchange rate and its PPP value exceeds some threshold, the level of which we do not prespecify. Thus, although our model of exchange rate swings does not predetermine when a swing will begin or end, it does imply that a prolonged swing away from PPP will eventually be reversed.[3]

We show that if one were to follow the vast majority of contemporary economists and presume that individuals' forecasting strategies are invariant, then a monetary policy rule that sets money supply to grow at a fixed rate would imply an unbounded swing in the exchange rate away from PPP. Thus, *under imperfect knowledge*, invariant representations not only presume gross irrationality on the part of market participants, but reliance on them is contrary to the fact that exchange rate swings are bounded.

REH sticky-price models imply that the process driving exchange rate movements is stable around a long-run equilibrium level given by PPP: market forces invariably push the exchange rate back to PPP and, in the absence of shocks, the exchange rate will come to settle at this equilibrium level. The IKE model that we develop in this chapter leads to a fundamentally different view. It implies that the exchange rate process is essentially unstable, but boundedly so. The exchange rate may move persistently away from PPP for extended periods of time and, if this price happens to equal PPP, there are no market forces that necessarily work to maintain it at this level. Nevertheless, PPP acts as an anchor for the exchange rate. With IKE and endogenous prospect theory, market participants relate the riskiness of holding a long or short position in foreign exchange not to the conditional variance of returns, but to the degree to which the exchange rate diverges from PPP. This alternative specification of risk implies that, although the exchange rate may move persistently away from PPP for extended periods of time, such movements are self-limiting: a growing gap from PPP eventually triggers revisions of forecasting strategies that lead to movements in the exchange rate in the direction of PPP.

14.1. A Monetary Model

The model that we develop in this chapter builds on the traditional monetary models of Dornbusch (1976), Frenkel (1976), and Frankel (1979). It assumes that there are two countries and consists of equilibrium conditions for the money, goods, and foreign exchange markets. Our specification of the goods markets allows for both flexible and sticky goods prices. The

---

3. IKE recognizes that it is impossible to fully prespecify "historical developments to the extent to which they may be influenced by the growth of our knowledge" (Popper, 1957, p. xii).

equilibrium condition for the currency market and the model's aggregate forecasts of the return and potential unit loss on foreign exchange are based on explicit IKE representations of individual behavior. But as in the traditional literature, the other components of the model are only loosely related to individual behavior.

Macroeconomists using NOEM have pursued a different line of research. They have built complete microfoundations into traditional sticky-price models and, on the whole, continued to use REH to represent individual forecasting behavior. To date, NOEM models have been unsuccessful in explaining swings in the exchange rate away from PPP. In this chapter, we show that the problem with the traditional monetary models is not their lack of complete microfoundations. Rather, the problem lies in how they represent an individual's forecasting behavior.

14.1.1. Money Markets

We follow much of the literature and specify the demand for domestic and foreign money symmetrically.[4] This assumption allows us to express equilibrium in the money markets in terms of relative—domestic minus foreign—magnitudes:

$$m_t = p_t + \phi y_t - \lambda i_t, \tag{14.1}$$

where m_t, and p_t, y_t denote the relative log levels of the money supply, goods prices, and income, respectively, and i_t denotes the relative nominal rates of interest.

14.1.2. Goods Markets

Traditional flexible-price monetary models assume that domestic and foreign goods are perfect substitutes and that there are no barriers to the trade of goods internationally. In this one-good world, the assumption of flexible goods prices is tantamount to the assumption that PPP holds at every point in time. By contrast, traditional sticky-price monetary models assume that domestic and foreign goods are imperfect substitutes. In specifying the behavior of goods prices, these models assume that the excess demand for goods depends on international price competitiveness, as given by the real exchange rate, as well as on other factors, such as interest rates and income levels. We follow this latter approach and assume that the excess demand

---

4. For a monetary model that allows for asymmetirc money demand specifications, see Goldberg (1995, 2000).

for domestic goods relative to foreign goods is given by:[5]

$$EDG_t = \alpha \left(s_t - p_t - q^{\mathrm{PPP}}\right) - \eta \left(i_t - \hat{\pi}\right), \qquad (14.2)$$

where s_t is the log level of the spot exchange rate; $\hat{\pi}$ denotes the aggregate of market participants' assessments concerning the relative rates of inflation that would prevail if goods markets cleared; q^{PPP} is a historical benchmark real exchange rate, which we take to be PPP; and α and η represent the sensitivity of excess demand to movements in the real exchange rate and interest rates, respectively. We assume that $\hat{\pi}$ and q^{PPP} are exogenous to the model and constant.[6]

To allow for sluggish adjustment of goods prices in our model, we follow the traditional literature and assume that the movement of goods prices depends on excess demand and some underlying rate of inflation:

$$\Delta p_{t+1} = \delta \left[\alpha \left(s_t - p_t - q^{\mathrm{PPP}}\right) - \eta \left(i_t - \hat{\pi}\right)\right] + \Delta \bar{p}_{t+1}, \qquad (14.3)$$

where Δ is the first-difference operator and the overbar denotes a value associated with goods-market clearing.

The assumption of flexible goods prices is tantamount to assuming that the excess demand for goods equals zero at every point in time. With excess demand given in equation (14.2), therefore, the assumption of flexible goods prices implies PPP if either one of two conditions holds: domestic and foreign goods are perfect substitutes (that is, $\eta = 0$), or equilibrium in the goods markets is associated with an equality between the real rates of interest across countries (that is, $i_t - \hat{\pi} = 0$). Under the usual no-bubbles REH solution, the latter condition, which is called *international Fisher parity,* holds. Consequently, under REH, the assumption of flexible goods prices implies PPP regardless of whether domestic and foreign goods are assumed to be perfect or imperfect substitutes.[7] By contrast, under IKE, equilibrium in the goods markets is not associated with international Fisher parity. Thus,

---

5. On purely empirical grounds, imperfect rather than perfect substitutability of goods across countries is clearly the more plausible assumption.

6. Dornbusch (1976), Frankel (1979), and many others set q^{PPP} to be consistent with absolute PPP; that is, $q^{\mathrm{PPP}} = 0$. However, with distinct domestic and foreign baskets of goods, $q^{\mathrm{PPP}} \neq 0$. In general, IKE restrictions could be used to model $\hat{\pi}$ as a function of causal variables. But doing so would not alter the ability of the model to generate exchange rate swings away from PPP. We therefore abstract from this complication.

7. The equilibrum models of Stockman (1980, 1987), Lucas (1982), and others generalize the traditional flexible-price monetary models in part by assuming imperfect substitutability between domestic and foreign goods. In these models, permanent movements in the real exchange rate occur because of shocks in preferences and technology. As we pointed out in chapter 7, it is diffcult to reconcile these models with the large and frequent swings in real exchange rates that have occurred in currency markets.

with IKE and imperfect substitutability, the assumption of flexible goods prices does not imply PPP.

14.1.3. Foreign Exchange Market

To specify equilibrium in the foreign exchange market, we replace the usual assumption of UIP with UAUIP, which we developed in chapter 11:

$$\widehat{s}_{t|t+1}\left(s_t, x_t\right) - s_t - i_t = \widehat{up}_t, \tag{14.4}$$

where

$$\widehat{up}_t = \left(1 - \lambda_1\right) \hat{l}_{t|t+1}\left(s_t, x_t\right). \tag{14.5}$$

$\widehat{s}_{t|t+1} = \frac{1}{2}\left(\hat{s}^L_{t|t+1} + \hat{s}^S_{t|t+1}\right)$ represents the aggregate of bulls' and bears' point forecasts of S_{t+1} at time t given their time-t information and forecasting strategies. The information set x_t includes current and past realizations on a set of causal variables that represents the union of factors that market participants use in forming their forecasts, and $\widehat{up}_{t|t+1}$ is the aggregate uncertainty premium at time t, which depends on bulls' and bears' degree of loss aversion, $\lambda_1 > 1$, and their forecasts of the potential unit loss from holding speculative positions, $\hat{l}_{t|t+1}\left(s_t, x_t\right) = \frac{1}{2}\left(\hat{l}^L_{t|t+1} - \hat{l}^S_{t|t+1}\right)$. Recall that superscripts L and S refer to long and short positions, respectively. As with short-run portfolio-balance models, we assume that asset supplies are exogenous and, for simplicity, set the international financial position *IFP* equal to zero in equation (14.4).

As in previous chapters, we represent an individual's forecasting strategy at each time t with any one of the conditional probability distributions for R_{t+1} that satisfy the partially predetermining restrictions of the model. UAUIP shows that there are two aspects of these partially predetermined distributions that are important for the analysis: their mean and expected loss. The expected loss for bulls and bears, $\hat{l}^L_{t|t+1} = E^L_t[R_{t+1} < 0|s_t, x^L_t]$ and $\hat{l}^S_{t|t+1} = E^S_t[R_{t+1} < 0|s_t, x^S_t]$, depend on the first and all higher moments of the distributions for $R^L_{t+1} = S_{t+1} - s_t - i_t$ and $R^S_{t+1} = i_t + s_t - S_{t+1}$, respectively.[8] In general, as market participants revise their forecasting strategies for R_{t+1}, they alter how their point forecasts of the future exchange rate and potential unit loss depend on s_t and x_t. In our model of swings, we also consider the case in which revisions of individuals' forecasting strategies for R_{t+1} involve

---

8. Because the return on short positions is $-R_{t+1}$, the aggregate expected return in equation (14.4)—$\hat{s}_{t|t+1} - s_t - i_t$—is defined as $\hat{r}_{t|t+1} = \frac{1}{2}(\hat{r}^L_{t|t+1} - \hat{r}^S_{t|t+1})$.

revisions in the way $\hat{l}_{t|t+1}$ depends on s_t and x_t, but not so with $\hat{s}_{t|t+1}$. We refer to this case as involving invariant forecasting strategies for the mean of S_{t+1}.

We specify the aggregate point forecast $\hat{s}_{t|t+1}$ to consist of an autonomous component, $\hat{s}^a_{t|t+1}$, which depends solely on a set of causal variables, and an endogenous component, which depends on the level of the exchange rate. Moreover, for tractability, we treat both components as linear:

$$\hat{s}_{t|t+1} = \hat{\beta}_t x_t + \hat{\rho} s_t. \tag{14.6}$$

The assumption of linearity allows us to interpret the $\hat{\beta}_t$ and $\hat{\rho}$ parameters as weighted averages of the parameters used to represent the forecasting strategies of the bulls and bears. To simplify our analysis, without altering our main conclusions, we assume that x_t does not include i_t or p_t. The t subscripts on the $\hat{\beta}_t$ parameters allow for the possibility that when market participants revise their forecasting strategies for R_{t+1}, they may change the way they forecast the mean of S_{t+1}.[9] In general, such revisions may also involve changes in the way s_t influences these forecasts. However, we simplify and assume that $\hat{\rho}$ does not vary over time. We also appeal to the partially predetermining price-level restriction that we motivated in chapter 10 and constrain $\hat{\rho}$ to lie between zero and unity. As for the $\hat{\beta}_t$ parameters, we constrain neither their magnitudes nor their algebraic signs.[10]

In specifying the aggregate—bulls minus bears—expected loss, we suppose that revisions of forecasting strategies for R_{t+1} are consistent with the gap restrictions developed in chapters 10 and 12. These restrictions motivate the following specification for the aggregate $\widehat{up}_t$ in terms of the aggregate gap, $\widehat{gap}_t = \hat{s}_{t|t+1} - \hat{s}^{\text{HB}}_t$:

$$\widehat{up}_t = \hat{\sigma} \left(\hat{s}_{t|t+1} - \hat{s}^{\text{HB}}_t \right), \tag{14.7}$$

where $\hat{\sigma} > 0$, and $\hat{s}^{\text{HB}}_t$ represents the aggregate of bulls' and bears' assessments of the historical benchmark level of the exchange rate around which they believe swings, which are of uncertain duration, revolve. We represent this benchmark level by PPP and set:

$$\hat{s}^{\text{HB}}_t = \hat{q}^{\text{PPP}} + p_t, \tag{14.8}$$

---

9. Allowing the $\hat{\beta}$ parameters in equation (14.6) to change over time leads to a piecewise linear specification of forecasting behavior. Contemporary economists sometimes use such a specification as an approximation to a more general nonlinear specification. However, when they do, they fully prespecify the piece-wise linearity. By contrast, we impose only partially predetermining restrictions on our representation.

10. In the next chapter, we impose TCEH restrictions on the algebraic signs of the $\hat{\beta}_t$ parameters. Such restrictions, however, are not needed to generate long swings in the monetary model.

where $\hat{q}^{\mathrm{PPP}}$ denotes the aggregate of market participants' assessments concerning the PPP level of the real exchange rate. We assume that this aggregate assessment is constant.[11]

The specification in equation (14.7) implies that even if revisions of market participants' forecasting strategies for R_{t+1} involve invariant strategies for forecasting the mean of S_{t+1} (that is, unchanged $\hat{\beta}_t$ and $\hat{\rho}$ parameters), the new forecasting strategies for R_{t+1} are associated with gap effects: the magnitude of the expected loss of the bulls (bears) moves positively (negatively) with their evaluation of the gap. In general, the way that an individual's expected loss can vary with her evaluation of the gap may change from one time period to another. We simplify, however, and assume that $\hat{\sigma}$ remains unchanged over time. We also assume that $\hat{\sigma} < 1$, which implies that an increase (decrease) in $\hat{s}_{t|t+1}$ will lead to an excess demand (supply) for foreign exchange. This assumption, along with $\hat{\rho} < 1$, helps to ensure stability in the model.

While we specify $\hat{\rho}$ and $\hat{\sigma}$ as constants, our representation of forecasting behavior is partially predetermined.[12] In our model, a change in the aggregate forecast $\hat{s}_{t|t+1}$ can arise either because of new realizations of the causal variables and the exchange rate or because of partially predetermined changes in the parameters of its autonomous component. The latter source of change, in general, could involve a change in the composition of the variables in x.

We express the total change in $\hat{s}_{t|t+1}^a$ between two adjacent points in time as follows:

$$\mathcal{D}\hat{s}_{t|t+1}^a = \Delta\hat{\beta}_t' x_t + \hat{\beta}_{t-1}' \Delta x_t = \mathcal{D}^R \hat{s}_{t|t+1}^a + \Delta^U \hat{s}_{t|t+1}^a, \qquad (14.9)$$

where $\mathcal{D}^R \hat{s}_t^a$ denotes the change in $\hat{s}_t^a$ that occurs because of revisions of forecasting strategies at time t and $\Delta^U \hat{s}_t^a$ denotes the change in $\hat{s}_t^a$ that would occur between $t - 1$ and t if individuals left their forecasting strategies for the mean of S_{t+1} unchanged and only new realizations of the causal variables led them to revise their forecasts.[13] If the composition of the causal variables in x changes at time t, then this set can be defined as comprising the variables that appear in the representations of the aggregate

---

11. The key here is that the benchmark varies less than the exchange rate, rather than its constancy. A more general specification could, for example, allow $\hat{s}_t^{\mathrm{HB}} = \hat{q}_t^{\mathrm{HB}} - p_t$, where $\hat{q}_t^{\mathrm{HB}}$ could depend on a Balassa (1964)–Samuelson (1964) effect or on current account balances, as in Hooper and Morton (1982).

12. We make clear below that these assumptions do not alter the basic conclusions of our analysis.

13. We recall from chapter 10 that $\mathcal{D}$ and $\mathcal{D}^R$ are not total and partial differentials, respectively: with IKE, a change in $\hat{s}_{t|t+1}^a$ may result from a change in the relationship between market participants' forecasts and the causal variables and not just from a change in x.

forecast at both t and $t - 1$. To represent the absence of some variables, the parameter values associated with them in the vectors $\hat{\beta}_t$ or $\hat{\beta}_{t-1}$ would be constrained to zero.

14.1.4. Social Context

Institutional and other changes occur in the economy that may influence individuals' decisions to hold money or affect how goods prices evolve over time. But the pace of such structural change is slow relative to the frequency of revisions of forecasts in the foreign exchange market. We thus abstract from these kinds of changes in the social context and assume that the parameters of the money demand and goods markets specifications in equations (14.1) and (14.3), respectively, are constant.

In deriving the implications of the monetary model under IKE, we need to represent how its causal variables—m, y, and those in x—evolve over time. A common practice in the literature is to approximate the processes driving m and y as random walks with drift:

$$M_t = \mu_t + m_{t-1} + \eta_t \text{ and } Y_t = g_t + y_{t-1} + v_t, \qquad (14.10)$$

where μ_t and g_t are drift terms and η_t and v_t denote white-noise errors. We represent the possibility that the processes driving these causal variables may change from one subperiod to another by allowing for shifts in their drift components.

The set of causal variables in x, in general, may include both macroeconomic and nonfundamental variables. We examine the case in which the processes driving these variables are also approximated by random walks with drifts whose values may change intermittently. We refer to a subperiod in which the deterministic trends in m, y, and the variables in x do not vary over time as involving a fixed policy environment.

14.2. Invariant Representations and an Unbounded Swing Away from PPP

We now show that traditional monetary models of the exchange rate have very different implications once REH is replaced with restrictions on forecasting behavior that recognize the imperfection of knowledge. We begin with the case in which revisions of forecasting strategies for R_{t+1} involve no changes in the way that individuals forecast the mean of S_{t+1}; that is, we assume that the $\hat{\beta}$ parameters in equation (14.6) are invariant. We show that macroeconomic fundamentals can drive exchange rate swings in the model with either flexible or sticky goods prices as long as market participants are presumed to have imperfect knowledge and the policy environment is assumed to be fixed. Thus, even with an invariant $\hat{s}_{t|t+1}$ representation, one can explain a persistent movement of the exchange rate away from PPP without abandoning the insight that exchange rate movements depend on macroeconomic fundamentals.

Examining the implications of the model in which $\hat{\beta}$ is constant provides insight into the case in which we allow for partially predetermined changes in these parameters. We show in the next section that the logic behind an exchange rate swing under an invariant $\hat{s}_{t|t+1}$ representation is preserved when revisions of the $\hat{\beta}$ parameters are assumed to satisfy a set of qualitative conservative or reinforcing restrictions.

14.2.1. Solution of the Model

The solution of the model under the assumptions of invariant representations for individuals' forecasts of the mean and policy environment is:

$$q_t = c_1 (1 - \theta)^t + \bar{q}_t, \qquad (14.11)$$

where

$$\bar{q}_t = q^{\text{PPP}} + \frac{\eta (1 - \hat{\sigma})}{G} \left(\hat{s}^a_{t|t+1} - \hat{s}^{\text{RE}\,a}_t \right)$$

$$+ \frac{\eta (1 - \hat{\sigma}) [\lambda (1 - \hat{\rho}) - 1]}{G} \left(\hat{\pi} - \hat{\pi}^{\text{RE}} \right) - \frac{\eta \hat{\sigma}}{G} \hat{\pi}^{\text{RE}} + \frac{\eta \hat{\sigma}}{G} \left(\hat{q}^{\text{PPP}} - q^{\text{PPP}} \right) \quad (14.12)$$

$$\theta = \frac{\delta \left[\alpha + \eta h + \alpha \lambda \left(h - \hat{\sigma} \right) \right]}{h \lambda},$$

where $G = (\alpha + h\eta) + \alpha\lambda(h - \hat{\sigma}) > 0$, $h = 1 - \hat{\rho}(1 - \hat{\sigma}) > 0$, the superscript RE denotes the solution that would be obtained under REH, and the constant parameter c_1 is equal to zero if goods prices are assumed to be flexible, whereas with sticky goods prices, it depends on an initial condition for p. The autonomous component of the aggregate forecast of the mean of S_{t+1} under REH is

$$\hat{s}^{\text{RE}\,a}_t = \rho^{\text{RE}} \left(m_t - \phi y_t + q^{\text{PPP}} \right) + \left(\rho^{\text{RE}} \lambda + 1 \right) \hat{\pi}^{\text{RE}}, \qquad (14.13)$$

since $\hat{s}^{\text{RE}}_t - s_t = \rho^{\text{RE}}(\bar{s}^{\text{RE}}_{t-1} - s_{t-1}) + \hat{\pi}^{\text{RE}}$, where ρ^{RE} is one minus the stable root of the model, $\bar{s}^{\text{RE}}_t = m_t - \phi y_t + \lambda \hat{\pi}^{\text{RE}} + q^{\text{PPP}}$, and $\hat{\pi}^{\text{RE}} = E[\Delta \bar{s}^{\text{RE}} | m, y] = \mu - \phi g$.

The time path in equation (14.11), and those for the nominal exchange rate, relative goods prices, and relative interest rates in equations (14.24), (14.25), and (14.26) in appendix A, are standard in form. They depend on a short-run adjustment term if goods prices are assumed to be sticky and a corresponding medium-run—goods-market-clearing—level. We use the term "medium-run" instead of the more common term "long-run" to describe goods-market-clearing values for the endogenous variables because these values are not invariant functions of the causal variables when we allow for revisions of the $\hat{\beta}$ parameters below. Consequently, there is no single set of values, given the causal variables, toward which the endogenous variables will adjust.

When goods prices are assumed to be flexible, the time path for the real exchange rate is given by its medium-run level in equation (14.12). With $\hat{\rho}$ and $\hat{\sigma}$ both between zero and unity, $\theta > 0$, so that the root of the system, $1 - \theta < 1$. To ensure stability and non-oscillatory behavior, we assume that $\theta < 1$.[14]

The medium-run value in equation (14.12), and those for the nominal exchange rate, relative goods prices, and relative interest rates in equations (14.27), (14.28), and (14.29) in appendix A, show that the time paths for the endogenous variables of the model depend not only on the underlying structural parameters of the economy but also on the forecasting behavior of market participants, as represented by $\hat{s}^a_{t|t+1}, \hat{\pi}, \hat{q}^{\mathrm{PPP}}, \hat{\rho}$ and $\hat{\sigma}$. This dependence also holds for the REH solution, but because REH jointly determines aggregate outcomes and individual behavior, the structural parameters of the economy and those used to represent forecasting behavior are one and the same, that is, $\hat{s}^a_{t|t+1} = \hat{s}^{\mathrm{RE}a}_t, \hat{\pi} = \hat{\pi}^{\mathrm{RE}}, \hat{q}^{\mathrm{PPP}} = q^{\mathrm{PPP}}$, and $\hat{\rho} = \rho^{\mathrm{RE}}$.[15]

Under REH, the model ties its representations of exchange rate and inflation forecasts rigidly to the market-clearing PPP exchange rate. Goods market clearing, therefore, implies that real interest rates are equal across countries, $\bar{i}^{\mathrm{RE}} - \hat{\pi}^{\mathrm{RE}} = 0$, and that the real exchange rate equals its PPP level, $\bar{q}^{\mathrm{RE}}_t = q^{\mathrm{PPP}}$. Thus, under REH, the assumption of flexible goods prices is tantamount to the assumption of PPP and international Fisher parity even with imperfect substitutability of domestic and foreign goods.

14.2.2. Imperfect Knowledge and Flexible Goods Prices

The REH representation of forecasting behavior relies on a particular set of parameters and macroeconomic variables. It is just one of myriad possible representations that could be used to model individual behavior. However, with imperfect knowledge, market participants make use of diverse strate-

---

14. In the case of REH, stability and non-oscillatory behavior requires

$$\frac{\delta \left[\alpha + (\eta + \alpha\lambda) \left(1 - \rho^{\mathrm{RE}} \right) \right]}{(1 - \rho^{\mathrm{RE}}) \lambda} < 1.$$

15. With no persistent swings in the exchange rate away from PPP under REH, there is no uncertainty as to whether a swing may continue or end. As such, $\hat{\sigma}^{\mathrm{RE}} = 0$.

gies in forming their forecasts of next period's exchange rate and potential unit loss. Moreover, even if all market participants were to base their assessments of the historical benchmark on PPP, we would expect a diversity concerning their assessment of q^{PPP}. Thus, in general, with imperfect knowledge, the aggregate of individuals' point forecasts of the exchange rate and potential unit loss are not characterized by the REH representation. We assume, therefore, that $\hat{s}^a_{t|t+1} \neq \hat{s}^{\text{RE}a}_t$, $\hat{\pi} \neq \hat{\pi}^{\text{RE}}$, $\hat{q}^{\text{PPP}} \neq q^{\text{PPP}}$, and $\hat{\rho} \neq \rho^{\text{RE}}$. Also, if the fixed policy environment involves deterministic trends, then movements in the $\hat{s}^a_{t|t+1}$ and $\hat{s}^{\text{RE}a}_t$ representations will also involve deterministic trends. Again, because imperfect knowledge implies a diversity of forecasting strategies, $E[\Delta \widehat{S}^a_{t|t+1}|x_{t-1}]$ and $E[\Delta \widehat{S}^{\text{RE}a}_t|m_{t-1}, y_{t-1}]$ are, in general, not equal.

Consider first the case of flexible goods prices, so that $q_t = \bar{q}_t$. We note that equation (14.12) can be expressed as the time path of the nominal exchange rate relative to its PPP level, since $q_t - q^{\text{PPP}} = s_t - s^{\text{PPP}}_t$, where $s^{\text{PPP}}_t = p_t + q^{\text{PPP}}$. Equation (14.12) shows, therefore, that the presumption of imperfect knowledge on the part of market participants implies that the exchange rate will deviate from its PPP level. Taking first differences of equation (14.12) delivers the key equation of the model:

$$\Delta \left(s_t - s^{\text{PPP}}_t\right) = \frac{\eta \left(1 - \hat{\sigma}\right)}{G} \left(\Delta \hat{s}^a_{t|t+1} - \Delta \hat{s}^{\text{RE}a}_t\right), \qquad (14.14)$$

which shows that persistent trends in the causal variables will lead market participants to push the exchange rate persistently toward or away from PPP.

If the policy environment involves no deterministic trends in m, y, and the variables in x, then the divergence between the exchange rate and its PPP level will neither grow nor shrink on average; that is,[16]

$$E\left[\Delta \hat{s}^a_{t|t+1} - \Delta \hat{s}^{\text{RE}a}_t | x_{t-1}, m_{t-1}, y_{t-1}\right] = 0.$$

However, if the policy environment does involve deterministic trends, so that:

$$E\left[\left(\Delta \hat{s}^a_{t|t+1} - \Delta \hat{s}^{\text{RE}a}_t\right) | x_{t-1}, m_{t-1}, y_{t-1}\right] \neq 0,$$

then a persistent swing in the exchange rate either away from or toward PPP will, on average, arise in the model. If the persistent movement of the exchange rate is initially toward PPP, then eventually the exchange rate will shoot through this benchmark level and begin trending away from PPP from the other side. Thus, as long as the representation of forecasting behavior

---

16. Nevertheless, the stochastic trends in the causal variables will still lead to persistent deviations from PPP.

presumes imperfect knowledge, and this representation and the policy environment remain unchanged, the monetary model with flexible goods prices implies a persistent movement of the exchange rate away from PPP.

Equation (14.14) also shows that this persistent movement can arise if the forecasting strategies attributed to market participants depend solely on macroeconomic fundamentals. This conclusion is true even if x is specified to include only those fundamentals that drive the REH forecast, that is, m and y. As long as market participants' knowledge is imperfect, so that the weights attached to the variables in $\hat{s}^a_{t|t+1}$ differ from those in $\hat{s}^{RE_a}_t$, the model implies a persistent movement in the exchange rate away from PPP.

It is not difficult to understand the intuition behind this result. Market participants' point forecasts of the exchange rate influence the equilibrium exchange rate, as represented by UAUIP in equation (14.4). Once one recognizes that knowledge is imperfect, the aggregate of these point forecasts is, in general, not equal to the PPP exchange rate.

Suppose, for example, that the spot exchange rate lies above its PPP level at some time t. Further suppose, without loss of generality, that the deterministic trends in m and y are such that, on average, $\hat{s}^{RE_a}_t$ is constant, while $\hat{s}^a_{t|t+1}$ rises. An increase in $\hat{s}^a_{t|t+1} - \hat{s}^{RE_a}_t$, ceteris paribus, implies an increase in the aggregate expected return on holding foreign exchange, which leads market participants to bid up the exchange rate. This domestic currency depreciation, in turn, leads to an incipient excess demand for domestic goods, which then bids up p_t. It is clear from equation (14.2) that if nominal interest rates did not change, or if domestic and foreign goods were perfect substitutes, p_t would have to rise one-for-one with s_t to ensure equilibrium in the goods market. But the rise in p_t leads to a rise in the demand for money, and thus, to a rise in i_t. With imperfect substitutability between domestic and foreign goods, the rise in i_t works together with the rise in p_t to reduce the demand for domestic goods. Thus, in general equilibrium, goods prices rise less than one-for-one with the spot exchange rate, thereby implying a greater divergence from PPP.

This movement of the exchange rate away from PPP will continue as long as market participants' forecasting strategies for the mean of S_{t+1} and the policy environment are assumed to remain unchanged. Consequently, with imperfect knowledge and invariant representations for forecasting behavior and the policy environment, the monetary model with flexible goods prices implies an unbounded swing away from PPP.

14.2.3. Imperfect Knowledge and Sticky Goods Prices

The implication of an unbounded swing in the exchange rate away from PPP carries over to the case involving sticky goods prices. This is because the medium-run levels toward which the exchange rate and relative goods prices adjust, as we have just shown, can themselves imply an unbounded exchange rate swing away from PPP.

Using equations (14.11) and (14.12), we can express the change in the nominal exchange rate relative to its PPP level as:

$$\Delta \left(s_t - s_t^{\text{PPP}}\right) = \theta \left(\bar{q}_{t-1} - q_{t-1}\right) + \frac{\eta \left(1 - \hat{\sigma}\right)}{G} \left(\Delta \hat{s}_{t|t+1}^{a} - \Delta \hat{s}_t^{\text{RE}_a}\right).$$

(14.15)

The excess demand and secular trend components—the first and second terms in the equation, respectively—can, in general, imply real exchange rate movements that are in opposite directions, regardless of whether q or $\bar{q}$ is above or below PPP. But, with an invariant $\hat{s}_{t|t+1}^{a}$ representation and a fixed policy environment, the magnitude of any excess demand in the goods market falls over time as the endogenous variables of the model adjust to their medium-run levels. Consequently, any trends in the secular component $\hat{s}_{t|t+1}^{a} - \hat{s}_t^{\text{RE}_a}$ eventually dominate the effect of the excess demand term.

There are thus two cases to consider. Again we suppose that:

$$E\left[\Delta \widehat{S}_{t|t+1}^{a} | x_{t-1}\right] \neq E\left[\widehat{S}_t^{\text{RE}_a} | m_{t-1}, y_{t-1}\right] \neq 0$$

and $\eta \neq 0$. If the excess demand and secular trend terms influence q in the same direction, or the magnitude of the latter is greater, then the exchange rate will, on average, move persistently either toward or away from PPP. If the persistent movement of the exchange rate is initially toward PPP, then eventually the exchange rate will shoot through this benchmark level and begin trending away from PPP from the other side.

If the excess demand and secular trend terms influence q in opposite directions and the magnitude of the former is greater, then a swing in q in one direction will eventually be followed by a swing in the opposite direction as the size of the excess demand term steadily falls. Therefore, in this case, too, the exchange rate will eventually begin trending away from PPP.

Hence, as with flexible goods prices, the invariant monetary model with sticky goods prices implies an unbounded movement of the exchange rate away from PPP as long as market participants are presumed to have imperfect knowledge and the policy environment involves secular trends. Moreover, such an unbounded swing would occur in the model even if all market participants are presumed to base their forecasts solely on macroeconomic fundamentals.

14.3. Fixed Policy Rules and Invariant Representations?

In part I, we argued that the microfoundations of invariant models are flawed: they presume gross irrationality on the part of market participants. The analysis in the preceding section highlights another important implication of imperfect knowledge for economic analysis, this time for examining the consequences of government policies.

The vast majority of contemporary economists presume that, once the policy environment is fixed, invariant models adequately represent market participants' behavior. This belief leads them to advocate that policy officials should be constrained to follow fixed rules. This practice presumably improves macroeconomic outcomes according to some measure of social welfare by limiting departures of market outcomes from their "desirable" levels, such as PPP in the case of currency markets.

The analysis in this section indicates that these conclusions may depend crucially on the presumption that imperfect knowledge is unimportant for understanding market outcomes and the consequences of government policies. If invariant models were indeed to represent adequately individual behavior, then, a monetary policy rule that sets money supply to grow at a fixed rate would imply, in the context of our model, an unbounded swing in the exchange rate away from PPP.

The exchange rate experience of the past three decades is characterized by exchange rate swings that, although protracted, are bounded and eventually reverse themselves over subsequent time periods. To generate such self-limiting swings in our monetary model, we need to allow for change in the representations of forecasting behavior and/or the policy environment. This brings us to an IKE model of swings.

14.4. An IKE Model of Exchange Rate Swings

Although our IKE model does allow for changes in the policy environment, our main focus is on developing partially predetermining restrictions on revisions of forecasting strategies. We ask whether there are qualitative regularities in the way strategies are revised so that, if they persist for an extended period of time and the policy environment remains unchanged during this period, the causal variables will drive persistent movements of the exchange rate either away from or toward PPP.

We find that there are two sets of such restrictions. These restrictions constrain revisions of forecasting strategies for R_{t+1} to be either conservative or reinforcing, in that the resulting change in the point forecast for S_{t+1} is either not too different from or reinforces the change that would arise in the model if forecasting strategies for the mean remained unchanged.

In representing revisions of forecasting strategies for R_{t+1}, we assume that $\hat{\sigma}$ and $\hat{\rho}$ are constant, and allow the $\hat{\beta}_t$ parameters to change. It is clear from the analysis based on an invariant $\hat{s}_{t|t+1}$ representation, however, that if revisions of forecasting strategies between adjacent points in time were to result in point forecasts for S_{t+1} that did not differ too much from those that would be obtained if the $\hat{s}_{t|t+1}$ representation remained unchanged, then the causal variables would continue to drive exchange rate swings regardless of whether $\hat{\rho}$ and $\hat{\sigma}$ were also permitted to change.

As in the invariant case discussed in the previous section, our IKE model can generate exchange rate swings that are driven by movements in the causal variables regardless of whether goods prices are assumed to be fully flexible or sticky. However, unlike before, the excess demand term that arises under sticky prices can grow over time when the $\hat{\beta}_t$ parameters are allowed to change, which complicates the analysis. We thus analyze the sticky-price case in appendix B.

In the case of flexible goods prices, the total change in the real exchange rate, and thus in the nominal exchange rate relative to its PPP level, between $t-1$ and t can be expressed as the sum of two components: the change that would occur if strategies for forecasting the mean of S_{t+1} remained unchanged at time t—$\Delta^U(s_t - s_t^{\mathrm{PPP}})$—and the change that stems solely from revisions of these strategies given new realizations of the causal variables x_t—$\Delta^R(s_t - s_t^{\mathrm{PPP}})$:

$$\Delta\left(s_t - s_t^{\mathrm{PPP}}\right) = \Delta^U\left(s_t - s_t^{\mathrm{PPP}}\right) + \Delta^R\left(s_t - s_t^{\mathrm{PPP}}\right). \qquad (14.16)$$

Under the assumption of flexible goods prices, we have, from equation (14.14):

$$\Delta^U\left(s_t - s_t^{\mathrm{PPP}}\right) = \frac{\eta\left(1-\hat{\sigma}\right)}{G}\left(\Delta^U\hat{s}_{t|t+1}^a - \Delta\hat{s}_t^{\mathrm{RE}a}\right), \qquad (14.17)$$

and from equation (14.12):

$$\Delta^R\left(s_t - s_t^{\mathrm{PPP}}\right) = \frac{\eta\left(1-\hat{\sigma}\right)}{G}\mathcal{D}^R\hat{s}_{t|t+1}^a, \qquad (14.18)$$

where we recall from equation (14.9) that $\Delta^U\hat{s}_{t|t+1}^a = \hat{\beta}_{t-1}\Delta x_t$ and $\mathcal{D}^R\hat{s}_{t|t+1}^a = \Delta\hat{\beta}_t x_t$.

We showed in the preceding section that if individuals' forecasting strategies for the mean of S_{t+1} and the policy environment were to remain unchanged, persistent trends in the causal variables would lead to persistent movements in the real exchange rate in one direction on average. This result followed from the fact that, with invariant representations, the effect of the trends on individual forecasts did not change over time.

With IKE, however, revisions of forecasting strategies will also influence individual forecasts and the exchange rate. Consider the movement of the real exchange rate between $t-1$ and t and suppose that the trends in the causal variables and $\hat{\beta}_{t-1}$ are such that, in the absence of revisions of forecasting strategies, the real exchange rate would tend to move up, that is, $\Delta^U \left(s_t - s_t^{PPP} \right) > 0$. It is clear that revisions of forecasting strategies at t, $\mathcal{D}^R \hat{s}_{t|t+1}^a$, can either reinforce or impede the upward movement of q due to the movements of the causal variables. But, even if these revisions are impeding, as long as their impact on the real exchange rate does not dominate the influence from the trends in the causal variables, q will still move up between $t-1$ and t.

Revisions of forecasting strategies at t impact the movement of q not only between $t-1$ and t, but also between t and $t+1$. This is because revisions of $\hat{\beta}_t$ affect how the trends in the causal variables will influence individuals' forecasts between t and $t+1$, that is, they affect $\Delta^U \left(s_{t+1} - s_{t+1}^{PPP} \right)$ through $\Delta^U \hat{s}_{t+1|t+2}^a = \hat{\beta}_t' \Delta x_{t+1}$. Consequently, to ensure that trends in the causal variables drive a persistent movement in q over successive time periods, we need to restrict how revisions of forecasting strategies at each time t influence individuals' forecasts at t, $\mathcal{D}^R \hat{s}_{t|t+1}^a$, and how they affect the movement of these forecasts between t and $t+1$, $\Delta^U \hat{s}_{t+1|t+2}^a$.

14.4.1. *Conservative and Reinforcing Forecasting Behaviors*

Consider first restrictions on $\mathcal{D}^R \hat{s}_{t|t+1}^a$ and suppose again, without loss of generality, that the deterministic trends in the causal variables and the $\hat{\beta}_{t-1}$ parameters are such that, between two points in time, $t-1$ and t, $E_{t-1}[\Delta^U (S_t - S_t^{PPP})|x_{t-1}, m_{t-1}, y_{t-1}] > 0.$[17] We also suppose that the policy environment remains unchanged for an extended period of time. Given this setup, if forecasting strategies remain unchanged at t $(\mathcal{D}^R \hat{s}_{t|t+1}^a = 0)$, the trends in the causal variables would drive the real exchange rate up between $t-1$ and t. In general, however, $\mathcal{D}^R \hat{s}_{t|t+1}^a$ is nonzero. But even if the influence of revisions in $\hat{\beta}_t$ impede the upward movement of q, this price would, nonetheless, tend to rise between $t-1$ and t as long as the following conservative restriction held:

---

17. The subscript $t-1$ on the expectations operator reflects the fact that with revisions of forecasting strategies, the influence of trends in x on individuals' forecasts changes over time.

$$\left| \mathcal{D}^R \hat{s}^a_{t|t+1} \right| < \left| E_{t-1} \left[\Delta^U \left(S_t - S^{\text{PPP}}_t \right) | x_{t-1}, m_{t-1}, y_{t-1} \right] \right|, \qquad (14.19)$$

where $|\cdot|$ denotes absolute value. Because

$$E_{t-1}[\Delta^U (S_t - S^{\text{PPP}}_t) | x_{t-1}, m_{t-1}, y_{t-1}] > 0$$

this partially predetermining restriction implies that the real exchange rate has a tendency to move up between $t-1$ and t. It also implies that the trends in the causal factors are the dominant factor driving this movement, in that their influence is larger than the influence of revisions in forecasting strategies.

By imposing only a qualitative condition on change, the conservative restriction in equation (14.19) is consistent with myriad possible revisions of forecasting strategies. It is compatible with large changes in the $\hat{\beta}_t$ parameters, which could involve a change in the composition of the causal variables in x. Also, because equation (14.19) constrains only the partial change in $\hat{s}^a_{t|t+1}$, it does not rule out a large change in this forecast. If changes in the causal variables were large, then the change in $\hat{s}^a_{t|t+1}$ may also be large.

The model could imply a tendency for q to rise between $t-1$ and t even if the revisions of forecasting strategies at t were not conservative. This possibility would arise if revisions in $\hat{\beta}_t$ reinforced the influence of the trends in the causal variables on individuals' forecasts:

$$\text{sign} \left(\mathcal{D}^R \hat{s}^a_{t|t+1} \right) = \text{sign} \left(E_{t-1} \left[\Delta^U \left(S_t - S^{\text{PPP}}_t \right) | x_{t-1}, m_{t-1}, y_{t-1} \right] \right), \qquad (14.20)$$

where sign$(\cdot)$ denotes the algebraic sign of the argument. It is possible, of course, for revisions of forecasting strategies to be reinforcing and either conservative or nonconservative. As such, the reinforcing restriction in equation (14.20) implies that the trends in the causal factors would, at a minimum, contribute positively to the tendency of the real exchange rate to rise between $t-1$ and t.

Now consider the movement of the real exchange rate between t and $t+1$:

$$\Delta \left(s_{t+1} - s^{\text{PPP}}_{t+1} \right) = \Delta^U \left(s_{t+1} - s^{\text{PPP}}_{t+1} \right) + \Delta^R \left(s_{t+1} - s^{\text{PPP}}_{t+1} \right). \qquad (14.21)$$

If trends in the causal variables continue to influence the real exchange rate positively ($\Delta^U (s_{t+1} - s^{PPP}_{t+1}) > 0$) and revisions of forecasting strategies at $t+1$ remain conservative and/or reinforcing as defined by equations (14.19) and (14.20), then the tendency for q to rise would continue. Of course, $\Delta^U (s_{t+1} - s^{\text{PPP}}_{t+1})$ would be positive if forecasting strategies remain unchanged at t, $(\hat{\beta}_t = \hat{\beta}_{t-1})$. In this case, the trends in the causal variables between t and $t+1$ exert the same influence on individuals' forecasts as they did between $t-1$ and t, that is,

$$E_t\left[\Delta^U \widehat{S}^a_{t+1|t+2}|x_t\right] = E_{t-1}\left[\Delta^U \widehat{S}^a_{t|t+1}|x_{t-1}\right] = E_t\left[\hat{\beta}_{t-1}\Delta x_{t+1}|x_t\right].$$

As we pointed out, revisions of $\hat{\beta}_t$, in general, imply a change in how the trends in the causal variables influence individuals' forecasts. But, if this influence between t and $t+1$ is not too different from the influence between $t-1$ and t, that is, $E_t[\Delta^U \widehat{S}^a_{t+1|t+2}|x_t]$ and $E_{t-1}[\Delta^U \widehat{S}^a_{t|t+1}|x_{t-1}]$ do not differ too much, then $\Delta^U(s_{t+1} - s^{\mathrm{PPP}}_{t+1})$ would indeed continue to be positive:

$$\left|E_t\left[\Delta^U \widehat{S}^a_{t+1|t+2}|x_t\right] - E_{t-1}\left[\Delta^U \widehat{S}^a_{t|t+1}|x_{t-1}\right]\right|$$

$$< \left|E_{t-1}\left[\Delta^U\left(S_t - S^{\mathrm{PPP}}_t\right)|x_{t-1}, m_{t-1}, y_{t-1}\right]\right|. \qquad (14.22)$$

It is also possible for $\Delta^U(s_{t+1} - s^{\mathrm{PPP}}_{t+1})$ to remain positive even if this conservative restriction is not satisfied. This condition holds if the positive influence of the trends in the causal variables becomes stronger between t and $t+1$:

$$\mathrm{sign}\left(E_t\left[\Delta^U \widehat{S}^a_{t+1|t+2}|x_t\right] - E_{t-1}\left[\Delta^U \widehat{S}^a_{t|t+1}|x_{t-1}\right]\right)$$

$$= \mathrm{sign}\left(E_{t-1}\left[\Delta^U \widehat{S}^a_{t|t+1}|x_{t-1}\right] - E\left[\Delta \widehat{S}^{\mathrm{RE}_a}_t|m_{t-1}, y_{t-1}\right]\right). \qquad (14.23)$$

We note that, as with the qualitative restrictions in equations (14.19) and (14.20), the conservative and reinforcing restrictions in equations (14.22) and (14.23), respectively, constrain the revisions of forecasting strategies only partially. They are thus consistent with myriad possible revisions of forecasting strategies.

It is clear that if we were to represent revisions of forecasting strategies over T consecutive points in time as conservative or reinforcing and if the policy environment were to remain unchanged over this subperiod, then the exchange rate would move either toward or away from PPP on average.[18] If movements of the exchange rate were initially toward PPP, and the subperiod of conservative or reinforcing forecasting behavior and a fixed policy environment endured, then this price would shoot through PPP and begin

---

18. A real exchange rate swing would also occur in the model if the conservative restriction in equation (14.19) and the reinforcing restriction in equation (14.23) both held.

trending away from this benchmark level from the other side. As before, persistent trends in the causal variables would lead market participants to revise their forecasts of the mean of S_{t+1} away from PPP, and thereby bid the exchange rate away from this benchmark. Such representations of forecasting behavior and the policy environment imply that, if all market participants were to base their forecasts of the future exchange rate solely on macroeconomic fundamentals, then trends in these variables would not only help drive the real exchange swing, but they may be the dominant factor behind this movement.

It is important to emphasize that the above conservative and reinforcing restrictions require an economist to fully prespecify neither the potential set of causal variables that underpin change in the exchange rate nor their influence in his representations. Nevertheless, they place enough structure on the analysis to model exchange rate swings: such behavior arises from persistent trends in the causal variables, whatever they may be, and from forecasting behavior that is conservative or reinforcing.

14.4.2. Limited Movements in Flexible Goods Prices

Figures 7.1–7.3 in chapter 7 show that large swings in nominal exchange rates are associated with movements in relative goods prices that are small by comparison. This experience is widely viewed as evidence that goods prices adjust sluggishly.[19] As we now point out, however, our IKE monetary model with flexible goods prices is compatible with this kind of behavior.

Equations (14.27) and (14.28) in appendix A show that the decomposition of changes in the real exchange rate into movements of the nominal exchange rate and relative goods prices depends on the relative magnitudes of α and η, that is, on the sensitivity of excess demand in the goods markets to changes in the real exchange rate and relative rates of interest, respectively. If, for example, α is small relative to η, which the extensive literature on exchange rate pass-through suggests is the case, then a swing in $\hat{s}^a_{t|t+1}$ will lead to movements in the spot exchange rate that are large relative to movements in relative goods prices, and therefore in relative interest rates as well. The time paths for relative goods prices and interest rates given in appendix A imply that in the limit, as $\alpha \rightarrow 0$, the impact of changes in $\hat{s}^a_{t|t+1}$ on p_t and i_t, approaches zero. Thus, although goods prices are assumed to be fully flexible, swings in $\hat{s}^a_{t|t+1}$ in the model can cause large swings in the exchange rate while goods prices and nominal interest rates change very little.

---

19. For example, see chapter 9 in Obstfeld and Rogoff (1996).

14.5. Conventional and Behavioral
Views of Reversals

The exchange rate experience depicted in figures 7.1–7.3 of chapter 7 suggests that although swings in currency prices away from PPP can occur for extended periods of time, they are ultimately bounded. Eventually sustained countermovements occur in which exchange rates move persistently back to PPP. These sustained countermovements, as with swings away, are irregular. Sometimes they involve only a partial movement of the exchange rate back to PPP, while at other times they involve a complete return to and a shooting through this benchmark level. Extant accounts of sustained reversals back to PPP fall into one of two categories: some rely on exogenous factors, whereas others presume that a large gap from the benchmark itself will trigger such behavior.

In traditional REH monetary models, as well as their NOEM successors, persistent exchange rate swings away from PPP do not arise. These models, therefore, provide no explanation of why such swings are ultimately bounded. The bubble solutions of these models generate swings. They suggest that swings are bounded because market participants at some point, for reasons that are exogenous to the model, collectively abandon their belief in a further continuation of the bubble and equate their forecasts to the unique fundamental time path of the model. However, these models not only lack plausible microfoundations, but as we pointed out in chapter 7, they cannot account for sustained countermovements that involve only partial movements back to PPP.

The noise-trader models of Brock and Hommes (1998), De Grauwe et al. (2005), and others provide a similar view of why exchange rate swings are ultimately bounded: a large exogenous shock to fundamentals leads market participants increasingly to abandon their chartist forecasting rule in favor of one based on fundamentals. However, as with other behavioral models, these models embody an inconsistency between their representations on the aggregate and individual levels. On the aggregate level, these models imply exchange rate swings away from PPP, but the two types of forecasting strategies that are attributed to individuals assume that they are endlessly unaware of the long-swings nature of exchange rate movements. These models presume, therefore, gross irrationality on the part of market participants.

Recent studies that estimate nonlinear univariate specifications of the real exchange rate have relied on transactions-cost models.[20] Although these models provide no explanation of why swings away from PPP arise, they do offer a different view of why they are eventually bounded. According to

---

20. See chapter 7 for a discussion and references.

this view, swings away are self-limiting: when the gap from PPP grows larger than the transactions costs associated with international trade, commodity arbitrage works to push the exchange rate and goods prices back to PPP. However, such an explanation of why real exchange rate swings are self-limiting is odd because more than 95 percent of the volume in currency markets is widely known to stem from trade in assets rather than in goods.

14.6. Imperfect Knowledge and Self-Limiting Long Swings

In contrast to transaction-cost models, the IKE model that we develop in this chapter provides an asset market view of exchange rate swings. Moreover, unlike the REH-bubble and noise-trader models, in which reversals are triggered by exogenous factors, reversals in our IKE model arise endogenously from our representations of forecasting behavior and risk.

A swing away from PPP occurs in the model because trends in the causal variables and revisions of forecasting strategies lead point forecasts of the exchange rate to move away from this benchmark level. Nevertheless, PPP acts as an anchor for exchange rate movements in the model. With IKE and endogenous prospect theory, market participants are presumed to relate the riskiness of holding an open position in foreign exchange not to the conditional variance of returns, but to the degree to which the exchange rate deviates from PPP. This alternative specification of risk implies that a growing gap from PPP eventually triggers revisions of forecasting strategies that lead to countermovements in the exchange rate back to PPP. Moreover, policymakers become concerned about large misalignments from PPP; this concern prompts them to alter policy in ways that are aimed at reducing the gap.

14.6.1. An IKE Asset Market View of Reversals

Evidence from psychology indicates that conservatism is a regularity that may characterize forecasting behavior over extended periods of time. We have shown that such behavior can lead to exchange rate swings in both directions, that is, with persistent movements either toward or away from PPP. We now consider a transition between two subperiods that involve conservative (or reinforcing) forecasting behavior and a stable policy environment, and thus exchange rate swings, but where these swings are in opposite directions. We show that, if revisions of forecasting strategies become nonconservative and nonreinforcing or there is a shift in the policy environment between two adjacent points in time, such a transition can occur in the model.

Consider first a transition in the model that is triggered by revisions of forecasting strategies. To fix ideas, we suppose again that the deterministic trends in the causal variables and market participants' forecasting strategies are such that, at an initial point in time, t_0

$$E_{t-1}\left[\Delta^U \hat{S}^a_{t|t+1}|x_{t-1}\right] - E\left[\Delta \hat{S}^{\mathrm{RE}_a}_t|m_{t-1}, y_{t-1}\right] > 0.$$

We also suppose that the policy environment remains unchanged and that forecasting behavior is conservative and/or reinforcing for T time periods, where T is large enough so that at some point in time between t_0 and $t_0 + T$, the exchange rate begins to move, on average, persistently away from PPP.

A movement in q back to PPP at time $t_0 + T + 1$ would arise in the model if, in the aggregate, revisions of forecasting strategies at this point were neither conservative nor reinforcing, that is, the magnitude of $\mathcal{D}^R \hat{s}^a_{t|t+1}$ was negative and large and $E_t[\Delta^U \hat{S}^a_{t+1|t+2}|x_t] - E[\Delta \hat{S}^{\mathrm{RE}_a}_{t+1}|m_t, y_t] < 0$. Such behavior could arise, for example, if bulls' concern about a countermovement led them to revise considerably their forecasting strategies. To represent such shifts, we may need to replace some causal variables in our $\hat{s}^L_{t|t+1}$ representation whose movements impact q positively (say rising foreign income levels) with other causal variables that impact q negatively (say growing foreign current account deficits).

The shift in forecasting strategies at $t_0 + T + 1$ does not ensure that the reversal will continue beyond this point. However, if forecasting behavior were once again to become conservative and/or reinforcing, then the reversal would continue. Indeed, as we noted in chapter 10, the psychological findings indicate that individuals need substantial evidence before they would revise their strategies in nonconservative ways. This suggests that, having revised their forecasting strategies in significant ways at $t_0 + T + 1$, market participants would hold off altering their strategies for some time, as they monitored how they were performing. In our model, this conservative behavior would lead to a sustained reversal in the exchange rate toward PPP beyond $t_0 + T + 1$.

Shifts in the policy environment could also lead to a transition between subperiods of a generally rising and falling real exchange rate. Suppose that revisions of forecasting strategies remained conservative and/or reinforcing beyond $t_0 + T$. It is clear that if policy officials were able to alter the processes driving some of the causal variables, so that $E_t[\Delta^U \hat{S}^a_{t+1|t+2}|x_t] - E[\Delta \hat{S}^{\mathrm{RE}_a}_t|m_{t-1}, y_{t-1}]$ became negative, then the real exchange rate would fall beyond $t_0 + T$.

Revisions of forecasting strategies and shifts in the policy environment stem from the decisions of individuals who act creatively in coping with ever-imperfect knowledge. Consequently, our IKE model does not prespecify how long forecasting behavior may be conservative or reinforcing or how long the policy environment may remain unchanged. Hence, it does not prespecify when protracted exchange rate swings away from or toward PPP might begin or end. However, we argue in the next section that eventually, if the gap from PPP grows large enough, revisions of forecasting strategies will be nonconservative and nonreinforcing or the policy environment will shift.

14.6.2.   Self-Limiting Long Swings

The IKE monetary model of this chapter assumes that market participants are aware of the long-swings nature of exchange rate movements and take this behavior into account when forming their forecasts of the return and potential unit loss from holding speculative positions in the market. If trends in the causal variables and conservative or reinforcing forecasting behavior last long enough, both $\hat{s}_{t|t+1}$ and s will eventually diverge from PPP from any starting point. But we characterize market participants as endogenously loss averse and model their expected unit loss to depend on the gap from PPP. Thus, as the divergence from PPP grows larger, say from above, bulls become more concerned about the losses that they would suffer from a possible countermovement back to PPP, while bears grow less concerned about the losses that would be associated with a possible continuation of the swing.[21] Such behavior, were the exchange rate swing away from PPP to continue, would eventually lead to an end of the swing and persistent exchange rate movements back to PPP.

   Consider first the bulls. The persistent trends in the causal variables and their conservative or reinforcing forecasting behavior lead them to raise their $\hat{s}_{t|t+1}^{\text{L}}$ and, while their $-\hat{l}_{t|t+1}^{\text{L}}$ also increases, their desire to hold long positions increases as well. But there must be a point at which, if the swing above PPP continues, their concern about capital losses grows so large that their desire to take on long positions would no longer increase. Our model represents such a shift in behavior by assuming that $\hat{s}_{t|t+1}^{\text{L}}$ decreases. For this shift to occur, revisions of forecasting strategies would have to become nonconservative and nonreinforcing.

   As for the bears, the persistent trends in the causal variables and their conservative and/or reinforcing forecasting behavior also lead them to raise their $\hat{s}_{t|t+1}^{\text{S}}$ and, while $-\hat{l}_{t|t+1}^{\text{S}}$ falls, their desire to hold short positions falls.

---

   21. We are assuming that an upward swing in $\hat{s}_{t|t+1}$ and s is associated with a rise in both $\hat{s}_{t|t+1}^{\text{L}}$ and $\hat{s}_{t|t+1}^{\text{S}}$. It is also possible in our model for the forecasts of one side of the market to fall over time as the aggregate $\hat{s}_{t|t+1}$ rises. But because we need the forecasting behavior of only one side of the market to become nonconservative and nonreinforcing, our argument concerning the self-limiting nature of swings away from PPP also applies to this case.

But there must be a point at which, if the swing above PPP continues, their concern about capital losses grows so small that their desire to take on short positions would no longer fall. Our model represents such a shift in behavior by assuming that $\hat{s}^{s}_{t|t+1}$ decreases. Again, for this shift to occur, revisions of forecasting strategies would have to be nonconservative and nonreinforcing.

We thus assume that if the size of the aggregate gap were to exceed some threshold, which we do not prespecify, market participants' forecasting behavior would become nonconservative and nonreinforcing. This behavior, in turn, would lead to the end of the exchange rate swing away from PPP and a subperiod in which the exchange rate moved persistently toward PPP.

Policymakers too worry about large and protracted misalignments from PPP. Such misalignments pose challenges for firms and workers that are engaged in international business. They lead to changes in competitiveness and require costly resource allocation. These effects, in turn, prompt calls for protectionist measures on the part of business and the public. Consequently, we assume that there exists some threshold beyond which, if the size of the aggregate gap grows, policymakers would alter policy in an attempt to push the exchange rate back toward PPP. The coordinated intervention by central banks and the changes in policy that were aimed at bringing down U.S. dollar rates in 1985 and yen rates in 1995 provide just two examples.

The assumption of thresholds beyond which forecasting behavior and policymaking work to limit exchange rate swings implies that such movements are ultimately self-limiting. The point at which the size of the aggregate gap grows too large, triggering market participants to revise their forecasting strategies in nonconservative and nonreinforcing ways or policymakers to alter policy, is not prespecified in the model. This threshold varies from one period of time to another and depends on market conditions, the course of economic change, and political events that no one can fully foresee.

Unlike the behavioral models, our IKE model of exchange rate swings does not embody an inconsistency between its representations on the aggregate and individual levels. On the aggregate level, the model generates long swings in the exchange rate that revolve, in irregular ways, around PPP. On the individual level, market participants are assumed to take this long-swings behavior into account when forming their forecasts of returns and potential losses. It recognizes that individuals cannot fully foresee the duration of any swing, and so its representations on the individual level allow for the existence of both bulls and bears at every point in time. Thus, by recognizing the imperfection of knowledge, the IKE model of exchange rate swings that we have developed in this chapter allows for bulls and bears without the presumption of gross irrationality.

Appendix 14.A:
Solution with an Invariant Representation

The time paths for the exchange rate, relative goods prices and relative interest rates are:

$$s_t = c_1 (1 - \theta)^t + \bar{s}_t \tag{14.24}$$

$$p_t = c_2 (1 - \theta)^t + \bar{p}_t \tag{14.25}$$

$$i_t = c_2 (1 - \theta)^t + \bar{i}_t \tag{14.26}$$

where:

$$
\bar{s}_t = \bar{s}_t^{RE} + \frac{\left(\rho^{RE} - \hat{\rho}\right)\left(1 - \hat{\sigma}\right)\alpha\lambda}{G} \bar{s}_t^{RE} + \frac{(\eta + \alpha\lambda)\left(1 - \hat{\sigma}\right)}{G}\left(\hat{s}_t^a - \hat{s}_t^{RE_a}\right)
$$
$$
+ \frac{\eta\left(\hat{\sigma}\lambda - 1\right)}{G}\left(\hat{\pi} - \hat{\pi}^{RE}\right) - \frac{(\eta + \alpha\lambda)\hat{\sigma}}{G}\hat{\pi}^{RE} + \frac{(\eta + \alpha\lambda)\hat{\sigma}}{G}\left(\hat{q}^{PPP} - q^{PPP}\right)
$$
$$\tag{14.27}$$

$$
\bar{p}_t = \bar{p}_t^{RE} + \frac{\left(\rho^{PPP} - \hat{\rho}\right)\left(1 - \hat{\sigma}\right)\alpha\lambda}{G} \bar{p}_t^{RE} + \frac{\alpha\lambda\left(1 - \hat{\sigma}\right)}{G}\left(\hat{s}_t^a - \hat{s}_t^{RE_a}\right)
$$
$$
+ \frac{h\eta\lambda}{G}\left(\hat{\pi} - \hat{\pi}^{RE}\right) - \frac{\hat{\sigma}\alpha\lambda}{G}\hat{\pi}^{RE} + \frac{\hat{\sigma}\alpha\lambda}{G}\left(\hat{q}^{PPP} - q^{PPP}\right) \tag{14.28}
$$

$$
\bar{i}_t = \hat{\pi}^{RE} + \frac{\left(\rho^* - \hat{\rho}\right)\left(1 - \hat{\sigma}\right)\alpha}{G} \bar{p}_t^{RE} + \frac{\alpha\left(1 - \hat{\sigma}\right)}{G}\left(\hat{s}_t^a - \hat{s}_t^{RE_a}\right)
$$
$$
+ \frac{h\eta}{G}\left(\hat{\pi} - \hat{\pi}^{RE}\right) - \frac{\alpha\hat{\sigma}}{G}\hat{\pi}^{RE} + \frac{\alpha\hat{\sigma}}{G}\left(\hat{q}^{PPP} - q^{PPP}\right). \tag{14.29}
$$

Appendix 14.B:
Exchange Rate Swings and Sticky Goods Prices

The implication that trends in the causal variables can drive swings in the real exchange rate carries over to the model with sticky goods prices. In this case, the total change in the real exchange rate continues to be described by equation (14.16). However, the changes in $s_t - s_t^{PPP}$ that stem from movements in the causal variables and revisions of forecasting strategies between $t - 1$ and t are now given by:

$$\Delta^U \left(s_t - s_t^{\text{PPP}} \right) = \theta \left(\bar{q}_{t-1} - q_{t-1} \right) + \frac{\eta \left(1 - \hat{\sigma} \right)}{G} \left(\Delta^U \hat{s}_{t|t+1}^a - \Delta \hat{s}_t^{\text{RE}_a} \right) \quad (14.30)$$

$$\Delta^R \left(s_t - s_t^{\text{PPP}} \right) = \frac{\left(1 - \hat{\sigma} \right)}{h} \mathcal{D}^R \hat{s}_{t|t+1}^a, \quad (14.31)$$

Equation (14.31) follows directly from UAUIP in equation (14.4), since relative goods prices, and thus relative interest rates, remain constant at any point in time at which forecasting strategies are revised.

Equation (14.30) shows that, with sticky goods prices, $\Delta^U(s_t - s_t^{\text{PPP}})$ involves an excess demand term. This term complicates our IKE analysis of exchange rate swings relative to the flexible-price case: there are now three factors—excess demand, movements in the causal variables through their effect on $\Delta^U(\hat{s}_{t|t+1}^a - \Delta \hat{s}_t^{\text{RE}_a})$, and revisions of forecasting strategies— that can drive change in the real exchange rate. Consequently, although movements in the causal variables may be the largest of the three factors, they may not help to determine the direction of change of q. We define the "dominant factor" behind real exchange rate movements as the largest influence on q that also contributes positively to its direction of change.

As in the invariant case considered in this chapter, the influence of the excess demand term can, in general, imply a real exchange rate movement that is in the same or opposite direction to the one implied by the secular trend term, regardless of whether q or $\bar{q}$ is above or below PPP. Consequently, as before, conservative or reinforcing forecasting behavior may initially not imply a swing in the real exchange rate. However, unlike the invariant case, the magnitude of $\bar{q}_{t-1} - q_{t-1}$ can grow over time with revisions of forecasting strategies.

The expression for the change in $\bar{q} - q$ between adjacent points in time is:

$$\Delta \left(\bar{q}_t - q_t \right) = -\theta \left(\bar{q}_{t-1} - q_{t-1} \right) - \psi \mathcal{D}^R \hat{s}_{t|t+1}^a, \quad (14.32)$$

where

$$\psi = \frac{\alpha \left(1 - \hat{\sigma} \right) \left[1 + \left(h - \hat{\sigma} \right) \lambda \right]}{hG} > 0.$$

If there are no changes in forecasting strategies, so that $\mathcal{D}^R \hat{s}_{t|t+1}^a = 0$, then, as in the invariant case, q and $\bar{q}$ necessarily move closer together between $t - 1$ and t at the rate θ. Even if $\mathcal{D}^R \hat{s}_{t|t+1}^a \neq 0$, the size of $\bar{q}_t - q_t$ could still fall. This result would occur if changes in forecasting strategies were limited:

$$\left| \mathcal{D}^R \hat{s}_{t|t+1}^a \right| < \frac{1}{\psi} \left| \theta \left(\bar{q}_{t-1} - q_{t-1} \right) \right|, \quad (14.33)$$

or if revisions of forecasting strategies also influenced the size of $\bar{q}_t - q_t$ in the downward direction, that is, if:

$$\text{sign}\left(\bar{q}_{t-1} - q_{t-1}\right) = \text{sign}\left(\mathcal{D}^R \hat{s}^a_{t|t+1}\right). \qquad (14.34)$$

However, if the conditions in expressions (14.33) and (14.34) are not satisfied, so that revisions of forecasting strategies work to increase the size of $\bar{q}_t - q_t$, and this effect is greater than the initial level of excess demand, then the magnitude of $\bar{q}_t - q_t$ would grow.

The possibility that the excess demand term in equation (14.30) may grow over time further complicates our analysis. We consider first a set of conservative restrictions that lead to exchange rate swings in the model.

14.B.1. *Conservative Forecasting Behavior*

The conservative restrictions that imply that the causal variables are the dominant factor inducing swings depend on whether the excess demand and secular trend terms influence the real exchange rate in the same direction or in opposite directions. Swings will occur in the model if these terms work in the same direction and

$$\left|\frac{(1-\hat{\sigma})}{h} \mathcal{D}^R \hat{s}^a_{t|t+1}\right| < |STT_t| \qquad (14.35)$$

and

$$\left|E_t\left[\Delta^U \hat{S}^a_{t+1|t+2}|x_t\right] - E_{t-1}\left[\Delta^U \hat{S}^a_{t|t+1}|x_{t-1}\right]\right|$$
$$< \left|E_{t-1}\left[\Delta^U \hat{S}^a_{t|t+1}|x_{t-1}\right] - E\left[\Delta \hat{S}^{RE\,a}_t|m_{t-1}, y_{t-1}\right]\right|, \qquad (14.36)$$

or if they work in opposite directions:

$$\left|\frac{(1-\hat{\sigma})}{h} \mathcal{D}^R \hat{s}^a_{t|t+1}\right| \le \tfrac{1}{2} \left|\theta\left(\bar{q}_{t-1} - q_{t-1}\right) + STT_t\right| \qquad (14.37)$$

and

$$\left|E_t\left[\Delta^U \hat{S}^a_{t+1|t+2}|x_t\right] - E_{t-1}\left[\Delta^U \hat{S}^a_{t|t+1}|x_{t-1}\right]\right|$$
$$< \tfrac{1}{2} \left|\theta\left(\bar{q}_{t-1} - q_{t-1}\right) + STT_t\right|, \qquad (14.38)$$

where

$$STT_t = \frac{\eta\left(1-\hat{\sigma}\right)}{G}\left(E_{t-1}\left[\Delta^U \hat{S}^a_{t|t+1}|x_{t-1}\right] - E\left[\Delta \hat{S}^{RE_a}_t|m_{t-1}, y_{t-1}\right]\right)$$

denotes the secular trend term.

To see how these conservative restrictions imply swings in the real exchange rate that depend on the causal variables, suppose, without loss of generality, that the deterministic trends in these variables and market participants' forecasting strategies are such that, at an initial point in time, t_0,

$$E_{t-1}\left[\Delta^U \hat{S}^a_{t|t+1}|x_{t-1}\right] - E\left[\Delta \hat{S}^{RE_a}_t|m_{t-1}, y_{t-1}\right] > 0.$$

Further suppose that, initially, excess demand is also positive and larger in size than the secular trend term; that is, $\theta\left(\bar{q}_{t-1} - q_{t-1}\right) - STT_t > 0$. Finally, we assume that revisions of forecasting strategies at t_0 are consistent with the conservative restriction in expression (14.35). In this case, q tends to rise between $t_0 - 1$ and t_0, and although the causal variables are not the dominant factor behind this rise, they contribute positively to the movement.

Consider now what happens in the model if the conservative restrictions in expressions (14.35) and (14.36) characterize forecasting behavior for an extended period of time beyond t_0, say, for T_1 time periods. The restriction in expression (14.36) ensures that STT_{t+1} will be positive.[22] Thus, as long as $\theta\left(\bar{q}_t - q_t\right)$ is also positive, $\Delta^U\left(s_{t+1} - s^{PPP}_{t+1}\right) > 0$. In this case, the real exchange rate moves up on average over T_1 time periods, and the causal variables contribute positively to this swing.

However, the excess demand term could fall and eventually become negative. Initially, excess demand will have a tendency to fall if, at each point in time, revisions of forecasting strategies have a larger impact on q than on $\bar{q} - q$, that is, if:

$$\psi < \frac{\left(1-\hat{\sigma}\right)}{h}. \tag{14.39}$$

In this case, the inequality in (14.33) is, on average, initially satisfied, because $\left|\theta\left(\bar{q}_{t-1} - q_{t-1}\right)\right|$ is assumed to be larger than $\left|STT_t\right|$ and $\left|\frac{(1-\hat{\sigma})}{h}\mathcal{D}^R\hat{s}^a_{t|t+1}\right|$ cannot be larger than the secular trend term when expression (14.35) is assumed to hold.

---

22. The reinforcing restriction in equation (14.23) also ensures that the secular trend term remains positive beyond t.

The magnitude of ψ depends on the sensitivity of price adjustment in the goods markets to changes in the real exchange rate and relative interest rates, that is, on α and η, respectively. Equation (14.32) shows that if α/η is small, which is consistent with empirical evidence (see section 14.4.2), then ψ is small and revisions of forecasting strategies have little effect on $\bar{q}_t - q_t$. In what follows, we assume that α/η is small enough so that the inequality (14.39) holds.

This condition ensures that the magnitude of the excess demand term will eventually become smaller than that of the secular trend term if T_1 is large enough. This situation could occur because revisions of forecasting strategies could lead to a rise in the secular trend term that, although consistent with the conservative restriction in expression (14.36), implies a value greater than that of the excess demand term, that is, $\Delta STT_{t+1} > \theta \left(\bar{q}_{t-1} - q_{t-1} \right) - STT_t$.[23] Or, even if forecasting behavior did not lead to a rise in the secular trend term, the condition (14.33) implies that $\theta \left(\bar{q}_{t-1} - q_{t-1} \right)$ would fall until it was equal to or smaller than $|\psi \mathcal{D}^R \hat{s}^a_{t|t+1}|$. But expression (14.35) ensures that $|\psi \mathcal{D}^R \hat{s}^a_{t|t+1}| < |STT_t|$, since

$$\left| \psi \mathcal{D}^R \hat{s}^a_{t|t+1} \right| < \left| \frac{(1 - \hat{\sigma})}{h} \mathcal{D}^R \hat{s}^a_{t|t+1} \right|.$$

The restrictions in expressions (14.35) and (14.36) imply that there are two possibilities once excess demand falls below the secular trend term. Forecasting behavior could be such that excess demand on average remains below the value of STT_t, in which case, if STT_t remains positive, the causal variables would be the dominant factor driving the upward swing in the real exchange rate over T_1 time periods. It is also possible that, while the secular trend term continues to be positive, its value falls sufficiently so that it is again below the magnitude of the excess demand term. In this case, however, the condition (14.33) would necessarily be satisfied, so that $\theta \left(\bar{q}_{t-1} - q_{t-1} \right)$ would fall until its size was once again smaller than that of STT_t. Consequently, it is possible that the role of the causal variables may alternate between merely contributing positively to the upward swing in the exchange rate and being the dominant factor behind this movement.

Although the restrictions in expressions (14.35) and (14.36) are consistent with an excess demand term that remains positive, they are also consistent with the possibility that this term falls and eventually becomes

---

23. Since intially $\Delta(\bar{q}_t - q_t) < 0$, if $\Delta STT_{t+1} > \theta(\bar{q}_{t-1} - q_{t-1}) - STT_t$, then $STT_{t+1} > \theta(\bar{q}_t - q_t)$.

negative. This scenario would occur if forecasting behavior, while conservative, was also consistently reinforcing, that is, $\mathcal{D}^R \hat{s}^a_{t|t+1} > 0$. If $\theta \left(\bar{q}_{t-1} - q_{t-1} \right)$ becomes negative, however, then this term would influence q in the opposite direction to the one implied by the secular trend term. In this case, the more stringent conservative restrictions in expressions (14.37) and (14.38) are needed to ensure that the causal variables remain the dominant factor behind the upward swing in the real exchange rate.[24]

For the causal variables to remain the dominant factor if $\theta(\bar{q}_{t-1} - q_{t-1}) < 0$, the excess demand term cannot grow large enough or the secular trend term become small enough to violate

$$ STT_t > \theta \left(\bar{q}_{t-1} - q_{t-1} \right) + \frac{(1 - \hat{\sigma})}{h} \mathcal{D}^R \hat{s}^a_{t|t+1}. \tag{14.40} $$

To see how the restrictions in expressions (14.37) and (14.38) imply inequality (14.40), suppose that forecasting behavior is consistently reinforcing beyond t_0 so that $\theta \left(\bar{q}_{t-1} - q_{t-1} \right)$ becomes negative at time $t_0 + T_1$. We note that, as the value of the excess demand term crosses the zero line and becomes negative, its size is necessarily smaller than that of the secular trend term, since STT_t remains positive because of expression (14.38). We need to show that the restrictions in expressions (14.37) and (14.38) imply that, as long as $\theta \left(\bar{q}_{t-1} - q_{t-1} \right)$ remains negative, the condition (14.40) holds.

The expression for the change in the excess demand term follows directly from equation (14.32):

$$ \theta \Delta \left(\bar{q}_t - q_t \right) = -\theta^2 \left(\bar{q}_{t-1} - q_{t-1} \right) - \theta \psi \mathcal{D}^R \hat{s}^a_{t|t+1} \tag{14.41} $$

In the absence of revisions of forecasting strategies, $\theta \Delta \left(\bar{q}_t - q_t \right) > 0$ in our example: excess demand always works to push prices back to their medium-run values. Thus, for the size of $\theta \left(\bar{q}_{t-1} - q_{t-1} \right)$ to grow, forecasting behavior must remain reinforcing beyond time $t_0 + T_1$; that is, $\mathcal{D}^R \hat{s}^a_{t|t+1}$ must stay positive. Suppose that $\mathcal{D}^R \hat{s}^a_{t|t+1}$ is consistently equal to the maximum value permitted by the conservative restriction in expression (14.37) for some extended period of time—say, for T_2 time periods;

$$ \mathcal{D}^R \hat{s}^a_{t|t+1} = \frac{h}{2 \left(1 - \hat{\sigma} \right)} \left[\theta \left(\bar{q}_{t-1} - q_{t-1} \right) + STT_t \right]. $$

24. These restrictions are more stringent not only becasue the right-hand-side terms are mutiplied by $\frac{1}{2}$, but because the sign of the excess demand term is assumed to be opposite to that of the secular trend term. We assume that $\frac{\eta(1-\hat{\sigma})}{2G} < 1$, which ensures that the secular trend term necessarily remains positive if the restriction in expression (14.38) holds.

This assumption implies that the size of the excess demand term will grow by its maximum value each time period, and that it will be smaller than half of STT_t.[25]

It also implies that the change in the value of the excess demand term between t and $t+1$ will be less than half the value of $\Delta^U(s_t - s_t^{\text{PPP}})$ on average:

$$\theta \Delta \left(\bar{q}_t - q_t \right) < \frac{1}{2} \left| \theta \left(\bar{q}_{t-1} - q_{t-1} \right) + STT_t \right|, \tag{14.42}$$

since

$$\psi \mathcal{D}^R \hat{s}_{t|t+1}^a < \frac{1}{2} \left| \theta \left(\bar{q}_{t-1} - q_{t-1} \right) + STT_t \right|$$

and $\theta < 1$. But the conservative restriction in expression (14.38) implies that the change in the size of the secular trend term between t and $t+1$ is also less than half of $\Delta^U(s_t - s_t^{\text{PPP}})$ on average. Consequently, if $\Delta^U(s_t - s_t^{\text{PPP}}) > 0$ on average, then $\Delta^U(s_{t+1} - s_{t+1}^{\text{PPP}})$ is also positive on average. And because $\left| \theta(\bar{q}_{t-1} - q_{t-1}) \right|$ and $\frac{(1-\hat{\sigma})}{h} \mathcal{D}^R \hat{s}_{t|t+1}^a$ will both be less than half of STT_t on average in any time period, expression (14.40) holds, that is, the real exchange rate continues to move up beyond $t_0 + T_1$ for T_2 time periods and the causal variables continue to be the dominant factor behind this swing.

It is clear from our discussion that if the excess demand term is initially negative and larger in size than $STT_t > 0$, then, although the conservative restrictions in expressions (14.37) and (14.38) are assumed to hold, the causal variables may, initially, not even contribute positively to real exchange rate movements. However, as before, with $\theta(\bar{q}_{t-1} - q_{t-1}) > 0$, the conservative restriction in expression (14.37) implies that the size of the excess demand term would initially fall. This fall would continue until movements of the causal variables become the dominant factor driving the real exchange rate.

We note that the conservative restrictions in expressions (14.35), (14.37), and (14.38) are more stringent than those in expressions (14.19) and (14.22) that we used for the flexible-price case. This difference is partly because of the possibility that the excess demand term can grow over time and because, with sticky goods prices, revisions of forecasting strategies have a larger effect on $s_t - s_t^{\text{PPP}}$ than with flexible goods prices. This result can be seen by comparing equations (14.31) and (14.18) and noting that:

$$\frac{\left(1 - \hat{\sigma} \right)}{h} \mathcal{D}^R \hat{s}_{t|t+1}^a > \frac{\eta \left(1 - \hat{\sigma} \right)}{G} \mathcal{D}^R \hat{s}_{t|t+1}^a, \tag{14.43}$$

---

25. As before, equation (14.32) implies that the size of $\theta(\bar{q}_{t-1} - q_{t-1})$ can grow only to a maximum equal to $\psi \mathcal{D}^R \hat{s}_t^a$, which is less than $\frac{(1-\hat{\sigma})}{h} \mathcal{D}^R \hat{s}_t^a$.

since $0 < \frac{\eta h}{G} < 1.$[26] Because revisions of forecasting strategies have a greater impact on the real exchange rate, more stringent conservative restrictions are needed to ensure that the causal variables will be the dominant component behind changes in q.

The foregoing discussion makes clear that, if the conservative restrictions in expressions (14.35)–(14.38) characterize forecasting behavior for an extended period of time, and we assume that the policy environment remains unchanged over this subperiod, then the exchange rate will, at least eventually, move either toward or away from PPP on average. If movements of the exchange rate are initially toward PPP, and the subperiod of conservative forecasting behavior and an unchanging policy environment is assumed to endure, then this price will shoot through PPP and begin trending away from this benchmark level from the other side. Moreover, if all market participants base their forecasts of the exchange rate solely on macroeconomic fundamentals, then these variables will not only contribute positively to the real exchange rate swing, but they will be the dominant factor behind this movement.

14.B.2. Reinforcing Forecasting Behavior

The reinforcing restrictions in equations (14.20) and (14.23), together with a fixed policy environment, may also lead to a swing in the real exchange rate that depends positively on the causal variables. But, unlike the flexible-price case, these restrictions do not ensure that such a swing will continue.

To see this, suppose again that, at an initial point in time t_0,

$$E_{t-1}\left[\Delta^U \hat{S}^a_{t|t+1} | x_{t-1}\right] - E\left[\Delta \hat{S}^{\mathrm{RE}a}_t | m_{t-1}, y_{t-1}\right] > 0.$$

Further suppose that $\theta(\bar{q}_{t-1} - q_{t-1}) - STT_t > 0$. Finally, we assume that revisions of forecasting strategies at t_0 are consistent with the reinforcing restriction in equation (14.20). In this case, q tends to rise between $t_0 - 1$ and t_0, and although the causal variables are not the dominant factor behind this rise, they contribute positively to it.

Consider now what happens in the model if the reinforcing restrictions in equations (14.20) and (14.23) characterize forecasting behavior for an extended period of time beyond t_0. The restriction in equation (14.23)

---

26. With sticky goods prices, p_t and i_t remain constant when forecasting strategies are revised at any time t. Consequently, the exchange rate must do all of the adjustment to maintain equilibrium in the foreign exchange market. By contrast, with flexible goods prices, revisions of forecasting strategies trigger an instantaneous equilibrium adjustment not only in the exchange rate but also in goods prices and interest rates. The adjustments of p_t and i_t help in restoring equilibrium in the foreign exchange market, thereby implying a smaller movement in s_t for flexible goods prices.

ensures not only that STT_{t+1} is positive, but that this term grows over time, that is, $STT_{t+1} > STT_t$. As for the excess demand term, its value initially falls over time because with reinforcing forecasting behavior, revisions of forecasting strategies work to push $\bar{q}_{t-1} - q_{t-1}$ down. Initially, then, the real exchange rate rises on average and the causal variables contribute positively to this swing. Eventually, these variables become the dominant factor driving this swing.

However, with reinforcing forecasting behavior, the excess demand term eventually becomes negative and, unlike the case with conservative forecasting behavior, $\theta(\bar{q}_{t-1} - q_{t-1})$ could grow larger than STT_t. As long as

$$\left| STT_t + \frac{(1-\hat{\sigma})}{h} \mathcal{D}^R \hat{s}^a_{t|t+1} \right| > \left| \theta \left(\bar{q}_{t-1} - q_{t-1} \right) \right|, \tag{14.44}$$

the real exchange rate continues to move up and the causal variables continue to contribute positively to this swing.

However, the reinforcing restrictions in equations (14.20) and (14.23) do not ensure that inequality (14.44) is satisfied. For example, suppose that the size of $\frac{(1-\hat{\sigma})}{h} \mathcal{D}^R \hat{s}^a_{t|t+1}$ is consistently large enough so that the excess demand term, although negative, becomes larger in size than the secular trend term. It is clear that beyond this point, a range of "small" positive values of $\frac{(1-\hat{\sigma})}{h} \mathcal{D}^R \hat{s}^a_{t|t+1}$ exist for which inquality (14.44) does not hold. Thus, if the value of $\frac{(1-\hat{\sigma})}{h} \mathcal{D}^R \hat{s}^a_{t|t+1}$ falls into this range consistently, the upward swing in q ends.

15 Exchange Rates and Macroeconomic Fundamentals

Abandoning the Search for a Fully
Predetermined Relationship

We have argued throughout this book that outcomes in many markets in capitalist economies, especially those for assets, are not governed by a fully predetermined causal mechanism; the search for fully predetermined models is therefore misguided. Nowhere is this problem more evident than in the numerous empirical studies that attempt to find a connection between exchange rates and macroeconomic fundamentals.

In the previous chapter, we showed that long swings in the exchange rate can be modeled without prespecifying either the causal variables or how these variables may influence the exchange rate. However, to address the question of whether exchange rate movements depend on macroeconomic fundamentals, an economist must represent these aspects of the causal mechanism. In examining whether macroeconomic fundamentals are among the causal factors driving the exchange rate, with few exceptions, economists have relied on models that are invariant. They have estimated these models over sample periods that, in some cases, span three decades. The failure to find an invariant relationship that is consistent with the data has led to the widespread belief among economists that exchange rates do not depend on macroeconomic fundamentals.[1]

The study that is most often cited as illustrating the supposed disconnection between the exchange rate and fundamentals is Meese and Rogoff (1983). This study found that three traditional REH-based monetary models did not outperform the random walk model in out-of-sample fore-

---

1. See chapter 7 for a discussion of this evidence and references.

casting, even when the forecasts of the structural models were predicated on the actual future values of their explanatory variables. This exercise of pitting the forecasting performance of exchange rate models against that of the random walk model has become an important litmus test in the literature for judging whether the causal mechanism behind exchange rate movements depends on macroeconomic fundamentals.[2] There are dozens of studies that have tried to overturn the Meese and Rogoff result by examining other time periods, using more sophisticated estimation techniques, or testing additional models. But the results have been disappointing. In reviewing the evidence, Frankel and Rose (1995, p. 1704) concluded that "The Meese and Rogoff analysis at short horizons has never been convincingly overturned or explained. It continues to exert a pessimistic effect on the field of empirical exchange rate modeling and international finance in general."

In this chapter, we show that if economists acknowledge the limits of their knowledge, as we have argued they should, we can begin to understand the relationship between exchange rates and macroeconomic fundamentals. Indeed, as we discussed in chapter 7, the Meese and Rogoff "exchange rate disconnect puzzle" is an artifact of the search for a fully predetermined relationship between the exchange rate and fundamentals. We find that, once one allows for temporal instability, the monetary models dominate the random walk model in out-of-sample forecasting.

Although we expect the relationship between the exchange rate and macroeconomic fundamentals to be unstable, there may be subperiods during which this relationship is statistically stable, that is, any changes in individual forecasting strategies are not detectable in aggregate data in those subperiods. We investigate this possibility in the context of the traditional monetary models used by Meese and Rogoff (1983) over their sample, which runs from March 1973 through June 1981. Because no one can fully prespecify how or when the relationship between the exchange rate and macroeconomic fundamentals might change, we rely on recursive test procedures similar to the ones that we used in chapter 12. These procedures constrain neither the timing of structural change nor which macroeconomic fundamentals of the monetary model may be needed to explain the data.

---

2. Recently, Engel and West (2006) have questioned the Meese and Rogoff out-of-sample forecasting experiment as a criterion for judging the merit of exchange rate models. They point out that the monetary models imply random walk behavior for the exchange rate because their fundamentals are widely found to be integrated of order 1, $I(1)$. One would not expect, therefore, that the monetary models would have predictive power over the random walk in a true forecasting experiment. Even so, the monetary models should dominate the random walk in out-of-sample forecasting when this experiment is based on the actual future values of the macroeconomic fundamentals.

Our structural-change analysis, which is based on monthly data for the DM/$ exchange rate, reveals that a composite monetary model experiences structural change on three occasions over the Meese and Rogoff (1983) sample.[3] It also indicates that there is one extended subperiod of floating in the 1970s during which the null of no structural change cannot be rejected: July 1974–September 1978.

We then examine whether, during this subperiod of "statistical parameter stability," exchange rate movements depended on some or all of the macroeconomic fundamentals of the monetary models. We find that a subset of these fundamentals are cointegrated with the exchange rate. We show that, under IKE, this finding indicates that the exchange rate was adjusting to a momentary equilibrium relationship based on macroeconomic fundamentals during the 1970s.

We also compare the forecasting performance of the monetary models with that of the random walk model when the forecasting experiment is allowed to run only until September 1978 and not, as in the original Meese and Rogoff study, until June 1981. We find that these models outperform the random walk model by considerable margins, especially at the longer forecasting horizons.

While our in-sample and out-of-sample results indicate that macroeconomic fundamentals matter for the exchange rate, an open question is whether they do so in ways that can be rationalized by the traditional monetary models. To examine this question in a world of imperfect knowledge, we make use of the theories consistent expectations hypothesis that we outlined in chapter 10. We find that all of the variables that enter our estimated relationship—and for which TCEH implies a constraint—do so with parameter signs that are consistent with TCEH. However, although the qualitative features of traditional models under TCEH are useful in shedding light on exchange rate movements, we also find that they provide an incomplete explanation of the data: the money supply variables are insignificant.

We conclude this chapter by investigating whether this class of TCEH-based models helps explain other episodes of the modern period of floating exchange rates. To this end, we extend the original Meese and Rogoff sample to include the remainder of the 1980s. We find that the composite monetary model is also structurally unstable during the 1980s. The structural change results imply another extended subperiod of statistical parameter constancy, which runs from November 1979 through August 1984. As in the 1970s, we find that a subset of the macroeconomic fundamentals of the monetary models are co-integrated and that these models outperform the

---

3. Most of the empirical work presented in this chapter is taken from Goldberg and Frydman (1996b).

random walk model in out-of-sample forecasting by considerable margins. We also find that many of the macroeconomic fundamentals enter our estimated relationship with parameters whose signs are "theories consistent." However, unlike the results for 1970s, some of the variables that enter significantly do so with parameters whose signs are inconsistent with the traditional monetary models under TCEH.

Although TCEH only aims to partially represent the causal mechanism underpinning the exchange rate, we find that our TCEH-based composite monetary model provides an incomplete explanation of exchange rate movements. It is not surprising, therefore, that Meese and Rogoff's search for an invariant model failed to produce positive results.

15.1. Structural Change in the Causal Mechanism

Meese and Rogoff (1983) examine the forecasting performance of three monetary models of the exchange rate: the FB model of (Frenkel, 1976; Bilson, 1978a,b), the DF model (Dornbusch, 1976; Frankel 1979), and the HM model (Hooper and Morton, 1982). The reduced forms of these models are embedded in equation (7.1), which we reproduce here:

$$s_t = \beta_0 + \beta_1 \left(m_t - m_t^* \right) + \beta_2 \left(y_t - y_t^* \right) + \beta_3 \left(i_t - i_t^* \right)$$
$$+ \beta_4 \left(\pi_t - \pi_t^* \right) + \beta_5 \left(TB_t - TB_t^* \right) + \epsilon_t. \tag{15.1}$$

Table 15.1 summarizes the qualitative predictions that are implied by the three monetary models.[4]

Causal relationships in economics are temporally unstable in ways and at times that no one can fully foresee. To test the temporal stability of the composite model in equation (15.1), without fully prespecifying either the location of any break point or the explanatory variables that may be relevant for explaining market outcomes in any one subperiod of the data, we use two recursive procedures: the cusum test and the Quandt ratio (QR) technique.[5] Our analysis is sequential. We first run the cusum test starting at the beginning of our sample in March 1973. When the cusum test indicates that a break has occurred, we use the QR technique to locate the most likely point of the break. Once the first break point is found, we re-run the cusum test and QR technique, but with a subsample that begins immediately after the location of the first break point. Additional break points are found

---

4. Hooper and Morton specify their model in terms of cumulative deviations of the current account balance from trend. The specification in equation (15.1) follows Meese and Rogoff (1983).

5. See Brown et al. (1975) and the discussion on testing for structural change in section 12.3.1.

**Table 15.1   Qualitative Predictions of the
Monetary Models**[a]

Variables[b]	FB	DF	HM
m-m^*	+	+	+
y-y^*	−	−	−
π-π^*	+	+	+
i-i^*		−	−
TB-TB^*			−

Source: Reprinted from Goldberg and Frydman
(1996b), copyright © 1996, with permission of
Elsevier.
[a] The symbols '+' and '−' denote predictions of
positive and negative parameter values, respectively. Blank entries indicate not applicable.
[b] m and y denote log levels of the domestic
money supply and income, i, π, and TB are the
domestic nominal interest rate, expected secular
rate of inflation, and cumulative trade balance,
respectively, and a superscript * denotes a
foreign value.

in a similar way. In carrying out the analysis, we drop the usual symmetry
restrictions on the domestic and foreign variables.[6]

Findings of structural change and the location of break points depend
on the particular test procedures that one uses and the confidence levels
chosen. There is thus no completely objective way to test the structural
stability of economic models. The results of our structural change analysis,
therefore, can be viewed only as an approximation to the frequency and
location of the temporal instability in the data.

The results of our analysis are summarized in figure 15.1, where break
points are indicated by dotted vertical lines.[7] We find that the composite
monetary model in equation (15.1) undergoes structural change on six
occasions over a sample that runs from March 1973 to December 1989.
Three of these break points are found in the original Meese and Rogoff

---

6. There is much evidence in the literature that these symmetry restrictions are inconsistent with
the data and will, if imposed, lead to biased estimates. Although relaxing the symmetry restrictions on
the money, income, secular inflation, and cumulative trade balance variables is straightforward, this
is not the case with the interest rate variables. Goldberg (2000) shows that the symmetry restriction
on the interest rate variables can be traced to the assumptions of perfect capital mobility and REH.
See also section 15.3.

7. The appendix provides a description of the data. For the cusum and QR plots, see Goldberg
(1991).

Figure 15.1   Structural Change Results Composite Monetary Model

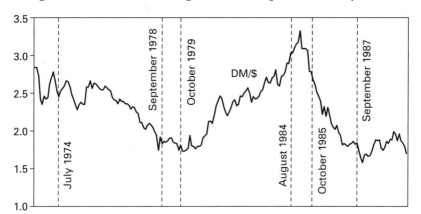

sample. Our structural change results imply that there are two extended time periods of statistical parameter constancy: July 1974–September 1978 and November 1979–August 1984.

An interesting aspect of our results is that several of the break points are proximate to a major shift in economic policy. The break in October 1978 preceded by a month the Carter bond program of active intervention to stem the fall in the value of the dollar (the level of intervention in November was $6.86 billion, a record at that time) and a tightening of monetary policy. In August 1979, Paul Volcker was appointed as chairman of the Federal Reserve and, in October (the third break in our sample), the Fed announced that it would de-emphasize the federal funds rate in favor of growth in nonborrowed reserves as its primary operating target. The break in September 1984 corresponds to when Treasury Secretary Donald Regan changed his stated policy toward the dollar of laissez-faire to one of actively trying to talk its value down, and the break in October 1985 occurs right after the Plaza accord in September of that year. These timings suggest that major changes in economic policy have an important influence on market participants' decisions to revise their forecasting strategies. However, as is evident from the other break points in our sample, such revisions also arise independently of policy changes.

15.2. Macroeconomic Fundamentals and the Exchange Rate in the 1970s

Meese and Rogoff found that the traditional REH-based monetary models provided no more help in forecasting the exchange rate in the 1970s than flipping a coin. But one would not expect these invariant models to perform well over a time period in which the causal mechanism undergoes structural change on several occasions. We now reexamine the connection between the exchange rate and macroeconomic fundamentals in Meese and Rogoff's sample, but confine our analysis to the first subperiod of statistical parameter constancy, July 1974–September 1978. We first provide the results of a reduction analysis that deletes all insignificant variables from the composite model in equation (15.1). We then test whether the variables of the reduced model are co-integrated and compare the forecasting performance of this model and the HM model with that of the random walk.

15.2.1. *Reduction and Co-integration Analysis*

The explanatory variables in equation (15.1) are commonly modeled as unit-root processes.[8] To deal with the problems associated with regressions involving such variables, we use the systems approach of Phillips (1991). This approach applies full information maximum likelihood (FIML) estimation to a triangular system that specifies the unit roots explicitly.[9]

One of the problems with unit-root variables is that they tend to be highly collinear. With collinearity, a parameter whose estimate is found to be insignificant when estimating the full model may become significant when one of the regressors is deleted. To deal with this problem, we begin by deleting one explanatory variable at a time, starting with the variable that has the lowest t-value. Once we have deleted all insignificant variables in this step wise fashion, we add these variables back into the regression one at a time to check whether they may be significant once they are included as part of the reduced model.[10] The estimated reduced model that results from this analysis is:

$$s_t = -.92y_t + 1.12y_t^* - 1.33i + 2.23i_t^* - .07TB + .62TB_t^* + \epsilon_t,$$

$$(.10) \quad (.11) \quad\quad (.23) \quad (.38) \quad\quad (.02) \quad\quad (.04) \quad\quad\quad (15.2)$$

where figures in parentheses are standard errors.

Inference from the regressions of our reduction analysis requires that the variables in equation (15.2) be co-integrated. In table 15.2, we report the results of co-integration tests based on the Engle and Granger (1987) two-

---

8. See Juselius (2007), among many others.

9. See Goldberg and Frydman (1996b) for more detail on the empirical specification estimated. Papell (1997) also uses Phillips (1991) to estimate a monetary model of the exchange rate.

10. A similar general-to-specific methodology is behind the econometrics of PcGets, which was developed by Hendry and Krolzig (2001). Hendry and Krolzig (1999) show that PcGets's general-to-specific methodology does remarkably well in finding the underlying data-generating process.

Table 15.2   Residual-Based Tests of Co-integration
ADF and Z Tests

Model[b]	p^c	n^d	t_a	$Z(t_a)$	$Z(\alpha)$
			Test statistics[a]		
RM_{70}	3	6	−2.08	−6.00***	−41.97**
RM_{80}	3	7	−3.73	−5.52***	−39.58
FB	5	3	−1.00	−1.59	−6.34
DF	3	4	−2.15	−1.93	−9.36
HM	5	6	−3.22	−4.57	−37.13
C	7	10	−3.29	−5.19	−46.27

Source: Reprinted from Goldberg and Frydman (1996b), copyright © 1996, with permission of Elsevier.
[a] All co-integrating vectors are estimated using ordinary least squares. t_a and $Z(t_a)$ are the augmented Dickey and Fuller (ADF) and Phillips and Perron Z t-statistics, respectively, and $Z(\alpha)$ is the Phillips and Perron Z α-statistic. Critical values are obtained from Phillips and Ouliaris (1990) for the cases where the number of regressors (n) is less than or equal to 5. When n is greater than five, critical values are obtained through extrapolation. *** and ** denote significance at the 1 and 5 percent levels, respectively.
[b] RM_{70} and RM_{80} denote the reduced models for the 1970s and 1980s, respectively; and C is the composite model in equation (15.1).
[c] Figures are the number of lagged first difference terms found to be significant in obtaining the ADF statistics.
[d] Figures are the number of regressors in the co-integrating vector.

step procedure, where we label the reduced model for the 1970s subperiod "RM_{70}." We use augmented Dickey and Fuller (1981) (ADF) and Phillips (1987) and Perron (1988) Z tests and ordinary least squares (OLS) residuals from the reduced model, as well as OLS residuals from the FB, DF, and HM models estimated over the full Meese and Rogoff sample.[11] Other studies that use the Engle and Granger two-step procedure to test for co-integration between the exchange rate and macroeconomic fundamentals include Meese (1986), Meese and Rogoff (1988), Meese and Rose (1991), and Papell (1997). All of these studies, which estimate co-integrating vectors

---

11. The co-integration results are unchanged if we use the FIML estimates in equation (15.2) to obtain the residuals of the reduced model.

over sample periods that include the 1970s and 1980s, are unable to reject the null hypothesis of no co-integration.

The results in table 15.2 are consistent with the earlier studies. We find that when the sample period includes the 1970s and the early part of the 1980s, the null hypothesis of no co-integration cannot be rejected even at the 10 percent level when based on any of the monetary models. However, when we restrict the analysis to the July 1974–September 1978 subperiod, we can reject this null hypothesis at the 1 percent level. We thus find evidence that during much of the 1970s' floating-rate experience, the exchange rate was adjusting to a momentary equilibrium relationship based on macroeconomic fundamentals.

15.2.2. The Exchange Rate Disconnect "Puzzle": An Artifact of Ignoring Structural Change

Although the foregoing in-sample regression results provide evidence that exchange rate movements in the 1970s are related to macroeconomic fundamentals, the belief in the disconnect between them largely arose from the failure of monetary models to dominate the random walk in forecasting out of sample. In their 1983 study, Meese and Rogoff first estimate FB, DF, and HM monetary models over an initialization period that begins in March 1973 and ends in November 1976. They then combine the in-sample parameter estimates of these models with the actual future values of the explanatory variables to generate "forecasts" of the exchange rate at the 1-, 6-, and 12-month horizons beyond November 1976.[12] The authors generate additional forecasts by updating the in-sample estimation period one observation at a time and computing forecasts at all four time horizons after each update. To measure the forecasting performance of the structural models, as well as the random walk model, Meese and Rogoff rely on root mean square error (RMSE), which averages together the squared forecasting errors generated by each model over the entire forecasting period, from December 1976 through June 1981.

The aim of their exercise is to test the forecasting performance of models with invariant structures. With such models, additional observations lead to better estimates of the underlying parameters, which are presumed to be fixed. But the structural change results in figure 15.1 reveal that this assumption is inconsistent with the data: Meese and Rogoff's initialization period straddles two distinct subperiods characterized by different exchange rate processes, whereas their forecasting experiment straddles three such distinct subperiods.

---

12. Meese and Rogoff also examine the performance of univariate and multivariate time-series models.

Figure 15.2   Pre- and Post-Break Performance of Monetary Models

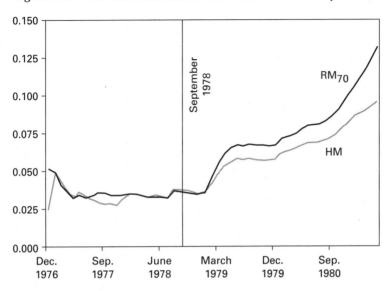

In figure 15.2, we plot the recursive RMSE generated by the HM and RM_{70} models based on the three-month forecasting horizon and Meese and Rogoff's initialization period. The observations plotted in the figure at each time t average the squared forecasting errors generated by the monetary models between t and the start of the forecasting experiment in November 1976. Consequently, the time plots are exactly what we would expect to see given our structural change findings. Prior to the break point in October 1978, the recursive RMSE for both monetary models is stable and below that of the sample average for the random walk model (5.83 percent). However, after the break point, the superior forecasting performance of the monetary models markedly deteriorates.[13]

In their study, Meese and Rogoff report only the RMSE generated by each model for the entire forecasting period. Consequently, their measure of forecasting performance masks the superior forecasting ability of the monetary models during the first half of their forecasting period. Summary statistics for the forecasting performance of the structural models, which we report in table 15.3, bear this point out.

In the left half of the table, we replicate the dismal results of Meese and Rogoff (1983). When the analysis ignores the temporal instability of the exchange rate relationship, the structural models are unable to beat the

---

13. Time plots of the recursive RMSE for the FB and DF models show a similar pattern.

Table 15.3   Out-of-Sample Fit: 1970s[a]

| | End of forecasting period: June 1981[b] | | | | | | End of forecasting period: September 1978[c] | | | | | |
| | RMSE | | DCS | | | | RMSE | | DCS | | | |
Forecast horizon (months)	RW	RM_{70}	HM	RM_{70}	HM	Nob[d]	RW	RM_{70}	HM	RM_{70}	HM	Nob[d]
1	3.63	10.83	7.32	39	42	55	2.15	2.54	2.64	59	64	22
								2.28	3.08	59	59	
3	5.83	13.30	9.65	45	45	53	4.32	3.20	3.24	80[e]	80[e]	20
								2.87	3.68	80[e]	75[e]	
6	8.93	16.36	12.69	52	52	50	6.77	3.27	3.46	100[e]	100[e]	17
								2.47	3.65	100[e]	100[e]	
9	11.08	19.48	15.48	58	58	47	10.14	3.95	4.37	100[e]	100[e]	14
								3.56	4.03	100[e]	100[e]	
12	13.08	23.59	18.63	64	64	44	13.59	5.36	4.92	100[e]	100[e]	11
								4.67	6.82	100[e]	100[e]	

Source: Reprinted from Goldberg and Frydman (1996b), copyright © 1996, with permission of Elsevier.
[a] DCS figures are the percentage of correct predictions. The two structural models—the HM model and the reduced model for 1970s (RM_{70})—are estimated using ordinary least squares. RW denotes the random walk model.
[b] Figures are based on an initialization period that begins in March 1973 and runs through November 1976. Forecasting begins in December 1976.
[c] The figures on the top of each row are based on an initialization period that begins in March 1973 and runs through November 1976, whereas the figures on the bottom are based on an initialization period that begins in July 1974 and runs through November 1976. In both cases forecasting begins in December 1976 and ends in September 1978.
[d] Number of forecasting observations.
[e] Significant at the 5 percent level when based on the binomial distribution.

random walk model at any forecasting horizon.[14] But this influential conclusion is overturned when the forecasting experiment takes into account the structural change. These results are presented in the right half of table 15.3. The figures on the top of each row are based on the Meese and Rogoff initialization period, whereas the bottom figures are based on an initialization period that begins in July 1974 and ends in November 1976. In both cases, forecasting begins in December 1976 and ends in September 1978.[15] The results reveal that both the HM and reduced models outperform the random walk model by substantial margins when based on RMSE at every forecasting horizon save the one-month horizon. Furthermore, both models perform best at the longer forecasting horizons. For example, the RMSE generated by the reduced model at the 12-month forecasting horizon (4.67 percent) is roughly one-third of that produced by the random walk model (13.59 percent). This finding suggests that macroeconomic fundamentals play a greater role over longer horizons.

Table 15.3 also reports forecasting results based on a measure of performance not examined in Meese and Rogoff (1983). This measure, which has been called the "direction of change" statistic (DCS), computes the proportion of times that a model correctly predicts the direction of change of the exchange rate, or what market participants call the "right side of the market." Leitch and Tanner (1991) argue that the ability to predict the right side of the market may be more relevant for profitability than outperforming the random walk model in terms of RMSE.[16]

The results using DCS parallel those based on RMSE. When the forecasting experiment is allowed to run until June 1981, the structural models have no ability to predict the right side of the market: their prediction concerning direction is statistically indistinguishable from that of flipping a coin. But when the out-of-sample analysis ends prior to the break in October 1978, the performance of the structural models improves markedly, especially at the longer forecasting horizons. Both the HM and reduced models are able to correctly predict the right side of the market 100 percent of the time at the 6-, 9-, and 12-month forecasting horizons.

---

14. The results are more extreme than those reported in Meese and Rogoff (1983), which shows that the HM model performs slightly better than the random walk model at the 1-month horizon and slightly worse at the 3-, 6-, and 12-month horizons. This difference can be traced to the way we and Meesse and Rogoff estimate the monetary models. In their estimations, Meese and Rogoff correct for first-order serial correlation, which, in effect, amounts to adding the lagged value of the exchange rate as an additional regressor. We do not correct for first-order serial correlation because once we limit the analysis to the July 1974–September 1978 subperiod, this problem does not arise.

15. Forecasts generated by the random walk model require no estimation. Consequently, the RMSE generated by this model is unaffected by whether the intialization period begins in March 1973 or July 1974.

16. Chinn and Meese (1995) and Cheung et al. (2005) also make use of the DCS.

The results presented in table 15.3 indicate that the large forecasting errors reported by Meese and Rogoff are the result of forecasting errors amassed after the break in October 1978.

15.3. Are the Monetary Models Consistent with Empirical Evidence?

The results of the preceding section provide evidence that, for much of the 1970s' floating-rate experience, exchange rate movements were connected to macroeconomic fundamentals. But the question remains whether the macroeconomic fundamentals enter the estimated relationship in ways that can be rationalized by the monetary models. To examine this question, we make use of TCEH. To implement TCEH, we first specify the qualitative features of each of our monetary models. In doing so, we follow the procedure that we outlined in chapter 10.

It is common in the literature to specify the flexible-price FB model with the assumption that domestic and foreign goods are perfect substitutes. With this assumption, however, the model is unable to explain deviations from PPP, even under IKE.[17] Moreover, this model, and the sticky-price DF and HM models are based on UIP. As we discussed in chapters 12 and 13, UIP is grossly inconsistent with the data. Thus, in deriving the qualitative features of our three monetary models, we make use of the assumptions of imperfect substitutability between domestic and foreign goods and UAUIP.

15.3.1. Qualitative Features of the Monetary Models

We consider first the qualitative features of the FB model. We need to derive the reduced-form equation of this model for S_{t+1} in terms of information at time t. The medium-run solution for the exchange rate in equation (14.27) in appendix A to the previous chapter implies a semi-reduced form in terms of information at $t + 1$, which we express as:

$$\bar{S}^{\mathrm{FB}}_{t+1} = \beta_1 M_{t+1} - \beta_2 Y_{t+1} \pm \beta_3 \hat{\pi}_{t+1} + \varphi \hat{S}^{a,\mathrm{FB}}_{t+1|t+2}, \qquad (15.3)$$

where sign restrictions are made explicit, $\hat{S}^{a}_{t+1|t+2}$ denotes the aggregate of market participants forecasts of S_{t+2} conditional on their time $t + 1$ forecasting strategies and information sets, and, for convenience, we define

---

17. See the previous chapter.

M, Y, and $\hat{\pi}$ as relative (domestic minus foreign) values.[18] Because the FB model under IKE does not constrain the sign of the parameter on $\hat{\pi}_{t+1}$, we leave it unconstrained in equation (15.3), which we denote by $\pm$. Also because the FB model assumes that the benchmark real exchange rate that is relevant for goods market flows is constant and given by absolute PPP, we set $q^{\mathrm{PPP}} = \hat{q}^{\mathrm{PPP}} = 0$.

To obtain the qualitative features implied by this model, we set specification of $\hat{s}^{a,\mathrm{FB}}_{t|t+1}$ to be a function of the causal variables in the semi-reduced form:

$$\hat{s}^{a,\mathrm{FB}}_{t|t+1} = \hat{\beta}_{1,t} m_t + \hat{\beta}_{2,t} y_t + \hat{\beta}_{3,t} \hat{\pi}_{t+1}, \tag{15.4}$$

where we assume that, while the values of the $\hat{\beta}$ parameters may vary over time, their signs do not. As before, we specify the money and income variables to follow random walks with drift and assume that $\hat{\pi}_{t+1}$ is expected to remain constant. These assumptions, together with equation (15.4) shifted forward one period, yield the following reduced-form equation for $\bar{S}_{t+1}$:

$$\bar{S}^{\mathrm{FB}}_{t+1} = \left(\varphi \hat{\beta}_{1,t+1} + \beta_1 \right) m_t + \left(\varphi \hat{\beta}_{2,t+1} - \beta_2 \right) y_t + \left(\varphi \hat{\beta}_{3,t+1} \pm \beta_3 \right) \hat{\pi}_{t+1}, \tag{15.5}$$

where we suppress the drift and error terms.

Equation (15.5) shows that, to ensure that the qualitative predictions of the model on the individual and aggregate levels are not inconsistent, we set $\hat{\beta}_{1,t+1} > 0$ and $\hat{\beta}_{2,t+1} < 0$ for all t. Because the semi-reduced form in equation (15.3) does not constrain the sign of β_3, the FB model under IKE does not imply a sign restriction on this variable. Thus, the FB model embodies the following qualitative features: (1) S_{t+1} depends on domestic and foreign money, income, and secular rates of inflation and (2) ceteris paribus, an increase in domestic (foreign) money at time t leads to an increase (decrease) in the price of domestic currency at time $t + 1$, whereas an increase in domestic (foreign) income leads to a fall (rise) in S_{t+1}.

As for the sticky-price models (denoted by superscript SP), their semi-reduced forms for S_{t+1} follow from the solution for s_t in equation (14.24) in appendix A to chapter 14, which we express as:

$$S^{\mathrm{SP}}_{t+1} = \theta \bar{s}_t + (1 - \theta) s_t + \Delta \bar{S}_{t+1}, \tag{15.6}$$

18. With asymmetric money demand specifications, the signs of the parameters attached to the causal variables would be the same as in equation (15.3), but the values of these parameters would be distinct across countries.

where $0 < \theta < 1$. The DF and HM models differ in terms of their specification of the benchmark real exchange rate. The DF model follows the FB model and sets this benchmark equal to absolute PPP. We thus use equation (15.3) to specify its medium-run value for the exchange rate. By contrast, the HM model assumes that the benchmark q is a function of cumulative trade balances:

$$q_t^{\text{HB}} = -\psi \, TB_t.$$

We thus express $\bar{s}_t$ for this model as:

$$\bar{s}_t^{\text{HM}} = \beta_1 m_t - \beta_2 y_t \pm \beta_3 \hat{\pi}_{t+1} - \beta_4 TB_t + \varphi \hat{s}_{t|t+1}^{a,\text{HM}}, \tag{15.7}$$

where we set $\hat{q}_t^{\text{HB}} = -\hat{\psi} \, TB_t.$[19]

As before, to obtain the qualitative features implied by the DF model in equations (15.6) and (15.3) and the HM model in equations (15.6) and (15.7), we set their specifications for the autonomous component of the market's point forecast of S_{t+1} to be functions of the causal variables in these semi-reduced forms. For the DF model, this specification is the same as for the FB model in equation (15.4), whereas for the HM model we have:

$$\hat{s}_{t|t+1}^{a,\text{HM}} = \hat{\beta}_{1,t} m_t + \hat{\beta}_{2,t} y_t + \hat{\beta}_{3,t} \hat{\pi}_{t+1} + \hat{\beta}_{4,t} TB_t. \tag{15.8}$$

Plugging equations (15.7) and (15.8) into equation (15.6) yields the following reduced forms implied by the sticky-price DF and HM models under imperfect knowledge for S_{t+1}:

$$S_{t+1}^{\text{SP}} = \theta \left(\varphi \hat{\beta}_{1,t} + \beta_1 \right) m_t + \theta \left(\varphi \hat{\beta}_{2,t} - \beta_2 \right) Y_t + \theta \left(\varphi \hat{\beta}_{3,t} \pm \beta_3 \right) \hat{\pi}_{t+1}$$

$$+ \theta \left(\varphi \hat{\beta}_{4,t} - \beta_4 \right) TB_t + (1 - \theta) s_t, \tag{15.9}$$

where $\hat{\beta}_{4,t} = \beta_4 = 0$ for the DF model.[20]

Imposing that $\text{sign}(\hat{\beta}_{i,t}) = \text{sign}(\beta_i)$ for $i = 1$ to 4 in equation (15.9) reveals that the reduced forms for the DF and HM models share the following qualitative features: (1) S_{t+1} depends on the exchange rate and domestic

---

19. The sign restriction on TB_t in equation (15.7) assumes that the magnitude of $\psi \left(\alpha + \hat{\sigma} \eta \right)$ is greater than $\alpha \hat{\sigma} \lambda \left(\hat{\psi} - \psi \right)$ in equation (14.27). Recall that the superscript HB denotes a historical bench mark level

20. Using the same specifications for the money, income, and secular inflation variables as before, the $\Delta \bar{s}_{t+1}$ term in equation (15.6) equals a constant plus an error term and a term that captures any change in the $\hat{\beta}$ parameters between t and $t+1$. Because these terms play no role in the analysis, we omit them from equation (15.9).

and foreign money, income, and secular rates of inflation and (2) ceteris paribus, an increase in domestic (foreign) money or the exchange rate at time t leads to an increase (decrease) in S_{t+1}, whereas an increase in domestic (foreign) income leads to a fall (rise) in S_{t+1}. In addition, the HM model implies that S_{t+1} depends on domestic and foreign cumulative trade balances with negative and positive weights, respectively.

15.3.2. A TCEH Representation of Forecasting Behavior

TCEH uses the common qualitative features of a set of extant models to constrain the representation of market participants' forecasting strategies. A comparison of the qualitative features implied by the FB, DF, and HM models reveals that there are no conflicts among models. Consequently, TCEH implies the following representation of the aggregate forecast of S_{t+1}:

$$\hat{s}_{t|t+1} = \hat{\beta}_{1,t} m_t - \hat{\beta}_{2,t} y_t \pm \hat{\beta}_{3,t} \hat{\pi}_{t+1} - \hat{\beta}_{4,t} TB_t + \hat{\rho}_t s_t, \qquad (15.10)$$

where we note that the sticky price models under IKE imply that $\hat{\rho}_t$ is not only positive, but less than one; see equation (15.9). We express equation (15.10) with symmetry restrictions for convenience only.

It is important to emphasize that TCEH presumes that, in forming their forecasts, market participants may decide to focus on different sets of variables during different time periods. TCEH thus assumes that only a subset of the variables implied by any one theory, or the variables from several theories, may be needed to approximate the data in any one time period. Moreover, it recognizes that the set of variables that are relevant may change from one subperiod to another. Consequently, TCEH does not preselect the set of variables an economist should use to represent forecasting behavior at any point in time. However, the variables that are used at any point are restricted to come from those implied by the extant models he chooses and to enter his representation with theories consistent weights.

15.3.3. A Monetary Model under TCEH

In the present setup, the reduced-form exchange rate equation under TCEH follows directly from the representation of the aggregate forecast equation (15.10) and the UAUIP equilibrium condition for the foreign exchange market:

$$\hat{s}_t - s_t - i_t = \hat{\sigma}_t \left(\hat{s}_t - \hat{s}_t^{\text{HB}} \right),$$

where the market's historical benchmark value may depend on cumulative trade balances, $\hat{s}_t^{\text{HB}} = \hat{\beta}_{5t} TB_t + p_t$. These specifications imply the following momentary equilibrium exchange rate relationship:

$$s_t = \frac{\left(1 - \hat{\sigma}_t\right)\hat{\beta}_{1t} + \hat{\sigma}_t}{h_t}m_t - \frac{\left(1 - \hat{\sigma}_t\right)\hat{\beta}_{2t} + \hat{\sigma}_t\phi}{h_t}y_t$$

$$\pm \frac{\left(1 - \hat{\sigma}_t\right)\hat{\beta}_{3t}}{h_t}\hat{\pi}_{t+1} - \frac{\left(1 - \hat{\sigma}_t\right)\hat{\beta}_{4t} + \hat{\sigma}_t\hat{\beta}_{5t}}{h_t}TB_t \pm \frac{\left(1 - \hat{\sigma}_t\lambda\right)}{h_t}i_t, \quad (15.11)$$

where we also use the money demand specification in chapter 14 to sub-stitute for relative goods prices, and $h_t = 1 - \hat{\rho}_t\left(1 - \hat{\sigma}_t\right) > 0$. We note that because the TCEH representation in equation (15.10) allows for any one of its parameters to be zero, the model in equation (15.11) is consistent with the possibility that the exchange rate may not depend on either the inflation or cumulative trade balance variables during some subperiod of floating. This case would obtain if $\hat{\beta}_{3t}$ or $\hat{\beta}_{4t}$ and $\hat{\beta}_{5t}$ were equal to zero. However, it is not the case with the money, income, and interest rate variables: even if $\hat{\beta}_{1t} = \hat{\beta}_{2t} = \hat{\sigma}_t = 0$, the model implies that these macroeconomic fundamen-tals should influence the exchange rate.

With TCEH, the money, income, and cumulative trade balance variables enter equation (15.11) with parameters that are constrained to take on particular signs, whereas the inflation and interest rate variables enter with unrestricted parameters.[21] Although the parameters in equation (15.11) vary with time, our structural-change analysis has identified two subperiods of floating in which the null of no structural change cannot be rejected. It is in those subperiods that we examine the question of whether our empirical results can be rationalized by the monetary models under IKE.

A comparison of the qualitative predictions embedded in equation (15.11) with the parameter estimates in equation (15.2) reveals that during the July 1974–September 1978 subperiod, a subset of the macroeconomic variables that enter the traditional monetary models has a significant influ-ence on the exchange rate and the signs of all parameter estimates are not inconsistent with the monetary models under TCEH. However, although these models help in rationalizing the connection between the exchange rate and macroeconomic fundamentals during the 1970s, this class of mod-els cannot be reconciled completely with the data.

Even though our TCEH model does allow for the possibility that some of the macroeconomic fundamentals implied by the monetary models may not matter for the exchange rate, this is not the case for the money sup-

---

21. A rise in relative interest rates, ceteris paribus, has two offsetting effects. It raises the expected return on holding domestic currrency, which works to push down the exchange rate. But it also causes $\hat{s}_t^{HB}$ to rise, through its effect on relative prices, which works to push up the exchange rate.

ply variables. The theory indicates that domestic and foreign money should enter the estimated equation with positive and negative coefficients, respectively. However, the momentary equilibrium relationship estimated for the 1970s does not include either of these variables. The absence of the money supply variables in equation (15.2) suggests that the monetary models examined by Meese and Rogoff (1983) under TCEH provide an incomplete explanation of exchange rate dynamics in the 1970s.[22]

15.4. Macroeconomic Fundamentals and the Exchange Rate in the 1980s

Our finding that macroeconomic fundamentals matter for exchange rate movements in the 1970s in ways that are largely consistent with the qualitative features of the traditional monetary models raises the question of whether these models also help in understanding other episodes of floating exchange rates. This possibility leads us to consider the November 1979–August 1984 subperiod of statistical parameter constancy.

Using the systems approach of Phillips (1991) and the same method of reduction as before, we estimate the following reduced model for this subperiod:

$$s_t = -.41m_t + .91m_t^* - .87y_t + .31y_t^* + 1.8i + .70i_t^* - .29\pi_t^* + \epsilon_t.$$

$$(.12) \quad (.14) \quad (.10) \quad (.12) \quad (.27) \quad (.23) \quad (.04) \quad (15.12)$$

Again, we test for co-integration using the Engle and Granger two-step procedure. These results are reported in table 15.2, where the reduced model for the 1980s subperiod is labeled RM_{80}. The table shows that the null hypothesis of no co-integration can be rejected at the 5 percent significance level. Thus, we find evidence that, for the first half of the 1980s as well, the exchange rate was adjusting to a momentary equilibrium relationship based on macroeconomic fundamentals.

Table 15.4 reports the results of out-of-sample forecasting exercises for the HM, RM_{80}, and random walk models.[23] Although these results are somewhat less impressive than those for the 1970s subperiod, they again underscore the importance of allowing for structural change in examining the

22. Perhaps the problem stems from the assumption that the money supply variables are exogenous during a period in which they clearly are not. Additional research is needed to determine whether and how the TCEH-based monetary models might be modified to better match the empirical evidence.

23. The initialization period runs from October 1979 through June 1982.

Table 15.4 Out-of-Sample Fit: 1980s[a]

Forecast horizon (months)	End of forecasting period: March 1988						End of forecasting period: August 1984[b]					
	RMSE			DCS			RMSE			DCS		
	RW	HM	RM_{78}	HM	RM_{80}	Nob[c]	RW	HM	RM_{80}	HM	RM_{80}	Nob[c]
1	3.51	10.10	16.93	35	30	69	2.80	4.30	3.95	54	62	26
								4.45	3.27	73[d]	73[d]	
3	6.46	12.96	18.80	30	30	67	4.57	5.92	4.39	58	67[d]	24
								6.18	3.60	75[d]	83[d]	
6	10.62	17.44	21.38	33	26	64	5.69	7.44	4.54	67	62	21
								8.27	3.55	81[d]	86[d]	
9	14.56	22.15	23.87	33	30	61	6.90	8.63	5.17	94[d]	66	18
								10.38	4.12	100[d]	83[d]	
12	18.59	27.26	26.13	28	33	58	8.41	11.12	5.89	93[d]	87[d]	15
								13.98	4.98	100[d]	100[d]	

Source: Reprinted from Goldberg and Frydman (1996b), copyright © 1996, with permission of Elsevier.

[a] DCS figures are the percentage of correct predictions. The two structural models—the HM model and the reduced model for 1970s (RM_{70})—are estimated using ordinary least squares. RW denotes the random walk model.

[b] Figures on the top of each row are for the models indicated, whereas the figures on the bottom of each row are based on adding to the indicated model first differences of the exchange rate and all explanatory variables.

[c] Number of forecasting observations.

[d] Significant at the 5 percent level when based on the binomial distribution.

forecasting performance of aggregate models. When the forecasting experiment is allowed to run until the end of our sample, the performance of the monetary models is everywhere inferior relative to the random walk.[24] These results are presented in the left half of table 15.4. But when we stop the exercise in August 1984, the performance of the structural models improves considerably, especially at the longer forecasting horizons. These results are presented in the right half of table 15.4. The figures on the bottom of each row are based on estimating an equation that includes among its regressors first differences of the exchange rate and each explanatory variable. The addition of such stationary, $I(0)$, variables explains the autocorrelated residuals produced by the structural models during the second exchange rate regime and thus captures the short-run dynamics of the system. We note that the reduced model for the 1980s performs well relative to the random walk when based on both the RMSE and DCS measures, whereas the HM model performs well only with respect to its ability to predict the right side of the market.

A comparison of the *qualitative* predictions embedded in equation (15.11) with the parameter estimates in equation (15.12) reveals that the traditional monetary models under IKE also help in explaining exchange rate movements in the 1980s. During the November 1979–August 1984 subperiod, German and U.S. money, income, and interest rates and U.S. inflation enter the estimated relationship, and the income variables do so with parameters whose signs are theories consistent.

However, again, the monetary models under TCEH provide an incomplete view of exchange rate movements. The results in equation (15.12) show that the money supply variables enter with signs that are inconsistent with theory. The event studies of Cornell (1982), Engel and Frankel (1984), Hardouvelis (1984), and Frankel and Hardouvelis (1985) are suggestive of where the problem may lie. These studies find that changes in U.S. money supply that breach central bank targets from above were associated with subsequent tightening and higher interest rates during the 1980s. If this central bank behavior was understood by market participants, then they may have attached a negative weight to U.S. money in forming their exchange rate forecasts, rather than the positive weight implied by the monetary models considered here. Equation (15.10) shows that if the magnitudes of the $\hat{\beta}_{1,t}$ and $\hat{\beta}_{2,t}$ parameters are large enough, the reduced-form parameters for the money supply variables could have signs that are opposite to those implied by the monetary models under TCEH. Thus, beyond the qualitative implications of extant models, economists may have to rely on extra-model

---

24. These results are from Goldberg and Frydman (1996b), which uses a sample that runs from March 1973 through March 1988.

considerations, such as the historical context within which market participants form their forecasts, to understand outcomes in real world markets.

Finally, comparing the results for the 1970s in equation (15.2) with those
for the 1980s in equation (15.12) reveals that the relationship between the
exchange rate and macroeconomics fundamentals is not only unstable, but
this instability takes on a striking form: different sets of macroeconomic
fundamentals matter for the exchange rate during different time periods.
More broadly, the empirical results presented in this chapter illustrate one of
the main implications of the IKE approach: to construct empirically relevant
models, economists have to allow for the possibility that the structure of any
representation of the causal mechanism that underpins market outcomes
may change at moments of time and in ways that cannot be fully prespecified.

Appendix 15.A:
Description of Data

All data are monthly. The data set begins in March 1973 and ends in December 1989. Trade balance data are from the Organisation for Economic
Cooperation and Development Main Economic Indicators data bank. All
other time series are from the International Monetary Fund's International
Financial Statistics data bank. An * denotes a foreign variable.

s	nominal exchange rate, end of month, DM/$
i	nominal interest rate, end of month three-month treasury bill rate
i^*	nominal interest rate, end of month three-month interbank deposit rate
π, π^*	average CPI inflation rate over the preceding 12 months
y, y^*	index of industrial production, seasonally adjusted
m, m^*	M_1, end of month, in billions of local currency
TB, TB^*	cumulative trade balance, billions of local currency, cumulative sum started January 1970

References

Abel, Andrew B. (1990), "Asset Prices under Habit Formation and Catching Up with the Joneses," *American Economic Review*, 80, 38–42.

Akerlof, George A., and Janet L. Yellen (1985), "Can Small Deviations from Rationality Make Significant Differences to Economic Equilibria?" *American Economic Review*, 75, 708–21.

Alexander, Don, and Lee R. Thomas, III (1987), "Monetary/Asset Models of Exchange Rate Determination: How Well Have They Performed in the 1980s?" *International Journal of Forecasting*, 3, 53–64.

Allen, Helen, and Mark P. Taylor (1990), "Charts, Noise and Fundamentals in the London Foreign Exchange Market," *Economic Journal*, 100, 49–59.

Ang, Andrew, Geert Bekaert, and Jun Liu (2004), "Why Stocks May Disappoint," *Journal of Financial Economics*, 76, 471–508.

Atkins, Ralph (2006), "Central Banks Eye Norway's Clarity on Rates," *Financial Times*, May 25, 15.

Azariadis, Costas, and Roger Guesnerie (1986), "Sunspots and Cycles," *Review of Economic Studies*, 53, 725–38.

Backus, David (1984), "Empirical Models of the Exchange Rate: Separating the Wheat from the Chaff," *Canadian Journal of Economics*, 17, 824–46.

Backus, David, Allan Gregory, and Chris Telmer (1993), "Accounting for Forward Rates in Markets for Foreign Exchange," *Economic Journal*, 100 (suppl.), 49–59.

Baillie, Richard T., and Rowena A. Pecchenino (1991), "The Search for Equilibrium Relationships in International Finance: The Case of the Monetary Model," *Journal of International Money and Finance*, 10, 582–93.

Balassa, Bela (1964), "The Purchasing Power Parity Doctrine: A Reappraisal," *Journal of Political Economy*, 72, 584–96.

Barberis, Nicholas C., and Ming Huang (2001), "Mental Accounting, Loss Aversion, and Individual Stock Returns," *Journal of Finance*, 56 1247–92.

Barberis, Nicholas C., and Richard H. Thaler (2003), "A Survey of Behavioral Finance," in George Constantinides, Milton Harris, and Rene Stulz (eds.), *Handbook of the Economics of Finance*, Amsterdam: North-Holland, 1051–121.

Barberis, Nicholas C., Andrei Shleifer, and Robert Vishny (1998), "A Model of Investor Sentiment," *Journal of Financial Economics*, 49, 307–43.

Barberis, Nicholas C., Ming Huang, and Tano Santos (2001), "Prospect Theory and Asset Prices," *Quarterly Journal of Economics*, 116, 1–53.

Basci, Erdem, and Mehmet Caner (2005), "Are Real Exchange Rates Nonlinear or Nonstationary? Evidence from a New Threshold Unit Root Test," *Studies in Nonlinear Dynamics and Econometrics*, 9(4), 1–19.

Baxter, Marianne, and Alan C. Stockman (1989), "Business Cycles and the Exchange-Rate System," *Journal of Monetary Economics*, 23, 377–400.

Bekaert, Geert, and Robert J. Hodrick (1993), "On Biases in the Measurement of Foreign Exchange Risk Premiums," *Journal of International Money and Finance*, 12, 115–38.

Bekaert, Geert, Robert J. Hodrick, and David A. Marshall (1997), "The Implications of First-Order Risk Aversion for Asset Market Risk Premiums on Biases in the Measurement of Foreign Exchange Risk Premiums," *Journal of Monetary Economics*, 40, 3–39.

Benartzi, Shlomo, and Richard H. Thaler (1995), "Myopic Loss Aversion and the Equity Premium Puzzle," *Quarterly Journal of Economics*, 110, 73–92.

Benigno, Gianluca (2004), "Real Exchange Rate Persistence and Monetary Policy Rules," *Journal of Monetary Economics*, 51, 473–502.

Betts, Caroline, and Michael B. Devereux (1996), "The Exchange Rate in a Model of Pricing-to-Market," *European Economic Review*, 40, 1007–22.

—— (2000), "Exchange Rate Dynamics in a Model of Pricing-to-Market," *Journal of International Economics*, 50, 215–44.

Bilson, John F. O. (1978a), "The Monetary Approach to the Exchange Rate: Some Empirical Evidence," *International Monetary Fund Staff Papers*, 25, 48–75.

—— (1978b), "Rational Expectations and the Exchange Rate," in Jacob Frenkel and Harry Johnson (eds.), *The Economics of Exchange Rates*, Reading, Penn.: Addison-Wesley, 75–95.

—— (1981), "The Speculative Efficiency Hypothesis," *Journal of Business*, 54, 435–51.

Blanchard, Olivier J., and Stanley Fischer (1989), *Lectures on Macroeconomics*, Cambridge, Mass.: MIT Press.

Blanchard, Olivier, J., and Mark Watson (1982), "Bubbles, Rational Expectations and Financial Markets," in P. Wachtel (ed.), *Crises in the Economic and Financial Structure*, Lexington, Mass.: Lexington Books, 295–316.

Blanchard, Olivier J., Francesco Giavazzi, and Filipa Sa (2005), "The U.S. Current Account and the Dollar," NBER, Working Paper 11137, Cambridge Mass.: National Bureau of Economic Research.

Bollerslev, Tim, Ray Y. Chou, and Kenneth F. Kroner (1992), "ARCH Modeling in Finance: A Review of Theory and Empirical Evidence," *Journal of Econometrics*, 52, 5–59.

Boothe, Paul, and Debra Glassman (1987), "Off the Mark: Lessons for Exchange Rate Modelling," *Oxford Economic Papers*, 39, 443–57.

Boughton, John M. (1987), "Tests of the Performance of Reduced-Form Exchange Rate Models," *Journal of International Economics,* 23, 41–56.

Branson, William H., and Dale W. Henderson (1985), "The Specification and Influence of Asset Markets," in Ronald W. Jones and Peter B. Kenen (eds.), *Handbook of International Economics,* vol. II, Amsterdam: North-Holland, 749–805.

Brock, William, and Cars H. Hommes (1998), "Heterogeneous Beliefs and Routes to Chaos in a Simple Asset Pricing Model," *Journal of Economic Dynamics and Control,* 22, 1235–74.

Brown, R. L., J. Durbin, and J. M. Evans (1975), "Techniques for Testing the Constancy of Regression Relationships over Time (with discussion)," *Journal of the Royal Statistical Society,* B, 37, 149–92.

Cagan, Phillip (1956), "The Monetary Dynamics of Hyperinflation," in Milton Friedman (ed.), *Studies in the Quantity Theory of Money,* Chicago: University of Chicago Press, 25–117.

Calvo, Guillermo A. (1983a), "Staggered Prices in a Utility-Maximizing Framework," *Journal of Monetary Economics,* 12, 983–98.

——— (1983b), "Staggered Contracts and Exchange Rate Policy," in Jacob A. Frenkel (ed.), *Exchange Rates and International Macroeconomics,* Chicago: University of Chicago Press, 235–52.

Camerer, Colin F., and George Loewenstein (2004), "Behavioral Economics: Past, Present, Future," in Colin F. Camerer, George Loewenstein, and Matthew Rabin (eds.), *Advances in Behavioral Economics,* Princeton, N.J.: Princeton University Press, 3–51.

Campbell, John Y., and John H. Cochrane (1999), "By Force of Habit: A Consumption-Based Explanation of Aggregate Stock-Market Behavior," *Journal of Political Economy,* 107, 205–51.

Campbell, John Y., and Robert J. Shiller (1988), "Stock Prices, Earnings and Expected Dividends," *Journal of Finance,* 43, 661–76.

——— (1998), "Valuation Ratios and the Long-Run Stock Market Outlook," *Journal of Portfolio Management,* 24, 11–26.

Cecchetti, Stephen G., Pok-sang Lam, and Nelson C. Mark (2000), "Asset Pricing with Distorted Beliefs: Are Equity Returns Too Good to Be True?" *American Economic Review,* 90, 787–805.

Chari, V. V., Patrick J. Kehoe, and Ellen R. McGrattan (2002), "Can Sticky Price Models Generate Volatile and Persistent Real Exchange Rates?" *Review of Economic Studies,* 69, 533–63.

Charness, Gary, and Matthew Rabin (2002), "Understanding Social Preferences with Simple Tests," *Quarterly Journal of Economics* 117, 817–69.

Cheung, Yin-Wong, and Menzie D. Chinn (2001), "Currency Traders and Exchange Rate Dynamics: A Survey of the U.S. Market," *Journal of International Money and Finance,* 20, 439–71.

Cheung, Yin-Wong, and Clement Yuk-Pang Wong (1999), "Foreign Exchange Traders in Hong Kong, Tokyo and Singapore: A Survey Study," *Advances in Pacific Basin Financial Markets,* 5, 111–34.

——— (2000), "A Survey of Market Participants' Views on Exchange Rate Dynamics," *Journal of International Economics,* 51, 401–19.

Cheung, Yin-Wong, Menzie D. Chinn, and Ian Marsh (1999), "How Do UK-Based Foreign Exchange Dealers Think Their Market Operates?" CEPR Discussion Paper 2230, London: Center for Economic Policy Research.

Cheung, Yin-Wong, Menzie D. Chinn, and Antonio Garcia Pascual (2005), "Empirical Exchange Rate Models of the Nineties: Are Any Fit to Survive?," *Journal of International Money and Finance*, 24, 1150–75.

Chinn, Menzie, and Richard Meese (1995), "Banking on Currency Forecasts: Is Change in Money Predictable?" *Journal of International Economics*, 38, 161–78.

Clark, Peter B., and Ronald MacDonald (1999), "Exchange Rates and Economic Fundamentals: A Methodological Comparison of BEERs and FEERs," in Ronald MacDonald and Jerome Stein (eds.), *Equilibrium Exchange Rates*, Amsterdam: Kluwer, 285–322.

Constantinides, George M. (1990), "Habit Formation: A Resolution of the Equity Premium Puzzle," *Journal of Political Economy*, 98, 519–43.

Cornell, Bradford (1982), "Money Supply Announcements, Interest Rates, and Foreign Exchange," *Journal of International Money and Finance*, 1, 201–8.

Cumby, Robert E., and Maurice Obstfeld (1981), "A Note on Exchange-Rate Expectations and Nominal Interest Rate Differentials: A Test of the Fisher Hypothesis," *Journal of Finance*, 36, 697–703.

Cushman, David, Sang S. Lee, and Thorsteinn Thorgeirsson (1996), "Maximum Likelihood Estimation of Cointegration in Exchange Rate Models for Seven Inflationary OECD Countries," *Journal of International Money and Finance*, 15, 337–68.

De Bont, F. M. Werner (1993), "Betting on Trends: Intuitive Forecasts of Financial Risk and Return," *International Journal of Forecasting*, 9, 355–71.

De Grauwe, Paul, and Marianna Grimaldi (2005), "Heterogeneity of Agents, Transactions Costs and the Exchange Rate," *Journal of Economic Dynamics and Control*, 29, 691–719.

De Grauwe, Paul, Hans Dewachter, and M. Embrechts (1993), *Exchange Rate Theories: Chaotic Models of the Foreign Exchange Markets*, Oxford: Blackwell.

De Grauwe, Paul, Roberto Diece, and Marianna Grimaldi (2005), "Fundamental and Non-Fundamental Equilibria in the Foreign Exchange Market: A Behavioral Finance Framework," CESIFO Working Paper 1431, Munich, Germany: Center for Economic Studies and Information and Research.

——— (2006), "Exchange Rate Puzzles: A Tale of Switching Attractors," *European Economic Review*, 50, 1–33.

DeLong, Bradford J., Andrei Shleifer, Lawrence H. Summers, and Robert J. Waldman (1990a), "Noise Trader Risk in Financial Markets," *Journal of Political Economy*, 98, 703–38.

——— (1990b), "Positive Feedback Investment Strategies and Destabilizing Rational Speculation," *Journal of Finance*, 45, 375–95.

Devereux, Michael B., and Charles Engel (2002), "Exchange Rate Pass-Through, Exchange Rate Volatility, and Exchange Rate Disconnect," *Journal of Monetary Economics*, 49, 913–40.

Dickey, David A., and Wayne A. Fuller (1981), "Likelihood Ratio Statistics for Autoregressive Time Series with a Unit Root," *Econometrica*, 49, 1057–72.

Dooley, Michael P., and Peter Isard (1982), "A Portfolio-Balance Rational Expectations Model of the Dollar-Mark Exchange Rate," *Journal of International Economics*, 12, 257–76.

Dornbusch, Rudiger (1976), "Expectations and Exchange Rate Dynamics," *Journal of Political Economy*, 84, 1161–74.

—— (1980), "Exchange Rate Economics: Where Do We Stand?" *Brookings Papers on Economic Activity*, 143–94.

—— (1983a), "Comment on Shafer and Lopesko," *Brookings Papers on Economic Activity*, 1983, 79–85.

—— (1983b), "Exchange Rate Risk and the Macroeconomics of Exchange Rate Determination," in R. Hawkins, R. Levich, and C. G. Wihlborg (eds.), *The Internationalization of Financial Markets and National Economic Policy*, vol. 3, Greenwich, Conn.: JAI Press, 3–27.

—— (1987), "Exchange Rates and Prices," *American Economic Review*, 77, 93–106.

—— (1989), "Real Exchange Rates and Macroeconomics: A Selective Survey," *Scandinavian Journal of Economics*, 91, 401–32.

Dornbusch, Rudiger, and Jeffrey A. Frankel (1995), "The Flexible Exchange Rate System: Experience and Alternatives," in Jeffrey A. Frankel (ed.), *On Exchange Rates*, Cambridge, Mass.: MIT Press, 25–39. Originally published in Silvio Borner (ed.), *International Finance and Trade*, London: International Economics Association and Macmillan Press, 1988.

Dougherty, Peter J. (2002), *Who's Afraid of Adam Smith? How the Market Got Its Soul!* Hoboken, N.J.: John Wiley & Sons.

Dumas, Bernard (1992), "Dynamic Equilibrium and the Real Exchange Rate in a Spatially Separated World," *Review of Financial Studies*, 5, 153–80.

Edwards, Ward (1968), "Conservatism in Human Information Processing," in Benjamin Kleinmüth (ed.), *Formal Representation of Human Judgement*, New York: John Wiley & Sons, 17–52.

Eichenbaum, Martin, and Charles L. Evans (1995), "Some Empirical Evidence on the Effects of Monetary Policy Shocks on Exchange Rates," *Quarterly Journal of Economics*, 110, 975–1009.

Ellsberg, Daniel (1961), "Risk, Ambiguity and the Savage Axioms," *Quarterly Journal of Economics*, 75, 643–69.

Engel, Charles M. (1993), "Real Exchange Rates and Relative Prices," *Journal of Monetary Economics*, 32, 35–50.

—— (1996), "The Forward Discount Anomaly and the Risk Premium: A Survey of Recent Evidence," *Journal of Empirical Finance*, 3, 123–91.

—— (1999), "Accounting for U.S. Real Exchange Rate Changes," *Journal of Political Economy*, 107, 507–38.

—— (2000), "Local-Currency Pricing and the Choice of Exchange-Rate Regime," *European Economic Review*, 44, 1449–72.

Engel, Charles M., and Jeffrey A. Frankel (1984), "Why Interest Rates React to Money Supply Announcements: An Explanation from the Foreign Exchange Market," *Journal of Monetary Economics*, 13, 31–39.

Engel, Charles M., and James D. Hamilton (1990), "Long Swings in the Exchange Rate: Are They in the Data and Do Markets Know It?" *American Economic Review*, 80, 689–713.

Engel, Charles M., and Anthony P. Rodrigues (1989), "Tests of the International CAPM with Time-Varying Covariances," *Journal of Applied Econometrics,* 4, 119–38.

Engel, Charles M., and John H. Rogers (1996), "How Wide Is the Border?" *American Economic Review,* 86, 1112–25.

——— (2001), "Deviations from Purchasing Power Parity: Causes and Welfare Costs," *Journal of International Economics,* 55, 29–57.

Engel, Charles M., and Kenneth West (2006), "Exchange Rates and Fundamentals," *Journal of Political Economy,* 3, 485–517.

Engle, Robert F. (1982), "Autoregressive Conditional Heteroskedasticity with Estimates of the Variance of United Kingdom Inflation," *Econometrica,* 50, 987–1007.

——— (2003), "Risk and Volatility: Econometric Models and Financial Practice," Nobel Lecture, http://nobelprize.org/economics/laureates/2003/engle-lecture.pdf.

Engle, Robert F., and C. W. J. Granger (1987), "Co-Integration and Error Correction: Representation, Estimation, and Testing," *Econometrica,* 55, 251–76.

Epstein, Larry G., and Stanley E. Zin (1989), "Substitution, Risk Aversion and the Temporal Behavior of Consumption and Asset Returns: A Theoretical Framework," *Econometrica* 57, 937–69.

——— (1990), "First Order Risk Aversion and the Equity Premium Puzzle," *Journal of Monetary Economics,* 26, 387–407.

——— (1991), "Substitution, Risk Aversion, and the Temporal Behavior of Consumption Growth and Asset Returns II: An Empirical Analysis," *Journal of Political Economy,* 99, 263–86.

Evans, George W. (1986), "A Test for Speculative Bubbles in the Sterling-Dollar Exchange Rate: 1981–84," *American Economic Review,* 76, 621–36.

Evans, George W., and Seppo Honkapohja (2001), *Learning and Expectations in Macroeconomics,* Princeton, N.J.: Princeton University Press.

——— (2005) "An Interview with Thomas J. Sargent," *Macroeconomic Dynamics,* 9, 561–83.

Evans, Martin D. D., and Karen K. Lewis (1995), "Do Long-Term Swings in the Dollar Affect Estimates of the Risk Premia?" *Review of Financial Studies,* 8, 709–42.

Fama, Eugene F. (1984), "Forward and Spot Exchange Rates," *Journal of Monetary Economics,* 14, 319–38.

——— (1998), "Market Efficiency, Long-Term Returns, and Behavioral Finance," *Journal of Financial Economics,* 49, 283–306.

Farmer, Roger E. A. (1999), *The Macroeconomics of Self-Fulfilling Prophecies,* 2nd edition, Cambridge, Mass.: MIT Press.

Fellner, William (1961), "Distortion of Subjective Probabilities as a Reaction to Uncertainty," *Quarterly Journal of Economics,* 75, 670–89.

——— (1965), *Probability and Profit: A Study of Economic Behavior along Bayesian Lines,* Homewood, Ill.: Richard D. Irwin.

Finn, Mary G. (1986), "Forecasting the Exchange Rate: A Monetary or Random Walk Phenomenon?" *Journal of International Money and Finance,* 5, 181–93.

Fleming, Marcus J. (1962), "Domestic Financial Policy under Fixed and under Floating Exchange Rates," *International Monetary Fund Staff Papers,* 9, 369–79.

Flood, Robert P., and Andrew K. Rose (1995), "Fixing Exchange Rates: A Virtual Quest for Fundamentals," *Journal of Monetary Economics,* 36, 3–37.

—— (1999), "Understanding Exchange Rate Volatility without the Contrivance of Macroeconomics," *Economic Journal*, 109, F660–72.

—— (2002), "Noise Trading and Exchange Rate Regimes," *Quarterly Journal of Economics*, 117, 537–69.

Foley, Duncan K. (2003), "Rationality and Ideology in Economics," mimeo, New York: New School University.

Frankel, Jeffrey A. (1979), "On the Mark: A Theory of Floating Exchange Rate Based on Real Interest Differentials," *American Economic Review*, 69, 610–22.

—— (1982), "In Search of the Exchange-Rate Risk Premium: A Six Currency Test Assuming Mean Variance Optimization," *Journal of International Money and Finance*, 1, 255–74.

—— (1983), "Monetary and Portfolio Balance Models of Exchange Rate Determination," in Jagdeep Bhandari and Bluford Putnam (eds.), *Economic Interdependence and Flexible Exchange Rates*, Cambridge, Mass.: MIT Press, 84–115.

—— (1984), "Tests of Monetary and Portfolio Balance Models of Exchange Rate Determination," in John F. O. Bilson and Richard Marston (eds.), *Exchange Rate Theory and Practice*, Chicago: University Chicago Press, 239–60.

—— (1985), "The Dazzling Dollar," *Brookings Papers on Economic Activity*, 1, 190–217.

Frankel, Jeffrey A., and Kenneth A. Froot (1986), "Understanding the U.S. Dollar in the Eighties: The Expectations of Chartists and Fundamentalists," Special issue *Economic Record*, 24–38. Reprinted in Jeffrey A. Frankel (ed.), (1995) *On Exchange Rates*, Cambridge, Mass.: MIT Press, 295–316.

—— (1987), "Using Survey Data to Test Standard Propositions Regarding Exchange Rate Expectations," *American Economic Review*, 77, 133–53.

Frankel, Jeffrey A., and G. A. Hardouvelis (1985), "Commodity Prices, Money Surprises and Credibility," *Journal of Money, Credit, and Banking*, 17, 425–38.

Frankel, Jeffrey A., and Andrew K. Rose (1995), "Empirical Research on Nominal Exchange Rates," in Gene Grossman and Kenneth Rogoff (eds.), *Handbook of International Economics*, vol. III, Amsterdam: North-Holland, 1689–729.

Frenkel, Jacob A. (1976), "A Monetary Approach to the Exchange Rate: Doctrinal Aspects and Empirical Evidence," *Scandinavian Journal of Economics*, 78, 200–24.

Friedman, Milton (1953), *Essays in Positive Economics*, Chicago: University of Chicago Press.

—— (1956), *A Theory of the Consumption Function*, Princeton, N.J.: Princeton University Press.

—— (1961), "The Lag in Effect of Monetary Policy," *Journal of Political Economy*, 69(5), 447–66.

Frömmel, Michael, Ronald MacDonald, and Lukas Menkhoff (2005), "Markov Switching Regimes in a Monetary Exchange Rate Model," *Economic Modeling*, 22, 485–502.

Froot, Kenneth R., and Jeffrey A. Frankel (1989), "Forward Discount Bias: Is It an Exchange Risk Premium?" *Quarterly Journal of Economics*, 104, 139–61. Reprinted in Jeffrey A. Frankel (ed.), (1995) *On Exchange Rates*, Cambridge, Mass.: MIT Press, 245–60.

Froot, Kenneth A., and Kenneth Rogoff (1995), "Perspectives on PPP and Long-Run Real Exchange Rates," in Gene Grossman and Kenneth Rogoff (eds.), *Handbook of International Economics*, vol. III, Amsterdam: North-Holland, 1647–88.

Froot, Kenneth A., and Richard H. Thaler (1990), "Anomalies: Foreign Exchange," *Journal of Economic Perspectives,* 4, 179–92.

Frydman, Roman (1982), "Towards an Understanding of Market Processes: Individual Expectations, Learning and Convergence to Rational Expectations Equilibrium," *American Economic Review,* 72, 652–68.

—— (1983), "Individual Rationality, Decentralization and the Rational Expectations Hypothesis," in Roman Frydman and Edmund S. Phelps (eds.), *Individual Forecasting and Aggregate Outcomes: "Rational Expectations" Examined,* New York: Cambridge University Press, 97–122.

Frydman, Roman, and Michael D. Golberg (2003), "Imperfect Knowledge Expectations, Uncertainty Adjusted UIP and Exchange Rate Dynamics," in Philippe Aghion, Roman Frydman, Joseph Stiglitz, and Michael Woodford (eds.), *Knowledge, Information and Expectations in Modern Macroeconomics: In Honor of Edmund S. Phelps,* Princeton, N.J.: Princeton University Press, 145–82.

—— (2004), "Limiting Exchange Rate Swings in a World of Imperfect Knowledge," in Peter Sorensen (ed.), *European Monetary Integration: Historical Perspectives and Prospects for the Future. Essays in Honour of Niels Thygesen,* Copenhagen: DJOEF Publishing, 35–49.

—— (2008), *Economic Policy in a World of Imperfect Knowledge,* manuscript in preparation.

Frydman, Roman, and Edmund S. Phelps (1983), "Introduction," in Roman Frydman and Edmund S. Phelps (eds.), *Individual Forecasting and Aggregate Outcomes: "Rational Expectations" Examined,* New York: Cambridge University Press, 1–30.

—— (1990), "Pluralism of Theories Problems in Post-Rational-Expectations Modeling," paper presented at the 1990 Siena Summer Workshop on "Expectations and Learning," June 20–30.

Frydman, Roman, and Andrzej Rapaczynski (1993), *Markets by Design,* unpublished manuscript.

—— (1994), *Privatization in Eastern Europe: Is the State Withering Away?,* Budapest and Oxford: Central European University Press in cooperation with Oxford University Press.

Frydman, Roman, and Peter Rappoport (1987), "Is the Distinction between Anticipated and Unanticipated Money Growth Relevant in Explaining Aggregate Output?" *American Economic Review,* 77, 693–703.

Frydman, Roman, Cheryl Gray, Marek Hessel, and Andrzej Rapaczynski (1999), "When Does Privatization Work? The Impact of Private Ownership on Corporate Performance in Transition Economies," *Quarterly Journal of Economics,* 114 1153–92.

Frydman, Roman, Marek Hessel, and Andrzej Rapaczynski (2006), "Why Ownership Matters?" in Merritt Fox and Michael Heller (eds.), *Corporate Governance Lessons from Transition Economy Reforms,* Princeton, N.J.: Princeton University Press, 194–227.

Frydman, Roman, Michael D. Goldberg, and Nevin Cavusoglu (2007), "Imperfect Knowledge Economics of Managed Floating: Theory and Evidence," in preparation.

Frydman, Roman, Michael D. Goldberg, and Katarina Juselius (2007), "Imperfect Knowledge and the PPP Puzzle," in preparation.

Gertner, Robert (1993), "Game Shows and Economic Behavior: Risk Taking on 'Card Sharks,' " *Quarterly Journal of Economics*, 108, 507–21.

Giovannini, Alberto, and Philippe Jorion (1989), "Time Variation of Risk and Return in the Foreign Exchange and Stock Markets," *Journal of Finance*, 44, 307–26.

Goldberg, Michael D. (1991), "Reconsidering the Basic Relationships between Exchange Rates, Exchange Rate Expectations and Macroeconomic Fundamentals," Ph.D. dissertation, New York University, New York.

―――― (1995), "Symmetry Restrictions and the Semblance of Neutrality in Exchange Rate Models," *Journal of Macroeconomics*, 17, 579–99.

―――― (2000), "On Empirical Exchange Rate Models: What Does a Rejection of the Symmetry Restriction on Short-Run Interest Rates Mean?" *Journal of International Money and Finance*, 19, 673–88.

Goldberg, Michael D., and Roman Frydman (1996a), "Imperfect Knowledge and Behavior in the Foreign Exchange Market," *Economic Journal*, 106, 869–93.

―――― (1996b), "Empirical Exchange Rate Models and Shifts in the Co-Integrating Vector," *Journal of Structural Change and Economic Dynamics*, 7, 55–78.

―――― (2001), "Macroeconomic Fundamentals and the DM/$ Exchange Rate: Temporal Instability and the Monetary Model," *International Journal of Finance and Economics*, 6, 421–35.

Gollier, Christian (2001), *The Economics of Risk and Time*, Cambridge, Mass.: MIT Press.

Gomes, Francisco J. (2005), "Portfolio Choice and Trading Volume with Loss-Averse Investors," *Journal of Business*, 78, 675–706.

Goodhart, Charles (1988), "The Foreign Exchange Market: A Random Walk with a Dragging Anchor," *Economica*, 55, 437–60.

Gourinchas, Pierre-Olivier, and Aaron Tornell (2004), "Exchange Rate Puzzles and Distorted Beliefs," *Journal of International Economics*, 64, 303–33.

Granger, Clive W. J., and Timo Teräsvirta (1993), *Modeling Nonlinear Economic Relationships*, Oxford: Oxford University Press.

Greenspan, Alan (2004), "Risk and Uncertainty in Monetary Policy," *American Economic Review, Papers and Proceedings*, 94, 33–40.

Grosfeld, Irena, and Gérard Roland (1997), "Defensive and Strategic Restructuring in Central European Enterprises," *Journal of Transforming Economies and Societies*, 3, 21–46.

Gul, Faruk (1991), "A Theory of Disappointment Aversion," *Econometrica*, 59, 667–86.

Hahn, Frank, and Robert Solow (1995), *A Critical Essay on Modern Macroeconomic Theory*, Cambridge, Mass.: MIT Press.

Hamilton, James D. (1988), "Rational-Expectations Econometric Analysis of Changes in Regime: An Investigation of the Term Structure of Interest Rates," *Journal of Economics Dynamics and Control*, 12, 385–423.

―――― (1989), "A New Approach to the Economic Analysis of Nonstationary Time Series and the Business Cycle," *Econometrica*, 57, 357–84.

―――― (1990), "Analysis of Time Series Subject to Changes in Regime," *Journal of Econometrics*, 45, 39–70.

―――― (1994), *Time Series Analysis*, Princeton, N.J.: Princeton University Press.

Hansen, Lars P., and Robert J. Hodrick (1980), "Forward Exchange Rates as Optimal Predictors of Future Spot Rates: An Econometric Analysis," *Journal of Political Economy*, 88, 829–53.

Hardouvelis, Gikas A. (1984), "Market Perceptions of the Federal Reserve Policy and the Weekly Monetary Announcements," *Journal of Monetary Economics*, 14, 225–40.

Hau, Harald (2000), "Exchange Rate Determination: The Role of Factor Price Rigidities and Nontradeables," *Journal of International Economics*, 50, 421–47.

Hayek, Friedrich A. (1945), "The Use of Knowledge in Society," *American Economic Review*, 35, 519–30.

——— (1978), "The Pretence of Knowledge," Nobel Lecture, 1974, in *New Studies in Philosophy, Politics, Economics and History of Ideas*, Chicago: University of Chicago Press, 23–34.

Helpman, Elhanan (1981), "An Exploration of the Theory of Exchange Rate Regimes," *Journal of Political Economy*, 89, 865–90.

Henderson, Dale W., and Kenneth Rogoff (1982), "Negative Net Foreign Asset Positions and Stability in a World Portfolio Balance Model," *Journal of International Economics*, 13, 85–104.

Hendry, David (1980), "Econometrics: Alchemy or Science?," *Economica*, 47, 387–406. Reprinted in David Hendry (1993), *Econometrics: Alchemy or Science?*, Oxford: Blackwell.

Hendry, David, and Katarina Juselius (2000), "Explaining Cointegration Analysis. Part 1," *Energy Journal*, 21, 1–42.

——— (2001), "Explaining Cointegration Analysis. Part 2," *Energy Journal*, 22, 75–120.

Hendry, David, and Hans-Martin Krolzig (1999), "Improving on 'Data Mining Reconsidered' by K. D. Hoover and S. J. Perez," *Econometrics Journal*, 2, 202–19.

——— (2001), *PcGets*, London: Timberlake Consultants.

Hodrick, Robert (1978), "An Empirical Analysis of the Monetary Approach to the Determination of the Exchange Rate," in Jacob A. Frenkel and Harry G. Johnson (eds.), *The Economics of Exchange Rates*, Reading, Mass.: Addison-Wesley, 97–116.

Hong, Harrison, and Jeremy C. Stein (1999), "A Unified Theory of Underreaction, Momentum Trading, and Overreaction in Asset Markets," *Journal of Finance*, 54, 2143–84.

Hooper, Peter, and John Morton (1982), "Fluctuations in the Dollar: A Model of Nominal and Real Exchange Rate Determination," *Journal of International Money and Finance*, 1, 39–56.

Ito, Takatoshi (1990), "Foreign Exchange Rate Expectations: Micro Survey Data," *American Economic Review*, 80, 434–49.

Jeanne, Olivier, and Andrew K. Rose (2002), "Noise Trading and Exchange Rate Regimes," *Quarterly Journal of Economics*, 104, 139–61.

Juselius, Katarina (2007), *The Cointegrated VAR Model: Methodology and Applications*, London: Oxford University Press.

Kahneman, Daniel, and Amos Tversky (1979), "Prospect Theory: An Analysis of Decision under Risk," *Econometrica*, 47, 263–91.

Kaminsky, Graciela L. (1993), "Is There a Peso Problem?: Evidence from the Dollar/Pound Exchange Rate 1976–1987," *American Economic Review*, 83, 450–72.

Kaminsky, Graciela L., and Rodrigo Peruga (1990), "Can a Time-Varying Risk Premium Explain Excess Returns in the Forward Market for Foreign Exchange?" *Journal of International Economics*, 28, 47–70.

Kay, John (2004), "Obliquity," *Financial Times,* January 17, 16.

Keynes, John M. (1921), *A Treatise on Probability*, London: Macmillan.

——— (1936), *The General Theory of Employment, Interest and Money*, New York: Harcourt, Brace and World.

Kilian, Lutz, and Mark Taylor (2001), "Why Is It So Difficult to Beat the Random Walk Forecast of Exchange Rates?" Tinbergen Institute Discussion Paper TI 2001–031/4, Amsterdam: Tinbergen Institute.

——— (2003), "Why Is It So Difficult to Beat the Random Walk Forecast of Exchange Rates?" *Journal of International Economics*, 60, 85–107.

King, Mervyn (2005), "Monetary Policy—Practice Ahead of Theory," Mais Lecture 2005, www.bankofengland/news/2005/056.htm.

Knight, Frank H. (1921), *Risk, Uncertainty and Profit*, Boston: Houghton Mifflin.

Kollmann, Robert (2001), "The Exchange Rate in a Dynamic-Optimizing Business Cycle Model with Nominal Rigidities: A Quantitative Investigation," *Journal of International Economics*, 55, 243–62.

——— (2005), "Macroeconomic Effects of Nominal Exchange Rate Regimes: New Insights into the Role of Price Dynamics," *Journal of International Money and Finance*, 24, 275–95.

Kouri, Pentti J. K. (1976), "The Exchange Rate and the Balance of Payments in the Short Run and in the Long Run," *Scandinavian Journal of Economics*, 2, 2280–304.

——— (1978), "The Determinants of the Forward Premium," unpublished manuscript, University of Stockholm.

Kouri, Pentti J. K., and Jorge B. De Macedo (1978), "Exchange Rates and the International Adjustment Process," *Brookings Papers on Economic Activity*, 111–57.

Krugman, Paul R. (1981), "Consumption Preferences, Asset Demands, and the Distribution Effects in International Financial Markets," NBER, Working Paper 651, Cambridge, Mass.: National Bureau of Economic Research.

——— (1986), "Is the Strong Dollar Sustainable?" NBER Working Paper 1644, Cambridge Mass.: National Bureau of Economic Research.

——— (1987a), "The Narrow Moving Band, the Dutch Disease, and the Competitive Consequence of Mrs. Thatcher: Notes on Trade in the Presence of Dynamic Scale Economies," *Journal of Development Economics*, 27, 41–55.

——— (1987b), "Pricing to Market When the Exchange Rate Changes," in Sven W. Arndt and J. David Richardson (eds.), *Real-Financial Linkages among Open Economies*, Cambridge, Mass.: MIT Press, 49–70.

Kydland, Finn E., and Edward C. Prescott (1977), "Rules Rather than Discretion: The Inconsistency of Optimal Plans," *Journal of Political Economy*, 85, 473–91.

——— (1996), "A Computational Experiment: An Econometric Tool," *Journal of Economic Perspectives,* 10, 69–85.

Lane, Philip R. (2001), "The New Open Economy Macroeconomics: A Survey," *Journal of International Economics*, 54, 235–66.

Leijonhufvud, Axel (1968), *Keynesian Economics and the Economics of Keynes*, Oxford: Oxford University Press.

Leitch, Gordon, and J. Ernest Tanner (1991), "Economic Forecast Evaluation: Profits versus the Conventional Error Measures," *American Economic Review*, 81, 580–90.

Levich, Richard M. (1985), "Empirical Studies of Exchange Rates: Price Behavior, Rate Determination and Market Efficiency," in Ronald W. Jones and Peter B. Kenen (eds.), *Handbook of International Economics*, vol. II, Amsterdam: North-Holland, 979–1040.

Lewis, Karen K. (1989a), "Can Learning Affect Exchange Rate Behavior? The Case of the Dollar in the Early 1980s," *Journal of Monetary Economics*, 23, 79–100.

———— (1989b), "Changing Beliefs and Systematic Rational Forecast Errors with Evidence from Foreign Exchange," *American Economic Review*, 79, 621–36.

———— (1995), "Puzzles in International Financial Markets," in Gene Grossman and Kenneth Rogoff (eds.), *Handbook of International Economics*, vol. III, Amsterdam: North-Holland, 1913–71.

Liu, Peter C., and G. S. Maddala (1992), "Using Survey Data to Test Market Efficiency in the Foreign Exchange Markets," *Empirical Economics*, 17, 303–14.

Lucas, Robert E., Jr. (1972), "Expectations and Neutrality of Money," *Journal of Economic Theory*, 4, 101–24.

———— (1982), "Interest Rates and Currency Prices in a Two-Country World," *Journal of Monetray Economics*, 10, 335–59.

———— (1995), "Monetary Neutrality," Nobel Lecture, Stockholm: Nobel Foundation.

———— (2001), "Professional Memoir," mimeo. http://home.uchicago.edu.

———— (2002), *Lectures on Economic Growth*, Cambridge, Mass.: Harvard University Press.

———— (2003a), "Macroeconomic Priorities," *American Economic Review*, 93, 1–14.

———— (2003b), "General Comments on Part I," in Philippe Aghion, Roman Frydman, Joseph Stiglitz, and Michael Woodford (eds.), *Knowledge, Information and Expectations in Modern Macroeconomics: In Honor of Edmund S. Phelps*, Princeton, N.J.: Princeton University Press, 137–41.

Lui, Yu-Hon, and David Mole (1998), "The Use of Fundamental and Technical Analysis by Foreign Exchange Dealers: Hong Kong Evidence," *Journal of International Money and Finance*, 17, 535–45.

MacDonald, Ronald, and Ian W. Marsh (1997), "On Fundamentals and Exchange Rates: A Casselian Perspective," *Review of Economics and Statistics*, 79, 655–64.

MacDonald, Ronald, and Mark P. Taylor (1993), "The Monetary Model to the Exchange Rate: Rational Expectations, Long-Run Equilibrium, and Forecasting," *International Monetary Fund Staff Papers*, 40, 89–107.

———— (1994), "The Monetary Model of the Exchange Rate: Long-Run Relationships, Short-Run Dynamics and How to Beat a Random Walk," *Journal of International Money and Finance*, 13, 276–90.

MacDonald, Ronald, and Thomas S. Torrance (1988), "On Risk, Rationality and Excessive Speculation in the Deutschemark–U.S. Dollar Exchange Market: Some Evidence Using Survey Data," *Oxford Bulletin of Economics and Statistics*, 50, 107–23.

Mankiw, Gregory N. (1985), "Small Menu Costs and Large Business Cycles: A Macroeconomic Model of Monopoly," *Quarterly Journal of Economics*, 100, 529–39.

Mark, Nelson C. (1985), "On Time Varying Risk Premia in the Foreign Exchange Market: An Econometric Analysis," *Journal of Monetary Economics*, 16, 3–18.

——— (1988), "Time Varying Betas and Risk Premia in the Foreign Exchange Market: An Econometric Analysis," *Journal of Financial Economics*, 22, 335–54.

——— (1995), "Exchange Rates and Fundamentals: Evidence on Long-Horizon Predictability," *American Economic Review*, 85, 201–18.

——— (2001), *International Macroeconomics and Finance*, Malden, Mass.: Blackwell.

Mark, Nelson C., and Doo-Yull Choi (1997), "Real Exchange Rate Prediction over Long Horizons," *Journal of International Economics*, 43, 29–60.

Mark, Nelson C., and Yangru Wu (1998), "Rethinking Deviations from Uncovered Interest Parity: The Role of Covariance Risk and Noise," *Economic Journal*, 108, 1686–786.

Martin, J. P., and P. Masson (1979), "Exchange Rates and Portfolio Balance," NBER Working Paper 377, Cambridge, Mass.: National Bureau of Economic Research.

Meese, Richard A. (1986), "Testing for Bubbles in Exchange Markets: A Case of Sparkling Rates?," *Journal of Political Economy*, 94, 345–73.

——— (1990), "Currency Fluctuations in the Post–Bretton Woods Era," *Journal of Economic Perspectives*, 4, 117–34.

Meese, Richard A., and Kenneth Rogoff (1983), "Empirical Exchange Rate Models of the Seventies: Do They Fit out of Sample?" *Journal of International Economics*, 14, 3–24.

——— (1988), "Was It Real? The Exchange Rate–Interest Differential Relation over the Modern Floating-Rate Period," *Journal of Finance*, 43, 993–48.

Meese, Richard A., and Andrew K. Rose (1991), "An Empirical Assessment of Non-Linearities in Models of Exchange Rate Determination," *Review of Economic Studies*, 58, 603–19.

Mehra, Rajnish, and Edward C. Prescott (1985), "The Equity Premium: A Puzzle," *Journal of Monetary Economics*, 15, 145–61.

Michael, Panos, A. Robert Nobay, and David A. Peel (1997), "Transaction Costs and Non-Linear Adjustment in Real Exchange Rates: An Empirical Investigation," *Journal of Political Economy*, 105, 862–79.

Milesi-Ferretti, Assaf Razin (2000), "Current Account Reversals and Currency Crises: Empirical Regularities," in Paul Krugman (ed.), *Currency Crises*, Chicago: Univeristy of Chicago Press, 285–325.

Modjtahedi, Bagher (1991), "Multiple Maturities and Time-Varying Risk Premia in Forward Exchange Markets: An Econometric Analysis," *Journal of International Economics*, 30, 69–86.

Morgenstern, Oskar (1949), "Economics and the Theory of Games," *Kyklos*, 3, 294–308.

Mundell, Robert A. (1963), "Capital Mobility and Stabilization Policy under Fixed and Flexible Exchange Rates," *Canadian Journal of Economics and Political Science*, 29, 475–85.

Muth, John F. (1961), "Rational Expectations and the Theory of Price Movements," *Econometrica*, 29, 315–35.

Obstfeld, Maurice (1994), "The Logic of Currency Crises," *Cahiers Économiques et Monétaires (Banque de France)*, 43, 189–213.

—— (1996), "Models of Currency Crises with Self-Fulfilling Features," *European Economic Review*, 40, 1037–47.

—— (2002), "Exchange Rates and Adjustment: Perspectives from the New Open Economy Macroeconomics," *Monetary and Economic Studies* (Bank of Japan), 20, 23–46.

Obstfeld, Maurice, and Kenneth Rogoff (1995), "Exchange Rate Dynamics Redux," *Journal of Political Economy*, 103, 624–60.

—— (1996), *Foundations of International Macroeconomics*, Cambridge, Mass.: MIT Press.

—— (1998), "Risk and Exchange Rates," NBER Working Paper 6694, Cambridge Mass.: National Bureau of Economic Research.

—— (2000a), "New Directions for Stochastic Open Economy Models," *Journal of International Economics*, 50, 117–53.

—— (2000b), "The Six Major Puzzles in International Macroeconomics: Is There a Common Cause?" in Ben Bernanke and Kenneth Rogoff (eds.), *NBER Macroeconomics Annual 2000*, Cambridge, Mass.: MIT Press, 339–90.

—— (2005), "Global Current Account Imbalances and Exchange Rate Adjustments," *Brookings Papers on Economic Activity*, 1, 67–146.

Obstfeld, Maurice, and Alan Taylor (1997), "Nonlinear Aspects of Goods-Market Arbitrage and Adjustment: Heckscher's Commodity Points Revisited," *Journal of the Japanese and International Economies*, 11, 441–79.

Papell, David H. (1997), "Cointegration and Exchange Rate Dynamics," *Journal of International Money and Finance*, 16, 445–60.

Parsley, David, and Shang-Jin Wei (2001), "Explaining the Border Effect: The Role of Exchange Rate Variability, Shipping Costs and Geography," *Journal of International Economics*, 55, 87–105.

Peirce, Charles S. (1878), "The Doctrine of Chances," in C. J. Loesel et al. (eds.), *Writings of Charles S. Peirce: A Chronological Edition*, vol. 3, 1872–1878, Indianapolis: Indiana University Press, 238–42.

Perron, P. (1988), "Trends and Random Walks in Macroeconomic Time Series," *Journal of Economic Dynamics and Control*, 12, 297–332.

Phelps, Edmund S. (1968a), "Money Wage Dynamics, and Labor Market Equilibrium," *Journal of Political Economy*, 76, 687–711.

—— (1968b), "Population Increase," *Canadian Journal of Economics*, 1, 497–518.

—— (1972), *Inflation Policy and Unemployment Theory*, New York: Norton.

—— (1983), "The Trouble with 'Rational Expectations' and the Problem of Inflation Stabilization," in Roman Frydman and Edmund S. Phelps (eds.), *Individual Forecasting and Aggregate Outcomes: "Rational Expectations" Examined*, New York: Cambridge University Press, 31–41.

—— (1994), *Structural Slumps: The Modern-Equilibrium Theory of Unemployment, Interest and Assets*, Cambridge, Mass.: Harvard University Press.

—— (2006a), "Prospective Shifts, Speculative Swings: 'Macro' for the Twenty-First Century in the Tradition Championed by Paul Samuelson," in Michael Szenberg, Lall Ramrattan, and Aron A. Gottesman (eds.), *Samuelsonian Economics*, Oxford: Oxford University Press, 66–87.

——— (2006b), "Economic Prosperity and Dynamism of Economic Institutions," in Winston T. H. Koh and Roberto S. Mariano (eds.), *Economic Prospects of Singapore*, Singapore: Addison-Wesley, 299–333.

Phelps, Edmund (2007), "Macroeconomics for a Modern Economy," Nobel Prize Lecture, forthcoming in *American Economic Review*.

Phelps, Edmund S., et al. (1970), *Microeconomic Foundations of Employment and Inflation*, New York: Norton.

Phillips, Peter C. B. (1987), "Time Series Regression with Unit Roots," *Econometrica*, 55, 277–302.

——— (1991), "Optimal Inference in Cointegrated Systems," *Econometrica*, 59, 283–86.

Phillips, Peter C. B., and S. Ouliaris (1990), "Asymptotic Properties of Residual Based Tests for Cointegration," *Econometrica*, 58, 165–93.

Polanyi, Michael (1958), *Personal Knowledge*, Chicago: University of Chicago Press.

Popper, Karl R. (1945), *The Open Society and Its Enemies*, London: Routledge and Kegan Paul.

——— (1957), *The Poverty of Historicism*, London and New York: Routledge.

Quandt, Richard (1960), "Tests of the Hypothesis that a Linear Regression System Obeys Two Separate Regimes," *Journal of the American Statistical Association*, 53, 873–80.

Rabin, Matthew (2002), "A Perspective on Psychology and Economics," *European Economic Review*, 46, 657–85.

Rogoff, Kenneth (1996), "The Purchasing Power Puzzle," *Journal of Economic Literature*, 34, 647–68.

Roubini, Nouriel (2006), "Global Imbalances, the U.S. Dollar and Globalization Challenges at Davos," January 27th blog, http://www.rgemonitor.com/blog /roubini/.

Sachs, Jeffrey (1981), "The Current Account and Macroeconomic Adjustment in the 1970s," *Brookings Papers on Economic Activity*, 1981, 201–82.

——— (1982), "The Current Account in the Macroeconomic Adjustment Process," *Scandinavian Journal of Economics*, 84, 147–59.

Samuelson, Paul (1964), "Theoretical Notes on Trade Problems," *Review of Economics and Statistics*, 46, 145–64.

Sargent, Thomas J. (1987), *Macroeconomic Theory*, New York: Academic Press.

——— (1993), *Bounded Rationality in Macroeconomics*, Oxford: Oxford University Press.

——— (2001), *The Conquest of American Inflation*, Princeton, N.J.: Princeton University Press.

Sarno, Lucio, and Mark P. Taylor (1999), "Moral Hazard, Asset Price Bubbles, Capital Flows, and the East Asian Crisis: The First Tests," *Journal of International Money and Finance*, 18, 637–57.

——— (2002), *The Economics of Exchange Rates*, Cambridge: Cambridge University Press.

Schinasi, Garry J., and P. A. V. B. Swamy (1989), "The Out-of-Sample Forecasting Performance of Exchange Rate Models When Coefficients Are Allowed to Change," *Journal of International Money and Finance*, 8, 375–90.

Schulmeister, Stephan (1983), "Exchange Rates, Prices and Interest Rates: Reconsidering the Basic Relationships of Exchange Rate Determination," C. V. Starr Center For Applied Economics Working Paper 83-13, New York: C. V. Starr Center For Applied Economics.

———— (1987), "Currency Speculation and Dollar Fluctuations," *Banca Nazionale del Lavoro Quarterly Review*, 167, 343–65.

———— (2006), "The Interaction between Technical Currency Trading and Exchange Rate Fluctuations," *Finance Research Letters*, 3, 212–33.

———— (2007), "Components of the Profitability of Technical Currency Trading," forthcoming in *Applied Financial Economics*.

Schulmeister, Stephan, and Michael D. Goldberg (1989), "Noise Trading and the Efficiency of Financial Markets," in Giacomo Luciani (ed.), *The American Financial System: Between Euphoria and Crisis*, Rome: Quaderni della Fondazione Adriano Olivetti, 117–53.

Schumpeter, Joseph A. (1911), *Theory of Economic Development*, English trans, Revers Opie, Cambridge, Mass.: Harvard University Press, 1932.

Sercu, Piet, Raman Uppal, and Cynthia Van Hulle (1995), "The Exchange Rate in the Presence of Transactions Costs: Implications for Tests of Purchasing Power," *Journal of Finance*, 50, 1309–19.

Shiller, Robert J. (1978), "Rational Expectations and the Dynamic Structure of Macroeconomic Models: A Critical Review," *Journal of Monetary Economics*, 4, 1–44.

———— (1979), "The Volatility of Long-Term Interest Rates and Expectations Models of the Term Structure," *Journal of Political Economy*, 87, 1190–219.

———— (1981), "Do Stock Prices Move Too Much to Be Justified by Subsequent Changes in Dividends?" *American Economic Review*, 71, 421–36.

———— (1990), "Speculative Prices and Popular Models," *Journal of Economic Perspectives*, 4, 55–65.

———— (2000), *Irrational Exuberance*, Princeton, N.J.: Princton University Press.

Shleifer, Andrei (2000), *Inefficient Markets*, Oxford: Oxford University Press.

Sibert, Anne (1996), "Unconventional Preferences: Do They Explain the Foreign Exchange Risk Premia?," *Journal of International Money and Finance*, 15, 149–65.

Sims, Christopher A. (1996), "Macroeconomics and Methodology," *Journal of Economic Perspectives,* 10, 105–20.

Smith, Adam (1759), *The Theory of Moral Sentiments*, 1976 Edition, Oxford: Oxford University Press.

———— (1776), *An Inquiry Into the Nature and Causes of the Wealth of Nations*, 1994 Modern Library Edition, New York: Random House.

Solnik, Bruno H. (1974), "An Equilibrium Model of the International Capital Market," *Journal of Economic Theory*," 89, 500–524.

Somanath, V. S. (1986), "Efficient Exchange Rate Forecasts: Lagged Models Better than the Random Walk," *Journal of International Money and Finance*, 5, 195–220.

Soros, George (1987), *The Alchemy of Finance*, New York: Wiley.

———— (1998), *The Crisis of Global Capitalism: Open Society Endangered*, New York: Public Affairs.

———— (2006), *The Age of Fallibility: Consequences of the War on Terror*, New York: Public Affairs.

Stein, Jerome L. (1995), "The Natural Real Exchange Rate of the United States Dollar, and Determinants of Capital Flows," in Jerome Stein and Polly Reynolds Allen (eds.), *Fundamental Determinants of Exchange Rates*, Oxford: Clarendon Press, 38–84.

Stockman, Alan C. (1980), "A Theory of Exchange Rate Determination," *Journal of Political Economy*, 88, 673–98.

———— (1987), "The Equilibrium Approach to Exchange Rates," *Federal Reserve Bank of Richmond Economic Review*, 73, 12–30.

Svensson, Lars E. O. (1985), "Currency Prices, Terms of Trade, and Interest Rates: A General Equilibrium Asset Pricing Cash-in-Advance Approach," *Journal of International Economics*, 18, 17–41.

Svensson, Lars E. O., and Sweder van Wijnbergen (1989), "Excess Capacity, Monopolistic Competition, and International Transmission of Monetary Disturbances," *Economic Journal*, 99, 785–805.

Takagi, Shinji (1991), "Exchange Rate Expectations: A Survey of Survey Studies," *International Monetary Fund Staff Papers*, 38, 156–83.

Taylor, Alan, and Mark P. Taylor (2004), "The Purchasing Power Parity Debate," *Journal of Economic Perspectives*, 4, 135–58.

Taylor, John (1979a), "Aggregate Dynamics and Staggered Contracts," *Journal of Political Economy*, 88, 1–24.

———— (1979b), "Staggered Price Setting in a Macro Model," *American Economic Review*, 69, 108–13.

Taylor, Mark P. (1988), "What Do Investment Managers Know? An Empirical Study of Practitioners' Predictions," *Economica*, 54, 429–38.

Taylor, Mark P., and Helen Allen (1992), "The Use of Technical Analysis in the Foreign Exchange Market," *Journal of International Money and Finance*, 11, 304–14.

Taylor, Mark P., and David A. Peel (2000), "Nonlinear Adjustment, Long-Run Equilibrium and Exchange Rate Fundamentals," *Journal of International Money and Finance*, 19, 33–53.

Taylor, Mark P., David A. Peel, and Lucio Sarno (2001), "Nonlinear Mean-Reversion in Real Exchange Rates: Towards a Solution to the Purchasing Power Parity Puzzles," *Internationl Economic Review*, 42, 1015–42.

Thaler, Richard H., and Eric Johnson (1990), "Gambling with the House Money and Trying to Break Even: The Effects of Prior Outcomes in Risky Choice," *Management Science*, 36, 643–60.

Tirole, Jean (1982), "On the Possibility of Speculation Under Rational Expectations," *Econometrica*, 50, 1163–81.

Tobin, James (1958), "Liquidity Preference as Behavior Towards Risk," *Review of Economic Studies*, 25, 15–29.

———— (1981), "Money and Finance in the Macro-Economic Process," Nobel Lecture, Stockholm: Nobel Foundation.

Tversky, Amos, and Daniel Kahneman (1986), "Rational Choice and the Framing of Decisions," *Journal of Business*, 59, S251–78.

———— (1991), "Loss Aversion in Riskless Choice: A Reference-Dependent Model," *Quarterly Journal of Economics*, 106, 1039–61.

———— (1992), "Advances in Prospect Theory: Cumulative Representation of Uncertainty," *Journal of Risk and Uncertainty*, 5, 297–323.

Von Neumann, John, and Oscar Morgenstern (1944), *Theory of Games and Economic Behavior*, Princeton, N.J.: Princeton University Press.

Weber, Max (1897), *Sociological Writings*, 1994 Edition, Wolf Heydebrand (ed.), New York: Continuum.

———— (1930), *The Protestant Ethic and the Spirit of Capitalism*, 2001 Edition, London: Routledge.

———— (1968), *Economy and Society*, New York: Bedminster Press.

Weitzman, Martin L. (2007), "Subjective Expectations and Asset-Return Puzzles," forthcoming in *American Economic Review*.

Wible, James R. (2007), *The Economics of Charles S. Peirce: How the Philosophy of the Metaphysical Club Intersects with the Economics of the Cambridge Scientific Club*, manuscript in preparation.

Wolf, Christian C. P. (1987), "Time-Varying Parameters and the Out-of-Sample Forecasting Performance of Structural Exchange Rate Models," *Journal of Business and Economic Statistics*, 5, 87–98.

Woo, Wing T. (1985), "The Monetary Approach to Exchange Rate Determination under Rational Expectations," *Journal of International Economic*, 18, 1–16.

Woodford, Michael (1984), "Indeterminacy of Equilibrium in the Overlapping Generations Model: A Survey," mimeo, Columbia University, May.

———— (1990), "Learning to Believe in Sunspots," *Econometrica*, 58, 277–307.

———— (2003), *Interest Rates and Prices: Foundations of a Theory of Monetary Policy*, Princeton, N.J.: Princeton University Press.

Zeuthen, Frederik (1955), *Economic Theory and Method*, translated by Else Zeuthen. London: Longmans.

Index

Page numbers followed by *f* indicate figures; those followed by *n* indicate notes; those followed by *t* indicate tables.